P9-CKA-171

Lone Stars and State Gazettes

Lone Stars

☆ AND ☆

State Gazettes

Texas Newspapers before
the Civil War

By Marilyn McAdams Sibley

Foreword by John H. Murphy

Texas A&M University Press
COLLEGE STATION

Copyright © 1983 by Marilyn McAdams Sibley
All rights reserved

Library of Congress Cataloging in Publication Data

Sibley, Marilyn McAdams.
    Lone Stars and state gazettes.

    Bibliography: p.
    Includes index.
    1. American newspapers—Texas—History—19th
    century. I. Title.
PN4897.T43S5   1983   071'.64   82-45898
ISBN 0-89096-149-2

Manufactured in the United States of America
FIRST EDITION

To the memory of my grandmother
Ida Barnett Stuart
unrusted and undaunted

Contents

List of Illustrations

Foreword

THIS book, which for the first time brings together the history of the newspapers and the persons who made them live from the earliest days of what is now Texas through the War Between the States, is an epic of dedication on several dimensions.

First, of course, it chronicles and preserves for future generations the dedication—many times at the risk of life itself—of the publishers, editors, and others of the newspapers of that era.

Secondly, the book itself and the years of intensive, meticulous research required to make it a reality are tributes of the highest kind to the author, Dr. Marilyn Sibley of Houston. Her devotion to the task and her ability are evident in the quality of her work.

Finally, their dedication to the newspaper business moved Harte-Hanks Communications, Inc., and the Southland Division of St. Regis Paper Company to make the generous grants that made this work possible. So, as an expression of our thanks to Harte-Hanks and St. Regis, the Texas Daily Newspaper Association would like to single out three men whose impact on the newspapers of Texas, through those two organizations, grows with the passing years:

Houston H. Harte, of San Angelo, and Marshall Bernard Hanks, of Abilene, founders of the original Harte-Hanks Newspapers, from which has grown one of the great communications groups of America. The original newspapers of that group and the many others that have been added in recent years were built and have prospered by following their creed—that a good newspaper's first responsibility is to serve its community.

Ernest L. Kurth, the man whose vision, sacrifices, and driving determination made the original newsprint mill at Lufkin the first to produce newsprint from Southern pine, revolutionized the newsprint industry and bequeathed to the newspapers of the South an economic benefit of inestimable dimensions.

The Texas Daily Newspaper Association (TDNA), which has sponsored the publication of this book, was initiated at Waco on January 24, 1921, as the Texas Newspaper Publishers Association. The association was formally organized in Dallas on March 10, 1921. Fifteen newspapers were charter members. Originally based in Houston, the organization moved its offices to Dallas in 1936, then back to Houston in 1952, following its reorganization as the Texas Daily Newspaper Association.

Today, TDNA has 95 member-newspapers, including papers in Louisiana, New Mexico, and Oklahoma, and is the largest single-state daily newspaper association in the nation.

JOHN H. MURPHY, Executive Vice-President
Texas Daily Newspaper Association

Acknowledgments

THIS book has placed me in debt to many people, foremost of whom are John H. Murphy and Frank Wardlaw. John Murphy, executive vice-president of the Texas Daily Newspaper Association, conceived the idea and arranged for publication of the book. Frank Wardlaw, incomparable man of Texas letters and first director of Texas A&M University Press, drafted me for the task of translating the idea into a book. The finished product is not what either of them expected, and I alone must accept full responsibility for it. Even so, without them it would not have been. For the challenge and for an interesting sojourn among old newspaper files I am grateful to them.

Along the way others made notable contributions. Ernest Wallace gave me a copy of his rare *Charles DeMorse, Pioneer Editor and Statesman*; Ron C. Tyler, an autographed copy of his *Joseph Wade Hampton, Editor and Individualist*; Max Lale, a copy of his paper on R. W. Loughery. James A. Creighton loaned his copious notes on Brazoria County papers; Marie Whitehead of the *Rusk Cherokeean* sent a copy of her history of that paper; Betty Seerden of the *Bay City Tribune* contributed a history of Matagorda County papers. Margaret S. McLean, an assistant to Thomas W. Streeter in the compiling of his *Bibliography of Texas*, gave both notes and advice. D. D. Tidwell advised on Masonic newspapers. Marcelle Hull sent information on Fort Worth newspapers.

As is their custom in research projects, a number of librarians rendered special service. The staffs of Houston Public Library, Texas State Library, Rice University, and the Newspaper Collection, University of Texas at Austin, went above the call of duty in making old newspapers available. J. C. Martin and the staff at San Jacinto Museum of History dispensed memorable hospitality along with rare journals; Catherine McDowell of the Daughters of the Republic of Texas Library at the Alamo called my attention to material on San Antonio papers; Sharon Crutchfield of the same library went to much trouble to locate a photograph. Jane Kenamore of Rosenberg Library at Galveston searched for fugitive items.

I am indeed grateful to all of these whose interest, efforts, and contributions made the book a reality.

Lone Stars and State Gazettes

CHAPTER 1

Of Press and Printers

THE pioneer printer marched not far to the rear in the procession of civilization that moved westward across the North American continent in the nineteenth century. One printer and his press reached Texas in 1813 in the very vanguard of the westward movement, and from then until the Civil War more than four hundred newspapers appeared there. In style and format those papers represented an extension of the Anglo-American frontier press. At the same time, they peculiarly reflected the course of history in Texas. Sometimes they shaped that history, and always they were interwoven with it. "Texas is a newspaper state," Charles DeMorse, a veteran editor and old Texian, observed correctly on the eve of the war.[1]

Only a fraction of the journals that appeared qualified as newspapers in the modern sense. Most were propaganda or special-purpose sheets that owed their appearance to the printer's monopoly on mass communication and the dissemination of news. When one wanted to convey a message to the public, to promote, discredit, or protest a cause, he simply founded a newspaper on the most convenient printing press. When the cause succeeded or failed, he discontinued the paper as promptly as he had begun it. Thus the papers taken together reflect the assorted fears and hopes of a people.

The first press came to Texas to promote a filibustering expedition, and, although the paper it produced went to press in Louisiana, it set a pattern followed by many later ones. Politics, personal or party, accounted for the founding of more papers than any other single factor. Military adventures and national crises inspired a spate of papers. Reli-

---

[1] Clarksville [*Northern*] *Standard*, January 19, 1861.

gious organizations, ethnic groups, and businessmen founded sheets to
serve their purposes. The *Alarm Bell of the West*, for example, warned
Texans in 1842 that a Mexican army approached; the *Sword of Gideon*
in 1861, that secession constituted treason. The *San Luis Advocate*
promoted the founding of a paper town near Galveston in 1841; the
Meridian and Pacific Railway Advocate, the building of a railroad in
northeast Texas in 1854. The *Texas Free Press* at Quitman worked
against slavery; the *White Man* at Jacksboro, for the defense of the
northwest frontier against Indians.

Often a single printing press produced a number of papers, some
of which appeared simultaneously. For example, the *Central Texian*
and *Texas Baptist* came from the same press at Anderson during the
mid-1850s, and two papers, one Democratic and one Whig, shared a
press at Henderson in 1854.

More often the papers appeared in succession as circumstances—
usually a change in ownership or relocation of the press—prompted
the discontinuing of one title and the beginning of another. Thus the
press at Matagorda changed hands several times between 1837 and
1861, producing some eight papers: the *Bulletin, Letter-Sheet Prices
Current, Colorado Gazette and Advertiser, Despatch, Colorado Herald, Colorado Tribune, Chronicle of the Times*, and *Gazette*. And a single press skipping across north Texas brought forth the *Advertiser* at
Bonham, the *Frontier Patriot* at Paris, and the *Patriot* at Sherman.

Charles DeMorse, a perceptive observer, summed up the course
of many of the pioneer papers. "Almost every little county town which
could properly pay the promiscuous expense of a printer's devil . . .
gets up a public journal with a pretentious title, and the affair goes on
with great vigor for a few months—languishes and changes hands," he
wrote. "A new aspirant for fame, perhaps two or three successively,
conduct it onward to its inevitable goal—it languishes again and ex-
pires. After a while, the establishment is sold out, goes to some new
locality, hitherto untouched by the tempter, and again the same play
is performed until the type wears out and natural death ensues—
finality."[2]

The first printing presses in Texas were of the screw variety, hand
operated, with two leather pads called ink balls used to ink the type.

[2]Ibid.

The Washington hand press, a lever variety patented by Samuel Rust in 1829, superceded the screw during the 1830s. Easily transported, the Washington hand press turned out some 240 sheets an hour and became the standard press in most offices until the Civil War.

The Houston *Telegraph and Texas Register* in 1838 acquired a double-cylindered Napier press built by Richard M. Hoe Company. The *Telegraph* billed it as a "power press," but in fact strong workmen furnished the power by turning cranks. The *Galveston News* in 1852 boasted of a Hoe cylinder press operated by horse power, "an ancient equine" driven by one of the proprietor's slaves. And another Galveston newspaper, the *Civilian*, installed the first steam-powered press in the state in 1857. The *Galveston News* acquired a steam engine in 1859, and in that same year the *San Antonio Herald* with considerable difficulty transported steam machinery from Indianola and put it to double duty—operating a press and grinding corn for the local farmers. The larger offices often boasted of more than one press.[3]

Those wishing to publish a newspaper customarily issued first a prospectus, which neighboring editors published as a professional courtesy. The prospectus gave the title and place of publication of the proposed paper, listed the names of those connected with it, and stated its purpose and policies. Publishers as a rule chose titles in common use in the United States—Gazette, Herald, Times, or Journal. Appropriately, a number of them used "Star" in their titles. Several *Lone Stars* appeared, along with the *Morning Star, Alamo Star, Bright Star, Southern Star, Western Star, Star Spangled Banner, Star State Jeffersonian*, and a sprinkling of plain Stars. The *Star State Patriot* welcomed the *Texas Star* in 1853 with the comment that the state had a "constellation of stars."[4]

The prospectus served as a test of public interest, and for lack of that interest or for other reasons, a number of proposed papers never appeared. If the publisher did pursue the matter, he found that despite the printer's monopoly on mass communication, his course did not run smoothly. He faced in full measure the problems common to others of his calling on the American frontier—a chronic shortage of newsprint, a lack of fresh news, an inadequate labor force, precarious financing,

[3] Frank Luther Mott, *American Journalism: A History, 1690–1960*, pp. 203–204; E. W. Winkler, *Check List of Texas Imprints, 1846–1860*, p. xix.

[4] Marshall *Star State Patriot*, March 19, 1853.

and, finally, unsatisfactory means of distributing his paper. The editor of the *Dallas Herald* in 1858 summed up several of the recurring problems in explaining the late appearance of an issue. "A combination of circumstances have delayed us again this week," he wrote. "In the first place our paper did not reach us until Tuesday; in the next, one of our workmen quit us on Monday . . . and lastly, a cold norther has been blowing."[5]

The shortage of newsprint stemmed from the primitive transportation. Customarily, Texan printers placed orders with dealers in New Orleans, who in turn ordered the paper from the northeast. The newsprint traveled to New Orleans and then to Texas by water on vessels that regularly ran afoul of tropical storms, shifting sand bars, and other hazards of navigation. Until late in the period the paper moved to the interior of Texas by temperamental rivers or by freight wagons drawn by oxen or mules and subject to the vagaries of weather and pioneer roads. The building of the railroads in the 1850s expedited transportation, but newsprint still remained scarce and expensive. The *Bastrop Advertiser* estimated in 1857 that Texan printers spent $180,000 annually for paper and launched a campaign to build a paper mill in Texas.[6] Several other journals endorsed the idea, yet when the Civil War came the state had not a single mill. The federal blockade of the coast and the consequent shortage of newsprint closed down all but a few printing offices and effectively ended an era of Texas journalism.

Primitive communication joined with primitive transportation to account for the lack of fresh news. The telegraph came later than the railroad to Texas and remained a novelty at the beginning of the Civil War. In the absence of the wire, the editor depended on age-old means of communication, and as a rule he looked upon his paper primarily as a means of expressing his views and only secondarily as a means of disseminating news. Occasionally during times of crisis, he received dispatches from a correspondent at a strategic location, but otherwise he made little effort to gather news. In this he followed the pattern of his colleagues in the United States, for the age of the great reporter lay in the future, and the editor rather than the reporter dominated the newspaper of the era.

[5] *Dallas Herald*, November 3, 1858.
[6] Austin *Texas State Gazette*, January 17, 1857.

The age of the sensational news story also lay in the future. Texan editors generally avoided stories of scandal or personal feuds, especially those within their own orbit. Robert W. Loughery of the Marshall *Texas Republican* printed the details of a case that rocked Harrison County in 1859. A husband, accusing his wife of adultery, killed her alleged paramour. In the ensuing murder trial, a local teacher, W. D. Gillespie, testified to the wife's bad reputation, whereupon her two sons, aged fifteen and eighteen, killed him.[7] But such details rarely appeared in print and for good reason. Most of the papers appeared weekly in towns of a few hundred population. Houston boasted only 2,073 inhabitants in 1837, and Galveston, the largest town in the state, only 4,177 in 1850. In towns of that size, any sensational local news and much important news from afar circulated by word of mouth before the newspaper appeared. This relieved the editor of the responsibility of bearing news and cleared the way for him to voice his opinions, which he did freely in regard to state or national matters.

But prudence dictated that he handle local items with care. By merely noticing certain events, he could antagonize advertisers and subscribers or possibly involve himself in personal vendettas not his own. Typically, he gave only a few words to such vendettas, maintaining a detachment and often using the passive tense. Thus, the short-lived *Texas Telegraph* at Sulphur Springs reported "that a personal rencontre occurred . . . between W. F. Scott and J. M. Brown in which the latter was killed at the time and the former subsequently died," and the Palestine *Trinity Advocate* regretted that "an unfortunate collusion took place between two youths . . . Messrs. Pinkney and Marcus Mallard in which the former was severely if not fatally wounded." Even Robert W. Loughery, who gave more coverage than most editors to such stories, often lapsed into the passive tense, as when he wrote that "Mr. J. O. Shook, editor and proprietor of the Democrat, Waco, Texas, was killed on the morning of the 25th ult. The report states that he was killed by a printer."[8]

Local news often being unprintable, the editor seldom went in search of it, and instead waited in his office for acceptable news to come to him. He received it by letters, sometimes addressed to him

[7] Marshall *Texas Republican* November 5, 1859.
[8] Ibid., May 22, 1858, and June 14 and November 10, 1860.

and sometimes to local citizens who shared their news with him. Travelers from distant points stopped at the press office to inform him of happenings at their point of departure or along their route. Most importantly, fellow editors in other towns sent him exchange papers, from which he clipped enough items to fill his pages.

The United States postal law permitted editors to exchange papers with each other without paying postage. This privilege had the desired effect of speeding the circulation of information, and it became the early editor's primary means of gathering news, serving him in the same way that the press association or wire service served a later generation.

The Republic of Texas adopted an exchange system similar to that of the United States, but provided further for each Texan editor to exchange postage-free as many as thirty papers with his fellows in foreign countries. At the time, of course, the United States qualified as a foreign country, and the Texans looked there for much of their news. For a few years after the founding of the republic, the United States extended the exchange privilege to Texan editors, but to the journalists' dismay, a new regime halted the practice in 1842. "The Post Master at New Orleans will not permit papers to the Editors of Texas to be taken out of that office until the postage is paid," Francis Moore informed readers of the Houston *Telegraph and Texas Register*. Then he made a play on the story that circulated widely in the United States of refugees who crossed the Sabine River in haste after scrawling "Gone to Texas" or "G.T.T." on their doors. "We shall be perfectly happy if he will send on the exchange papers as heretofore and make due return to the General Post Office by filling in his blanks with G.T.T."[9] The United States postal service did not relent to the pleas of the Texan editors, but a few years later annexation brought them again within the larger circle of privilege.

The exchange system created a fraternal network among the editors. They welcomed new journals, noted changes in management or location, and paid last respects to those that failed. Thus, they sketched the newspaper history of the period, leaving a record of many papers of which no copies survive. In periods of slow news, the editors sent greetings or insults to each other by way of their papers, often engaging in paper feuds that occasionally developed into real ones.

[9] Houston *Telegraph and Texas Register*, April 6, 1842.

Because Texas was a land of newcomers, the exchange papers turned the press office into a social center. Even by 1860, three-fourths of the state's inhabitants were born elsewhere, and throughout the period many of them, eager for news from former homes, flocked to the press office to read the exchange papers. Sometimes these hangers-on became a nuisance, and sometimes the editor took advantage of the situation by establishing a reading room or reading club in conjunction with the press office. Members paid an annual fee that gave them access to the reading room, where they could browse through the exchanges and also purchase refreshments. The *Morning Star* at Houston recruited members in the editorial columns. "In the Reading Room attached to the Star Coffee House, gentlemen, you will find a good variety of periodicals and a very gentlemanly and accommodating proprietor," the editor wrote on one occasion, and on another, "A good glass, an interesting paper and a pleasant cigar may always be found at the Star."[10]

The editor usually needed the extra funds brought in by the reading room. Only a few enjoyed secure financing, and even editors of the more stable journals complained of the poor return for their efforts. "The publishers of newspapers in Texas do not receive the same equivalent for their labor and means expended that other people do," complained the editor of the *Morning Star* in 1841; while John Marshall of the powerful *Texas State Gazette* in Austin declared in 1857 that "if we were to spend the next fifty years at the types, we can do no more than live and die poor."[11]

Sometimes special interests underwrote a paper. A group of Germans in San Antonio formed a stock company to establish a press; a group of prominent citizens at Clarksville backed DeMorse's press. Religious sheets expected but did not always get support from their denominations; political parties inspired the founding of a number of sheets, but because of the predominance of the Democrats and the weakness of other parties these sheets rarely received substantial support from party organizations.

More often than not the paper represented the initiative of one man or a few, with the proprietor filling several roles. Of economic necessity, many papers, like the *Crockett Printer*, were "edited by the

---

[10] Houston *Morning Star*, December 29, 1839, and January 15, 1840.
[11] Ibid., November 13, 1841; *Texas State Gazette*, March 28, 1857.

publisher" and "published by the printer." "There are but two printers in our office—one ourself," wrote George Robinson of the *Huntsville Item*, "but one pressman, ourself; but one writer, ditto; but one financial agent, ditto; yet this economy is absolutely necessary, or we should soon have to 'shut up shop.'"[12]

The typical office not only issued a newspaper, but also printed job orders, handbills, pamphlets, and, on occasion, books. The more fortunate obtained public printing contracts—national, state, or local—for which they engaged in lively contests with rivals. The Republic of Texas passed the printing around to various offices, depending on the faction in power and the location of the government at the time. The state contract went early to the *Texas State Gazette* at Austin, which fended off all challengers during the 1850s to become in effect the official printer for the state. The republic and state both granted certain printers in various areas contracts to print laws, a practice also followed by the United States after annexation.

The pioneer newsman, like his successors, looked upon advertising as an important source of income, but, unlike them, he often placed the advertisements on his front page. This custom stemmed in part from the principle of putting first things first and in part from practical considerations. The printer who worked all week setting type for a four-page weekly paper found it expedient first to set the advertisements that rarely changed from week to week and to place them on the first and last pages. Then he set the editorials, usually on the second page, and filled the space remaining with communications, clippings from the exchanges, and additional advertisements. At the bottom of the editorial page, he saved space for any late news that arrived before press time. Thus the news that Texas had declared independence appeared at the bottom of an inside page of the *Telegraph and Texas Register* in 1836, not because the editor failed to recognize an important story, but because that was the only space left when the news arrived.

The editor of the *San Antonio Herald* in 1857 commented that few people read his advertisements, and he probably spoke for other papers as well. Most advertisements were pedestrian by modern standards, consisting primarily of simple cards or notices enlivened by an

[12] Cited in *Texas State Gazette*, September 18, 1858; *Texas Republican*, December 17, 1853.

occasional woodcut. Even so, when read in sequence over the years, the advertisements picture the transition of society as clearly as the news stories.

Real estate promotions filled the pages of the earlier papers and remained numerous throughout the period. Planters posted notices of runaway slaves, and merchants advised the public of the arrival of new shipments of merchandise. J. W. Parker advertised for information about members of his family who had been captured by the Indians, and John H. Matthews recruited men to go with him to the California goldfields. Medicine men hawked their wares, suggesting by their remedies the ailments that afflicted the citizenry and sometimes foretelling methods of the future. One entrepreneur, for example, offered Texian Universal Pills designed especially to help newcomers cope with the endemic diseases of Texas. Another induced General Thomas J. Rusk to give a testimonial for "Dr. Hardeman's Vegetable Ointment for the Piles." Late in the period woodcuts advertising railroads, sewing machines, harvesters, and windmills announced the approach of the industrial age.

Advertising sold by the square, the *Telegraph and Texas Register* counting eight lines to a square in 1838 and charging two dollars for the first insertion and one dollar for each continuance. Editors gauged the success of their competitors by the number of advertisements they carried, and many of them had trouble selling advertisments despite persistent efforts. One old Texian told of a local editor's nagging a widow who kept a hotel to advertise her house in his paper. At first she declined politely, but finally, growing weary of his efforts, she informed him that her house was better known than his paper.[13]

Subscriptions ranged from two dollars to ten dollars annually, depending on the time, place, and frequency of publication. Some editors such as DeMorse in Clarksville and Thomas Johnson of Washington on the Brazos accepted produce in lieu of cash. Most editors announced a policy of cash in advance for all transactions, but in practice they extended credit freely with predictable results. They continually dunned their debtors and drew object lessons by reporting the demise of papers because of failure to pay the printer. "The subscribers of the Weekly Despatch are respectfully reminded that three dollars in advance does not mean twelve months credit," said a Matagorda

[13] Zachariah N. Morrell, *Flowers and Fruits in the Wilderness*, p. 300.

editor in 1844. "We have many accounts and want something really more substantial—something that will pay the board and wages of our hands, that will buy ink, paper, type, and other indispensable necessities," wrote the editor of the *Star State Patriot* in 1851.[14]

Robert W. Loughery once threatened to list his delinquent debtors along with the amount each owed and print the list in the *Texas Republican* each week until he received his pay. Then adopting another approach, he announced his imminent departure for New Orleans on a buying trip and invited his debtors to pay up so he could continue the paper. "Come up to the scratch, Gentlemen, and enable us to lay in a large supply of material."[15]

Editors themselves placed virtually all the help-wanted advertisements, thus pointing up another of their problems. "Another apprentice will be received in this office," read a notice in the *Northern Standard*. "He must have a plain English education and be of good habits and disposition. None need apply who are not willing to be bound for a term of years."[16] Similar advertisements appeared regularly throughout the period, for journeymen printers maintained in Texas the reputation they had won in the United States—a reputation for independent natures, itchy feet, and dry throats. "From high to low, they are the same careless, well informed, good hearted men—knowing how to act better than they do," wrote A. W. Canfield after some exasperating experiences with printers on the San Augustine *Red-Lander*. "We have seen one and the same individual of the craft a minister in Georgia, a boatmaster on the western canal, a sheriff in Ohio, a sailing master on the board a privateer, a dandy on Broadway, a pressman in a garret printing office, a fiddler in a bawdy house!"[17]

The printers pioneered the labor movement in Texas, organizing the Texas Typographical Association in Houston in 1838 and maintaining local organizations in all of the larger printing centers by 1860. The association sometimes took on the aspects of a social club, but it insisted on New Orleans wages for printers and did not hesitate to call a strike if necessary to obtain them. The *San Luis Advocate* missed a few issues in 1841 because of a printers' strike, and journeymen printers in

---

[14] Matagorda *Weekly Despatch*, April 6, 1844; *Star State Patriot*, March 13, 1851.
[15] *Texas Republican*, March 8, 1856.
[16] *Northern Standard*, September 25, 1847.
[17] San Augustine *Red-Lander*, November 13, 1845.

Galveston and San Antonio struck for New Orleans wages in 1857. The 1857 strikes lasted for some time, prompting unemployed printers in both cities to found papers of their own. A group in Galveston founded the *Daily and Weekly Herald*; a group in San Antonio, the short-lived *Mallet and Shooting Stick.*[18]

Once a publisher overcame all the other problems of producing a newspaper, he still faced that of distributing it to his subscribers. He depended primarily on the postal service, which in turn depended on the same primitive means of transportation that delivered the printing supplies. Both subscribers and editors made few allowances for the hazards of road and river. The subscribers complained that they did not receive their papers for weeks or months at a time, and the editors continually criticized the postal service.

The Houston *Morning Star*, the first daily in Texas, initiated home delivery service to local patrons in 1839. The same carrier that delivered the *Star* also delivered the weekly *Telegraph and Texas Register*, which came from the same office, and the *Intelligencer* from the rival office. Even then problems occurred. The editor once asked subscribers of all three papers to pick them up at the press offices "in consequence of our Carrier Boy having been slightly injured by the machinery of the power press."[19]

Editors and publishers made no secret of the problems they encountered. The papers abound with their tales of woe. On several occasions some of them talked of forming an association to deal with their common problems. As early as 1840, George K. Teulon, the English-born editor of the *Austin City Gazette*, proposed that publishers meet in a convention to consider establishing standard rates and the cash system and to become better acquainted with one another. The Austin *Texas State Gazette* took up the cause in 1853 and promoted it for about a year, gaining support from some nine editors. The matter came up again in 1857 when the printers agitated for New Orleans wages, but nothing came of the publishers' efforts.[20]

Nor did the obvious hazards of the business discourage would-be

[18] *Morning Star*, July 29, 1840; *Texas Republican*, May 16, August 26, 1857; *San Antonio Herald*, October 20, 1857; Stuart, "Newspapers in Texas," p. 98.

[19] *Morning Star*, December 12, 1839.

[20] Cited in the *Telegraph and Texas Register*, July 1, 1840; *Texas State Gazette*, April 2, 1853, and March 22 and May 27, 1854; Austin *Texas State Times*, April 4, 1857.

newsmen. When one publisher failed, another waited to take his place. No matter the problems involved, the monopoly on public communication proved an irresistible attraction to a succession of literate, opinionated, and often remarkable men. As a group they gravitated to the center of action, military or political, and they rarely backed away from a controversy. Otherwise, they had little in common, for they represented the varied population of frontier Texas. Only a few like Hamilton Stuart and Charles DeMorse made lifetime careers in journalism, and even they did not depend solely on their newspapers for a livelihood. Most conducted a newspaper for only a season, in conjunction with other pursuits, and for a specific purpose. Many proved their ability—and their diversity—by their successes in other areas. Mirabeau B. Lamar served as president of the Republic of Texas; Gail Borden made a fortune in condensed milk; Legs Lewis helped lay the foundation of the King Ranch; Ferdinand Lindheimer distinguished himself as a botanist. Often their neighbors disagreed with them on issues; yet editors and publishers held a unique position in the community. The paper gave each the opportunity not enjoyed by his neighbors of presenting his views to a wide audience and of possibly molding public opinion. The press office, moreover, even the most financially strapped, served as a clearing house of news and a focal point of the community. Thus, men continued to accept the challenge, and newspapers continued to appear.

Editors alternately applauded and deplored the proliferation of newspapers, pointing out on the one hand that newspapers signaled the advance of civilization and on the other that the sheer numbers made it impossible for any newsman to earn an adequate livelihood. From the 1840s editors declared that no city in the United States had more papers per capita than Galveston, and in 1859 one noted that Crockett, with a population of 464—"not as many persons really" as in the Saint Charles Hotel at New Orleans during the busy season— boasted two newspapers. "The business has been overdone," admitted one editor, while another observed with resignation that Texas had a "passion" for newspapers.[21]

[21] *Texas Republican*, January 21, 1859; *San Antonio Herald*, October 20, 1857.

CHAPTER 2

Gaceta de Texas

THE first newspaper prepared in Texas was spawned by war and revolution on a grand scale. In 1813 Europe neared the end of that quarter of a century of turmoil that began as the French Revolution and continued as the Napoleonic Wars. The long trauma caused repercussions across the Atlantic. The United States, an emerging nation, prospered by trading with the warring powers and doubled in size when military considerations prompted Napoleon to part with Louisiana.

These fringe benefits from Europe's troubles made the Americans bold and greedy. They threatened war against any power that interfered with their European shipping and cast proprietary glances at additional territory. To the southeast lay Florida and to the southwest Mexico, both held by a decadent Spain and both inviting to American intrigue. Florida, isolated from the remainder of the Spanish-American empire, was an obvious target for expansionists, while northern Mexico as far as the Rio Grande was claimed by the United States under the vague terms of the Louisiana Purchase.

Already the southwestern border had seen a full measure of intrigue. Philip Nolan died at the hands of Spanish soldiers during an adventure in Texas in 1799, and in 1806, three years after the purchase, young Lieutenant Zebulon Pike set out on a western journey that brought him home across Texas as a Spanish prisoner.

Almost simultaneously with the Pike adventure, Aaron Burr played games of uncertain stakes that most certainly involved southwestern territory. The charges and countercharges that came in the wake of the Burr affair lulled the spirit of intrigue in the southwest without quenching it. The intriguers simply bided their time awaiting a propitious moment, their sentiments expressed by none less than Thomas Jefferson. "They are ours," Jefferson wrote of the adjacent territories in 1809, "the first moment that any war is forced upon us."[1]

By early 1812 the war they awaited seemed at hand. On the high seas Great Britain, still fighting Napoleon, continued to stop American shipping, and along the western border rumors circulated of British guns in the hands of marauding Indians. Public indignation grew to fever pitch and, as Spain was Britain's ally, observers reasoned that war with Britain would also mean war with Spain, a war that would clear the way for American ambitions in the southwest. That assumption underlay American thought and action along the border as the War of 1812 approached.

But American expansionists were not the only threat to Spanish power in the southwest. Latin America no less than the United States had felt the impact of events in Europe. The French Revolution and Napoleonic Wars stirred the spirit of independence and hastened the disintegration of the Spanish-American empire. In 1810 Father Miguel Hidalgo y Costilla launched the movement that resulted eleven years later in Mexican independence, an independence he did not live to see. After initial successes, he met with reverses and then treachery, and in the summer of 1811 he and other leading patriots were executed by Spanish Loyalists. Among the revolutionary leaders who escaped was Bernardo Gutiérrez de Lara, who fled across Texas and emerged in the safety of Louisiana in September, 1811.

Gutiérrez found a warm welcome in the United States, for he and the American expansionists had a common enemy, if for different reasons, and each hoped to use the other. He went to Washington, where he met with high government officials, including Secretary of State James Monroe, and sojourned in Philadelphia at the house of Ira Allen, where he plotted with other Spanish-American revolutionaries, among them José Alvarez de Toledo. Then in early 1812, as war with Britain drew nearer, Gutiérrez returned to the southwestern border, there to give his name to the expedition that was the southwestern version of the War of 1812, just as that war was the American version of the Napoleonic conflict. A by-product of that expedition was a two-page propaganda sheet, the *Gaceta de Texas*, the first newspaper prepared in Texas.

[1]Thomas Jefferson, *The Writings of Thomas Jefferson*, XII, 261.

It was Gutiérrez's sometime friend Toledo who furnished the press and co-edited the *Gaceta*. Cuban-born, Toledo was educated in Spain and served in the Spanish navy with distinction. In 1810–11 he represented Santo Domingo in the Cortes, but his advocacy of Spanish-American independence brought him trouble. Forced into exile, he found refuge in the United States in the fall of 1811, bringing with him a commission from the Spanish-American delegation to the Cortes to revolutionize the Spanish Empire.

Like Gutiérrez, Toledo found encouragement in Washington. Described as an artist with words, he became an eloquent propagandist for his cause. He published articles in newspapers and issued various tracts and pamphlets that inspired Gutiérrez before the two met. "He is a man of great talents, and passionately devoted to the cause of liberty of Mexico," Gutiérrez wrote of Toledo in his diary. "The discourses of this gentleman are admirably great and just."[2]

The two revolutionaries struck up a warm, if brief, friendship, and Toledo, who saw himself as coordinator of all activities against Spain in the western hemisphere, gave Gutiérrez advice on how to proceed in Mexico. At the time Gutiérrez departed for the Texas-Louisiana border, Toledo planned a similar expedition to the Antilles, and the two talked of eventually coordinating their activities.

When Gutiérrez reached New Orleans on his way to the border, he joined forces with William Shaler, the other man who would co-edit the *Gaceta de Texas*. Shaler too had an interesting career behind him. Born in Connecticut in 1773, he became a sea captain and engaged in adventures in South America and China. In 1810 he published an account of his experiences in the China trade. Fluent in several languages, he then entered the diplomatic service, being appointed consul to Havana, Cuba, in 1810. But in January, 1812, as action loomed in the southwest, he went to Louisiana as a special agent, officially to observe events in Texas and unofficially to orchestrate the Magee-Gutiérrez expedition. His reports kept James Monroe well informed of events on the border.

Shaler and Gutiérrez met at Governor W. C. C. Claiborne's office and then proceeded to Natchitoches, arriving on April 28, 1812. After their adventure ended, Gutiérrez described Shaler as "a man of great

---

[2] Elizabeth West, trans. and ed., "Diary of José Bernardo Gutiérrez de Lara, 1811–1812," *American Historical Review* 34 (October, 1928): 76.

genius but also a great scoundrel," but at the time he accepted both
Shaler's money and his advice.[3] The Spanish consul at Natchitoches,
Félix Trudeaux, kept a perceptive eye on the pair. "Bernardo Gutie-
rrez has returned from the United States," Trudeaux reported. "With
him is an American, whom I believe to be a person of some importance. I suppose his intention is to find every means possible for starting a revolution in the Internal Provinces."[4]

One of Gutiérrez's first acts upon arriving in Natchitoches was to
seek the services of a printing press. At that time republican doctrines
circulated in Texas, but, wrote a correspondent from San Antonio to
the *Niles Weekly Register*, "for want of printing presses they are copied
by itinerant monks and posted up by the creoles to animate their
countrymen."[5]

Gutiérrez's acquaintance with Toledo had taught him the effec-
tiveness of the printing press, and he wrote the State Department asking assistance in obtaining a printer with whom Toledo was acquainted.
His efforts were fully reported by the watchful Trudeaux. "It is said
that there will soon be a printing press here," Trudeaux wrote, "and it
is thought that it will be used exclusively to publish proclamations and
lies provoking insurrection. There are two printers; one is a Spaniard
and the other a Portuguese. Since, I believe, they cannot make a living
at it, there is no doubt that they are being paid by someone who wants
to see the shedding of blood."[6]

Before Gutiérrez and Shaler had been in Natchitoches a month,
the printing press—probably the first in western Louisiana—was in
operation, and Gutiérrez could write in his diary on May 25, 1812, "I
went to the printing office to see printed a thousand copies of the proclamation which goes to the Realm of Mexico; I was much interested in
seeing the dexterity of the printers."[7]

During the early summer an extralegal army of Mexican patriots,
American frontiersmen, and assorted adventurers collected on the

[3]Charles A. Gulick et al., eds., *The Papers of Mirabeau Buonaparte Lamar*, I, 17.
For full accounts of the expedition, see Julia Kathryn Garrett, *Green Flag Over Texas*,
and Harris Gaylord Warren, *The Sword Was Their Passport*.

[4]As quoted in Ike H. Moore, "The Earliest Printing and First Newspaper in
Texas," *Southwestern Historical Quarterly* 39 (October, 1935): 92.

[5]Ibid.

[6]Ibid.

[7]"Diary of Gutiérrez," p. 293.

border, and on June 22 Augustus William Magee, who had graduated third in his class at West Point and was then only twenty-four years old, resigned his commission as lieutenant in the United States Army to lead them. In the last week of July news reached Natchitoches that the United States had declared war on Britain on June 18. That news was the signal for action. Magee led his men across the Sabine in early August and marched on Nacogdoches, which fell easily. Gutiérrez joined him shortly thereafter, issuing a proclamation of congratulations to "Fellow Soldiers and Volunteers in the Mexican cause." The filibusters did not have access to a printing press in Texas. All reports emanating from the expedition were handwritten. But the proclamation was taken to Alexandria, about fifty miles downstream from Natchitoches. There it was printed—probably on the press that Gutiérrez had previously used at Natchitoches—with the heading "The Herald Extra. Alexandria, (Louis.), August 31, 1812."[8] Shaler, watching events from Natchitoches, forwarded a copy of the printed proclamation to Monroe, along with news of the success of the expedition.

The news also reached Toledo, who waited in Philadelphia and whose plans and loyalties had undergone changes since Gutiérrez's departure for the southwest. Toledo's plans for the expedition to the Antilles had not materialized and, in discouragement, he had become convinced of the error of his ways.

On October 5, 1812, about the time he learned of Gutiérrez's success, he approached Luis de Oñis, the unrecognized minister from Spain to the United States, professing repentance for his past revolutionary activity and offering to give proof of his regeneration by betraying the filibusters in Texas. He proposed to take command of 2,000 men recruited on the Louisiana border, join with the revolutionaries in Mexico, and deliver the entire force, including 12,000 guns and other equipment supplied by the United States, to Spanish Loyalist commanders in Texas. Along with this plan, he included a request for money.[9]

Oñis had little money to contribute and was too cynical and sea-

[8]Thomas W. Streeter, *Bibliography of Texas, 1795–1845*, pt. 3, vol. I, 31. The only known copy of the proclamation is in State Department Manuscripts, Special Agents, William Shaler, 1810, II, in the National Archives, Washington, D.C.

[9]Harris Gaylord Warren, "José Alvarez de Toledo's Initiation as a Filibuster, 1811–1813," *Hispanic American Historical Review* 20 (February, 1940): 65.

soned an observer to be taken in by sudden and unproven conversions. But Toledo's later actions proved his sincerity. He embarked on a course of deception that brought disaster to the Gutiérrez-Magee expedition and ultimately returned him to the bosom of Spain as an honored and wealthy citizen. Incidentally along the way he introduced the printing press to Texas.

Professing his determination to cooperate with Gutiérrez, Toledo rallied a few followers in Philadelphia, including Henry Adams Bullard, a scion of the famous Adams family of Massachusetts, and Juan Mariano Picornell, a native of Majorca with a long record of revolutionary activities.

The party, consisting of ten or twelve men, embarked at Pittsburgh in December, 1812, on board a small flatboat that had been constructed for the purpose, and floated down the Ohio River toward Natchez. "Nothing can be conceived more heterogeneous than this little party," wrote Bullard, who remained in Louisiana to become a distinguished citizen and who years later wrote his recollections of the adventure. "They took with them, among other things, a printing-press and a font of types, and the printer himself." The printer was Aaron Mower of Philadelphia, who would set the type for the *Gaceta de Texas*. Bullard, who rendered the printer's name as "Moore," had highest praise for him, describing him as "a man of singular versatility of talent, possessing a vast amount of practical knowledge, and at the same time brave, enthusiastic and enterprising."[10]

By the time the party reached the Texas frontier, it also included Godwin Brown Cotten, another man of consequence in Texas journalism.[11] Twenty-two years old in 1812, Cotten would in 1829 establish the *Texas Gazette*, the first newspaper in Stephen F. Austin's colony and the first permanent newspaper in Texas. Oñis kept an eye on Toledo as he and his men made their way downstream toward Natchez. "He has with him, so I have been told, plans, instructions and printed incendiary proclamations, the printer of them who is probably Picornel, and a printing press," he reported to the viceroy.[12]

Others also watched Toledo, and his double-dealing did not go un-

[10] Book review from the *North American Review* (1836); cited in Moore, "Earliest Printing," p. 87.
[11] Moore, "Earliest Printing," p. 98.
[12] Ibid., p. 94.

suspected. Among those drawn to his standard in the fall of 1812 was Nathaniel Cogswell, also a printer. But Cogswell grew uneasy before the party left Pittsburgh and, abandoning Toledo, sent a letter to Gutiérrez and Magee warning them not to admit Toledo to Texas.[13] Not content with this warning, Cogswell also set off for Texas, voicing his suspicions along the way. Thus by the time Toledo's party reached Natchitoches, rumors circulated along the frontier about his doubtful loyalties.

But events in Texas worked to his advantage. Augustus Magee died under mysterious circumstances in February, 1813, and was succeeded by Samuel Kemper, under whose leadership the general success of the expedition continued. San Antonio fell to the filibusters on April 1, 1813; the populace rallied to their cause, and within a matter of days they issued a declaration of the independence of Texas.[14]

But success brought to the surface the irreconcilable differences between the Mexican and American factions. The Mexicans expected Texas to be a state in a Republic of Mexico; the Americans expected it to become one in the United States.

The advantage went to the Mexicans following the capture of San Antonio. Gutiérrez placed himself at the head of the civil government, excluding Americans from meaningful participation. He further antagonized them by ordering the execution of fourteen high Loyalist officials, including Governor Salcedo. Kemper and a number of Americans forthwith abandoned the expedition in disgust and carried news of the turn of events to Shaler. Outraged by what he considered Gutiérrez's betrayal, Shaler looked for a new leader and, turning to Toledo, who had recently arrived, proposed that he take the command.

Toledo seized the opportunity. In early May, he went to Nacogdoches, taking his entourage, printing press, and printer with him. After taking command of affairs in that outpost, he wrote Gutiérrez, announcing his presence and his willingness to assist. Shaler soon joined Toledo at Nacogdoches. They set up the printing press and together composed the *Gaceta de Texas*, which Aaron Mower set in type under the date May 25, 1813.

[13] Nathaniel Cogswell to Generals Gutiérrez and Magee, December 29, 1912, State Department Manuscripts, Special Agents.

[14] See Garrett, *Green Flag*, pp. 175–79; and Harris, *Sword Was Their Passport*, pp. 48–53.

Written in Spanish and bearing the motto "La Salud del Pueblo es
la Suprema Ley" ("The Safety of the People is the Supreme Law"), the
paper was conceived to further their cause. The contents fell into three
parts. The first, entitled "Reflections," was written in the heroic style
of Toledo and opened with a veiled slap at Gutiérrez: "If from the very
moment in which we began our political regeneration we had tried in
good faith to establish a system both in the military affairs as well as in
those that pertain to the civil side . . . we should now be entirely free."
Then the paper hailed the dawn of a new era:

> This is undoubtedly a glorious day in which for the first time the Press
> sheds its light in the State of Texas! Not only is it the first time that Texas
> prints in its territory, but it is also the first time in which throughout all of
> Mexican continent one may write freely. . . .
> Yes European peoples! Mexico now has also freedom of the press: it is
> the strongest fortress against the violence and the tyranny of despots, and
> one of the most precious and sacred rights of man. The right to think and
> to communicate to his equals the principles and most sublime ideas of
> philosophy, can only be attained through the medium of the freedom of
> the press.[15]

The second part of the *Gaceta*, headed "Foreign News," probably
the work of Shaler, gave reports from the United States and Spain that
were well calculated to encourage the revolutionaries in Mexico.

The last section, headed "The United States of Mexico," gave local
news from Nacogdoches and personal items regarding the three men
most instrumental in preparing the paper. One paragraph noted the
arrival of "Mr. William Shaler, with a commission from the government of the United States of North America accredited to the constituted authorities of Mexico." Another reported that "General J. A. de
Toledo, accompanied by all his general staff, conducted a general review of all the new cavalry detachments." The last item paid tribute to
Aaron Mower: "The citizen of the United States of America, A. Mower,
living in Philadelphia, and having a public press of considerable reputation, being informed of the motives of our noble war, and knowing of
the necessity in which we find ourselves for printing, abandoned all of

[15]Julia Kathryn Garrett, trans., "Gaceta de Texas: Translation of the First Number," *Southwestern Historical Quarterly* 42 (July, 1938): 21, 22. For an account of events
leading up to the publication of the paper, see Julia Kathryn Garrett, "The First Newspaper of Texas: Gaceta de Texas," *Southwestern Historical Quarterly* 40 (October,
1937): 200–15.

his interests, and tranquility which he enjoyed in the bosom of his family in order to come to offer his services to the Mexican patriots, and after a hard and long journey, he finds himself at this post where today he has the satisfaction to be the first to give to the public a paper printed in the State of Texas."[16] But Aaron Mower did not print a paper in the state of Texas. He only set type for one.

After the type was set but before the paper was printed, Toledo received a reply to his letter to Gutiérrez that terminated their friendship. Gutiérrez had earlier received Cogswell's letter of warning and taken it to heart. He asked Toledo to leave Texas and informed him that an officer was en route to take command at Nacogdoches and to negotiate with the printer to bring the press to San Antonio.[17]

Determined not to lose the press, Toledo promptly loaded it—with type still set—on four mules and carried it across the Sabine to the safety of Natchitoches. Shaler, firmly convinced of Toledo's innocence, followed him, and sometime before June 12 they again set up the small press and printed the *Gaceta de Texas* as it was originally set. Shaler sent a copy—two pages, printed on one side of the paper and measuring eight by twelve inches—to James Monroe and along with it a letter explaining the turn of events that prevented its being printed in Nacogdoches.[18]

Shaler and Toledo then composed and printed under the date of June 19 what was either the second issue of the *Gaceta* or the first issue of a new paper. Even they were not certain, for they continued the numbering begun in the *Gaceta* but entitled the second sheet *El Mexicano*. The difference in approach justified the new name, for, while the *Gaceta* had been veiled in its criticism of Gutiérrez, *El Mexicano* was blatant. Blaming "calamities, errors, weakness, and monstrous crimes" on the "despicable" Gutiérrez, it called for his removal. Again Shaler sent a copy to his government.[19]

Riders carried additional copies to San Antonio for distribution among the filibusters. Gutiérrez later wrote bitterly that Toledo "published innumerable calumnies about me on a printing press which he

[16] Garrett, "Gaceta de Texas," pp. 26, 27.

[17] Garrett, "First Newspaper," p. 212.

[18] Shaler to Monroe, June 12, 1813, State Department Manuscripts, Special Agents.

[19] Garrett, "First Newspaper," p. 214.

carried with him. He called this libel which he printed and dated Nacogdoches the 'Mexican.' He introduced copies of it to Bexar."[20]

Gutiérrez could well be bitter, for, if he did not already know the power of the press, *El Mexicano* proved it to him. The hard propaganda was all too effective. The American filibusters took it to heart and threatened to abandon the expedition in a body if Gutiérrez did not relinquish command. A vote not only forced him to resign his position but also to leave Texas.

In the meantime, Shaler stood down Toledo's accusers. On June 29 at a point on the Louisiana-Texas border, he confronted Cogswell and took depositions from Aaron Mower, Henry Bullard, and Samuel Alden that established, in Shaler's mind at least, the innocence of Toledo. Cogswell, according to the testimony, had simply disagreed with Toledo in regard to a business matter and was venting his spite.[21]

By the time Gutiérrez abandoned the command and started for Louisiana, Toledo waited not far from San Antonio—with press in tow—to replace him. Toledo assumed command on August 4. Two weeks later on August 18, he led the expedition to a decisive and final defeat in the Battle of Medina. As remnants of the expedition straggled back to the Sabine carrying news of the disaster, the Loyalists wreaked terrible vengeance on the native population that had supported the revolution. Some 200 were slaughtered and 1,200 fled to Louisiana for safety. As the population of the state numbered only a few thousand to begin with, Texas was virtually depopulated.[22]

In contrast to the treatment they accorded the natives, the Loyalists followed a conciliatory course toward the American invaders. Those captured were given horses and a gun for every five men and hastened on their way to the border with a reprimand. Clearly, the Spanish did not want to give the United States an excuse to intervene. Even more curious was the course of the Loyalists toward Toledo. He was in the vanguard of refugees and stopped at Nacogdoches, where, rumor had it, he intended to make a stand. But the Loyalist commander, Colonel Elizondo, delayed approaching that town. Instead he sent nine of the pardoned Americans to Nacogdoches with orders to

[20] Gulick et al., eds., *Papers of Lamar*, I, 18.

[21] Garrett, *Green Flag*, p. 194.

[22] Warren, "Toledo's Initiation," p. 77; Dunbar Rowland, ed., *Official Letter Books of W. W. C. Claiborne, 1801–1816*, VI, 273–74.

capture Toledo. By the time Elizondo advanced several days later, the Americans and Toledo had of course crossed into Louisiana. The Loyalists thus permitted Toledo to escape and at the same time retain his cover as a revolutionary.[23]

None of the participants on either side of the Battle of Medina charged Toledo with treason or credited him with the defeat of the filibusters. Nor have historians blamed him for it.[24] But the result was exactly what he had outlined to Oñis the previous October, and his later course followed the same pattern.

Still generally accepted as a revolutionary, he lingered on the border for another three years, frustrating several other filibustering efforts. In 1815 he participated in the venture that resulted in the capture and death of the Mexican patriot José María Morelos. In 1816 he returned to Philadelphia, where he tried to sabotage the designs of Jerome Bonaparte and Francisco Mina. By then he could no longer pose as a revolutionary, and Oñis was convinced of his regeneration. Toledo returned to Spain with a letter of recommendation from Oñis in his pocket and received a warm welcome. He entered the diplomatic service, married a wealthy widow, and lived out a long life in comfort.[25] With a few more of his ilk, the Spanish-American empire would have lasted a thousand years.

If Shaler ever realized his mistake in backing Toledo, he never admitted it. But he did accept as final the disaster of Medina. By then, events on the larger stage had made obvious the fact that the United States had declared war on Britain at the wrong moment. In the same month as the declaration, Napoleon marched his grand army toward its destiny in Russia, and by the summer of 1813 his long hold on Europe neared an end. The United States and France were not allies, but they were both fighting Britain, so Napoleon's defeat boded ill for American ambitions.

[23] Warren, "Toledo's Initiation," p. 80.

[24] Warren, *Sword Was Their Passport*, pp. 71–72; Harry McCorry Henderson, "The Magee-Gutiérrez Expedition," *Southwestern Historical Quarterly* 55 (July, 1951): 43–61; Mattie Austin Hatcher, ed., "Joaquín de Arredondo's Report of the Battle of the Medina, August 18, 1813," *Quarterly of the Texas State Historical Association* 11 (January, 1908): pp. 220–36.

[25] Warren, *Sword Was Their Passport*, pp. 73–95, 113–14, 120–45, 154–58; Harris Gaylord Warren, "José Alvarez de Toledo's Reconciliation with Spain," *Louisiana Historical Quarterly* 23 (July, 1940): 827–63.

Nor were affairs nearer home going well for the Americans. In New England opposition to the war threatened to break up the union, and on all fronts military operations proved generally disappointing. Clearly the United States did not need a war with Spain. The new circumstances cooled any sentiments for provoking one.

Shaler wrote off the southwestern adventure as a loss and left Louisiana for Washington in September. His conduct had evidently pleased his superiors, for he was promptly rewarded with an assignment to the peace delegation at Ghent. Within a few years he returned to Cuba as minister, where he died in 1833.

Thus the waters closed over the first attempt at printing a newspaper in Texas. Toledo and Shaler had not launched the "glorious day" they promised in the *Gaceta*, nor, despite their pronouncements, had the press yet shed "its light in the State of Texas."[26] Even their efforts in that direction were forgotten for over a century. The only surviving products of their press—the single copies of the *Gaceta de Texas* and *El Mexicano* that Shaler sent Monroe—lay unknown in the National Archives, while historians speculated about the beginnings of printing in Texas.

Then in the 1930s a scholar, Ike Moore, considered the question. Collecting the scattered evidence, he concluded that Toledo had indeed brought the first press into Texas. Moore even found a clue as to the fate of the little press after Toledo abandoned it during the debacle of Medina. In a history of Nuevo León first published in 1865, José Eleuterio Gonzáles quoted a historian of Monterrey, who said:

> Early in 1815 there was seen in this capital the first printing press. This caused considerable surprise even though it was a small one, a press for an army campaign, as they called it. On August 18, 1813, on the Medina River, Texas, General Arredondo won a celebrated battle from General Toledo, whose forces were completely routed. As part of the booty of war there was captured the aforementioned press, which had been brought along by the North Americans who accompanied the leader of the enemies' forces. There are two old documents printed by the press that confirm this fact besides many eyewitnesses who are still living.[27]

Moore drew his conclusions without knowledge of the imprints in the National Archives. But shortly after he published his paper, another

[26] Garrett, "Gaceta de Texas," p. 22.
[27] As quoted in Moore, "Earliest Printing," pp. 96–97.

scholar, Julia Kathryn Garrett, discovered the *Gaceta de Texas* and *El Mexicano* while doing research for a book on the Magee-Gutiérrez expedition. Along with them she discovered Shaler's letter, explaining why, despite its inscribed place and date, the *Gaceta* had missed the honor of being the first newspaper printed in Texas. Even so, the *Gaceta* marked a beginning. As Garrett put it, the *Gaceta* was "the first newspaper prepared in Texas, the first newspaper to have its type set within the limits of Texas, and the first newspaper addressed to Texans and devoted solely to Texas affairs."[28]

[28] Garrett, "First Newspaper," p. 15.

CHAPTER 3

More False Starts

THE second and third presses in Texas, like the first, came in connection with unsuccessful attempts to overthrow Spanish sovereignty. Francisco Xavier Mina brought the second in 1817; James Long, the third in 1819. Each of these claims a distinction that the *Gaceta* missed because of Toledo's hasty retreat to Louisiana. The Mina press struck the first Texas imprint, a proclamation issued at Galveston; the Long press printed the first Texas newspaper, the *Texas Republican*, at Nacogdoches. But no Texas imprint of either press has survived. It was left for a fourth press, one introduced to San Antonio by José Félix Trespalacios in 1823, to strike the earliest extant Texas imprint, and to yet another, one brought to San Felipe de Austin by Godwin Brown Cotten in 1829, to print on Texas soil the first newspaper of which copies survive.

Francisco Xavier Mina arrived on the American scene as Toledo was leaving it, and their paths crossed briefly in the northeast. A dashing Spanish patriot, Mina won renown as a guerrilla fighter during the struggle against Napoleon. But after Napoleon's defeat, he became disillusioned with the policies of the restored monarch, Ferdinand VII. When Ferdinand renounced the Constitution of 1812, Mina launched a resistance movement. That failed, and he fled to England, where he became the darling of the liberals. With encouragement from his new friends, he decided to cast his lot in the New World and organized an expedition to aid the Mexican revolutionaries. Only twenty-six years old when he sailed from Liverpool in May, 1816, Mina carried with him munitions, a small printing press, and a few European adventurers. He knew virtually nothing of the situation in Mexico, but he learned after arriving at Baltimore that José Manuel de Herrera, an

agent of the revolutionaries, resided in New Orleans, and that Luis
Aury, whom Herrera had appointed governor of Texas, had established
himself at Galveston. He thus determined to join them.[1]

Mina's reputation preceded him to the United States, and he received the same welcome as others of his ilk. The government ignored,
perhaps even encouraged, his activities; businessmen collected money
to outfit his ships; and recruits rallied to his banner—among them, two
boys, Samuel Bangs and John J. McLaren, who enlisted as printers to
help operate his printing press.

Luis de Oñis, ever faithful to Spain, again took what measures he
could to protect his monarch. He sent letter after letter to the American government, detailing Mina's activities, and, when that government showed no disposition to act, he turned to Toledo. Toledo had
done what damage he could to the cause of revolution in Mexico and
had come to offer proof of his allegiance to Oñis. Oñis accepted the
proof and gave him one additional assignment: that of sabotaging the
Mina expedition. Obligingly, Toledo tried to insinuate himself into
the expedition, but his reputation too had gone before him. His services were declined, and, hiring an assassin to kill Mina, he departed
for Spain to begin the next—and brighter—chapter in his life.[2]

Even without help from Toledo, the hired assassin, or the United
States government, the expedition failed as thoroughly as Oñis could
have wished. Bad weather, desertions, and disease plagued Mina as he
sailed for the southwest, and when he arrived at Galveston he received
a cool welcome from Aury, a French buccaneer who posed as a Mexican
revolutionary only at his convenience. A power struggle immediately
developed between the two leaders, and only after several days of negotiation did Aury permit Mina to land.

Along with some three hundred men, Mina landed his printing
press, and—with supervision from Joaquin Infante—Samuel Bangs
and John J. McLaren began printing orders of the day. Under the date
of February 22, 1817, they struck the first documented Texas imprint, a
proclamation by Mina similar to one he had issued earlier in Pennsylvania. In it he explained his reasons for coming to America and justified

[1] Harris Gaylord Warren, *The Sword Was Their Passport*, pp. 146–72. The standard firsthand account of the Mina Expedition is William Davis Robinson, *Memoirs of
the Mexican Revolution Including a Narrative of the Expedition of General Xavier Mina*.
[2] Warren, *Sword Was Their Passport*, pp. 154, 157.

his actions; on the back the young printers placed Spanish versions of their names, Juan J. M:Laran and S. Bancs. No original copy survives, but the proclamation is known from a reprint in Carlos María Busta-mante, *Cuadro histórico de la revolución de la América Mexicana.*[3]

After Mina's men had sojourned for several months at Galveston, Aury agreed to transport them to Mexico. Thus, on April 7, 1817, the entire force abandoned the island, burning their quarters as they left. The fleet stopped at the mouth of the Rio Grande to replenish the wa-ter supply, and while there Bangs and McLaren printed yet another version of Mina's proclamation, one bearing the notation "Rio Bravo del norte a 12 de abril de 1817." If this version was printed in Texas territorial waters, it stands as a second documented Texas imprint, but again no original has survived. It too was reprinted in Bustamante, *Cuadro histórico*, however, and two copies of a contemporary printing made by the Mina press at Soto la Marina have survived. Aury depos-ited Mina, his men, and the printing press at Soto la Marina in mid-April, and under the date "25 de abril de 1817" the Río Bravo procla-mation was printed again with the title *Boletin I de la Division Ausiliar de la Republica Mexicana.* Two copies of the *Boletin*, one in the Na-tional Museum of Mexico and the other in the Thomas W. Streeter Collection at Yale University, are among the extant products of the Mina printing press.[4]

After reaching Soto la Marina, the expedition disintegrated. Aury and his ships sailed away to other adventures; a group of Anglo-Ameri-cans abandoned Mina and headed for Texas; Mina and the majority headed for the interior of Mexico, where they eventually met defeat and Mina died before a Royalist firing squad. In the general disintegra-tion, John J. McLaren vanished forever from the pages of history, but Samuel Bangs proved of more durable stuff. Shortly after the landing he printed his first known separate imprint, a broadside entitled *Can-cion Patriotica—que, al desembarcar el general Mina y sus tropas en la Barra de Santander, compuso Joaquin Infante, auditor de la divi-*

[3]2nd ed., Mexico, 1843–46, IV, 317–23. For a translation of the proclamation, see Lota M. Spell, *Pioneer Printer: Samuel Bangs in Mexico and Texas*, pp. 154–59. See also Spell, *Pioneer Printer*, pp. 16–19; and Thomas W. Streeter, *Bibliography of Texas, 1795–1845*, pt. 1, vol. I, xxxiii–xxxiv.

[4]Streeter, *Bibliography of Texas*; Spell, *Pioneer Printer*, p. 25. For a translation of the *Boletin*, see Spell, pp. 159–63.

sion. A copy in the Streeter Collection at Yale is also among the extant imprints of the Mina press.[5]

Not long after the printing of the *Cancion*, the Royalists captured Bangs and the press. They welcomed it as a novelty in northern Mexico and, eager to put it to work, spared Bangs's life, for only he knew how to operate it. Most of his companions died before a firing squad. Ironically, the press and printer brought to Mexico to promote the revolution went to work for the opposition.

Bangs remained a prisoner-printer until the ultimate success of the Mexican Revolution freed him. For a time he served the new government. Then he returned to his home in New England, where he visited his family and married. Finding no satisfactory occupation there, he returned to Mexico and established himself as a printer in Tamaulipas. He was there in 1835 when an American abolitionist visited with him and described him as the "government printer," who enjoyed "in a high degree, the confidence of the Mexicans."[6]

In 1838, after the death of his first wife and after the success of the Texan Revolution, Bangs began a new career at Galveston. Acquiring a printing press, he became the printer, editor, or publisher of a list of newspapers, among them the *Galveston News*, the paper that boasts the longest continuous history in Texas. At the outbreak of the Mexican War, Bangs moved to Corpus Christi to found the *Gazette*. Later as the American army moved into northern Mexico, Bangs followed and established the *Reveille* at Matamoros.

Samuel Bangs made his mark as a pioneer printer and journalist in Texas, but he returned too late to print the first newspaper. While he languished as a prisoner-printer in northern Mexico, members of the James Long expedition achieved that distinction. Again international affairs furnished the leavening. In 1819 Luis de Oñis, still faithfully representing Spain, negotiated a treaty with John Quincy Adams, then secretary of state, by which the United States relinquished all claims to Texas in exchange for Florida and concessions in Oregon.

The agreement outraged frontiersmen and expansionists of the Mississippi Valley, for they had long looked covetously to the rich cotton lands of Texas. Moreover, the treaty came almost simultaneously

---

[5] Spell, *Pioneer Printer*, p. 22.

[6] Benjamin Lundy, *The Life, Travels and Opinions of Benjamin Lundy, including his Journeys to Texas and Mexico*, pp. 154–55.

with a severe panic that ruined many men and caused them to turn westward to recoup their fortunes. Indignation ran particularly high in Natchez, Mississippi, where in the late spring a group of malcontents gathered to abrogate the treaty on their own accord. The national government, in contrast to its stance on the Magee-Gutiérrez expedition, actively discouraged any new venture across the Sabine. Nevertheless, the leaders organized a filibustering expedition, recruiting men and collecting money and munitions. They offered the command to John Adair, who had been on the fringe of such activities since the days of the Burr conspiracy. He declined the honor, and it fell to James Long, a twenty-six-year-old doctor, soldier, merchant, and planter, who has been completely overshadowed in history by his wife, Jane Wilkinson Long.[7]

The vanguard of the expedition that crossed the Sabine in early June included Captain Eli Harris, who had some sixty men in his command and who brought with him a printing press and varied experience as a printer and publisher. Born in North Carolina, Harris had drifted westward, working first with one small newspaper and then another. In 1808–1809 he was a printer with the Athens, Georgia, *Express*; by 1810 he was with the Richmond, Kentucky, *Globe*; and by 1816, with the McMinnville, Tennessee, *Mountain Echo*. Somewhere along the way he worked with papers at Franklin, Tennessee, and Lexington, Kentucky.[8]

Long and the main body of filibusters followed Harris to Nacogdoches, and on June 22 they declared Texas an independent republic, with Long as president and a permanent council to assist him in governing. On the council were several old hands at border intrigue, among them Bernardo Gutiérrez. Also on the council was Horatio Bigelow, whom a source close to Mrs. Long later described as "a man of considerable intelligence and talents and not destitute of merit,

[7] Charles A. Gulick et al., eds., *The Papers of Mirabeau Buonaparte Lamar*, II, 51–134; Henry Stuart Foote, *Texas and the Texans*, II, 202–203; Anne A. Brindley, "Jane Long," *Southwestern Historical Quarterly* 56 (October, 1952): 211–38; Warren, *Sword Was Their Passport*, pp. 233–54.

[8] Clarence S. Brigham, *A History and Bibliography of American Newspapers, 1690–1820*, II, 1070; Douglas C. McMurtrie, "The First Texas Newspaper," *Southwestern Historical Quarterly* 36 (July, 1932): 41, 46; Biographical File, American Antiquarian Society, Worcester, Massachusetts.

apart from his inveterate habits of intoxication."[9] With Eli Harris, Bigelow would edit the newspaper of the expedition.

Bigelow did not serve with distinction on the council. The men suffered from shortages because United States troops confiscated supplies destined for them. Thus, the council determined to open a new supply route through Galveston, which Jean Laffite, the most notorious of the Gulf pirates, had appropriated for himself after Aury's departure. Bigelow was sent to negotiate with Laffite. "The specific instructions which he carried with him are not known," says an early history of the expedition. "It is only known that he disappointed the expectations of his Chief, and produced infinitely more mischief than good. . . . This unfortunate officer, instead of executing his mission with the punctuality and efficiency which its importance demanded, abandoned himself to dissipation as soon as he arrived at the Island; and by his continued intoxication, excited the disgust and contempt of Lafitte, to such an extent, that the latter would have no communication or connection with him."[10] Long himself went to Galveston to negotiate with Laffite, and Bigelow returned to Nacogdoches in disgrace, ousted for the moment at least from his position on the council but still associated with the prospective newspaper.

Years later Eli Harris wrote Mirabeau B. Lamar, who was then president of another Republic of Texas, that "I established the 'Star', The Single Star now the emblem of your Republic—I also established the Flag which you now use—I was proud of being the man to establish the Star and flag of Texas."[11] On the basis of that statement, Lamar wrote in his history of the Long expedition that Harris and Bigelow established a newspaper called the *Star*, which derived its name from the flag of the new nation—"which was of white silk, striped and fringed with red, having a single star in the center of a red ground in the upper corner."[12]

But Lamar misinterpreted Harris's meaning. A postscript to Harris's letter indicates that he referred to the star and the flag as the emblems of the Long republic. "There are many men living in your (or my

[9] Gulick et al., *Papers of Lamar*, II, 59.
[10] Ibid., II, 60.
[11] Ibid., III, 483.
[12] Ibid., II, 59.

country) who were present when I presented the Star and flag," he wrote Lamar. "There are men now living in this town and some beside who live in different parts of this parish who saw my draft of the Star and flag before I entered into the Texian Service."[13] Possibly the newspaper carried Harris's single star as a part of its masthead, and possibly, as he suggests, that star was the original Lone Star of Texas. But no copy of the paper survives to prove it.

The name of the paper, however, was definitely the *Texas Republican*, and the first number appeared dated "Nacogdoches, August 14th, 1819. In the first year of the Republic of Texas."[14] Harris, in accordance with journalistic custom, sent copies to other newspaper offices throughout the country. A number of the editors returned the courtesy by mentioning the new sheet in their own columns and reprinting excerpts from it. In doing so they unknowingly performed a more lasting service, for the *Texas Republican* is known only through those references.

Taken collectively, the references give an adequate description of the physical appearance, editorial policies, and content of the paper. "It is about a foot square, and reads only on one side," observed one editor. "In looking at the terms of this spunky little print, one could imagine it done in the neighbourhood of El Dorado, and that its subscribers are all of the Candidi. It contains four Advertisements, two General Orders, and one Declaration, besides some other articles."[15]

Other editors filled in the details. The advertisements, noted the *St. Louis Enquirer*, included "one which requests the citizens of the town and neighborhood to meet at the house of Mr. Cargill to choose trustees of a seminary of learning; another which shows that a Mr. Madden has engaged in building a grist and saw mill."[16] Another editor printed the two general orders, both issued by "James Long, Commander-in-Chief," and the Milledgeville, Georgia, *Republican* printed the "Declaration," a statement by three citizens testifying to the good conduct—despite reports to the contrary—of Long's soldiers.[17]

[13] Ibid., III, 485.

[14] Ernest W. Winkler, "The First Newspaper in Texas," *Quarterly of the Texas State Historical Association* 6 (October, 1902): 162.

[15] [Clarence S. Brigham], "From the Texas Republican," *Southwestern Historical Quarterly* 51 (April, 1948): 366–67.

[16] Winkler, "First Newspaper," p. 163.

[17] [Brigham], "From Texas Republican," p. 366.

The Milledgeville paper also printed in full a statement of purpose issued by the editors of the *Texas Republican* in their first issue:

> As this is the first Press established in this section of America, and owing to the many difficulties that arise in procuring the materials for carrying on a newspaper, the editor deems it a duty he owes to those who may be desirous to read his journal, to give them an idea of the object of the work.
>
> The paper will be liberal in its principles, and will give a description of this beautiful country, hitherto so little known; also, the proceedings of the present republican government, with a fair and impartial detail of its commencement and progress, together with the course of policy it has and may hereafter pursue. As our government has so lately come into existence, and has assumed a stand among the nations of the earth, it is a duty it owes to itself, and to the world, to encourage such periodical works as will clearly show their motives, their acts, and their means of maintaining the high ground they have already taken, as well as do away the false ideas and prejudices that may be entertained against them.
>
> The editor pledges himself, and that as soon as circumstances will admit, he will enlarge his paper, and forward it in the most regular manner to his subscribers.[18]

The content of the paper was summarized by the *St. Louis Enquirer*, which observed that "it is principally occupied with the military and political operations going on in that quarter." The collected excerpts confirm this generalization. Passages spoke hopefully of opening a port of entry and establishing a court of admiralty at Galveston, of alliances with friendly Indians, and of demoralized Royalists on the interior.[19]

But a running theme in many of the articles—and one that suggests the motivation of the expedition—was land. The council promised to reward privates who served with 6,400 acres of good quality land; the readers were advised of the promising settlements and land "of best Quality" in the area of Pecan Point on Red River; and families were urged to hasten to the republic to take first choice of land "the quality of which cannot be excelled." In addition, the editors quoted freely—but without giving credit—from Zebulon Pike's description of the state, including his verdict: "The country . . . is rich, prolific and possessing the most delightful temperature of air and climate in North

[18] Ibid., pp. 366–67.
[19] Winkler, "First Newspaper," p. 162.

America. The water is pure and clear and the country throughout very well watered."[20]

Frankly conceived to promote the interests of the venture, the *Texas Republican* nevertheless reported between the lines the weaknesses. The editors denied too often that the soldiers were behaving atrociously. Three citizens felt called upon to certify that the soldiers were so well behaved; General Long on the day his republic was declared issued a letter trusting "that no individual" would tarnish the character of the group; and the editors later advised sternly that "no persons, for the future, will be received into the Republican Army unless they are of good moral character and come well recommended or give sufficient assurance for their good conduct."[21]

Nor could the editors conceal their disappointment at the conduct of the United States—"a government to which we are all attached, and have long hoped that we should one day or another be governed by its laws." Recent hostile acts having disspelled those hopes, the *Texas Republican* promised "we will now try to govern ourselves and to have the laws as nearly assimilated to them as possible."[22]

Nor, one reads again between the lines, did recruits and settlers rally to the cause as the filibusters had hoped. The promise of land to soldiers provided for a sliding scale that sharply reduced the reward to those who failed to enlist immediately. A similar message went to prospective settlers, informing them that early arrivals would have "the most choice lands, in greater abundance, and on better terms, than those who wait to see our troubles over without shewing a disposition to effect the settlement of the country or contributing in any manner to advance the cause."[23]

The paper, a weekly, appeared August 14, August 28, and possibly a few times in September. Then it lapsed into a silence that told more eloquently than any words the fate of the Long Expedition. The several hundred men at Nacogdoches found themselves without supplies after confiscations by the United States, and no help came from Jean

[20] Ernest W. Winkler, "The Texas Republican," *Southwestern Historical Quarterly* 16 (January, 1913): 331; McMurtrie, "First Texas Newspaper," p. 43. Cf. Pike, *Sources of the Mississippi and the Western Louisiana Territory*, appendix to p. III, pp. 30–32.

[21] Ernest W. Winkler, "Note on the Texas Republican," *Quarterly of the Texas State Historical Association* 7 (January, 1904): 243.

[22] [Brigham], "From Texas Republican," p. 367.

[23] Winkler, "Texas Republican," p. 331.

Laffite, who unknown to them was in the pay of Spain—although, as usual, working only for himself. In order to survive, the men scattered into small groups that could live off the country.

In the meantime the Royalists collected a force to drive out the intruders. Colonel Ignacio Pérez marched from San Antonio, capturing small parties of filibusters as he advanced and taking Nacogdoches without a battle on October 28. Before he arrived, Eli Harris and his company abandoned the town, leaving the printing press to be destroyed. They fled to the vicinity of Galveston, where they remained for about a year, sustaining themselves by hunting and trading game to Laffite for powder and lead. They were still there in the spring of 1820 when an American ship, the *Enterprise*, arrived with an ultimatum for Laffite to depart. "I was there at the time with a Perogue load of Venison on a trading expedition and saw the whole affair," Harris recalled.[24]

Long retired to Natchitoches before Pérez reached Nacogdoches, but he still did not abandon the project. Going to New Orleans, he found new support from E. W. Ripley, who had recently retired as general in the United States army, Isaac Preston, a New Orleans businessman later involved in railroad building, and several other backers. He also enlisted new recruits, among them Ben Milam, Jim Bowie, and W. D. C. Hall. Then, accompanied by his wife, he sailed for Galveston, arriving on April 6, 1820, shortly before Laffite's departure, giving Mrs. Long the memorable experience of dining with the pirate.[25]

On June 4 Long convened the General Council of his republic again, and a committee headed by Horatio Bigelow, again a councilman in good standing, proclaimed that the new expedition was a continuation of the first and that the council still existed. The council elected Ripley the president of the republic, voting him an annual salary of $25,000 and granting him a large tract of land.[26] Ripley accepted the honor but never came to Texas to claim it. Instead, he and Long decided that the expedition needed the protective covering of Mexican patriotism and enlisted the aid of José Félix Trespalacios, a veteran of Mexican revolutionary activities who was then in exile in New Orleans. Trespalacios accepted the title of governor of the revolutionary

[24] Warren, *Sword Was Their Passport*, p. 224.
[25] Gulick et al., *Papers of Lamar*, II, 63, III, 483.
[26] Ibid., II, 82–84.

state of Texas and proceeded to Galveston with a small group of recruits to join forces with Long.

Trespalacios also took with him to Galveston the novel plan of paying the troops with treasury notes drawn on the Mexican revolutionary
government. A "tall, sedate and dignified man, gentlemanly in his deportment, kind in his expressions and liberal in his dealings," he and
his plan initially gave new life to the expedition. Then the men learned
that New Orleans merchants refused to honor the paper money. This
precipitated a crisis that had scarcely passed when word arrived that
the Mexican revolution had taken a dramatic new turn. Agustín de
Iturbide, a leading Royalist, had switched sides and placed himself at
the head of the revolution. Uncertain of the meaning of Iturbide's action, Trespalacios, accompanied by Ben Milam, sailed for Mexico in
August, 1821, in an attempt to contact the new leader. Long in the
meantime decided that the time had come to make his move. On September 19, he left his wife at Point Bolivar near Galveston, and led a
force of more than fifty men against La Bahía. He took that point easily
but met with failure when he advanced on San Antonio. On October 8
he surrendered to the Spanish governor, who promptly dispatched
him as a prisoner to Mexico City.[27]

But the wheels of fortune were turning rapidly in Mexico. While
Long was still en route, the revolution succeeded, and the cover of
Mexican patriotism served him well—at least, momentarily. He was
released from prison, but as he made ready to claim his reward for having helped the cause time ran out for him. In Mexico City, he died of a
bullet wound, inflicted either by a careless guard or by a henchman of
Trespalacios.[28]

At the time of Long's capture in San Antonio, most of the fifty-two
men with him were recent recruits. They were also of a cosmopolitan
character, representing at least eleven nations. The second in command was Simon Bourne, an Englishman who later wrote a book describing Texas, and in the group were seven Irishmen, five Prussians,
three Scots, two Swedes, two Frenchmen, a Pole, a Russian, a Dutch-
man, and a Spaniard. Missing from the captives were Ben Milam and
Jim Bowie, who would become martyrs of a later Texas revolution,
and durable W. D. C. Hall, who had already survived the Magee-

[27] Ibid., II, 96–98; Warren, *Sword Was Their Passport*, pp. 253–54.
[28] Gulick et al., *Papers of Lamar*, II, 120–23.

Gutiérrez republic and would outlive the next Republic of Texas. Missing, too, were Horatio Bigelow and Eli Harris. Bigelow lost confidence in the venture shortly after the second phase began and, writing a letter of explanation to Long, abandoned it. In 1829, according to one source, he appeared again in Nacogdoches in association with another newspaper, the *Mexican Advocate*.[29]

Eli Harris had his fill of filibustering before the second phase even began. He left Galveston for Alexandria, Louisiana, shortly after the *Enterprise* served notice on Laffite and before Long arrived to regroup his forces. "Capt. Crawford followed me and requested me to return to the Sea coast, stating that Commissioners were there from Mexico, and offered to each officer his regular pay, and to me double pay on account of the loss of my Printing Office which the Royalists had destroyed," he remembered. "And if I would go on to Mexico I should be maintained in my Rank with full pay as a Major." Harris declined to return. Later he moved to Ouachita Parish, where he married and "entered into the business of Deputy Sheriff—and then to writing for the Parish Judge." In 1835 the governor gave him a commission as a notary in Lake Providence, Carroll Parish. He was still there in 1841 when, "crippled and advanced in years" and with a young family to support, he wrote Mirabeau B. Lamar, setting forth his claims for early service to Texas and for designing the single star and Texas flag.[30]

The existence of Lamar's republic was none too secure at the time, and apparently he never answered the letter. Nor did Harris receive land or credit, if it was due, for his design. The third attempt at printing in Texas thus ended like the two earlier ones—in disaster for the expedition that brought the press and disappointment for the printers.

The next attempt was no more successful, though less disastrous, but, unlike the first three, it was associated with the success rather than the failure of the Mexican revolution. After José Félix Trespalacios and Ben Milam left James Long on the Texas coast, they contacted Iturbide in Mexico and allied themselves with him in time to share his triumph. In return, Iturbide upon declaring himself emperor appointed Trespalacios the governor of Texas on April 1, 1822.[31]

---

[29] Ibid., II, 81, III, 280–81; Walter Prescott Webb and H. Bailey Carroll, eds. *The Handbook of Texas*, I, 161.

[30] Gulick et al., *Papers of Lamar*, III, 484.

[31] Webb and Carroll, *Handbook of Texas*, II, 800.

Trespalacios established himself in San Antonio and launched an imaginative program to improve the state. He dispatched a young aide, Juan Nepomucino Almonte, to the United States to purchase a printing press and other supplies, and then, pursuing the course begun in the Long expedition, he created the Banco Nacional for the purpose of issuing paper currency.[32]

The printing press arrived at Matagorda Bay on the *Perseberencia* in late January or early February, 1823. About the same time printer George Asbridge arrived, accompanied by an assistant, probably Godwin Brown Cotten, and under the date of April 9 they printed the earliest extant Texas imprint, a prospectus for a newspaper, the *Correo de Texas* or *Texas Courier*. The prospectus was printed in two columns, one in Spanish and one in English, with both enclosed in a border of type ornamentation. Printed for the "Govierno de Texas, en San Antonio de Bexar," it was addressed "to the Advocates of Light & Reason, the friends to the Province of Texas, and the Mexican Empire." In words reminiscent of *Gaceta de Texas*, it denounced the oppressive tyrannical government that had deterred the development of Texas for three centuries and announced that "the town of Bexar, which, by its ancient rulers, was not thought deserving of a primary school, is now in possession of a Printing Press, the best organ of information and guardian of our dearest interests."[33]

The prospectus attracted attention abroad. The New Orleans *Louisiana Advertiser* published the full English text in an advertisement on May 23, and the Saint Louis *Missouri Republican* took note of it on July 9. Stephen F. Austin, in Monterrey working to establish his colony, heard of it and wrote his brother on May 20: "I am told you have a newspaper in Bexar which I am rejoiced to hear. It will be of incalculable advantage to Bexar and the whole province." Trespalacios sent a copy to the ayuntamiento of Sombrerete, along with a broadside describing a meeting at Bexar on April 15, and the ayuntamiento acknowledged receipt of the items by writing that both indicated "the

---

[32] J. W. Beretta, *The Story of Banco Nacional de Texas and 136 Years of Banking in San Antonio de Bexar, 1822–1958*, pp. [2–4].

[33] Streeter, *Bibliography of Texas*, pt. 1, vol. I, xx, xxxv–xxxvi; Eugene C. Barker, "Notes on Early Texas Newspapers, 1819–1836," *Southwestern Historical Quarterly* 21 (October, 1917): 127–28. The only extant copy of the prospectus is in the Bancroft Library. A facsimile appears in Streeter, *Bibliography of Texas*, pt. 1, vol. I, xxi.

love for humanity possessed by your Lordship and the unusual enlightenment which makes your Lordship illustrious."[34]

The editor proposed to issue the newspaper each Wednesday
morning, printed in both the Spanish and English languages. The
price was $6.50 per annum in Bexar or $10.00 elsewhere in the Mexican
empire, and the first issue was promised for the following Wednesday. It
is unlikely, however, that the *Correo de Texas* ever appeared.

The wheels were still spinning in Mexico, and about the time Asbridge printed the prospectus, word arrived in San Antonio that Emperor Iturbide had abdicated on March 19. Indeed, the meeting of
April 15, described in the broadside Trespalacios sent the ayuntamiento of Sombrerete, was held to deal with the change in circumstances. The citizens of Bexar did not approve the new plan of government Trespalacios presented at the meeting, and he resigned on
April 17.[35]

His resignation frustrated plans for the newspaper and left in
doubt the fate of the press and printers he had brought to San Antonio.
That he even proposed a newspaper is curious, for the total civilized
population of the state at the time was scarcely three thousand, and
only a handful of those were literate. The tone of the prospectus leaves
no doubt that the paper was envisioned as a propaganda sheet for the
government, and other items printed by Asbridge indicate that the
press expected government patronage. It is also likely that Trespalacios
originally intended that the press print the currency issued by the
Banco Nacional, but, if so, that intent was already frustrated by the
time the press arrived. Trespalacios issued hand-drafted bank notes in
late 1822, but the central government upon learning of his action ordered the withdrawal of the notes and the substitution of its own paper
money in their stead.[36]

Even more curious than the proposal to print a newspaper in the
wilds of Texas is the presence of George Asbridge there. The extant
imprints from his San Antonio press indicate that he was no ordinary

[34] Barker, "Notes on Newspapers," 128; Eugene C. Barker, ed., *The Austin Papers*,
I, 128, 635–36; Streeter, *Bibliography of Texas*, pt. 1, vol. I, 10; Ayuntamiento of
Sombrerete to Trespalacios, May 26, 1823, Bexar Archives, University of Texas, Austin.

[35] Streeter, *Bibliography of Texas*, pt. 3, vol. II, 613–14.

[36] Barker, "Notes on Newspapers," p. 128; Beretta, *Story of Banco Nacional de
Texas*, p. [5].

printer, and indeed he was not. A New Yorker printer, he had gained such a reputation in his field that in 1811 his fellows invited him to speak on a ceremonial occasion, and his speech, twenty-eight pages long, was printed as *An Oration, Delivered before the New York Typographical Society at Their Second Anniversary, etc.* By the following year he was publishing the weekly *Independent Mechanic* in New York.[37]

Asbridge's reasons for leaving New York are known only to himself, but it is clear he did not improve his fortunes in Texas. By June 13, 1823, Trespalacios had negotiated the sale of the press to the government at Monterrey for 3,500 pesos, and Stephen F. Austin wrote from that city that "Trespalacios is here and it is said will go to Mexico. The Govt here have bought the printing establishment that is in Bexar and will send for it immediately." By July 9, the authorities in Bexar still had not shipped the press because transportation was not available and because Asbridge and his assistant had been reluctant to release it, as they had received only a fraction of the salary promised them by Trespalacios. By July 17, however, pack mules were available and Asbridge had surrendered the press. It was taken "in seven loads, well packed and wrapped by Adbrig [*sic*], the printer," to Monterrey.[38]

Before the end of the year, George Asbridge and Godwin Brown Cotten were back in New Orleans, where Asbridge was listed as a broker and Cotten as a printer and "Collector of Marine Intelligence."[39] As late as 1840 Asbridge was still in business in New Orleans, but Cotten by 1824 was a printer in Tamaulipas and by 1829 was back in Texas to launch the *Texas Gazette* at San Felipe.

[37] Brigham, *American Newspapers*, I, 652. Asbridge's speech was published in New York by C. S. Van Winkle in 1811; copy is in the Library of Congress.

[38] Barker, *Austin Papers*, I, 672; Streeter, *Bibliography of Texas*, pt. 1, vol. I, xxxvi; Luciana García to Felipe de la Garza, July 9, 1823, Bexar Archives.

[39] John Adams Paxton, *Supplement to the New Orleans Directory and Register*, unpaginated. The speculation that Cotten was Asbridge's assistant is based on circumstantial evidence. The two simultaneously left and returned to New Orleans during this period, and Cotten was in and out of northern Mexico from 1812.

CHAPTER 4

The Permanent Press: Great Big Cotten

BETWEEN 1823 and 1829 no press operated in Texas. Yet those years were significant ones, for they prepared the way for a permanent press. Even as James Long gathered his forces at Galveston, Moses Austin trudged across Texas to present a plan of colonization to the Spanish governor, and even as George Asbridge envisioned the *Correo de Texas* at San Antonio, Stephen F. Austin labored in Mexico to confirm his deceased father's plan.

The Austins, like James Long, were pushed into Texas by the Panic of 1819, and for them, as for Long, the great attraction was land. But their approach was different. Where Long came as a military man, they came as displaced persons seeking a home, and their approach was as successful as his was disastrous. Mexico not only confirmed the grant Spain had given Moses Austin, but issued additional grants to others who agreed to bring settlers to Texas. Throughout the early 1820s a steady stream of Anglo-American pioneers poured into the state until their sheer numbers caused misgivings on the part of Mexican officials. Overtures by the United States to buy Texas added to those misgivings, and the abortive Fredonian revolution of 1827 turned the misgivings to alarm. In 1828 a Mexican official, Manuel de Mier y Terán, inspected the state and confirmed his government's worst fears. Unless "timely measures" were taken, Mexico would lose Texas, he warned. "Among these foreigners are fugitives from justice, honest laborers, vagabonds and criminals, but honorable and dishonorable alike travel with their political constitutions in their pockets, demanding the privileges, authority and officers which such a constitution guarantees."[1]

[1]Eugene C. Barker, *The Life of Stephen F. Austin, Founder of Texas, 1793–1836*, p. 261.

Freedom of the press was an integral part of the constitution the "foreigners" carried with them, and the pioneer printer never lagged far behind as they pushed westward. Even before the success of Austin's colony was assured, he recognized the advantage of a newspaper in the development of the country, and in the wake of the Fredonian rebellion he recognized the advantage of a newspaper that voiced his sentiments.

Austin strongly opposed the Fredonians and with justification feared the reaction of the Mexican government to them. Thus he was incensed when the *Natchitoches Courier* printed their proclamations and gave them a sympathetic hearing. Two other empresarios, David G. Burnet, later ad interim president of the Republic of Texas, and his partner Humphrey Fullerton of Ohio, were equally annoyed at the *Courier*, and Austin joined with them to plan a newspaper, the *Texas Gazette*, to be "devoted to Literature, News, and the general Politics of the day."

They enlisted J. A. Bingham as editor, and on April 2, 1827, he issued a prospectus that showed every evidence of hasty and imperfect planning. He proposed to publish the paper, a weekly, as soon as possible after "Messrs. Burnet and Fullerton or Col. Austin" had received deposits from three hundred subscribers. "The precise town or place where the Gazette would be published cannot at this time, be definitely selected," he wrote, "but St. Philip is named."[2]

Even before the prospectus appeared, Milton Slocum, who with Benjamin Buisson edited the *Courier*, learned of Austin's displeasure. As Austin and other Texans were patrons or potential patrons for the struggling press, Slocum tried to make amends. "I have understood from several persons that you were highly Displeased with the course which I have pursued relative to the late insurection In your province . . . in my paper," he wrote. "I can assure you Sir, if any eroneous statements have been made by me they were unintentional and that the columns of my paper will be open to any one who wishes to refute them."[3]

Austin accepted the apology and received an even more reassuring letter. "It gives me pleasure to learn that you do not attribute to me bad motives for the course I have pursued relative to the late unfortu-

---

[2] Thomas W. Streeter, *Bibliography of Texas, 1795–1845*, pt. 1, vol. II, 544.
[3] Eugene C. Barker, ed., *The Austin Papers*, I, 1616.

nate troubles which have been brought upon your province by the late Fredonians," Slocum wrote. "I can assure you that every person in this place is opposed to the conduct of these late renegades." Slocum then asked Austin for news from Texas and Mexico and offered to send northern papers in exchange. Austin subscribed to the *Courier* and later in the year sent Slocum an account of the adoption of a state constitution for Coahuila-Texas, along with a copy of the constitution.[4]

Either because of Slocum's conciliatory attitude or for lack of three hundred subscribers, Austin suspended plans for the *Texas Gazette* in 1827. But he kept a wary eye on Milton Slocum and eastern Texas. Two years later when Slocum brought his printing press to Nacogdoches, Austin promptly revived plans for the *Gazette*; and only weeks after Slocum began printing the *Mexican Advocate*, the first issue of the *Texas Gazette* appeared.

The almost simultaneous publication of the two papers ushered in the age of the permanent press in Texas, a milestone the *Niles Register* of November 28, 1829, noted with a few lines under "Interesting Items": "Mr. G. B. Cotton is about to commence a newspaper at St. Felipe de Austin in Texas. A newspaper has been recently commenced at Nacogdoches." Closer at hand, the newspapers also attracted attention. "I am happy to see the establishing of printing offices amongst us," Thomas McKinney wrote Austin from Nacogdoches on September 9, "and seriously hope that soon they may inform both the people of this and adjoining countries so that many existing evils may be eradicated."[5]

If Austin felt misgivings about Milton Slocum, they proved unfounded. Slocum arrived at Nacogdoches in early June, 1829, and shortly thereafter applied for citizenship, stating that he was a printer by trade, a native of Massachusetts, and a recent resident of Louisiana. In addition, he was unmarried, twenty-six years old, and a Roman Catholic. Slocum took the oath required of printers that he would not disturb the peace with seditious papers, and on August 4 the alcalde of Nacogdoches sent an *impreso*, either a prospectus or a copy of the newspaper, to the political chief.[6]

No copy of the *Mexican Advocate* survives, but it was definitely in

[4] Ibid., I, 1620, 1662.
[5] Ibid., II, 257.
[6] Eugene C. Barker, "Notes on Early Texas Newspapers 1819–1836," *South western Historical Quarterly* 21 (October, 1917): 130.

print by September 4 and probably earlier. Several contemporary newspapers in addition to the *Niles Register* took note of its appearance. The *Natchitoches Courier* cited a letter from the editor of the *Mexican Advocate*, which the *Arkansas Gazette* of Little Rock picked up and mentioned in the issue of September 9. The *Arkansas Gazette* of September 23 carried the additional information that "a newspaper has been established at Nacogdoches, Texas, and is published in the Spanish and English language, by Milton Slocumb," and on October 20, the *Gazette* reprinted a news item from the *Mexican Advocate*, dated September 4, and pertaining to Spain's efforts to regain Mexico. By October 23, the first number of the *Mexican Advocate* had reached New York and the *New York Courier* acknowledged receipt by confirming that the paper was printed in Spanish and English and commenting that it was "conducted with intelligence and success."[7]

Slocum came to Nacogdoches under the auspices of Joseph Durst, who had been at least on the fringes of the Fredonian rebellion, but his paper aroused no misgivings among government officials.[8] Durst had extensive business and real estate holdings in the environs of Nacogdoches and like other men in similar position wished to attract settlers. Slocum, while editor of the *Natchitoches Courier*, had received patronage from Durst and had printed for him separate copies of the constitution of Coahuila-Texas, which were distributed to stimulate immigration. The few excerpts available from the *Mexican Advocate* suggest that it too was aimed at prospective settlers. It mentioned land grants, reviewed the history of Nacogdoches, and described the town in terms worthy of a land promoter as being located "on the main road from Natchitoches to San Felipe de Austin and Bejar." "The situation of the town is beautiful," said an excerpt that probably came from the *Mexican Advocate*, "it being on an eminence just above the junction of two beautiful creeks, the Nano on the east and the Banito on the west—the waters of which are as clear as crystal."[9]

Both the newspaper and Slocum disappeared quietly. The paper ceased publication without fanfare about the time the Law of April 6,

[7] Ernest W. Winkler, "The Mexican Advocate," *Quarterly of the Texas State Historical Association* 7 (January, 1904): 243.

[8] Barker, *Austin Papers*, I, 1516, 1518, 1521, 1528.

[9] Ernest W. Winkler, "The Mexican Advocate," *Quarterly of the Texas State Historical Association* 8 (January, 1905): 273.

1830, halted immigration from the United States. Slocum appeared on the local census as a printer in 1831, and on March 10 of that year he printed a "Circular for the Board of Piety of Nacogdoches," the only surviving imprint attributed to him. The census of 1832 listed him as a farm hand for Joseph Durst and that of 1833 omitted him entirely.[10] His press did not vanish as quietly. It remained in Nacogdoches and after a few years of silence began operating anew as the Texan Revolution erupted.

Although the publication of the *Mexican Advocate* in late August or early September, 1829, marked the beginning of the permanent press in Texas, the *Texas Gazette*, published a few weeks later, became the first newspaper worthy of the name in the state. Godwin Brown Michael Cotten founded the *Gazette* under Stephen F. Austin's patronage, and the paper, in some measure at least, represented Austin's response to the Slocum press in Nacogdoches. Yet, ironically, the Cotten press in the long run created more problems for Austin than the Slocum.

Cotten was neither a novice printer nor a stranger to Texas when he opened his office at San Felipe de Austin in 1829. The son of Edwin B. Cotten, a veteran New Orleans newsman, he was a restless, gregarious man who had followed his trade from Mobile, Alabama, to northern Mexico. In 1813 he founded the *Mobile Gazette* but abandoned the paper almost at once to go to Texas with José Alvarez de Toledo in the final phase of the Magee-Gutiérrez Expedition. Upon the failure of that filibuster, he returned to New Orleans, where his father owned the *Louisiana Gazette and New Orleans Mercantile Advertiser*. Cotten began publishing the paper in late 1814 after his father's death but, because of debts, sold it to William Bruner on January 16, 1816.

On July 14, 1818, Cotten again became publisher of the *Mobile Gazette*. By April of the following year, he had a partner named Isaac Miller, and a few months later on June 23 he announced the sale of the paper to Daniel B. Sanderson. Still later, on August 7 of the same year, he advertised his intention of launching another paper, the *Mobile Alabamian*, but it never appeared. By 1823 Cotten was back in New Orleans—possibly after another adventure in Texas—and by the follow-

[10] Ibid., p. 272; Streeter, *Bibliography of Texas*, pt. 1, vol. II, 538.

ing year he was an "Impreso" in Tamaulipas, printing documents for the "Govierno del Estado." When he arrived in Austin's colony on August 10, 1829, he stated that he was a recent resident of Louisiana. He stated further that he was thirty-eight years old—but his years were telling on him, for a contemporary, Noah Smithwick, remembered him at the time as "a genial old bachelor of fifty or thereabouts."[11]

Cotten enlivened society at San Felipe. A man made conspicuous by his "aldermanic proportions," he customarily signed his name as G. B. Cotten, causing one acquaintance to ask the meaning of the initials. "Why d——n it, can't you see? Great Big Cotten, of course," he replied. He facetiously dubbed his paper the "Cotton Plant," a name that several later historians took seriously and entered in the roster of Texas newspapers.[12]

When Cotten established himself at San Felipe, women were in such short supply that Smithwick could not recall a party between 1829 and 1831 in which ladies had participated. Stag parties filled the void, many of them held in Cotten's printing office or nearby residence. He "was the host in many a merry bout; love feasts, he called them," Smithwick remembered. "Collecting a jovial set of fellows, he served them up a sumptuous supper in his bachelor apartments at which every guest was expected to contribute to the general enjoyment according to his ability. . . . Some sang, some told stories and some danced."[13]

A leading spirit among the revelers was Robert McAlpin Williamson, commonly called "Three-Legged Willie" because an affliction drew up one leg to a right angle at the knee, necessitating the use of a wooden leg. A gifted man and able lawyer, Williamson had a natural bent for comedy and on occasion staged one-man shows. "Willie was equally at home conducting a revival meeting or a minstrel show," recalled Smithwick, and he handled the banjo "like a professional." Another prominent reveler was Luke Lesassier, a Louisiana Frenchman and brilliant lawyer. Smithwick remembered him as "our champion

[11]Clarence S. Brigham, *A History and Bibliography of American Newspapers, 1690–1820*, II, 187; Alexandro Prieto Collection, Nettie Lee Benson Latin American Collection, University of Texas, Austin; *New Orleans City Directory*; Noah Smithwick, *The Evolution of a State*, p. 61.
[12]H. H. Bancroft, *A History of the Northern Mexican States and Texas*, II, 548; F. B. Baillio, *A History of the Texas Press Association*, p. 320.
[13]Smithwick, *Evolution of a State*, p. 71.

story teller," with Cotten and Doctor Robert Peebles as his worthy competitors. Smithwick himself was the "most nimble footed man in the place," paying his dues in "jigs and hornpipes."[14]

The differences in temperament between Stephen F. Austin and the newsman he brought to San Felipe surfaced early. The sober Austin never participated in the merriment at the printing office, although his secretary and close associate, Samuel May Williams, "sometimes looked in, took a glass and cracked a joke." When Cotten had been in San Felipe something more than a year, Austin expressed a distrust of him, asking Williams to have some sensitive documents printed at night when no one was present. "Take care of *my* signatures, don't put me in the power of the printer or his boys," Austin cautioned. Somewhat later Austin confided to Williams that the *Gazette* was "badly" conducted but conceded nevertheless that it had performed a service to the colony.[15]

Indeed, the *Gazette* served well at the time and preserved a wealth of historical data for later generations. Not only was it the first newspaper printed in Texas of which copies survive, but it was also the most important in the state before the Texan Revolution. In many respects, it was typical of the frontier newspaper of the era and the prototype of many other Texas newspapers before the Civil War. At the same time, it occupies a unique place in history in that it reflects the growing Anglo-American society in Texas, the development of tension between that society and the Mexican government, and Stephen F. Austin's reactions to the tension.

The first issue of the *Texas Gazette* appeared September 25, 1829, with the explanation that it would have appeared sooner had not the editor and his assistant suffered illness. The paper would be "dedicated to political and miscellaneous intelligence," Cotten announced. "It will chronicle events as they transpire within our own country, or may come to us from foreign parts." He promised further that it would advocate the national and state constitutions; indulge in no personalities or abuse; obtain and publish good translations of laws; and publish information of use to immigrants and news from interior Mexico. The first issue consisted of four pages, each measuring nine and one-half by

[14] Ibid., pp. 62–63, 71.
[15] Ibid., p. 72; Barker, *Austin Papers*, II, 568, 569, 599–600.

twelve inches and each divided into three columns. Subscriptions cost six dollars per annum in cash or produce; advertisements, one dollar for ten lines for the first insertion and fifty cents for each subsequent insertion.

In keeping with journalistic custom of the time, the first page of the *Gazette* usually carried an essay or article borrowed from an exchange. The second page carried editorials and news; the third, ordinances of the local government and advertisements; and the last, verse and more advertisements. Cotten, Austin, and Robert M. Williamson contributed editorials, none of which was signed but many of which are easily identified as to author.[16] Austin expounded on Mexican laws, giving ponderous explanations that placed the best possible light on Texan-Mexican relations; Williamson aimed at entertaining his readers; and Cotten took digs at the local establishment.

Although nominally a weekly, the *Gazette* led an irregular existence. After the appearance of the sixth issue on November 7, 1829, Cotten suspended publication for almost three months to free the press for the printing of Austin's *Translation of the Laws, Orders, and Contracts on Colonization . . .* , the first book published in Texas. He assured his subscribers that the suspension would result in no financial loss to them, for they would receive the full fifty-two issues of their year's subscription. Other problems inherent to pioneer journalism further interrupted publication so that the final issue of the first volume did not appear until January 15, 1831. One issue was delayed by a breakdown of the press, another by pied type, and on November 27, 1830, that bugaboo of the pioneer printer, lack of paper, caused a temporary suspension. "The Editor is now absent . . . , using every possible endeavor to procure paper," the subscribers were informed. "He has forwarded paper for the last four publications, and we are now entirely out."

Cotten, again like most pioneer newsmen, had trouble in the distribution of his paper. Eventually, several agencies, among them, McKinstry and Austin at Brazoria, Adolphus Sterne at Nacogdoches, and James W. Breedlove at New Orleans, handled the distribution of

---

[16] Barker, "Notes on Newspapers," p. 135; Duncan W. Robinson, *Judge Robert McAlpin Williamson: Texas' Three-Legged Willie,* pp. 48, 53–54; Charles A. Bacarisse, "*The Texas Gazette,* 1829–1831," *Southwestern Historical Quarterly* 56 (October, 1952): 242–44.

the *Gazette*, but problems abounded. Some subscribers complained that nonsubscribers pilfered their paper, causing Cotten to offer a reward of ten dollars for the apprehension of the thieves. Other subscribers failed to pay for the paper, prompting him to print plea after plea to the delinquents. "Printers like all other animals both eat and drink and have their wants which must be satisfied some way or other," he wrote.[17]

Cotten's natural restlessness and his differences with Austin further complicated the course of the *Gazette*. When it resumed publication after printing the *Translation of the Laws*, Robert M. Williamson assumed the position of editor, while Cotten became printer and publisher. About three months later with no explanation Cotten again became editor. During Williamson's tenure he adopted the motto "Dios y Libertad" ("God and Liberty"), which Cotten promptly changed to "Where Light Is, There is Liberty . . . Where Liberty Is, There is My Country." Otherwise the change in editors brought no changes in the paper, for one simple reason. Stephen F. Austin, the principal patron of the printing shop and its financial mainstay, set the policies of the paper on all major issues.[18]

Austin's own motto, reiterated time and again, was "Fidelity to Mexico," and repeatedly he urged his colonists to adopt the same motto. Almost as often he advised them to avoid the tangled web of Mexican politics. Internal dissension in Mexico was so chronic at the time that one seasoned observer predicted the nation would break up into little principalities, "each governed by a popular chief to the extent of his personal influence and no further." Austin warned the colonists that they could only lose by taking sides. "No matter which party gains, it would ruin the people of the colony to take part in any way," he said. "They must be mere spectators, and silent ones, hear and see everything they can, but without taking any part or expressing any opinion."[19] Austin saw the *Gazette* as a vehicle for promoting his viewpoints—on the one hand, quieting the suspicions of the Mexican government, and on the other, reminding the Texans of their debt to Mexico.

The *Gazette* appeared at an opportune time for his purposes, and

[17] San Felipe *Texas Gazette*, May 15 and June 5, 1830.
[18] Bacarisse, *"Texas Gazette,"* p. 244.
[19] Barker, *Austin Papers*, II, 450, 517, 765, 768, 783, 1080.

later he noted with satisfaction that, despite Cotten's bad management, the little paper had warded off some blows aimed at the country and corrected some erroneous opinions regarding the settlers. In the same month that Cotten published the first issue, President Vicente Guerrero issued a decree abolishing slavery throughout Mexico, a measure obviously aimed at slowing immigration from the United States to Texas. By the time news of the decree reached Texas, Cotten had suspended publication of the *Gazette* to print *Translation of the Laws*, and by the time the paper resumed publication, Austin had maneuvered to have Texas excluded from the decree. Thus, he soothed colonial anxieties by publishing in the issue of January 30, 1830, official letters relaying the good news.[20]

Austin had more trouble with the next measure. In response to Manuel de Mier y Terán's report, the Mexican government passed the Law of April 6, 1830, frankly designed to squelch any designs by the United States on Texas. One section of the law provided for the stationing of Mexican troops, some of them convicts, in the state; another section, for the development of economic bonds between Texas and the rest of Mexico by promoting coastal trade; another, for the populating of the state with Europeans and Mexicans; and Article 11, the most objectionable to the Texans, halted immigration from the United States.

Austin used the columns of the *Gazette* to give ingenious explanations of the law. He hailed the stationing of Mexican troops as a measure to protect the frontier and predicted the goods the soldiers purchased would stimulate the Texan economy. The development of coastal trade between Texas and Mexico he viewed as another boon to the economy, and he welcomed the prospect of settlers who would introduce new skills and trades. Austin postponed dealing with the obnoxious Article 11 until September, when, still holding officially to his Pollyanna viewpoint, he blamed newspapers in the United States for spreading rumors of a large immigration of renegades poised on the border to pour into Texas. Article 11, he implied, was passed to halt that immigration, which, of course, would have been disastrous for Texas.[21]

[20] Ibid., II, 599; Barker, *Life of Austin*, 213–14.

[21] *Texas Gazette*, June 26, July 3, and September 25, 1830; Barker, *Austin Papers*, II, 431, 437, 498.

In a more practical way, Austin succeeded in obtaining from the Mexican government a strained interpretation of the law that excluded his colony. Later he admitted privately that his editorials were for the benefit of Mexican officials. The law was "founded in error and unjust suspicion, but to have said so, would have been very impolitic," he wrote. "I have excused and even invented plausable [*sic*] reasons to justify, to explain away, all the policy errors of my adopted country." Still, he blamed newspapers in the United States for inciting the suspicions of the Mexican government. "It has been my policy to slide along without any noise," he said. "Had all others followed my system and kept Texas out of the newspapers, the law of 6 April, 1830, would not have been passed."[22] Many readers of the *Gazette* neither accepted nor understood Austin's reasoning. As Mexican troops and customs officials arrived to put the law into effect, his popularity declined. Eventually, the Texans divided into two factions, one labelled the War party and headed by William H. Wharton and John A. Wharton, and the other the Peace party, headed by Austin.

Cotten also had trouble understanding Austin, as much from their differences in temperament as from their disagreements over the issues at hand, and he grew weary of the problems of a country editor. He borrowed and printed a paragraph that described his tribulations:

A Country Editor—Is one who reads newspapers, selects miscellany, writes articles on all subjects; sets type, reads proof; works at press, folds papers; and sometimes carries them; prints jobs, runs on errands; cuts wood; toats water; talks to all his patrons who call; patiently receives blame for things that never were nor can be done; gets little money; has scarce time or materials to satisfy his hunger, or to enjoy the quiet of "nature's grand restorer" sleep; and esteems himself peculiar happy, if he is not assaulted and battered, (or bulletted and his ears cut off) by some unprincipled demagogue, who loves puppet shows, and hires the rabble with a treat of corn whiskey, (and that burnt), to vote him into some petty office.—A man who does all this and much more, not here recorded, you well know is rather a busy animal; and as he performs the work of so many different persons, he may justly be supposed their representative, and to have an indisputable right, when speaking of himself, to use the plural number, and to say "we," on all occasions and in all places.[23]

For Cotten, the rewards accruing to a country editor seemed meager considering the problems, and in a new country opportunity beck-

---

[22] Barker, *Austin Papers*, II, 600–601, 680.
[23] *Texas Gazette*, May 15, 1830.

oned elsewhere. He gave his subscribers the full year of the *Gazette* he had promised, but in issue number fifty-two, he announced the sale of the press to Robert M. Williamson. Cotten forthwith proceeded to the mouth of the Brazos, where he opened a hotel in partnership with William Chase.[24]

Williamson changed the name of the paper to the *Mexican Citizen* and began publishing it in association with John Aitken, a recent arrival from Florida, where he had been connected with the *Pensacola Gazette*. Austin was in Saltillo representing Texas in the state legislature when the change took place, but the new name obviously adhered to his wishes. "I am much pleased with the new arrangement," he wrote upon hearing of Cotten's departure. "That paper must be conducted with great prudence, you have no idea there, what importance is attached, even to trifles, coming from the Austinians." Austin's alter ego, Samuel May Williams, expressed equal pleasure with the change. "I assure you that it is an important one, and must prove beneficial to the country," he informed Austin. "Williamson, partner of Mr. Aitken is an excellent workman, and quite the gentleman, and they must succeed."[25]

Simultaneously with Williams's acquisition of the press and while Austin was still away, trouble erupted between hotheaded Texans and officials of the government sent to enforce the Law of April 6, 1830. Williamson's inclinations led him to side with the malcontents. Thus, only a few months after launching the *Mexican Citizen*, he sold it to a group headed by Austin and including Oliver Jones, Francis W. Johnson, Luke Lesassier, and Samuel May Williams.[26]

John Aitken operated the paper for the proprietors until late in 1831, when Cotten reacquired it as suddenly as he had sold it. He changed the name back to *Texas Gazette* and numbered it as a continuation of his original sheet. But again his differences with Austin proved

[24] [Asahel Langworthy], *A Visit to Texas*, p. 13.

[25] Barker, "Notes on Newspapers," p. 136; Barker, *Austin Papers*, II, 599, 629. The *Galveston Weekly News* of February 4, 1850, reported: "A rather eccentric gentleman, Mr. J. A. Aitken, called upon us as he passed through this city last week on his way to St. Paul, Minnesota, where he is engaged in publishing a paper. We learn from him that he was the publisher of the first paper ever printed in Texas. This paper was called the Mexican Citizen and was printed in San Felipe de Austin as long ago as 1829 and continued for one year."

[26] Streeter, *Bibliography of Texas*, pt. 1, vol. II, 543.

too great. In the spring of 1832, in what can only be interpreted as a slap at the empresario, Cotten moved his press to Brazoria, a hotbed of the War party. There he changed the name again, to *Texas Gazette and Brazoria Commercial Advertiser*, and began a new numbering.[27]

Cotten arrived in time to lend support to the firebrands who marched on Anahuac and fought the Battle of Velasco in the early summer. But he found pioneer journalism as troublesome and unrewarding in Brazoria as in San Felipe, and his actions lost forever any hope of patronage from Stephen F. Austin. On June 29, four days after the Battle of Velasco, Cotten sold his press for the last time—to Daniel W. Anthony, an ambitious newcomer to Texas. Anthony published an extra on July 23, 1832, announcing the change in ownership, and then changed the name of the paper to the *Constitutional Advocate and Texas Public Advertiser*. For a time, Cotten worked for Anthony, but controversy still marked his printing career. During Anthony's absence from the office because of illness, Cotten printed a handbill attacking "official conduct of the public agents." Anthony apologized in the newspaper upon his return, while Cotten cast about for another means of earning a livelihood. Some months later the successor to the *Constitutional Advocate* carried his decision. He announced his readiness to practice law in the different courts of Austin's colony, observing that he felt himself as capable as many others who were exercising the profession.[28]

Anthony's initial publication, the extra of July 23, 1832, won him the special notice of Stephen F. Austin, and for a time at least the newspaper received Austin's patronage and served his cause as well as the *Texas Gazette* ever had. The Texan agitations of 1832 coincided with Antonio López de Santa Anna's rise to power in Mexico, a circumstance the colonists and Austin turned to their advantage. While the agitators laid siege on Anahuac, they issued the Turtle Bayou Resolutions declaring themselves to be Santanistas. Austin, again in Mexico representing Texas in the legislature, heard of the disturbances with dismay but, departing from his previous admonitions against participation in Mexican politics, also followed the line that the agitators were Santanistas. When Colonel José Antonio Mexia, a supporter of Santa

[27] Ibid., pt. 1, vol. II, 512.

[28] Ibid.; Charles A. Gulick et al., eds., *The Papers of Mirabeau Buonaparte Lamar*, I, 96; *Advocate of the People's Rights*, March 27, 1834.

Anna, sailed from Matamoras to Texas to investigate the disturbances on behalf of the central government, Austin accompanied him. By the time they reached the mouth of the Brazos, Austin had convinced Mexia that the colonists were indeed Mexican patriots of his own political persuasion. Spokesmen for the Texans further reassured Mexia, whereupon he and Austin proceeded to Brazoria for a grand celebration.[29]

Anthony's extra of July 23 reported the occasion in terms well calculated to please Austin. The paper carried documents and speeches explaining the disturbances and told of "a splendid public dinner & ball" given "in celebration of the triumph of the cause of the Constitution and in honor of its distinguished advocate, Genl. Santa Ana." The dinner was "an occasion of patriotic rejoiceing . . . large, cheerful and convivial; and full of republican feeling and generous enthusiasm," said the paper.

John Austin and William H. Wharton, ringleaders in the disturbances, read prepared toasts, including one to Santa Anna—"He has started as the Washington of his country; may he continue so to the end"—and another to Mexia—"We are proud of his co-operation—for knowledge of his liberal and republican principles is not confined to the land of his nativity."

Other toasts conveyed additional messages to Mexia. The Texans drank to the "odious" law of the sixth of April—"Under its baleful influence, Texas would be a wilderness! and none but those who wish this can approbate it"—and to Coahuila and Texas—"They are dissimilar in soil, climate, and productions—the connection between them is unnatural and ought to be dissolved."

Mexia responded in kind, including among his toasts, "The liberty of the press without licentiousness." Then he departed, fully convinced of the loyalty of the settlers and leaving behind a state completely free of Mexican troops. Terán's solution of the Texas problem thus came to naught, but he never knew of it. The same extra that told of Mexia's triumphal reception at Brazoria noted in a postscript that Terán had died by his own hand a few weeks earlier.

Basking in Austin's favor and the excitement of the time, Anthony enjoyed a period of success as a newsman. The Texans called a conven-

[29] Barker, *Life of Austin*, p. 344.

tion to air their grievances and petition Santa Anna to repeal the Law of April 6. The delegates, meeting at San Felipe on October 1, elected Austin president over William H. Wharton, indicating the temper of the time and enabling Austin to throw more business Anthony's way. He printed *Proceedings of the General Convention of Delegates . . . Held at the Town of San Felipe*, the second book published in Texas, in December, 1832. He also made bold to ask the empresario for land for himself and his brothers, Henry and Jacob.[30]

But Anthony proved no mere mouthpiece for Austin. The paper carried the account of a party at Judge Cummins's house where the toasts carried disturbing overtones. "The United States of the North— Land of the free and home of the Brave," ran one toast, while another went, "Long corns and short shoes to the insidious enemies of Texas— whether they be from Amsterdam, Rotterdam, or any other dam place —dam them all in a heap."[31]

Anthony also displayed a fine balance toward the factions. When a controversy erupted over whether William H. Wharton had planned the Battle of Velasco or acted the coward in that regard, Anthony printed handbills for all the disputants, including one in which Wharton charged John Austin with belonging to the Austin faction trying "to curtail the rights of the citizens of Texas."[32]

Stephen F. Austin felt pangs of misgiving about the paper by the opening of 1833 and pointedly informed Anthony that the tone was "anti-Mexican and ought to be changed." Anthony responded with a tact equal to Austin's, thanking the empresario for his advice and asking that he continue giving it. "If I do not strictly adhere to it, rest assured it will be always a guide," he said. Then in another show of independence, Anthony pointed out that the tone of a paper reflected the united feelings of the people and was not easy to change: "The tone of the paper has been caught from, and formed by the events that have occured [sic], and the circumstances and necessary feelings which surround us."[33]

Anthony correctly interpreted public sentiment in early 1833. At

[30] Barker, *Austin Papers*, II, 910, 924.

[31] James A. Creighton, *A Narrative History of Brazoria County*, p. 73; Brazoria *Constitutional Advocate and Texas Public Advertiser*, August 22, 1832.

[32] Streeter, *Bibliography of Texas*, pt. 1, vol. I, 35–40.

[33] Barker, *Austin Papers*, II, 920.

a convention called for April 1, William H. Wharton defeated Austin for chairman, indicating the change in opinion from October. The delegates voted to ask the central government to repeal the Law of April 6 and to separate Texas from Coahuila. Then, turning back to Austin, they asked him to take their requests to Mexico City.

Austin agreed and set off on a long and fateful journey. He obtained the repeal of the Law of April 6, but before he could return home he was arrested and confined to prison. Shortly after his arrest, he wrote home imploring the Texans to remain quiet and stir up no agitation over his plight. But as the months passed, his countrymen took his instructions more literally than he expected. His health deteriorated, and he grew despondent. Not until September, 1835, did he return to Texas, and by then he had turned into a rebel, and many other things had also changed.

During the first summer of his absence, an outbreak of cholera spread panic along the Texas coast and took a fearful toll at Brazoria. The disease cut short Daniel W. Anthony's promising journalistic career and temporarily silenced his press. His estate lingered in the courts for years, and thereafter the title to his press, valued at $350 in the estate inventory, was never clear. John A. Wharton acquired use of the press, however, and in November, 1833, began publishing the *Advocate of the People's Rights*, with Oliver H. Allen as nominal editor.

The paper was rabidly anti-Austin and obviously intended as a vehicle for the Whartons to express their sentiments. Upon hearing of Austin's arrest, William H. Wharton took occasion to philosophize in the *Advocate*: "Whom the gods wish to destroy they first make mad." Wharton professed to wish Austin no harm, but, said he, "I do most sincerely hope that the Mexicans will hold on to him until he undergoes a radical change, and seriously repents having given the good people of Texas such damnable advice."[34]

Word of the Whartons' paper reached Austin in prison and plunged him deeper into despair. "It is said that a newspaper is bountifully supported in the colony by the great mass of the people for the express purpose of abusing me," he wrote. "They ought to remember that I am in a distant prison unable . . . to repel calumny, or defend myself—

---

[34] *Advocate of the People's Rights*, February 22, 1834; Creighton, *Brazoria County*, p. 82.

and that I am in this prison for having performed what I believed was my duty to my constituents.[35]

Although he heard correctly that the paper existed, it was never "bountifully supported," at least in part because it offended the readers' sense of fair play. By the time he heard of it, John Wharton had long since published his last issue, an extra dated March 27, 1834. The extra was published for the "sole purpose of laying before the public" Austin's January 17 letter from Monterrey, telling of his arrest, Wharton explained. He prefaced the letter with a two-edged statement, noting that he had condemned Austin previously. "Some have thought that my remarks were prompted by personal feelings. This was not the case. They were such as I would have made against my best friend under similar circumstances," he wrote. "The Col. will find in me a firm supporter, so long as he continues a true friend to Texas, . . . but should he be actuated by an inordinate ambition for wealth and power should he be disposed to sacrifice the interest of thousands to promote his own private views, he will find in me . . . a Brutus with an arm uplifted against him."

In the same issue he announced the suspension of the *Advocate*. Expressing the feelings of many pioneer newsmen (feelings that most of them had the professionalism to conceal), he vented his spleen on those who had failed to support his press. "The public . . . have refused that support necessary to secure the existence of this paper— and it is this consideration that makes me view its discontinuance with frigid indifference," he wrote. "If, in their opinion, it is best to have no Press . . . no friend and supporter of laws, and good order; if it is best to be led astray by every popular commotion—to be the dupes and victims of every factious demagogue—to be kept in a state of total ignorance: Be it so."

Then displaying no "frigid indifference" whatsoever, John Wharton launched into one of the impassioned tirades for which he and his brother were noted. "Have you not already endured Enough? Will you longer permit your rights to be trampled on? Are you determined to drain to the very dregs the bitter cup of oppression?" he asked. "Arise! Shake off the lethargy. . . . Contemplate for a moment our situation should we be deprived of the benefits of a press; would we not be in a state of total darkness?"

[35] Barker, *Austin Papers*, II, 1088.

Having proven himself thus temperamentally unfit to be a country editor, Wharton announced that Benjamin Franklin Cage and Franklin C. Gray, a printer and former foreman of the New Orleans *Commercial Bulletin*, would publish the next newspaper at Brazoria. Cage and Gray initially proposed naming the paper the *Emigrant*, but when the first issue appeared on July 5, 1834, it was called the *Texas Republican* and A. J. Harris had replaced Cage as Gray's associate.

In the first issue the editors acknowledged that their printing press had fallen into disrepute because of the "variable, uncertain and unfaithful manner" of its previous operation. "We are aware of the many disadvantages under which we labour in an effort to resuscitate and bring into notice and make useful an establishment so effectually dead as this press must be, at present, in the public estimation," they wrote. As if to atone for past misdeeds, they also carried an exposition by Robert M. Williamson regarding Austin's imprisonment.

Harris withdrew from the partnership in November, leaving Gray the sole proprietor. In the months that followed, Gray succeeded in restoring a measure of respectability to the little press. He printed the proceedings and resolutions of numerous public meetings and committees of safety, some of which are not found elsewhere. Thus, he continued the service to posterity begun by the *Texas Gazette*. The pages of the *Texas Republican* reflect the confusion of the Mexican nation at the national, state, and local levels on the eve of the Texan Revolution. At the national level, Santa Anna, departing from the liberalism that had won him support from Texans in 1832, made himself dictator; at the state, the government collapsed in a dispute over the location of the capital; at the local, Texans waxed indignant over a series of land speculations and divided among themselves when hotheads again precipitated trouble at Anahuac.

Gray tossed in a few items to entertain his readers, reported on local horse races, and sold a number of advertisements, one of which was at least as amusing as some of the items he borrowed from other presses.

> League and Ainsworth (formerly Attorneys at Law) being a second time "choked off" from the practice of their profession beg leave to inform their friends that they have remodeled their Law Office into a Barber Shop and having a plentiful supply of scissors and Razors are prepared to execute all work of their calling in a BARBER-OUS MANNER. Their patrons

may rest assured that if they call, they will be clipped and shaved to their heart's content.[36]

Over all, his paper compared favorably with the earlier newspapers printed on the same press. Yet the *Texas Republican* carried, if not the anti-Austin bias of its immediate predecessor, at least a definite pro-Wharton flavor. Gray vigorously denied that the Whartons controlled his paper, but the documents he printed usually featured at least one of them, and in late 1834 he printed, somewhat reluctantly to be sure, William H. Wharton's card attacking Austin. Austin had written his brother-in-law, James F. Perry, on August 25, 1834, expressing his despondence and blaming Wharton for his long imprisonment. Perry had the letter printed on Gray's press and circulated it. Incensed, Wharton wrote the card hotly denying having wronged Austin and insisted that Gray publish it. After calling Austin "this trumpeter of his own praises, this accuser of others, 'this disinterested benefactor of Texas,' this circular weathercock, this political Proteus, 'this innocent victim,' this maker of mottos, this organizer of parties, this presumtous [*sic*] dictator," Wharton pledged to brand Austin upon his return to Texas "on the forehand with a mark of political *perfidy* that shall outlast his epitaph." The card reached a number of readers, at least one of whom endorsed it. "William shewed me his *card* in answer to Austins ridiculous letter . . . ," Sam Houston, a relative newcomer to Texas, wrote John A. Wharton. "I think he has left the little Gentleman very few crumbs of comfort."[37]

But the card, together with Austin's letter, aroused Austin's friends anew, and within weeks after it appeared a group of them planned a new paper for Texas. Gail Borden, Jr., surveyor and the mainstay of Austin's land office during his absence, headed the group. He enlisted the support of Samuel May Williams and wrote James F. Perry and others asking for assistance.[38] *The Texas Republican* printed a prospectus for the rival paper in the issue of February 14, 1835. Joseph Baker, Gail Borden, Jr., and John P. Borden announced their intention of printing a weekly, the *Telegraph and Texas Planter*, at San Felipe. None of the prospective journalists had any experience whatever in printing, and all

[36] Brazoria *Texas Republican*, July 18, 1835.

[37] Gulick, *Papers of Lamar*, I, 175, 201.

[38] Barker, *Austin Papers*, III, 41.

had been close enough to observe the casualty rate of newspapers printed on the Cotten press. If they did not understand the problems of a pioneer newspaper, at least they entertained no illusions about the rewards. Their motivation, politely stated, can be read in their announcement that the paper would be "tool to no party, but would fearlessly expose crime and critical error wherever met with."

Before the new paper appeared, the *Texas Republican* reported Austin's return to Texas and the first battle of the revolution. The *Republican* reported too on the grand land speculations that blighted Austin's career. The state government of Texas-Coahuila passed laws in 1834–35 providing for a number of eleven-league land grants. Samuel May Williams and several other speculators immediately appropriated the grants, bringing cries of fraud and screams of wrath from the settlers in Texas. Austin, still held in Mexico City, had nothing whatsoever to do with the speculation, but, because of his close association with Williams, he came in for a full measure of criticism. Even though the grants were cancelled later, the scandal contributed to Austin's defeat for the presidency of the Republic of Texas in 1836 and brought a break in his friendship with Williams.

Austin's friends, not his enemies, created the situation, but the pages of the *Texas Republican* gave it full coverage in the spring of 1835. Then another crisis pushed it into the background. At Anahuac a dispute reminiscent of 1832 developed over the collection of customs. A group of hotheads led by William Barret Travis marched on the town, forcing the surrender of the Mexican garrison and bringing widespread condemnation on themselves from other settlers.

For once John A. Wharton came down on the side of moderation. As reported by the *Texas Republican*, he helped frame resolutions calling for unity among the Texans and deploring rash actions by a few men. Citizens' meetings throughout the state echoed his sentiments, prompting a chastised Travis to publish a notice in the paper asking that his fellows withhold judgment until he could present all the facts to them.[39]

The furor over the Anahuac affair turned into fear as the summer progressed. Word came from the south, first as rumor and then as fact, of Mexican troops converging on the state. Suddenly the Whartons and

[39] *Texas Republican*, July 18, 1835.

others who had been passing resolutions condemning the attack on Anahuac began calling for a consultation of all the people to meet at Washington on the Brazos on October 15 to determine their course.[40]

At this point, on September 1, 1835, Stephen F. Austin returned home from his long absence to receive a hero's welcome. He confirmed the movement of Mexican troops toward Texas, and at a dinner and ball in his honor at Brazoria on September 8 he let his fellows know the change made in his thinking by his sojourn in prison. Amid cheers, he endorsed the idea of a consultation of all the colonists, taking a position that for all practical purposes destroyed the Peace party in Texas.

Still a gap remained between the Austin and Wharton factions. The *Texas Republican* duly reported the festivities surrounding Austin's Brazoria visit, including a toast that ended: "The colonists of Texas, in him, acknowledge their founder. They hail his arrival as the angel of mercy and the harbinger of hope." But Editor Gray confessed that he found the "extolation of Col. Austin . . . too high." "That Col. Austin is 'the founder' of the colony, we all agree," he wrote. "That he is the 'Harbinger of hope,' we also agree, but that he is 'THE ANGEL OF MERCY,' all will agree is absurd and ridiculous."[41]

Austin in his own quiet way took his revenge on the pro-Wharton press. Almost simultaneously with his return, Gail Borden's new press arrived at San Felipe. Austin assumed responsibility for the consultation and arranged for it to meet at San Felipe instead of Washington so the new press could print its proceedings. Clearly, Gray could expect none of the patronage.

The controversy between the factions burst into print with the election of delegates to the consultation. The Whartons put forth the People's Ticket of candidates and elected them in a manner Thomas McKinney of the Austin side found high-handed. McKinney voiced his protest in the *Texas Republican*, to which John A. Wharton replied in his usual style, raising again the specter of the land speculations. "Mr. McKinney . . . when the greatest outrage that ever was committed upon the rights of any people was perpetrated, when more than a million of acres of their land was sold for a 'mere song,' by the Congress, was you at your post? Was your voice uplifted against that unhallowed

---

[40] Ibid., August 22, 1835.
[41] Ibid., September 19, 1835.

act? Did not your partner Williams make the purchase, and are you not interested in the speculation?" Gray ventured the editorial opinion that he saw nothing irregular about the election, causing McKinney to characterize him privately as "that slave Gray," meaning slave of Wharton.[42]

Even as the controversy over delegates raged in the *Texas Republican*, events postponed the consultation. On October 1, at Gonzales, Texans exchanged shots with Mexican soldiers, and the revolution began. William H. Wharton and Stephen F. Austin departed for the scene of action, where they continued their sparring—Austin as commander of the Texan forces and Wharton as one of his subordinates.

In the midst of the excitement, the Bordens and Joseph Baker brought forth the first issue of their long-awaited paper. Gray, struggling to keep his own press afloat, could hardly have relished the competition. Yet he interrupted his reports on the crisis to give a courteous welcome to the new press, at the same time hinting at the partisan considerations behind it. "We are highly gratified to perceive that the Press at San Felipe has commenced. . . . We hail its appearance as a new Star, in the Political firmament."[43]

Gray proved more prophetic than he knew. The "new Star" would become the super star among early Texas newspapers, the most historically important and venerable of them all.

[42] Ibid., October 10, 1835; Barker, *Austin Papers*, III, p. 286.
[43] *Texas Republican*, October 10, 1835.

CHAPTER 5

The Revolutionary Press:
The Unsinkable Telegraph and Texas Register

THE *Telegraph and Texas Register* appeared in the worst of times and the best—the worst in that war plus the natural hazards of the pioneer press made its survival improbable, and the best in that the same war gave it, if it did survive, a rare opportunity for immortality. The *Telegraph*, guided by a hand touched with genius, went the improbable route. It not only endured but became a part of the drama of the revolution and the birth of a new nation. Indeed, the *Telegraph* outlasted by three decades the republic whose birth coincided with its own. Under a second editor it helped bring about the end of that republic—by annexation to the United States; and under yet another editor, it helped lead the state out of the union and into the ill-fated Confederate States of America. Not until it had recorded the state's forcible return to the union and the subsequent rigors of reconstruction and redemption did the *Telegraph* cease to publish.

As the *Telegraph* ended its first volume, the editor looked back in awe at the events recorded—Austin's return from imprisonment, the meeting of the Consultation, the Grass Fight, the siege of San Antonio, the defense of the Alamo, the Declaration of Independence, the election of constitutional officers, the meeting of the first congress. "No public journal ever commenced and continued in a more eventful period," he declared with considerable justification.[1]

Appropriately, the first issue appeared on October 10, 1835, nine days after the first shot of the Texan Revolution. The partners, departing from their intentions announced in the prospectus, called the paper the *Telegraph and Texas Register*. They substituted the word

[1] *Telegraph and Texas Register*, January 18, 1837.

Register for *Planter*, they explained, because of the change in circumstances. Early in the year "the engrossing object was the accumulation of wealth and consequent aggrandizement of the country," but in October the "all absorbing question" was how to protect themselves and what they already possessed. They promised to make the paper what its new title suggested—the organ for communicating the most important news to the people and "a faithful *register* of passing events." Another change from the prospectus spoke more ominously of the times. Thomas H. Borden replaced his brother John in the partnership because John had already joined the army.

The partners brought no practical printing experience to the enterprise. Joseph Baker's chief contribution was his ability as a translator. Called Don José because of his fluency in Spanish, he had arrived in Texas from Maine in 1831 as a twenty-seven-year-old school teacher. The Bordens, natives of New York, had westered with their parents, following the traditional family occupation of surveying. Thomas Henry, born in 1804, reached Texas first, coming as one of Stephen F. Austin's Old Three Hundred in 1824. His father, Gail, Sr., and brothers, John Pettit, Paschal Pavolo, and Gail, Jr., joined him late in 1829 and settled in the environs of San Felipe. Of Quaker forebears and Baptist inclinations, the clan was longer on character and more sober of mien than the general run of settlers. The Bordens, like Austin, eschewed the revelries at Godwin Brown Cotten's printing office, and they found favor with the empresario for the same reasons that Cotten did not. First Thomas and then his brother Gail became Austin's surveyor. Gail manned Austin's land office during his imprisonment in Mexico. After many of Austin's old friends had failed him, he asked and answered a rhetorical question: "Who can I trust? I know of no one but Gail Borden. He can be trusted for he is conscientiously an honest man."[2]

Theoretically, Tom served as business manager and Gail as editor of the *Telegraph*, but Tom had come late to the partnership and had other interests. The burden of keeping the paper alive fell to Gail. The oldest of the brothers, Gail Borden was thirty-four years old when he turned his hand for the first and last time to journalism. If nothing in

[2]Ethel Mary Franklin, "Joseph Baker," *Southwestern Historical Quarterly* 36 (October, 1932): 130–43; William P. Zuber, *My Eighty Years in Texas*, p. 40; Eugene C. Barker, ed., *The Austin Papers*, III, 439.

his past prepared him for that task, certainly nothing suggested the phenomenal success of his later years. After sojourning with his family in Kentucky and Indiana, he had moved to Mississippi in search of relief for a lung ailment. There he surveyed and, although he himself had only a year and a half of formal schooling, taught school. There too he married. Then he joined his family in Texas, where, in addition to surveying, he farmed, opened a blacksmith shop, and participated in local affairs. In an era when the actuarial statistics warned men to bloom early if at all, Gail Borden was a late bloomer. He was already middle-aged by the standards of the time and with little in solid achievement to show for it when he launched the *Telegraph* and thus carved his place in the history of Texas. Not until he was fifty-seven (Stephen F. Austin at age forty-three and William Barret Travis at age twenty-six had been dead more than twenty years) did he flower again. Then his method of condensing milk, developed after years of fruitless experimentation and disappointment, brought him a fortune and made his name a household word for the generations that followed.[3]

Gail Borden was brushed with genius, but the *Telegraph* survived not because of his intellectual or journalistic brilliance but because of his inability to give up. He did not know the problems of operating a pioneer press when he began, but he soon learned. After producing the first issue, he wrote Austin, then with the Texas army, explaining some of the difficulties. Although the printers had worked day and night for two days, the paper still ran late. Major Ward, charged with distribution, refused to wait, so when the copies finally came from the press, Borden had to send them by express to catch him. In addition, Joseph Baker and Tom Borden yearned to join Austin on the front and felt embarrassed at what the neighbors would say about their remaining at home. "I shall endeavor to prevent their going." Gail Borden wrote with the singleness of purpose that characterized him, "for my maxim is Do the best for my country, praise or no praise."[4]

Despite Gail's best efforts, Thomas Borden joined Austin at the battle front and then sent letters pressing Gail to do the same. "If I should go, the business could not go on," Gail explained.[5] And indeed the *Telegraph* would have died young without him. With Tom in the

---

[3] For a biography, see Joe B. Frantz, *Gail Borden, Dairyman to a Nation*.
[4] Barker, *Austin Papers*, III, 170–71.
[5] Ibid., p. 228.

army and Joseph Baker eager to go, securing help became a chronic problem. The first issue of the *Telegraph* carried an advertisement, one of only four in the paper, asking for "an active and intelligent boy, as an apprentice to the printing business." The advertisement became a more or less permanent feature of the paper as long as Gail Borden was associated with it.

He also learned early the problems of distribution and financing. In the second issue, he noted that "a large number of our subscribers are absent from home in the service of the country. We know not where to direct their papers." In the third issue he reminded his readers of the hard economic facts: "Every one must be aware that the expense of an establishment of this kind is considerable, and that funds are necessary to carry it on properly. . . . We hope that those who have money for which they have no other use, will bear us in mind." By November 1, the partners had received less than $75 in subscriptions while wages and their costs were running $250 a month. "So long as the war lasts, it will be a dead and heavy weight upon us," Gail told Austin.[6]

Nor did the financial situation improve upon the convening of the Consultation on November 3. Before November 24 the press had printed fourteen separate items for the government for a total of $593.75 but had not received any payment. The proprietors submitted a petition along with their bill, explaining their situation. Because of the unsettled state of the country, they had not realized the benefits they expected; their expenses had been heavy; their collections of subscriptions almost nonexistent; and in order to hold workmen they paid the highest rates known in the United States. For this they had received no remuneration, and without it they would have to discontinue. Realizing that the government had no money, they asked only for a letter of credit in New Orleans. But even that was not forthcoming.[7]

The public printing in fact proved a liability rather than a benefit. Not only did Gail Borden receive no pay, but he printed so many public documents that he depleted his stock of newsprint. By mid-Decem-

---

[6] Ibid.

[7] Frantz, *Gail Borden*, p. 95; Baker & Bordens to Governor and Council of Texas, November 24, 1835, Republic of Texas, Records Relating to Public Printing, Archives, Texas State Library, Austin.

ber he was so short of paper that he reduced the size of the *Telegraph* from eight pages to four. Then he omitted an issue altogether. In the emergency, he appealed first to Tom, asking him to go to New Orleans for materials. But Tom, another stubborn Borden, refused to leave the army unless Austin deemed the newspaper business more vital to the country. Gail Borden then turned to Austin, asking that he furlough Tom. "I have written to brother Tom, that without we had more materials in our printing establishment, it was impossible to do work to any extent, that it was all important, as well for ourselves as the interest of the country to send an agent to N. Orleans for the purpose of getting what articles we want, and extend our subscription list," he wrote. "Without a great patronage, we cannot stand the heavy expense of carrying on the office."[8]

The lack of paper indeed hurt the country. Some citizens questioned the authority of the new provisional government, and others asked pointedly why the council did not print its acts. "The fault . . . is in a great measure ours," Borden explained to his readers after new supplies arrived in late December, "the delay having been occasioned by want of paper." In less than two months, he was again waiting for new supplies and again apologizing for delays in publication: "We did not anticipate the quantity of business nor so large a subscription list, which so soon exhausted our stock of paper."[9]

Of news there was no shortage in the fall of 1835. The Consultation at San Felipe decided against independence for Texas but created a provisional state government and issued a declaration of causes for taking up arms. The delegates then appointed Sam Houston commander in chief of the nonexistent regular army, designated Stephen F. Austin, William H. Wharton, and Branch T. Archer as agents to secure help for Texas in the United States, closed the land office, and arranged for another convention to meet at Washington on the Brazos the following March 1.

Because of Stephen F. Austin's maneuvering, the *Telegraph* enjoyed the advantage of location in reporting actions by the Consultation. In addition, Austin during his tenure as commander in chief sent reports from the field directly to the *Telegraph*. Others followed his example, and as the weeks passed the *Telegraph* gained patronage so

[8] Barker, *Austin Papers*, III, 228.
[9] *Telegraph and Texas Register*, January 2 and February 20, 1836.

that its pages reflected the times. James Bowie and James W. Fannin wrote of action before San Antonio; Sam Houston and Lorenzo de Zavala gave their opinions on the political situation; Sterling C. Robertson warned prospective buyers that Stephen F. Austin's claim to the Upper Colony was invalid; James B. Bonham announced the opening of a law office; and W. Barret Travis announced the end of one partnership and the beginning of another. Gail Borden included news from abroad when it was available and occasionally threw in items to amuse his readers, such as a discussion of the correct name for inhabitants of the state. Were they Texians, Texans, Texonians, Texasians, or Texicans? The *Telegraph* agreed with the New Orleans *Bee* on Texian, commenting that it was certainly preferable to the many "absurd epithets . . . which are frequently given us."[10]

Despite a few early indications to the contrary, no feud developed between the *Telegraph* and the *Texas Republican*. William H. Wharton sent his reports from the front to the *Republican*, and the Wharton-McKinney dispute continued in its pages until late October. But the military crisis and the convening of the Consultation brought cries for unity from all factions. Franklin C. Gray left for the front in late October, leaving his assistants to handle the problems of his press and Gail Borden to carry news of the Consultation.[11]

Borden, for his part, loftily refused to indulge in personalities. In an early issue of the *Telegraph* he set forth his philosophy that the press was one of the "greatest and most important inventions of man" if directed to the proper object of improving and enlightening the world and rendering "man in society more happy." "But if diverted from this object, it is productive of the greatest evil, and becomes a scourge to mankind," he said, with a backward glance to the *Advocate of the People's Rights*. "To render the press useful it should never be prostituted to misrepresentation, slander, and vituperation."[12]

In keeping with that philosophy, he gave no space to private quarrels, insisted on "decorous" language in communications, and from time to time lectured his readers: "The columns of the *Telegraph* are at all times open to the free and impartial discussion of political subjects

---

[10] Ibid., November 7 and 14, December 26, 1835, and January 16, 1836.
[11] Brazoria *Texas Republican*, October 28, 1835.
[12] *Telegraph and Texas Register*, November 7, 1835.

but can never stoop to low and scurrilous abuse of private character."[13]

Borden accepted paid notices setting forth the Robertson-Austin land grant dispute, but he steered away from the differences between the old Peace and War factions. The Consultation effectively squelched any remaining vestiges of the quarrel by sending Austin and Wharton to the United States, thus removing them from the scene for the duration of the conflict.

By doing so, the Consultation set the stage for another and more dangerous division among Texans. Shortly after the appointment of Austin and Wharton as ambassadors, the Texas army followed Ben Milam into San Antonio, took the city, and cleared the state of enemy soldiers. The victory was so complete that it left the citizens free to engage in their own squabbles again, but the departure of Austin and Wharton left Texas without leadership. Lesser men sought to fill the void, and the resulting struggle proved almost fatal to the Texan cause. For almost two months the provisional governor, Henry Smith, and the council wrangled over authority, while James W. Fannin planned a campaign against Matamoras and volunteers gathered to defend the Alamo. In face of the confusion, Sam Houston took a furlough from the army to negotiate with the Cherokees around Nacogdoches. Not until the next convention met on March 1 did a semblance of effective leadership emerge.

As the provisional government dissolved in acrimony and the new military crisis developed, the *Texas Republican* and the *Telegraph* adopted remarkably similar policies of restraint. Both avoided sensationalism or agitation. The *Telegraph* reported in early January that Santa Anna was approaching Texas with ten thousand men, promising "to leave nothing of us but the recollection that we once existed." But after panic-stricken settlers began rushing toward the United States border, both papers generally avoided editorial comment and confined themselves to printing letters and official documents. "We give news as received, and every man will be able to judge for himself," said the *Texas Republican* while the Alamo was under siege. "We have endeavored to present facts," said the *Telegraph*. Even after William H. Wharton and Stephen F. Austin had buried old animosities to call for independence, the two papers declined to agitate for that cause. "It

[13] Ibid., November 14 and December 12, 1835.

has never been the objective of this paper to forestall public opinion and to crowd upon the people our own views in a matter so important as that touching a change in government," said the *Telegraph*, stating a policy followed also by the *Texas Republican*.[14]

Late in 1835, another newspaper appeared in Texas, this one at Nacogdoches. William G. Logan, a merchant recently from Mississippi, purchased the Milton Slocum press and took steps to reactivate it. He persuaded David E. Lawhon, a Tennessee printer en route to the Texas army, to stop and operate the press. Lawhon began printing the *Texean and Emigrant's Guide* on November 28, offering yet another name for citizens of the state. Thus, at the opening of the fateful year 1836, three newspapers operated in Texas.[15]

Early in the year, William W. Gant and Andrew J. Greer planned yet another newspaper, the *Texas Reporter*, to be published at Washington on the Brazos. Their prospectus, printed in the *Texas Republican* on February 17 and later in the *Telegraph and Texas Register*, looked forward to the Convention of March 1 and accepted as a foregone conclusion that it would declare the independence of Texas. Gant and Greer suggested a promising future for Washington as an economic center and capital of the new republic. Obviously, in view of the haste with which they planned the paper, they intended to use Gray's press and steal a march on Borden by printing the public documents of the convention. Gail Borden considered moving his own press to Washington but, upon hearing of the proposed paper, abandoned his plans, a decision he later regretted.[16]

The convention met as scheduled on March 1 and, as expected, declared Texas an independent republic the following day. Then, as the delegates awaited news from the beleaguered Alamo, they took other action. They appointed Sam Houston commander of the volunteer as well as the regular army and sent him to Gonzales to organize the defense. They elected David G. Burnet president and Lorenzo de

[14] Ibid., February 20, 1836.

[15] Thomas W. Streeter, *Bibliography of Texas, 1795–1845*, pt. 1, vol. II, 530; Walter Prescott Webb and H. Bailey Carroll, eds., *The Handbook of Texas*, II, 38–39; R. B. Blake to E. W. Winkler, Ernest W. Winkler Papers, Archives, University of Texas at Austin.

[16] Streeter, *Bibliography of Texas*, pt. 1, vol. II, 549; Frantz, *Gail Borden*, p. 123; *Texas Republican*, February 17 and March 2, 1836; *Telegraph and Texas Register*, March 12, 1836.

Zavala vice-president of an ad interim government. They wrote a constitution and arranged for a general election in September to approve their actions. Gail Borden printed documents for the Convention of March 1, as he had done for the Consultation earlier—but under the handicap of being twenty pioneer miles distant.

Gant and Greer never printed the *Texas Reporter*, if, indeed, they seriously contemplated it. The times were inauspicious for any newspaper, and the fortunes of war eventually overwhelmed those already in existence. The *Texean and Emigrant's Guide* fell silent first, the last extant issue being that of January 2, 1836. David E. Lawhon probably published a few later issues, for on January 12 John Forbes wrote from Nacogdoches, where speculators vigorously opposed the closing of the land office, that "opponents of the Council" had tried to control the paper and had threatened to take the press away from Lawhon. "Mr. Lawhon pledges himself to conduct the Paper properly and in support of the Council," said Forbes. Ten days later, Forbes referred again to the subject: "The Press here will be neutral. As I have before advised you certain Individuals are endeavouring to control it." As late as January 25 government officials at San Felipe thought the paper still in operation, for James W. Robinson sent Lawhon some ordinances and decrees, asking that they be published "in your useful paper." Because of either those trying to control him or the general confusion, Lawhon ceased publication about that time. A document printed in late January is the last identified item under his imprint.[17]

Franklin C. Gray continued publishing the *Texas Republican* until early March. In the issue of March 2, he printed William Barret Travis's letter of February 24 from the Alamo, the letter beginning "I am besieged, by a thousand or more of Mexicans," and ending "Victory or Death!" A week later Gray printed the news that delegates at Washington had declared independence. He promised to issue handbills keeping the public informed of further developments and then suspended publication.

After the newly formed government of the Republic of Texas fled Washington in advance of the enemy, Gray approached President David G. Burnet at Harrisburg offering to move his press to that place.

[17] Charles Gulick et al., eds., *The Papers of Mirabeau Buonaparte Lamar*, I, 296, 303; Streeter, *Bibliography of Texas*, pt. 1, vol. I, 131–32, and pt. 1, vol. II, 539.

Burnet accepted the offer, promising him the public printing, and Gray made ready to move.[18] But he never did so. Instead, he left for the Bordens the distinction of establishing a press at Harrisburg and losing it to the enemy.

The Baker-Borden press won more desirable bibliographical laurels in February and March, 1836. Although the *Texas Republican* was the first newspaper to carry the Travis letter of February 24, Baker and the Bordens printed it first on February 29 in several different broadsheets. The letter arrived at San Felipe on February 27 and moved the citizens there, as it would move many later readers. Shortly after its arrival, Joseph Baker chaired a committee meeting that issued a call to arms. "You must read and act in the same moment, or Texas is lost," the committee warned the public. "You must rise from your lethargy, and march without a moment's delay to the field of war, or the next western breeze that sweeps over your habitations will bring with it the shrieks and wailings of the women and children of Guadaloupe and Colorado; and the last agonized shriek of liberty will follow." At the committee's order Baker and the Bordens printed two hundred copies of the proceedings, together with Travis's letter. In addition, the press struck a separate printing of the letter, printed another two hundred copies to which late news was added, and printed the letter again on three hundred copies of a proclamation issued by Provisional Governor Henry Smith calling on "Every Man to Do His Duty."[19]

The *Telegraph and Texas Register*, lagging behind the broadsheets, carried the letter in the March 5 issue, along with the proceedings of the committee meeting. News of the declaration of independence arrived just before the paper went to press and in time to be announced briefly at the bottom of a back page. Baker and the Bordens immediately printed a thousand copies of the declaration on order of the convention, working in such haste that the printers omitted two important names from the list of signers. One was that of George C. Childress, chairman of the committee that wrote the document; the

---

[18] A. Brigham to D. G. Burnet, March, 1836, Records Relating to Public Printing; D. G. Burnet to F. C. Gray, March 25, Executive Record Book, March–October, 1836, Archives, Texas State Library; F. C. Gray to D. G. Burnet, March 26, 1836, Republic of Texas, Domestic Correspondence, 1836, Archives, Texas State Library; Frantz, *Gail Borden*, p. 106.

[19] Streeter, *Bibliography of Texas*, pt. 1, vol. I, 126–27, 172. See also Gulick, *Papers of Lamar*, I, 339–41, 343–44.

other, that of Sterling C. Robertson, who had previously given notice of his dispute with Austin in the pages of the *Telegraph*. Both men represented Milam municipality, the disputed area, so a later generation might well call the omission a Freudian slip. At any rate, Gail Borden was embarrassed by it. The next issue of the *Telegraph* carried the text of the Declaration of Independence along with an apology and explanation to the two slighted signers.

The issue of March 12 also carried Travis's letter of March 3 to the president of the convention, "his last appeal from the Alamo." Baker and the Bordens printed separately a thousand copies of the letter on order of the convention, a fortunate circumstance, for the original letter disappeared in the course of the crisis. Except for the printing in broadsheet and newspaper, it would have been lost completely.[20]

With the printing of the Travis letter, Gail Borden could not restrain his irritation at the inconvenience of working for a convention so far removed. The convention, he explained to his readers, ordered the letter printed on Sunday, March 6, but it did not reach San Felipe until two days later, and, although he printed it the day received, he could not get a messenger to deliver the copies to Washington for another two days. Taking a swat at Gant and Greer, whose prospectus for the *Texas Reporter* appeared in the same issue, he pointed out that only the report of a press already at Washington had kept him from removing there in February.

Between issues of the paper, handbills kept the public apprised of the rush of events. One on March 2 advised that "Santa Ana, at the head of four thousand men, has crossed the San Antonio river leaving Goliad to his rear and is moving upon our public stores and thence to Gonzales." Another on March 16 relayed the information that the Alamo had fallen.[21]

The news sent families racing eastward to the safety of the United States. Men left the army to aid their families, and, to the dismay of Gail Borden and Sam Houston, the newly formed government of Texas abandoned Washington to join in the flight. As Houston's army melted away, he wrote the secretary of war: "For Heaven's sake, do not drop back again with the seat of Government! Your removal to Harrisburg has done more to increase the panic in the country than anything else

[20] Streeter, *Bibliography of Texas*, pt. 1, vol. I, 171–72.
[21] Ibid., pt. 1, vol. I, 127–28.

that has occurred in Texas, except the fall of the Alamo." Had the convention not struck panic throughout the country by moving, Houston wrote a friend on the eve of the Battle of San Jacinto, "Texas could have started at least four thousand men." As it was, he marched with about seven hundred. Houston could not fault Baker and the Bordens for undue panic. Although Gail Borden packed his papers in late February for removal in the event of disaster, he refused to join in the general rush eastward, believing that "so long as a paper should be printed *west* of the Brazos, the people *east* of it would not take alarm."[22] Instead, he and Tom Borden, like the good newsmen they had become, collected details of the Alamo as brought by Mrs. Almeron Dickinson and Travis's valet Joe, messengers sent by Santa Anna to bear the news. The *Telegraph* of March 17 carried the first newspaper announcement of the debacle; that of March 24, the details, including the names of the known dead, some of them familiar to the readers of the *Telegraph*: William Barret Travis, Jim Bowie, James B. Bonham.

Still, the Bordens refused to run. The *Telegraph* of March 24, the last newspaper ever printed at San Felipe, noted scornfully that "a great panic seized the citizens of this place and other neighborhoods and we are informed even the convention itself. Much bustle and scramble ensue which has been the cause of much loss of time and many turned heads."

Gail Borden steadfastly supported Sam Houston. "No general has ever had more to do," he wrote in the *Telegraph* when Houston took command. Nor did the *Telegraph* join in the criticism as Houston began his controversial retreat. "On hearing of the total destruction of Col. Travis' men, and reasonably calculating a sudden movement of the enemy, Gen. Houston found it advisable to fall back on the Colorado," commented the *Telegraph* of March 24.

Only when Houston's army retreated to San Felipe on the night of March 27 did the Bordens consider leaving. By then, they knew that the other presses in Texas had ceased operations and had received a message from the government asking them to move their press—"the last and only medium of publication they could possibly obtain"—to Harrisburg. "I shall endeavor to put it over the river today," Gail

[22] Eugene C. Barker and Amelia W. Williams, eds., *The Writings of Sam Houston*, I, 385, 413; *Telegraph and Texas Register*, January 18, 1837; William Fairfax Gray, *From Virginia to Texas*, p. 119.

Borden wrote Burnet. "If the government can send a team for it we will set it up in Harrisburg. It will require a large waggon & team. I have none. I send Mr. Magruder to inform you. If no team comes, it must be in the bottom."[23]

As Houston's army turned north to Jared Groce's plantation, Captain Moseley Baker and his company, mutinous at yet another retreat, remained behind at San Felipe and helped carry the press across the Brazos River. Even then the Bordens could take satisfaction at being in the rear guard. "The last to consent to move, we were resolved not to be in front," Gail Borden remembered proudly, taking a gratuitous dig at President Burnet, who could not make the same boast.[24]

As one contingent of Baker's force moved the press, another, scouting to the west, brought the report of Mexican cavalry within a few miles of San Felipe. Baker ordered the town fired, and the office of the *Telegraph* was the first put to the torch. With it went supplies the proprietors had not yet removed, and only later did they learn that Baker's scouts had erred. They had mistaken a drove of cattle for the enemy cavalry. The Mexican army did not arrive until a week later.

As Joseph Baker and the Bordens stood on the east bank of the Brazos with their heavy press and without means of moving it, they looked across at the smoldering ruins of San Felipe and pondered their future. For Baker, the decision was easy. He withdrew from the partnership and joined the army. The Bordens too considered giving up the publishing business. "The destruction of our buildings, and with them much of the valuable furniture which we could not remove; the great difficulty of procuring teams, . . . the payment of journeymen, having received but little from our subscribers, and nothing for the public printing, we felt for the moment discouraged," Gail Borden recalled later. But the government had no other means of printing and they felt obligated to continue. While they still waited for teams, the Brazos River began rising, and they built a raft to ferry the press through the backwater. At last they obtained a team from Eli Mercer, Gail Borden's father-in-law, and set out for Harrisburg over roads turned into quagmires by the spring rains.[25] En route they learned that the forces

[23]*Telegraph and Texas Register*, April 14, 1836; Gail Borden, Jr., to D. G. Burnet, March 28, 1836?, Records Relating to Public Printing.
[24]*Telegraph and Texas Register*, January 18, 1836.
[25]Ibid., April 14, 1836.

under James W. Fannin, another name familiar to *Telegraph* readers, had met with annihilation near Goliad.

The Bordens were not Burnet's first choice as public printers, something they never forgot, and Gail Borden could scarcely conceal his contempt for Burnet for his precipitous flight before the enemy. Nor did president and editor agree in regard to Houston's retreat, Borden continuing his staunch support of the general while Burnet was writing, "Sir: The enemy are laughing you to scorn. You must fight them. You must retreat no farther. The country expects you to fight."[26]

But the crisis left no time for pettiness. Burnet appointed G. and T. H. Borden public printers on April 13 and they published the first and last issue of the *Telegraph* at Harrisburg the following day, including in it Burnet's proclamations as president, extracts from the new constitution, and, significantly, the executive ordinance giving plenary powers to the ad interim government. Later, when Burnet's critics questioned his authority, the original ordinance could not be found, and only the copy in the *Telegraph* gave basis for his actions.

"Our subscribers on hearing of the ruin of San Felipe and seeing the delayed appearance of our Paper have perhaps thought it was an end," the Bordens told their readers in the historic Harrisburg issue. "We have been ourselves for several days irresolute whether we would pursue any more its publication." The very fact of the issue announced their decision. They explained the recent movements of Houston's army and reiterated their support of him, something he remembered later. "Foreseeing that if ever the enemy should come in this rear, he would have to starve on the bank of the Colorado, . . . or to share the fate of Fannin . . . , our General wisely ordered a retreat on San Felipe," they wrote.

The Bordens also reviewed their own trials, telling of their disastrous loss of property at San Felipe and their withdrawal to Harrisburg. They concluded with a ringing cry: "We promise the public of our beloved country that our press will never cease its operations til our silence shall announce to them that there is no more in Texas a resting place for a free press nor for the government of their choice."

Their press struck six copies at Harrisburg and then fell silent, thus redeeming their brave promise before their readers ever knew of

---

[26] Barker and Williams, *Writings of Houston*, I, 412.

it. Santa Anna's soldiers fell unexpectedly on Harrisburg while the paper was still at press. The Bordens snatched up the few copies already printed and fled by boat to join the ad interim government at Galveston Island. They left behind three printers—"a Frenchman and two North Americans"—who were still in the printing shop and the only persons in the town when Santa Anna himself arrived.[27]

Santa Anna remembered that several houses were burning when he entered the town and that the printers told him the fire had been accidental and they had been unable to extinguish it. But one of his soldiers wrote that Santa Anna ordered the town fired and personally lent a hand to the destruction. "Amidst the conflagration that ensued our establishment was consumed," Gail Borden wrote.[28]

Thus, the last revolutionary newspaper in Texas was silenced— but only temporarily. A week later Santa Anna met Sam Houston's army and disaster at the junction of Buffalo Bayou and the San Jacinto River. The Texans, screaming "Remember the Alamo, Remember Goliad," rushed across the prairie in mid-afternoon on April 21 to surprise and wreak vengeance on the Mexican general. When it ended, hundreds of his men lay dead, and he and hundreds more were prisoners.

The total victory of San Jacinto coming after the total defeats of the Alamo and Goliad became the very fabric of the Texan mystique. The victory gave life to a republic that had seemed stillborn, a future to a man whose career seemed behind him. It also gave Texas a leader to fill the void left by Austin's departure the previous winter. Sam Houston would dominate the next period of Texas history as Austin had dominated the previous one.

Caught up in the excitement of the victory, the Bordens forgot the problems of pioneer printing and the destruction of their property. The smoke had scarcely cleared from the big battle when they determined to continue the *Telegraph and Texas Register*. As they had lost their press in pursuit of government business, Burnet promised to underwrite the purchase of a new press and gave them letters of credit to agents in New Orleans.

Arriving in New Orleans, they met with new frustrations. The

[27] Carlos Eduardo Castañeda, ed., *The Mexican Side of the Texan Revolution, 1836, by the Chief Mexican Participants*, p. 74.

[28] Ibid.; José Enrique de la Peña, *With Santa Anna in Texas*, trans. and ed. Carmen Perry, p. 114; *Telegraph and Texas Register*, August 2, 1836.

government agent had only fifty dollars to advance them, and the Republic of Texas had no credit. For men who had been through the Texan Revolution, these proved trifling obstacles. Tom Borden left for Cincinnati to acquire a press by mortgaging their lands, while Gail Borden sold subscriptions to the paper for immediate funds and returned to Texas to prepare an office at Columbia, the temporary capital of the republic. In due time, Tom returned triumphantly; the new press arrived, and on August 2 the *Telegraph* again appeared to print government documents and tell how its first press "was consumed" in "the conflagration" at Harrisburg. "Santa Anna destroyed one press and printing establishment," Gail Borden boasted a few months later, "but this printing press rises from its ashes."[29]

Seven years later another editor of the *Telegraph* elaborated on these first accounts. When Santa Anna invaded Texas in 1836, wrote Francis Moore, "he burnt the office of the Telegraph at Harrisburgh and not satisfied with this threw the press and type into the bayou." Six decades later a historian of Texas newspapers elaborated still further. Santa Anna not only tossed the press into the bayou, said A. C. Gray, but a few years later the press was raised from the waters and another paper, the *Morning Star*, printed on it. Other historians followed Gray's line, asking few or no questions, and it became an article of faith in the lore of the period that Santa Anna dumped the *Telegraph* press into the bayou and that it was resurrected to print again.[30]

Santa Anna did indeed destroy a *Telegraph* press, and later the *Morning Star* was indeed printed on a *Telegraph* press. But Gray in attempting to reconcile those seemingly contradictory facts overlooked another key fact. The Bordens purchased a new press after the destruction of their first, and the next owners purchased yet another new press before the *Morning Star* appeared. The *Star* came, not from the press the Bordens had hauled from San Felipe to Harrisburg, but from one of the new presses. The Bordens undoubtedly would have raised the original press from the bayou had that been feasible. Both were inventive, ingenious, and mechanically inclined. Moreover, the firing of their property at San Felipe, Harrisburg, and Fort Bend had left

[29] *Telegraph and Texas Register*, November 19, 1836.
[30] Ibid., April 26, 1843; A. C. Gray, "A History of the Texas Press," in *A Comprehensive History of Texas, 1685–1897*, ed. Dudley G. Wooten, II, 370.

them in dire circumstances with only the clothes on their backs and a great deal of cheap land. Certainly, had there been the slightest chance of salvaging the press, they at least would have attempted to do so before they borrowed clothes, traveled to the United States, and mortgaged their lands to buy a new one. Possibly Santa Anna tossed their original press into the bayou, but only after effectively destroying it. It did not print again.

The *Telegraph and Texas Register* proved more durable than its press. By contrast, the *Texas Republican* and *Texean and Emigrant's Guide* proved less so. Both succumbed to the hazards of the time while their presses remained intact to print other newspapers under new proprietors. In the summer of 1837, Isaac W. Burton and William W. Bell acquired the Milton Slocum press and for a time printed the *Texas Chronicle* at Nacogdoches. About a year later W. W. Parker purchased the press and moved it to San Augustine, where he began printing the *Red-Lander* in September, 1838.[31]

Franklin C. Gray attempted to restore his press in the late spring and summer of 1836. After the destruction of the Borden press and the Battle of San Jacinto, Burnet turned again to Gray. Gray printed the treaty between Santa Anna and the Texas government in mid-May and shortly thereafter printed Santa Anna's letter to Burnet, defending the Mexican army in the Fannin massacre. Gray printed additional documents for the Texas government during June and July, but the restoration of the Borden press ended his patronage, for the Bordens still held the title of public printers.[32] Even so, Burnet showed marked favoritism toward Gray, a circumstance that joined with Gray's Santa Anna connection to bring about his downfall. Burnet's popularity dropped after the Battle of San Jacinto. The army refused to obey him; some elements violently opposed his move to release Santa Anna; and a few even threatened his life. Gray, who had printed for both Burnet and Santa Anna, found himself caught in the turmoil. Rumors accused his wife of intriguing to help Santa Anna escape, and he too fell under suspicion. Gray ran for sheriff of Brazoria County in the fall of 1836 but was defeated. In disgust he left Texas to seek his fortune elsewhere,

---

[31] Streeter, *Bibliography of Texas*, pt. 1, vol. II, 538, 539.
[32] Ibid., pt. 1, vol. I, 129, 142, 143, 162, 163, 164.

with mixed results. Word of him drifted back to interested old-timers. "F. C. Gray removed to California where he became wealthy, a circumstance so phenomenal to his craft as to unsettle his reason," wrote Noah Smithwick. "Gray died in New York by his own hand."[33]

The printing press Gray left behind had recorded a great deal of Texas history since Godwin Brown Michael Cotten had introduced it to San Felipe. Although its days of greatest glory were passed, it would yet record more. After an interval of silence, it began another checkered career—as a vehicle for promoting Mirabeau B. Lamar as president of the Republic of Texas.

The *Telegraph and Texas Register* experienced the revolution more directly than either of its contemporaries and was the only newspaper to lose its press to the enemy. Yet it appeared again on August 2 to boast of its trial by fire and prove its durability. The Bordens adopted the motto "We Go for Our Country" and reiterated their old position that the paper would advocate the interest of no party and would not publish articles "dictated by a spirit of private animosity, of malignant feelings or of party views." The paper shows their problems had not disappeared. An advertisement carried the old message "printer wanted at this office," while an editorial noted that the war had displaced many of their subscribers, leaving questions as to where to send the papers.

As earlier, the Bordens found no shortage of news. The first issue at Columbia carried Burnet's proclamation calling an election for September; the second listed the candidates for president—Stephen F. Austin, Henry Smith, and Branch T. Archer; the third noted Archer's withdrawal in favor of Austin; and the next, that Sam Houston had entered the race.

Old loyalties tied Gail Borden to Austin and new ones to Houston. While the *Telegraph* remained objective, Borden personally supported his old friend. As the election neared, however, he realized that Austin could not win. The empresario had been out of the country too long; too many voters had never known him; too many old-timers remembered the eleven-league land scandal. And there was the charisma of the hero of San Jacinto. Borden informed Austin bluntly that

[33] Noah Smithwick, *The Evolution of a State*, p. 61; Gray, "History of the Texas Press," p. 369.

he had little chance of winning unless he responded to the charges of land speculation, and Austin replied at length in broadsheet and newspaper. But to no avail. The *Telegraph* carried news of Houston's overwhelming victory and in succeeding issues carried the proceedings of the First Congress and Houston's inaugural address. Late in the year the *Telegraph* paid last tribute to Austin in a black-bordered page carrying the legend "The Patriarch is Gone."

In the meantime, new problems compounded the old, causing the Bordens to lose their zest for newspapering. Yellow fever struck late in the summer, leaving Gail Borden convalescent and carrying off one of the printers and Thomas's wife. The village of Columbia, turned into a boom town by those with government business, became too rowdy for the Bordens' taste. At the same time, they did not relish the task of moving their press yet again when congress chose the site of the next capital.

Worst of all, they received no pay from the government, and mortgages on their lands fell due in December. Time and again they presented bills to the government, and time and again the government delayed paying old printing bills, at the same time running up new ones. The government, of course, had no money, but that was poor consolation to men faced with the loss of their property.

Over all, newspapering offered too many problems and too few tangible rewards, and the Bordens turned back to surveying, which they had never given up altogether. They accepted the offer of the Allen brothers, A. C. and John, to survey a new city advertised in the *Telegraph*, a city named Houston for the new president and located at the head of navigation on the stream where he had won his great battle.

About the same time, they made the *Telegraph* a semiweekly and negotiated a new contract with the government, spelling out the responsibilities of each party. The contract offered more promises than immediate cash, but it enhanced the value of the business and they took advantage of the opportunity to offer the *Telegraph and Texas Register* for sale. The business, they informed prospective buyers, was in "the most prosperous condition" and had become "a matter of profit" to themselves and of "incalculable advantage to the community." The government contract assured business in the future, and their list of seven hundred subscribers was still growing rapidly. Even so, the bereavement of one partner and the poor health of the other forced them to sell.[34]

Although many citizens believed the newspaper to be as prosperous as the Bordens' offer suggested, they were six months in finding a buyer. Francis Moore, Jr., purchased Thomas H. Borden's interest in early March, 1836, took over the editorial duties from Gail, and moved the press to Houston in April. Two months later, on June 20, Gail sold his interest to Jacob W. Cruger, a seventeen-year-old friend of Francis Moore.

The Bordens retired forever from journalism. Thomas Borden returned to Fort Bend to rebuild his plantation. Gail Borden went on to serve as customs collector at Galveston and as agent for the Galveston City Company and to experiment with a terraqueous machine, a meat biscuit—and condensed milk.

[34] *Telegraph and Texas Register*, October 19, 1836; Frantz, *Gail Borden*, pp. 116–22.

CHAPTER 6

Presidents, Politics, and Public Printing

THE team of Francis Moore, Jr., and Jacob W. Cruger nursed the *Telegraph and Texas Register* to maturity, making it the voice of the Republic of Texas just as the Bordens had made it the voice of the revolution. For fourteen years, from 1837 to 1851, Moore edited the paper, while Cruger served as business manager. Then Moore bought Cruger's interest and continued as sole proprietor for three years until business reverses forced him to sell the *Telegraph* and retire from the publishing business.[1]

Throughout the Moore-Cruger period, the *Telegraph* retained its prominent position. Francis Moore's involvement in government—as mayor of Houston, representative in the Texas Congress, and delegate to the annexation convention of 1845—kept the paper close to the center of events, and his sharp pen kept his colleagues mindful of their behavior. As the number of papers in the republic increased, the importance of the *Telegraph* in no way diminished. On the contrary, its circulation increased and its influence spread. A fellow editor called Moore "the patriarch" of Texas newsmen, a title he modestly disclaimed, saying it belonged by rights to Gail Borden, but no one disputed the *Telegraph's* title as patriarch of Texas newspapers. Other newspapers, among them the *Civilian* and *Morning Star*, came from the *Telegraph* printing press; other newsmen, most notably Hamilton Stuart and Willard Richardson, began their Texas publishing careers in

[1] Unless otherwise noted, biographical information about Moore and Cruger is derived from Samuel Wood Geiser, "Note on Dr. Francis Moore (1808–1864)," *Southwestern Historical Quarterly* 47 (April, 1944): 420–21, and Madeleine B. Stern, "Jacob Cruger: Public Printer of Houston," in *Imprints on History: Book Publishers and American Frontiers.*

the *Telegraph* office; and Jacob Cruger, while maintaining his interest in the *Telegraph*, went to Austin to establish the *Texas Centinel*.

Moore and Cruger had already shared adventures before they acquired the *Telegraph*. Both resided near Bath, New York, in the fall of 1835, and when word arrived of the action in Texas, both were caught up in the excitement of the time. In company with Cruger's younger brother, James, they set off afoot to lend support to the Texan cause.

Moore, older by eleven years than Cruger, had a varied career behind him. The son of a medical doctor, he was born in Massachusetts on April 20, 1808, but moved with his family to New York when he was twenty years old. He studied medicine and law and by 1835 was teaching school at Bath, where one old-timer remembered him as "an accomplished scholar and gentleman." Described by another acquaintance as "tall and disproportioned" in stature, "a long slabsided, knock-kneed sixfooter," Moore had lost an arm in a youthful accident. This circumstance placed him at only minimal disadvantage. "The lying scribbler of the *Telegraph* is a one armed man," said Sam Houston, who often felt the bite of Moore's criticism. "You never would forgive me for abusing a cripple, but I must confess that one arm can write more malicious falsehoods than any man with two arms I ever saw. His one arm is more prolific for evil than the traditional bag that had seven cats and every cat had seven kits."[2]

A friendlier writer called him a "warm & devoted friend to the cause of the Revolutionists," who "abandoned fair prospects" when he set out afoot for Texas. After his death a fellow newsman called him "one of the purest men in the country, in whose nature patriotism was a passion," and an early historian of the press described him as "one of the most accomplished writers by whom the Texas press has been graced." Even Sam Houston, despite the epithets, respected him. "I found . . . in Moore's Telegraph some instructive and quite pretty moral articles," he once confessed. "I would as soon have found them in any other paper."[3] And on the eve of the Civil War, when both men had passed their prime and both opposed secession, Houston appointed his old critic Moore to the position of state geologist.

[2] Edward Stiff, *The Texian Emigrant*, p. 95; Eugene C. Barker and Amelia W. Williams, eds., *The Writings of Sam Houston*, VI, 11.
[3] William S. Speers, ed., *Encyclopaedia of the New West*, p. 580; A. C. Gray, "A History of the Texas Press," in *A Comprehensive History of Texas, 1685–1897*, ed. Dudley G. Wooten, II, 374, 385; Barker and Williams, *Writings of Houston*, V, 108.

Moore and the young Cruger brothers arrived in Texas too late to fight in the Battle of San Jacinto but in time to join in the activities of the troublesome Texas army in the summer of 1836. In June they enlisted in Captain James L. Allen's Buckeye Rangers, a command that protected Ad Interim President Burnet from elements of the army that threatened the civil government throughout the summer. The experience made them forever Burnet's partisans. They never forgot the scene of the beleaguered president "holding government in a miserable shanty about twenty-one feet square with one of his children shrouded for the grave and the other not expected to outlive the day." Throughout their journalism careers, they supported Burnet regardless of the issues. As volunteers, they also attracted favorable attention. On September 2, Moore became "warden" of a hospital at Velasco and on January 9, 1837, assistant surgeon of the army. In the same period Jacob Cruger advanced to assistant paymaster in the army.[4]

When Sam Houston solved the army problem by furloughing most of the soldiers in early 1837, the three New Yorkers left the army but resolved to cast their lots in Texas, for the purpose, as their later actions made clear, of adding the republic to the United States. Jacob Cruger joined his brother in a mercantile enterprise in Houston and briefly served as postmaster there. In the same period he and Francis Moore began the negotiations with the Bordens that led to the purchase of the *Telegraph*.

Like the original proprietors, Moore and Cruger had no experience in newspapering, but, says Jacob Cruger's biographer, "printers' ink ran in his veins," since he was related to Daniel Cruger, a prominent printer-lawyer in New York. Despite his youth, Jacob Cruger supplied a steady hand to the operation of the *Telegraph*, proving a perfect foil for the acidulous Moore. When they had been partners for several years, Moore paid him tribute: "Mr. Cruger has been for more than eight years, my bosom friend and almost constant companion. We have, by turns, nursed and sustained each other in sickness, and cheered and defended each other amid privations and perils; in adversity and prosperity shared alike. We are connected by bonds of attachment more strong than those of fraternal love."[5]

[4] Audited Military Claims, Archives, Texas State Library, Austin.

[5] Republic of Texas, *Journals of the Fourth Congress of the Republic of Texas, 1839–1840*, ed. Harriet Smither, III, 94.

Moore, for his part, promptly displayed the ability to cope with the challenges of pioneer journalism. He purchased Thomas Borden's interest in the *Telegraph* with the understanding that the firm, as public printer, would follow the government to Houston, where quarters awaited. Accordingly, after printing the final issue at Columbia on April 11, he and Gail Borden loaded the press aboard the steamer *Yellow Stone*, which also carried the government archives, and set out for the new capital. They confidently expected to print the next issue of the paper without interruption, but the *Yellow Stone* took a week to clear the bar at Velasco. Then the tide held it aground another day at Clopper's Bar before it "groped" its way through the meanderings of Buffalo Bayou to Houston.

"On landing we . . . immediately proceeded in search of the 'nearly finished building' intended for our press," Moore informed his readers when the *Telegraph* resumed publication on May 2. "Our search was fruitless. Like others who have confided in speculative things, we have been deceived: no building had ever been nearly finished at Houston intended for the press." Moore rented a "shanty," which he described as being like the capital: "Without a roof and without a floor,/Without windows and without a door." Even this did not solve his problem. "The shanty is falling about our ears," he reported, "two massive beams have dropped down upon the stands, made a most disgusting pi, and driven the workmen to seek safety outside, the devil alone looks smiling on the mischief."[6]

Shortly thereafter, the weather created additional problems. "The heavy rains of Monday night poured in torrents into our shanty and transformed the floor to a bed of mud in which our journeymen stuck so fast that they could not stick to their business," he wrote. "We are obliged to suspend our operations."[7] At that point, Moore purchased a house for the *Telegraph*, a move that signified his intentions. Despite the problems of the newspaper, and despite the rawness of the new town, his future would be interwoven with both.

The first issue at Houston showed the personal style that characterized him as editor. In a blistering editorial he decried the practice of electing men to office who had criminal records in the United States.

[6] Houston *Telegraph and Texas Register*, May 2, 1837.
[7] Ibid., May 16, 1837.

In a land where etiquette demanded that a stranger be asked not his name but "What do you want to be called?" the editorial hit several sensitive nerves, especially those of Moseley Baker. Moore received pointed inquiries, asking who wrote the editorial. "Those interested are hereby notified," he responded, "that the author of that article is the editor of the Telegraph, who is not too stupid to discharge *unassisted* his editorial duties, nor too cowardly to persist in the path where those duties lead; if in that path even death be lurking, *he will walk onward*."[8]

His editorial direction also emerged in the early issues. He favored annexation to the United States and opposed dueling. A vein of puritanism ran deep in his character—the legacy of his New England birth—and he looked on himself and his paper as instruments for the upgrading of Texas society in general and Houston society in particular.

The *Telegraph* reflected further his preoccupation and that of his fellows with land. The bulk of advertisements carried throughout 1837 dealt with real estate promotions. Indeed, the paper at times seemed primarily a brochure for land companies. The front page of the September 30 issue, for example, advertised no less than seven new towns and offered other lands for sale. In addition, Moore wrote a series of articles that systematically described the counties and natural features of Texas, articles that in 1840 formed the nucleus of a small book, *Map and Description of Texas*, published in the United States. The articles and book gave a more objective view than the advertisements but served the same purpose—that of attracting settlers. More settlers meant more readers and advertisers for the *Telegraph* and more inhabitants for the paper cities and a consequent rise in land prices. These facts did not escape Moore's notice, for his interest in developing the republic was tied to his own self-interest, and like many of his fellow citizens he had caught the fever of land speculation.

The *Telegraph* office became more than a newspaper establishment. During Moore's three terms as mayor—in 1838, 1843, and 1849 —he conducted much city business there, wearing even "during the intolerable hot weather in the summer of 1838, the same Kentucky jeans pants, the same pair of stitchdowns, the same long and flowing blue green robe, and the same redoubtable ancient drab beaver." If

[8] Ibid., May 9, 1837.

one wanted to buy or sell land, open a school, recover an escaped slave, or stage a theatrical production, he went first to the *Telegraph* office. Moore and Cruger printed tickets to dances, handbills, powers of attorney, sheriffs' summonses, and other forms needed in the city. From time to time they printed newspapers for other editors and did public printing for the republic. Their business thrived, and within six months after the beginning of their partnership they had enlarged their paper and within another year acquired a power press.[9]

Moore's running battle with Sam Houston, which lasted throughout his editorial career, began in the late summer of 1837. The president attempted to dismiss the secretary of the navy, Samuel Rhoads Fisher, citing among other shortcomings the "offensive character" of the secretary's publications in the *Telegraph*, which were "disrespectful" of the executive, "sneering—taunting—ironical." Moore sided with Fisher, thus incurring the wrath of the president, who had grown accustomed to the confidence shown him by the *Telegraph* under the Bordens. Sam Houston had it in his power to retaliate as other journalists entered the field and looked covetously at the public printing contract. But Moore did not recant. When "his excellency the President commenced hostilities with a certain officer of the Navy, we felt it our duty to oppose his measures and incurred his displeasure," he explained. "If in defending the reputation of faithful public servants, we should be compelled to combat executive influence and possibly forfeit government patronage, we should be cheered by the reflection that justice and truth would smile on our exertions."[10]

For roughly a year—from March, 1836 to March, 1837—the *Telegraph* remained the only newspaper of record printed in Texas, and for more than another year it completely dominated the field. Yet as early as the fall of 1836 hopeful journalists began planning other newspapers and announcing their intentions in the *Telegraph*. The issue of October 26 carried the prospectus of the *Texian Star*, which W. M. Savage of Oxford, North Carolina, proposed in order to make information about Texas available in the United States; the issue of December 17, the prospectus for the *Texian*, which Thomas Wilson planned for the new capital of Houston.

[9] Stiff, *Texian Emigrant*, p. 95; *Telegraph and Texas Register*, November 4, 1837; August 11, 1838; and January 5, 1839.

[10] Charles A. Gulick et al., eds., *The Papers of Mirabeau Buonaparte Lamar*, I, 586; *Telegraph and Texas Register*, May 12, 1838.

Neither of these proposals resulted in competition for the *Telegraph*, and even when the other two presses in Texas renewed activity in 1837 Francis Moore could afford to be generous. The old Godwin Brown Cotten press, the identity of its new owner carefully concealed, produced one of the most controversial Texana items of all time, but only the feeblest of newspapers, while the Milton Slocum press, acquired by Isaac Watts Burton, remained in Nacogdoches, removed by geography from real competition with the *Telegraph*. Moore hailed the reactivation of the older presses, especially the appearance of Burton's *Texas Chronicle* about June 7, 1837, as evidence of the growing prosperity of the republic.[11]

He extended a similar welcome when John Warren J. Niles, a newcomer, arrived with another press to launch the *Matagorda Bulletin* on August 7. He might well have withheld his greeting to Niles, for the arrival of a fourth press in the republic marked the opening of the age of competition in the newspaper industry. "We hope to contribute our mite to the development of the resources of Texas by disseminating useful information," said the prospectus of the Matagorda paper, which spoke particularly of the development of a trade route, possibly a railroad, between Matagorda and San Antonio. The prospectus also announced that the paper would take "the broad ground" in politics, serving as the organ of no party and being "free of the influence of any man or group of men." Despite these words, Niles plunged into politics within a few months after his arrival, challenging Moore for the public printing and involving himself in the campaign to elect Lamar.

Not too surprisingly, much of the new journalistic activity from late 1836 through the presidential campaign of 1838 centered around Vice-President Mirabeau B. Lamar, himself a former newsman. Lamar was behind Thomas Wilson's proposal of December, 1836, to establish the *Texian* at Houston and was the secret owner of the Godwin Brown Cotten press in 1837. If he did not have a financial interest in the Niles enterprises, some of his closest associates did and used those enterprises to promote his election to the presidency in 1838.

Born in Georgia in 1798, Lamar moved to Cahawba, Alabama, as a young man and about 1821 became joint publisher of the Cahawba *Press*. In 1828, after a fling in Georgia politics, he founded and edited

[11] *Telegraph and Texas Register*, June 20, 1837.

the Columbia *Inquirer*, a journal dedicated to furthering states' rights, especially as interpreted by Governor George M. Troup. Using the paper as a springboard, Lamar won election as state senator in 1829. Then defeats at the polls and a series of family deaths, including that of his wife, prompted him to leave Georgia for Texas in the summer of 1835. Lamar determined to settle in Texas and, selecting his land, returned to Georgia in the fall to arrange his affairs. News of the revolution drew him back to Texas in time to distinguish himself in the Battle of San Jacinto.

The following September, only fourteen months after he first set foot in Texas and when he had spent less than eight months there, the voters elected him vice-president of the republic. "He was a man of the French type, five feet seven or eight inches high, with dark complexion, black, long hair, inclined to curl, and gray eyes," wrote one who saw him about that time. "I found the Vice-President rather reserved in conversation; it was said, however, that he was quite companionable with his intimate friends."[12]

Lamar, like Houston, rode to high office on the smoke of San Jacinto, but there any similarity ended. Lamar advocated executing Santa Anna, while Houston granted him clemency; Lamar considered Indians vermin, while Houston considered them his blood brothers; more basically, Lamar advocated states' rights as set forth by the Nullifiers, while Houston supported the federal union of Andrew Jackson. In summary, Lamar found himself in an awkward position in late 1836. He belonged to an administration whose policies diametrically opposed his own. Moreover, he found himself already mentioned as Houston's successor, for the constitution provided that no president could succeed himself and limited the first president to two years in office.

There was no assurance, however, that the republic would last until the next presidential election. Mexico still threatened to reconquer the province, and the citizens had voted for annexation to the United States at the same time they had thrust Lamar into office. If Texas were reconquered by one nation or annexed by the other, Lamar stood in need of employment, and at best the office of vice-president gave him little power and made few demands on his time.

[12] Francis Richard Lubbock, *Six Decades in Texas; or, Memoirs of Francis Richard Lubbock*, ed. C. W. Raines, p. 43. For a biography of Lamar, see Herbert Gambrell, *Mirabeau Buonaparte Lamar, Troubadour and Crusader*.

Under these circumstances, Lamar held aloof from the administration and contemplated his future. Thoughtfully he began collecting documents for a history of Texas and looking into the possibilities of establishing a newspaper. Thomas Wilson, a printer recently from Mobile, shared Lamar's interest in a paper, and together they planned the *Texian* and submitted the prospectus to the *Telegraph* in December, 1836.

Wilson returned to Mobile in February, there to publish the prospectus again and arrange for a printing press. But after leaving Texas he had trouble contacting Lamar. "I wrote you in regard to our Press that a first rate elegant Office could be procured at Cincinnatti at $2,000 or 2,200 and that I would be enabled to put in from 7 to $800— and that it would be advisable to get it in operation as soon as possible," he wrote on March 20.[13]

Wilson returned to Texas in late October and remained to work as a printer and help organize the Texas Typographical Association.[14] But he and Lamar never published the *Texian*. Other journalistic endeavors diverted Lamar's attention, and by early 1837 he already owned a press, not a new one from Cincinnati but the old one Godwin Brown Cotten had introduced to San Felipe and Franklin C. Gray had used more recently at Brazoria.

For good reason, Lamar's ownership remained a closely held secret. The press, moved to Velasco, began printing the *Velasco Herald* in early March, 1837, about the same time that Moore purchased the *Telegraph*, and the paper appeared erratically until a tropical storm damaged the press and materials the following October. The only extant issue, an extra dated April 21, 1837, is crudely printed, and the paper attracted little attention except a few notices in the *Telegraph*. Even so, the little press maintained its historical reputation. Early in 1837 it printed an anonymous pamphlet entitled *Houston Displayed* that marked the division of the citizenry into pro-Houston and anti-Houston factions, a division that lasted as long as Sam Houston lived.

Allegedly written by a veteran of San Jacinto, the pamphlet charged Houston with cowardice and even treason, and its appearance created a stir. Knowing observers almost immediately attributed it to Robert M. Coleman, a hardshell ranger who had survived the Battle of San Jacinto and a number of Indian engagements. Most contempo-

---

[13] Gulick, *Papers of Lamar*, V, 134, 144, 162.
[14] *Telegraph and Texas Register*, October 20, 1838.

raries also conceded that Coleman had help from a ghost writer. "This pamphlet was written by Coleman—or rather by Algernon P. Thompson—the matter or facts being furnished by Col. Coleman. This I have from Thompson himself," one old-timer wrote on his copy.[15]

In the furor created by the appearance of *Houston Displayed*, the owner of the press escaped notice entirely, a circumstance fortunate for Lamar. The pamphlet so infuriated Houston that he arbitrarily clapped the alleged author into military prison and kept him there without trial for several months. The secret increased Lamar's discomfort within the administration, and in late April he departed for Georgia, pleading personal business. Congress convened in Houston only days after his departure, but he left it to ad interim officers to preside over the senate, the most important duty assigned him by the constitution. As the weeks of his absence lengthened into months, President Houston formally requested his presence in Texas, and friends pleaded with him to return and look after his interest in the presidential election of the next year.

Still Lamar lingered in Georgia and Alabama. While Houston wrestled with the problems of an emerging nation and empty treasury, Lamar attended receptions in his honor and paid court to an attractive widow. He also renewed some old acquaintances within the newspaper fraternity, among them, William Jefferson Jones, a twenty-seven-year-old native of Virginia who had once worked in Lamar's newspaper office and who about 1836 had founded the Mobile *Morning Chronicle*.[16]

Congress adjourned and met again before Lamar returned to take up his duties as presiding officer of the senate on November 9. His prolonged absence, despite the fears of his friends, helped rather than hurt his chances at the presidency, for he had dissociated himself from the sagging Houston administration and remained clear of the controversies that flared during the summer. In late 1837 he represented a familiar name but unknown quantity, and his return signaled the beginning of the Lamar boom for the presidency.

The campaign in turn created a boom in newspapering, with Lamar, as befitted an old newsman, receiving a decided advantage in

[15]John H. Jenkins, ed., *Houston Displayed*, p. 44.
[16]Gulick, *Papers of Lamar*, II, 21–22; Charles W. Hayes, *Galveston: History of the Island and the City*, II, 853–54; Walter Prescott Webb and H. Bailey Carroll, eds., *The Handbook of Texas*, I, 927.

the press coverage. Isaac Watts Burton of the *Texas Chronicle* signed a card that launched the campaign by asking him to stand for office, a card that appeared in the *Telegraph* of December 1, 1837. Francis Moore took editorial note of it and deplored the method of nominating a candidate, but gave a lukewarm endorsement to Lamar.

The other presses in the republic gave him considerably more support, for reasons that he prudently concealed. Early in the campaign he took steps to divest himself of his own potentially embarrassing press, by then removed to Brazoria, but at the same time to prevent its falling into hostile hands. He tried to sell it to James D. Cocke, a printer formerly with the Mobile *Chronicle* who in late 1837 planned a newspaper for Houston. A native of Virginia and about twenty-two years old, Cocke supported Lamar so enthusiastically that the opposition eventually dubbed him "the fighting Cocke," but he declined to buy the press and printing materials. "The expense of bringing them to Houston, by land, will be equal to their value, in their present damaged state," he explained. "I am of the opinion it would be most expedient to dispose of them at Auction, where they now are; I am sure I could with less difficulty, and in shorter time, procure materials from N. Orleans." Cocke considered joining forces with George W. Bonnell, who also planned a newspaper for Houston and who at the time expected "a complete printing establishment, which he sometime since ordered from Cincinnati." John Warren J. Niles, who had his own plans for Houston, discouraged his potential rivals, assuring them that "it must be a losing concern." Cocke nevertheless issued a prospectus for the *Banner of the Lone Star* in January, 1838. Concluding for himself that the project would indeed be a "losing concern," he abandoned it.[17]

After Cocke declined to buy his press, Lamar lent it to Algernon P. Thompson and Dr. Theodore Lèger on condition that they return it to him in Brazoria "whenever demanded." Thompson, a precocious nineteen-year-old, had already gained notoriety in connection with *Houston Displayed*. A native of England, he arrived in Texas from New York in time to fight in the Battle of San Jacinto, and for a time he served as Sam Houston's secretary. Lèger, a French physician with a

---

[17] Gulick, *Papers of Lamar*, II, 28–29; Thomas W. Streeter, *Bibliography of Texas 1795–1845*, pt. 1, vol. II, 526; Webb and Carroll, *Handbook of Texas*, I, 368.

connection to Benjamin Constant, settled at Brazoria just before the revolution and attended Stephen F. Austin in his last illness. The two used Lamar's press to found the *People* at Brazoria in early February, 1838, a paper "with a design entirely patriotick," to use Lèger's words. Moore, who had previously noted the first issue of the ephemeral *Single Star*, which appeared from the same press, waited a few weeks before paying the customary editorial courtesy to the new sheet. "A paper styled the People has been published at Brazoria during the last ten weeks," he wrote in the *Telegraph* of April 25. "We have hitherto neglected to notice it because we feared . . . it would prove a thing of a day."[18]

Thompson and Lèger invited Lamar to contribute his historical sketches of Moses Austin and James Long and promised, "We will devote our whole energies to advancement of your cause." They kept that promise only too well, taking so bitter an anti-Houston stand that they made themselves obnoxious and created uneasiness among other of Lamar's friends. "Do you not think it would be better for your cause if your Editorial friends would . . . exchange a small portion of gall and wormwood which they mingle in their publications for an equal quantity of courtesy?" asked one. Another warned, "Some of your friends in their over anxious zeal are likely possible to do you some injury."[19]

Lamar indeed entertained second thoughts after lending the press to Thompson and Lèger. He transferred ownership to James S. Jones, errand boy for his brother William Jefferson Jones and Niles and Company, and young Jones appeared at Brazoria about the first of May, demanding possession. "Messrs. Leger & Thompson obstinantly refused to deliver me the press and deny my authority to dispose of it in any manner whatever," he complained to Lamar. "They have rendered themselves so odious and unpopular that they have not a single friend to advance a dollar for them."[20]

Lèger and Thompson also appealed to Lamar. "A Mr. Jones has been here requiring immediate cash payment for the Press or its delivery into his hands," they wrote. "He represented himself to be the

---

[18] Gulick, *Papers of Lamar*, II, 13. See also Andrew Forest Muir, "Algernon P. Thompson," *Southwestern Historical Quarterly* 51 (October, 1947): 143–53.

[19] Gulick, *Papers of Lamar*, II, 38, 178, 196. See also Streeter, *Bibliography of Texas*, pt. 1, vol. I, 240.

[20] Gulick, *Papers of Lamar*, II, 154–55.

brother of Mr. Jones of Mobile, but as he brought no credentials from you, of course we refused to treat with him, knowing no one but you as the owner." They also gave a different view of their operation, complaining of a "few contemptible knaves and fools" who threw obstacles in the way of their paper. "Their motives for this conduct it is impossible to divine, unless jealousy for the powerful influence which we are daily acquiring with the poorer and more numerous class of the community. This they fear, at the approaching election, will militate against the choice of their favourites."[21]

The problem of ownership and possession of the press resolved itself shortly thereafter when Robert Eden Handy, another supporter of Lamar and the founder of the town of Richmond, purchased it from James S. Jones with the understanding that it would be delivered to him on August 1. "In payment I have given him several notes of hand on different individuals & merchants amounting in all to nine hundred Dollars," Handy wrote Lamar. "I hope there will be no difficulty about the matter."[22]

The *People* continued in operation until June or July, with the editors still maintaining their vigorous if controversial support of Lamar. On June 12, they claimed a circulation of 2,000, probably a grossly exaggerated figure, and "increasing popularity" for their paper.[23]

Thompson and Lèger never posed a serious threat to Francis Moore, but John Warren J. Niles proved another matter. Niles flashed brightly across the scene, for a few months looming as a major figure in Texas journalism. He lent his name to a group, Niles and Company, that set out to wrest the public printing from Moore and Cruger late in 1837. At that time Moore and Cruger still operated under the contract signed the previous year by the Bordens, a contract that allowed for the depreciation of Texas currency. The improved prospects of the republic enhanced the value of the contract by late 1837, and only then, Moore observed, did Niles discover "a remarkable aching to secure the public printing."[24]

Although Moore blamed Sam Houston for encouraging the budding competition, others also welcomed the opportunity to even a few

[21] Ibid.
[22] Ibid., II, 158.
[23] Ibid., II, 162–63.
[24] *Telegraph and Texas Register*, May 12, 1838.

scores. Moseley Baker still smarted from Moore's tirade against criminal legislators, and some of his fellows took umbrage at Moore's criticism of "those most base, most grovelling, and most despicable of creeping things—DRUNKEN LEGISLATORS."[25] For reasons of his own, Lamar for once allied himself with Sam Houston, thus adding his support to the Niles effort.

Because of the increased value of Texas currency and the stirrings of competition, Moore and Cruger negotiated a new contract in early December, 1837, that called for about half the amount of the previous one. They signed the contract with a committee of the house of representatives, but Secretary of State Robert Anderson Irion, a close friend of Sam Houston, ruled the new contract invalid because the senate had failed to sign it. Moore and Cruger thus continued with the old contract that left them open to charges of making undue profits at the expense of the government.

About the same time that Irion ruled Moore and Cruger's new contract invalid, he signed a contract with Niles and Company to publish the congressional journals in two volumes of 250 pages each, at $1,600 per volume. As Irion considered this price extremely low, he advanced Niles $2,000 for the purpose "of procuring paper, &c."[26]

The transactions of late 1837 caused some confusion, which a joint committee of the congress reviewed and attempted to clarify the following April. The committee report, signed by Sterling C. Robertson for the senate and Joseph Baker for the house, found that "the only valid contract for the execution of Printing for the Government" was that originally made with the Bordens, "since passed into the hand of Messrs. Cruger and Moore, who have fulfilled that contract." The committee then recommended that in the future public notice be given, that sealed proposals be received by the speaker of the house "for printing, stitching and folding in pamphlet form, the Laws and Journals of the Republic," and that the two houses elect the public printer.[27]

Niles and Company owned no equipment at the time of the negotiation, but with the $2,000 advanced by Irion and funds from the si-

[25] Ibid., September 30, 1837.

[26] Republic of Texas, *Journal of the House of Representatives. Second Congress—Adjourned Session*, p. 10.

[27] *Telegraph and Texas Register*, May 12, 1838.

lent members of the firm, Niles promptly sailed for New Orleans, where, as he confided to Lamar, he "completed arrangements for the purchase of an extensive office." His company planned not only to acquire the public printing but also to issue a newspaper in competition with the *Telegraph*. "My printing materials will be shipped shortly—consisting of I think 4 Presses—the requisite quantity of type—paper &c—I shall also I think buy a Lithographic Establishment & Book Binders," he wrote Lamar on January 1, 1838. "I shall be prepared for every & any description of work & am determined none shall *underbid* me in prices for work. . . . I am determined to do the paper & my patrons justice—let the expense be ever so much."[28]

The *Matagorda Bulletin* of March 28, 1838, carried a prospectus for the new paper, the *National Banner*, and carried too an advertisement for "six or eight good printers" for the Houston office. The first issue appeared April 25 and received Moore's editorial welcome: "We hail it as new evidence of the prosperity of our beloved country; may it never be soiled by the polluting touch of Government harpies, nor bend to the influence of sectional prejudice but ever be true to its beautiful name."[29]

The editor of the *Banner* took exception to the greeting, abusing the *Telegraph* "most unmercifully" in an article that occupied nearly a column of his paper. "His imagination or his *conscience* has awakened in his mind doubts whether we intended to insult or flatter him . . . ," Moore responded. "As our neighbor professes not to understand the friendly warning we gave him, we will explain. Certain officers of the Government are endeavoring to establish a hireling Press in this country." The *Banner* returned Moore's fire, accusing him of having "battened upon the Government" by overcharging for public printing and failing to do the work in a reasonable time. Thus was launched the first full-scale editorial war in the republic and the first of many for Francis Moore.[30]

When congress called for bids on printing only days after the *Banner* began publication, three firms—Moore and Cruger, Cocke and Simmons, and Niles and Company—responded. Niles and Com-

[28] Gulick, *Papers of Lamar*, II, 13.

[29] *Telegraph and Texas Register*, April 25, 1838. See also Streeter, *Bibliography of Texas*, pt. 1, vol. II, 528.

[30] *Telegraph and Texas Register*, May 9 and 12, 1838.

pany emerged the winner, but Moore charged that his rival submitted the low bid only "after the proposals of the others had been openly read." On the evening of their victory Niles and his friends celebrated with a "splendid champaign party" in the *Banner* office, a party that one of them admitted cost more than the profits they expected from the contract. Among those present, according to Moore, were the "heads of several departments of government, the clerks of those departments and about a dozen of the great land speculators of the country all carousing and 'sounding the notes of triumph' over the poor old *Telegraph* with an exultation hardly exceeded by that of the myrmidons of Santa Anna when the *Telegraph* once before fell under the torch of the tyrant."[31]

Moore later recalled (after "an upright and impartial Congress" had restored the *Telegraph* to its "former sphere") that he bore "in silence the taunts and jeers of an ungenerous opponent," confident that his day of retribution would arrive, but his memory played him false. At the time he freely vented his wrath in the *Telegraph*, writing that "when men secretly sneak in, like '*rats*,' to undermine our business and sustained by the means of our enemies, offer to do work lower than actual cost, in order that they may at some after period . . . raise their prices at pleasure . . . we shall say to them, go back . . . to 'your Masters, and learn better manners.'"[32]

Moore then raised the question of exactly who comprised Niles and Company, a question that remains a good one. About John Warren J. Niles there was no doubt. He carried a name well known in the annals of American journalism. A native of Maryland, he was one of the twenty children of Hezekiah Niles, founder and editor of the respected and influential *Niles National Register*. The younger Niles, thirty-three years old when he arrived in Texas, left an erratic record behind him in the United States. "In Houston, I met with John W. Niles, a personage with whom it was my misfortune some years ago to become acquainted in Baltimore, where he done me every possible injury within the compass of his power," wrote one contemporary. "But I outlived him and he eventually failed and decamped for Texas."[33]

Moore dismissed Niles as only a front man—"a person who 'with a

[31] Ibid., May 12 and November 17, 1838.
[32] Ibid., May 12, 1838.
[33] Stiff, *Texian Emigrant*, p. 83.

parrotlike smartness,' would repeat the abusive epithets" that his backers had "hitherto vented in secret" against an individual whom they considered "factious and refractory"—that is, Moore. He hinted darkly at their identity. "We know men who covertly wield that paper, men connected with that word 'Co.' who would soil the bright wings of an angel, could they reach them," he wrote, meaning Moseley Baker; "one of those worthies has advanced two thousand dollars of the public money for this purpose," he said, meaning Robert A. Irion; and yet another he identified as one of the "great land speculators of the country," meaning Sam Whiting.[34]

Somewhere in the background of Niles and Company, carefully screened from Moore's view, lurked Lamar and his friend William Jefferson Jones. From the time Niles determined to obtain the public printing contract, he kept Lamar informed; Niles's *Matagorda Bulletin* supported Lamar, and the *National Banner* when it appeared championed him as vigorously as it reviled Moore. Clearly, "and Company" expected returns in the form of patronage if Lamar were elected.

Interwoven with Lamar's connection with Niles and Company was that of William Jefferson Jones. Jones disposed of his interest in the Mobile *Morning Chronicle* early in 1838 and arrived in Texas at about the same time as the Niles and Company presses, there to assume the role, if not the title, of Lamar's campaign manager. Jones called Nicholas Biddle, erstwhile president of the Bank of the United States, his "warm personal friend" and relayed messages to Lamar from former Governor James Hamilton of South Carolina. Hamilton, who had lost both fortune and reputation in the economic panic that swept the United States the previous year, looked to Texas as a place to begin a new career and gave early support to Lamar, with Jones acting as his agent. Some of the controversy surrounding Hamilton spilled over into Texas and attached to Jones late in the presidential campaign. When rumor reported that Lamar had promised Jones a cabinet post, Jones saw a danger to the candidate and wrote an emphatic denial for the *Telegraph*.[35]

If Hamilton used William Jefferson Jones as his agent, Jones in turn used his young brother James as a front in journalistic endeavors.

---

[34] *Telegraph and Texas Register*, May 9 and 12, November 17, 1838.
[35] Gulick, *Papers of Lamar*, II, 22, 28, 142, 154, 170, 191, 192.

James Jones trailed in the wake of Lamar's and J. W. J. Niles's enterprises in 1837 and 1838. He purchased one-third interest in the
Matagorda Bulletin from Niles in December, 1837, and edited the paper until Niles repurchased the interest in February, 1838. He became
nominal owner of Lamar's press when the property became an embarrassment and later negotiated the sale of the press to Robert Eden
Handy. His name cropped up on the *National Banner* and then as editor of the *National Intelligencer*, the successor to the *Banner*. In June,
1838, James Jones appeared at Galveston with a Niles and Company
press, there to establish the *Commercial Intelligencer*, the first paper
on the island, for Moseley Baker. "Owing to unavoidable circumstances which I immagine have been communicated to you we have
not yet presented the public with the first number of our paper," he
wrote Lamar at the time. "I hope however such interesting and unexpected obstacles will not delay its appearance much longer."[36]

Despite influential friends and associates, Niles and Company
proved only a passing threat to Francis Moore. Indeed, John Warren J.
Niles's publishing empire collapsed almost by the time he won his big
contract. Economic debacle in the United States reached into Texas to
press his financial backers, and, far from possessing the 10,000 pounds
of type he claimed in his bid, he never had more than 4,000.[37] Political
and personality conflicts completed his ruin. A scant two months after
the "champaign frolic," Niles relinquished the editorial chair and
thereafter played no active role in the business. About the same time
Robert A. Irion and Moseley Baker abandoned the *Banner* to found
newspapers of their own. Only Sam Whiting remained of those whom
Moore had identified as being connected with "and Company," and he,
having no journalistic experience and being highly opinionated, had
trouble keeping help.

Francis Moore made no effort to hide his satisfaction as he observed the disintegration of his competition. After two editors had quit
Whiting within one month, he ventured an observation: "We wonder
the proprietors of the Banner do not keep a standing advertisement for
an editor similar to the one of ours for journeymen printers. Where
changes are made so frequently, fresh hands should be always in readiness to meet any emergency."[38]

[36] Ibid., II, 175.
[37] *Telegraph and Texas Register*, January 5, 1839.
[38] Ibid., June 16, 1838.

The two new papers founded by erstwhile *Banner* supporters or proprietors enlivened Moore's summer of 1838 without threatening the position of the *Telegraph*. Indeed, the *Civilian*, founded by Irion in conjunction with Levi Jones and Hamilton Stuart, was printed in the *Telegraph* office. Irion early repented of his patronage of Niles and Company and left in a huff. A staunch friend of Sam Houston, he found the editorial stand of the *Banner* intolerable as the political lines hardened between the Lamar and Houston factions. His irritation increased when he realized the company had not the equipment to fulfill the printing contract. Making a truce with Moore, he shifted a portion of the public printing to the *Telegraph*, thereby keeping both presses busy.[39] Then, incensed that every newspaper in the republic supported Lamar, he joined with Jones and Stuart to found a new paper in support of the Houston candidate, Peter W. Grayson. As he and his colleagues had no press, they rented that of the *Telegraph*, choosing a name for their paper that poked fun at the current custom of giving military titles to one and all, the rank reflecting the importance and wealth of the man awarded it.

The appearance of the *Civilian* on June 7, 1838, dismayed Lamar's friends, for, while the *Telegraph* continued its unenthusiastic support of Lamar, the new paper from the same press viciously attacked him. "How I wish I could have been in Houston on the day the paper was published to have told Doct Moore what I thought of his *Pledges*," fumed one. "He has forfeited them. He told me that the first article of a personal character they attempted to introduce into the Civilian would be the signal to cease to print it. G——d d——m him— He must either be treacherous or possessed of queer notions as to what is a PERSONAL attack."[40]

Hamilton Stuart, editor of the *Civilian*, continued the attack, showing himself a master at political invective and outraging Lamar's friends. "I saw the last Civilian yesterday and was both shocked and disgusted at the tone and substance of the Editorials," wrote one, while Thompson and Lèger of the *People* asked Lamar to send them copies of the sheet, promising, "We will reply to them in their own coin." When Stuart charged Lamar with "mental derangement" and made "allusions to his deceased lady," even Moore over the name "San Jacinto" issued a rebuke: "I had determined to notice the licentious-

[39] Ibid., January 5, 1839.
[40] Gulick, *Papers of Lamar*, II, 177.

ness of the 'Civilian' of Thursday last in this paper. But its editor has
been handled 'with gloves off' in the Banner of yesterday . . . and so
justly rebuked . . . that it would be a 'brute part' in me to add in the
lash."[41]

The *Civilian* did not survive the election, and no copies are
known. Yet it marked the beginning of the pro-Houston press. A fore-
runner of the *Civilian and Galveston Gazette*, it also launched the career of Hamilton Stuart, one of the important editors in Texas before
1860. Stuart, then twenty-five years old and the former editor of the
Sentinel of Georgetown, Kentucky, came to Texas seeking a milder climate in early 1838. He brought with him a letter of introduction to
Sam Houston, which he presented at a time when Houston was earning his reputation as a hard drinker. Stuart, a teetotaler, felt ill at ease
when the president offered him a drink, but he declined it, at the same
time explaining his position. "I never insist upon any one drinking
with me," said Houston, putting his hand on Stuart's shoulder. "I
sometimes think I drink too much myself. Probably it would have been
better for me if I had never acquired the habit." From such a beginning grew a lifelong friendship. Stuart served a brief stint as editor of
the *National Banner* but quit "in consequence of the proprietors sending articles to the press without submitting them to the scrutiny of the
editor." Then he allied himself with Sam Houston. First as editor of
the ephemeral *Civilian* at Houston and then of the important *Civilian
and Galveston Gazette*, Stuart advocated Houston's cause and often
spoke for him for the next quarter-century. "Hamilton Stuart expects to
go to General Houston when he dies," a rival editor once quipped.[42]

Because of Stuart's pro-Houston bias and his success in Galveston,
he eventually became one of Francis Moore's great rivals. But in 1838
Moseley Baker's new paper rather than Stuart's drew Moore's editorial
fire. A candidate for the house of representatives from Galveston
County, Baker appropriated one of the Niles and Company presses and
founded the *Commercial Intelligencer* to promote his election. Initially, he concealed his connection with the paper. James S. Jones carried the press to the island; the paper appeared under the heading

[41] Ibid., II, 163, 177, 178; *Telegraph and Texas Register*, June 30, 1838.
[42] Ben C. Stuart, "Hamilton Stuart: Pioneer Editor," *Southwestern Historical
Quarterly* 21 (April, 1918): 383; *Tri-Weekly Telegraph*, August 10, 1859.

"Published weekly by Samuel Bangs for the proprietors," and John S. Evans edited it.[43]

The heading held import for the history of printing in Texas, for it marked the reappearance of Samuel Bangs—appropriately, in time to publish the first newspaper on the island where as a boy he had helped strike the first documented Texas imprint. But that aspect of the paper attracted no attention whatever at the time. Rather, speculation centered on the identity of the proprietors. The paper gave such ardent support to Baker that Moore quickly guessed the answer and turned the full force of his fire from the *Banner* to the *Intelligencer*. Where previously he had only hinted at Baker's identity, he now used the name. "Moseley Baker is wholly unworthy to hold any office of profit or trust within the gift of the people of Texas," he stated bluntly. Moreover, Baker was a "Loafer"—a term that implied "self-degradation" and was "invariably applied to drunken Vagrants."[44]

Baker capitalized on the term, calling himself the "Prince of Loafers," and responded with some name-calling of his own: "The editor of the Telegraph is a man whose looks bespeak the villain—whose downcast appearance clearly betokens that in life he has been guilty of some awful crime, and the recollection of which deters him from encountering with a manly look, even his most intimate acquaintances." Overall, Moore held the edge in vituperation, but his attack backfired in that it made Baker a martyr in some circles. "The Telegraph is literally persecuting Mr. Baker," complained Bernard Bee, while the editor of the New Orleans *Picayune* ventured a few kind words for the Galveston paper. Professing to admire the spirit and industry with which Texas papers generally were conducted, he called special attention to the *Intelligencer* as the seventh newspaper in the republic and suggested that as "the youngest of the batch" it ought to be well patronized. "When the Intelligencer first made its appearance the oldest paper of the 'batch' was the first to greet it and to recommend it to public patronage," Moore assured the New Orleans editor, "but when its editor was found associated with Loafers and boasting of being a Loafer . . . his brother editors determined to leave him to his fate."[45] Despite

---

[43] *Telegraph and Texas Register*, September 8, 1838.
[44] Ibid., August 18 and September 15, 1838.
[45] Ibid., September 1, 1838; Gulick, *Papers of Lamar*, II, 219; *Telegraph and Texas Register*, October 13, 1838.

Moore's attack, or perhaps in a measure because of it, Baker won the election, bringing charges from the *Telegraph* of gross irregularities in the election.

Of the seven newspapers counted by the New Orleans *Picayune*, only the *Civilian* supported the Houston faction. The others supported Lamar to various degrees, ranging from the rabid partisanship of the *People* to the double-handedness of the *Telegraph*. Of the three Niles-related papers, the *National Banner* gave the most substantial support, with the *Matagorda Bulletin* and the *Commercial Intelligencer* following in that order. Isaac W. Burton's Nacogdoches *Chronicle* of course had been first on the Lamar bandwagon, but as the campaign progressed Burton's enthusiasm diminished. When William Jefferson Jones visited Nacogdoches in late June, he thought Burton "had done nothing" in his paper to aid the cause. "I have given him a spur and he will be idle no longer," Jones informed Lamar.[46]

The only real threat to Lamar's press supremacy came when questions arose over his eligibility to office. The constitution required that the president be a citizen of the republic at the time of the adoption of the constitution or an inhabitant for at least three years immediately preceding his election. Lamar's long absence the previous year and uncertainty as to his first arrival made him vulnerable. Francis Moore wrote, asking him to speak to the point, as did J. W. J. Niles and Sam Whiting. His reply, widely published in the journals that supported him, laid to rest any doubts.[47] On election day in early September, Lamar won a victory even greater than the relative press support had indicated, receiving 6,995 votes to his opponent's 252.

But his victory brought no ruminations about the power of the press. Tragic circumstances rather than his qualifications or newspaper support brought about his landslide. The Sam Houston faction first had trouble uniting behind a candidate and then settled on Peter W. Grayson. Grayson killed himself on July 9; the Houston faction then shifted to James Collinsworth, who before the election also committed suicide. Lamar thus won almost by default.

If the press did not materially affect the outcome of the election, the election did affect the press, both immediately and in the long

[46] Gulick, *Papers of Lamar*, II, 173.
[47] Ibid., II, 164, 165, 166–68.

range. Of the seven papers counted by the *Picayune* on June 18, 1838, only two—the *Telegraph*, and the Nacogdoches *Chronicle*—had existed at the same time the previous year, and only two—the hardy *Telegraph* and the *Matagorda Bulletin*—continued in existence for another full year. But even those figures do not accurately picture the volatility of the Texas press. Within three months after the *Picayune's* count, four of the papers had changed names, proprietors, or place of operation, and by early 1839 only the *Telegraph* remained intact. On June 28, Niles sold the *Matagorda Bulletin* to John G. Davenport. About August 1, Thompson and Lèger delivered the *People's* press to Robert Eden Handy, who died the following October, leaving the press again in limbo. On August 25, Isaac W. Burton wrote Lamar that "I have sold my press to Parker of San Augustine. Politicks the same— so that you will make no alteration in your estimation of course of the Paper."[48] In September Hamilton Stuart transferred his *Civilian* to Galveston. By mid-November John S. Evans emerged as the editor-proprietor of the Galveston *Intelligencer*, which he continued for several months; and about December 10 Sam Whiting changed the name of the *Banner* to the *National Intelligencer*. Obviously, the election stimulated the founding of newspapers, and just as obviously those newspapers were either designed as campaign organs or based on weak foundations.

More significant in the long run than the proliferation of newspapers was the dramatic increase in the number of presses within the year. In June, 1837, there were three; a year later, nine. But of the three in 1837, two were barely active and only one could be called a business proposition. The introduction of six additional presses in so short a time made for a gross oversupply and fostered keen competition. Even though the population increased rapidly, hopeful journalists for years to come found it easy to start a newspaper but hard to keep it going.

John Warren J. Niles, the most notable journalistic casualty of the year, accounted for five of the new presses—the one at Matagorda and the four introduced by Niles and Company. Eventually he salvaged one of the company presses as his interest in the business and took it to Washington on the Brazos. There he founded the *Texas Emigrant*

[48] Ibid., II, 209.

about July 6, 1839, but the paper met with indifferent reception and ceased publication in August or September of the following year. By 1844 Niles and his wife Alisanna had returned to Houston, where he ran Niles Coffee House and dabbled in local politics. When he died shortly thereafter, Francis Moore, who had never forgiven him for the public printing fight of 1838, took only the briefest notice: "Died in this city 26 November 1845, John W. Niles, aged 41. Baltimore papers please note."[49]

Niles became the forgotten man in Texas journalism—a fate undeserved regardless of personal shortcomings for he left a lasting mark through the presses he introduced. He published the first newspapers at Matagorda and Washington on the Brazos; one Niles and Company press published the first newspaper at Galveston in 1838, and another the first at Austin the following year. Yet another remained in Houston to give Francis Moore competition of sorts before traveling to Washington on the Brazos, then to Austin, and finally to San Antonio to print the first newspaper there in 1848.[50] Over the years the Niles presses produced a spate of newspapers, many of them short-lived but among them the durable *Galveston News*. These papers added a few chapters and numerous footnotes to the story of Texas journalism. After Niles, the story became more complex and could no longer be told simply by tracing the activity of three presses.

If Niles was the big loser, Francis Moore emerged as the big journalistic winner of the year. Not only did he face down the budding competition but the excitement of the election stimulated his business. By early summer he could return to his benign view that the number of newspapers in the country indicated the state of civilization, prosperity, and progress. By mid-summer he noted smugly that his advertisements had increased, calling for an enlargement of the *Telegraph*, and that his subscription list had lengthened.[51] Shortly after

[49] *Telegraph and Texas Register*, January 21, 1846. Additional biographical information about Niles was derived from Deed Records of Harris County, County Clerk's Office, Houston, Texas.

[50] The peregrinations of the presses may be traced in Streeter, *Bibliography of Texas*, pt. 1, vol. II, 506, 507, 509, 528–29; Larry Jay Gage, "The Editors and Editorial Policies of the *Texas State Gazette*, 1849–1879" (M.A. thesis, University of Texas, 1959), pp. 1–5; and Jacobina Burch Harding, "A History of the Early Newspapers of San Antonio, 1823–1874" (M.A. thesis, University of Texas, 1951), p. 15.

[51] *Telegraph and Texas Register*, August 11, 1838.

the election, he acquired a power press, the ninth press in the republic and apparently the one George Bonnell had ordered early in the year.

Moore first took note of the press when a new paper appeared in September: "The Courier & Enquirer of this city is now printed on a large double cylinder Napier press—procured at great cost by its proprietors. . . ."[52] The *Courier and Inquirer* proved a thing of a day, but in short order Moore and Cruger acquired the press and began boasting of the Telegraph Power Press in bidding on public printing. The acquisition also left their original press free to travel to various places to meet the competition. It probably sojourned in Galveston when Hamilton Stuart began his *Civilian and Galveston Gazette* in competition with Baker's *Commercial Intelligencer*; later it traveled to Austin with Jacob W. Cruger and George Bonnell to compete with Sam Whiting.

In addition to seeing Moore the winner and Niles the loser, the year saw the emergence of several other journalistic personalities. Hamilton Stuart began his long editorial career, and Sam Whiting his controversial one; Samuel Bangs returned to continue his unique role; and George Bonnell and James Decatur Cocke stepped briefly on stage before moving on to tragic fates.

The newspaper industry also saw the first stirrings of the labor movement in the republic. From the time of Godwin Brown Cotten, advertisements for journeymen printers had appeared regularly in Texas papers, the very frequency testifying to the poor working conditions and low wages. In order to promote the interest of the craft throughout the republic, journeymen printers organized the Texas Typographical Association in Houston on April 28, 1838. They adopted a uniform scale of prices and invited others of the craft in all parts of Texas to join them. J. Smith served as the first president, N. W. Travis as vice-president, and J. M. Wade as secretary. By October Thomas Wilson, who had hoped to publish the *Texian* with Lamar, had replaced Wade, and about that time the association successfully negotiated better wages. Before the end of 1838, Francis Moore raised the advertising rates for the *Telegraph* from one dollar "per square" for the first insertion and fifty cents for each continuance—a square being

[52] *Telegraph and Texas Register*, September 8, 1838. See also Streeter, *Bibliography of Texas*, pt. 1, vol. II, p. 527.

eight lines or less—to double that amount. "In consequence of the recent advance made by the typographical association upon the wages of journeymen printers, the publishers of this city have been compelled to increase the rates of advertising and other printing in proportion," he explained to his patrons.[53]

[53] *Telegraph and Texas Register*, May 2, October 20, and December 15, 1838.

CHAPTER 7

Westward the Press

SAM WHITING, early settler, old revolutionary, and sometime privateer, found himself awkwardly situated in late 1838. He had taken a
new wife, the widow Elizabeth Menson, in January; he had won the
government printing contract in the spring and backed the winner in
the fall presidential election, but he could count few other triumphs
for the year. Hard times threatened his land speculations; shin plasters
guaranteed by his newspaper proved worthless; and he had won the
printing contract at so low a bid that considering the increased wages
to printers, the high cost of materials, and the depreciation of Texas
currency he could scarcely afford to fill it.[1] Nor had his *National Banner* posed the threat to the *Telegraph and Texas Register* that he had
envisioned.

Born in Hartford, Connecticut, Major Whiting came from a line
that accepted adversity as a challenge, and he followed the ancestral
pattern. The first of his name in America, a Puritan clergyman, had left
England after suffering severe persecution and settled in Massachusetts in 1636. Descendants of that first Samuel Whiting clustered in
New England, winning reputations as strong-minded and outspoken
citizens, until three brothers of the line—William Henry, Levi, and
the current Samuel—settled in the south during the early part of the
nineteenth century. William Henry located at Augusta, Georgia,
where he became a partner in the firm of Latimer and Whiting; Levi
established himself in Biloxi, Mississippi, where he fathered a son who
became a Confederate general; about 1825 Samuel arrived in Texas,

[1] Houston *Telegraph and Texas Register*, January 27 and September 15, 1838.

where he acquired extensive acreage and participated in early revolutionary activities.[2]

In late 1835, Sam Whiting stood with Fannin and Bowie at the siege of San Antonio, and shortly thereafter he accepted a commission from the revolutionary government to issue letters of marque and reprisal. Journeying east to recruit men and aid for the revolutionary cause, he missed the major engagements of the revolution—the Alamo, Goliad, and San Jacinto. His property, however, aided the cause more than he appreciated. In his absence and without his permission, about one hundred Buckeye Rangers, commanded by Major James L. Allen, occupied his plantation house, fed themselves from his cattle herd, generally damaged his property, and interfered with "his negroes and the business of his farm." In addition, the government appropriated his wagon to transport ammunition from Liberty to San Felipe and borrowed his prized bay horse. Furious at the license taken with his possessions, Whiting filed claims against the government, claims not filled with as much dispatch as he desired.[3]

Having grievances to redress and holdings he wished to advertise in the public print, Whiting entered the publishing business, a calling for which he was not suited by talent, temperament, or experience. But he never gave up easily. Despite the disintegration of Niles and Company and the failure of the *National Banner*, he refused to concede defeat in late 1838. The inauguration of the new administration held promise for him. He could claim special attention from the president, and he knew that Lamar, in direct contrast to Sam Houston, favored the removal of the capital westward. The prospect of the move and the founding of a new city offered dazzling opportunities for an insider with an eye for land speculation as well as opportunities for establishing a press removed from competition. Resolutely turning his back on the frustrations of 1838 and looking to the future, Whiting changed the name of his paper from the *National Banner* to the *National Intelligencer*, a change that coincided with Lamar's inaugural and, he hoped, symbolized a new era in his publishing career.[4]

At the same time that Whiting looked to the future, he turned his

[2] See William Whiting, *Memoir of the Reverend Samuel Whiting*, for genealogy.
[3] Civil Claims, Archives, Texas State Library, Austin.
[4] *Telegraph and Texas Register*, December 15, 1838; Thomas W. Streeter, *Bibliography of Texas 1795–1845*, pt. 1, vol. II, 528–29.

attention to the more immediate problem, that of his low bid on the printing contract. Reviewing it, he arrived at an imaginative interpretation. The contract, he informed the government, applied only to printing. If the government wanted its printing on paper, then the paper came extra.

This novel interpretation created a stir in both government and printing circles. The secretary of state inquired of Francis Moore as to usual printing procedures and received Moore's assurances, both privately and editorially in the *Telegraph*, that printing contracts customarily included paper, that all printers assumed as much.[5]

Impervious to the commotion he created, Whiting directed his claim for paper to the president, who, either because of obligation or intimidation, ordered the claim paid, thus bringing a barrage of criticism on himself as well as Whiting. The *Intelligencer* was "the hireling organ of the administration," charged one rival editor, while another threatened to write a biography of Whiting that would expose all his shortcomings. Whiting not only drew money to which he was not entitled, said Hamilton Stuart of the *Civilian*, but he was "a man of no self respect or moral honesty . . . and so destitute of every feeling of shame that a recapitulation of his acts would make those who heard it blush with shame sooner than himself."[6]

The president fared only slightly better. "How little he deserved the ephemeral popularity by which he was elevated," exclaimed R. L. Weir, who had recently introduced a new press and founded the *Brazoria Courier*. Hamilton Stuart spoke of the "poor old lady" who had been "made president by accident," while John Eldredge warned that a man who "awoke one morning and found himself *famous*" might well awake "on a darker morning to find himself *infamous*."[7]

Still impervious to criticism, Whiting continued his new paper, making it his personal sheet just as the old one had been and with as little success. The *National Intelligencer* agitated for the removal of the capital, lambasted Whiting's enemies, promoted his candidacy for mayor of Houston, and advertised his private ventures—lands, houses, and stock for sale, horses strayed, printing services available. Nor did

[5] *Telegraph and Texas Register*, November 14, 1838.
[6] Charles A. Gulick et al., eds., *The Papers of Mirabeau Buonaparte Lamar*, V, 281–82; Houston *Morning Star*, October 15, 1839.
[7] See *Morning Star*, May 3 and 18 and October 15, 1839.

his luck with editors improve. Indeed, the turnover of editors esca-
lated until by August, 1839, no fewer than eight men had held the editorial chair of the *Intelligencer*. "No decent man has yet been found
who would retain the place," said Hamilton Stuart, who had served his
turn as Whiting's editor the previous year. "The *Intelligencer* is a miserable concern, a disgrace to the country."[8]

Francis Moore generally left Whiting to other newsmen after
early 1839. Whiting's paper posed little competition to the *Telegraph*,
and other projects diverted Moore's attention. His stint as mayor having given him a taste for politics, and the *Telegraph* having given him a
platform, he planned to run for senator in the fall elections. In addition, his book on Texas neared completion, and he planned a trip to the
United States to arrange its publication and to visit his family and old
friends.

In company with Jacob Cruger, Moore left Texas in June, 1839,
intending to spend about two months in the northeast, but pleasant
diversions caused him to forget his Texas interests and to extend his
visit. Cruger returned alone at the end of the summer, while Moore
lingered behind to pay court to Elizabeth Moffat Wood. During his absence his friends conducted his campaign for senator, and the voters
elected him by a resounding majority. Moore tore himself away from
the northeast in time to reach Houston on November 6. The next day
he set out for the new capital on the frontier to assume office. The Congress had scarcely adjourned when he again departed for the United
States to pursue his courtship. Thus for about a year he remained away
from his editorial duties and was only nominally the editor of the *Telegraph*.[9] During that year, Jacob Cruger not only conducted the partnership business but put together for his own account the most successful semblance of a publishing empire in Texas before 1860.

Early in 1839, Cruger envisioned and founded the *Morning Star*,
the first daily paper in Texas, and less than a year later he and George
Bonnell established the *Texas Centinel*, later *Sentinel*, at Austin. Thus,
at the age of twenty-one, Cruger held interest in three newspapers,
two of them among the most influential in the Republic of Texas. For
about a decade, he controlled a broader segment of the press than any

of his contemporaries. Yet he maintained a low profile, attracting less attention than his colorful partner or many of his more flamboyant rivals. Described as "enterprising and industrious, of sound judgment, kind, sympathetic, adaptable, possessed of a pleasant address, and the faculty of making friends wherever he happened for the moment to be," Cruger won a reputation as a humanitarian. "During the many epidemics of yellow fever which visited Houston during the twenty-five years of his residence there, Jacob Cruger was one of the most active and untiring in giving aid and comfort to the sick and afflicted," wrote one admirer. "Brave and undaunted in the hour of danger, and never flinching when duty called, he yet never had a personal difficulty, and was never known to carry a deadly weapon except when travelling where he might encounter the prowling savage."[10]

Cruger succeeded by focusing his attention on the management side of the printing business. "It is safer to do a small cash rather than a large credit business," he once informed his readers, at the same time asking them to pay cash in advance for all advertisements and subscriptions. Somewhat later, after Texas currency dropped to a fraction of its face value, he informed them further that the economics of the publishing business forced him to accept their money only at exchange value.[11]

Cruger generally left the name-calling and editorial feuds to others. Rather than attack the competition with words, he preferred to follow the more deadly policy of "occupying the field,"—that is, of filling the need for newspapers and printing offices so completely that no room remained for competitors.[12] To this end he founded the two new papers.

He envisioned the daily, to be printed on the *Telegraph* press, at about the same time he and Moore moved their printing office to new quarters, representing their success. Failing to win Moore's interest in the project, he turned to Ezekial Humphreys, foreman of the *Telegraph* printing plant. A native of Connecticut and about twenty-eight years old, Humphreys had emigrated first to Ohio and then to Mississippi, where he worked as a printer. In April, 1836, he joined

[10] A. C. Gray, "A History of the Texas Press," in *A Comprehensive History of Texas, 1685–1897*, ed. Dudley G. Wooten, II, 384–85.

[11] *Morning Star*, November 13, 1839 and June 3, 1840.

[12] Gray, "History of the Texas Press," p. 385.

John A. Quitman's volunteer cavalry company and came to Texas to
fight in the revolution. Arriving too late to participate in the major battles, he nevertheless remained in Houston, where he practiced his
trade. He and Cruger enlisted the assistance of John W. Eldredge, a
young man who had arrived at Galveston in the summer of 1837, and
the *Morning Star*, called the *Evening Star* in the planning stage, appeared on April 8, 1839, with "E. Humphreys & Co." as publisher and
Eldredge as editor. Consisting of four pages, each half the size of one of
the *Telegraph*, the daily focused more on local events than the *Telegraph* and aimed less at the national and international audience. That
it survived testifies to Jacob Cruger's management skills, for both of his
colleagues met untimely deaths only months after its appearance.
Humphreys fell victim to a yellow fever epidemic that swept the coastal
towns in late 1839, and Eldredge died of tuberculosis early in 1840.[13]
Cruger's name appeared as publisher immediately after Humphreys'
death, and D. H. Fitch replaced Eldredge as editor with the issue of
March 2.

Even without the loss of Humphreys and Eldredge, the paper
faced unusual problems because of the frequency of its publication. Indeed, the paper was a "rash experiment," the editor admitted as it celebrated its first six months of existence, for in a new country the
amount of news hardly justified a daily. To fill his pages, the editor
freely quoted from other papers, always giving credit when due, and
he implored his fellow editors, among them "Friend Niles" at Washington on the Brazos and "Plain John" Gladwin, who edited a "trifling
little paper called the Galvestonian," to send him exchange copies. He
chronically complained about the lack of news, but when a newcomer
called Texas newspapers "the dullest in the world" he took a bright
view. No states' rights or abolitionist fights tore Texas apart as in the
United States, he noted, and the very "dullness" indicated the general
well-being of the country.[14]

His attitude represented that of his fellow editors. In reality, serious problems threatened the very existence of the young republic.
Indian hostilities wracked the frontier; Mexico threatened invasions;
and the currency continued to drop. But Texas editors generally con-

[13] Walter Prescott Webb and H. Bailey Carroll, eds., *The Handbook of Texas*, I,
864; *Morning Star*, November 20, 1839, and February 26, 1840.
[14] *Morning Star*, October 8, 1839.

sidered it poor taste to print news that would "hurt the country," and they viewed optimistically, if they did not ignore, any problems that might deter immigration. Thus the editor of the *Morning Star* virtually ignored the yellow fever epidemic that took a fearful toll of lives and brought business in Houston to a standstill in the fall of 1839. Not until the epidemic subsided did he comment on it—even though it claimed among its victims one of his publishers and his fellow newsman "Plain John" Gladwin.

From the time the first issue of the *Morning Star* appeared, rumors circulated that it represented a daily edition of the *Telegraph*, but initially all parties denied as much. "Not the least possible political connection exists between the *Star* and *Telegraph*. . . . They are entirely separate and distinct," insisted Eldredge. Moore for his part brushed aside the suggestion that he controlled Cruger's editor. "We would be the last to attempt to control an editor," he declared, "even if he were in our employment."[15]

Still, the two papers emanating from the same printing office and sharing a publisher bore marked similarities. They often exchanged material, usually took similar stands on major issues, and never hurled barbs at each other as they did at other papers. After the deaths of Humphreys and Eldredge, Moore increasingly lent a hand to the *Star*, and his touch became evident on its editorial page. When he returned to Houston after one of his periodic sabbaticals, a rival editor punned, "The Morning Star of late . . . displays MOORE light than usual. We cannot account for it but presume that all have observed MOORE or less this to be the case."[16] The *Star* quoted the pun with amusement and without bothering to deny it. Somewhat later Moore became editor of the *Star* as well as the *Telegraph*.

The *Morning Star* counted ten newspapers in Texas by the summer of 1839 and observed, with perhaps some exaggeration, that they "would do credit to any section of older and more prosperous nations."[17] The location of the papers clearly indicated the most rapidly developing areas of the republic. Three—the two Cruger-Moore papers, and Whiting's *National Intelligencer*—were printed in Houston, two—the *Civilian* and *Galvestonian*—in Galveston, and one each in

[15] Ibid., July 19, 1839; *Telegraph and Texas Register*, June 23, 1841.
[16] *Morning Star*, July 14, 1840.
[17] Ibid., August 14, 1839.

five other towns, three of them along the Brazos River. The *Telescope and Register* was printed at Richmond; the *Texas Emigrant*, at Washington on the Brazos; the *Courier*, at Brazoria; the *Colorado Gazette and Advertiser*, at Matagorda; and the *Red-Lander* at San Augustine.

With few exceptions, most notably the Cruger-Moore papers and Hamilton Stuart's *Civilian*, the papers struggled to survive or ran erratic courses. Obviously newspapering held pitfalls for the unwary, and the various editors frequently explained their problems—high costs, low profits, uncertain mails, delinquent subscribers. Still, the field attracted a bevy of hopeful newsmen, and in the late summer of 1839 rumors ran rampant of new presses and new journals to be established. "We are told it is in contemplation to establish one or two more presses in this city," Hamilton Stuart wrote from Galveston, while Eldredge reported from Houston that "almost every person who has called upon us . . . has informed us that at least two new presses are to be put in operation."[18]

The rumors prompted Stuart to give a few words of advice, which Eldredge endorsed, to the would-be journalists. "Forty-nine out of Fifty papers in the United States are lingering along upon just business enough to induce their proprietors to *hope* that they may become profitable," he wrote, "and forty-nine out of fifty Publishers retire from the business, if not wholly ruined, so discouraged and crippled that few of them afterwards recover from the effects of having thus trifled away their labor and resources." When a friend told Eldredge that he anticipated starting a paper because he thought editors had "about the easiest times of anybody," Eldredge replied that editors reaped "more curses than coppers" and that, if editing were easy, "heaven keep us from the hard times."[19]

Although rumors swirled of new papers for Houston and Galveston, most of the action in late 1839 centered around the founding of Austin, the new capital city to the west. Early in the year a government committee selected a site on the Colorado River, where, according to tradition, President Lamar had once hunted and envisioned the permanent capital. The announcement of the choice set off a controversy, dividing the citizenry into camps for and against it. As the issue presumably would not "hurt the country," the newspapers joined in

[18] Ibid.
[19] Ibid., August 7, 13, and 31, 1839.

the fray, with the *Intelligencer* foremost among the advocates and the *Morning Star* the most vehement of the opponents.

Neither paper qualified as a disinterested party. Whiting saw the move as an opportunity to improve his fortunes, while Cruger saw it as potentially disastrous to his thriving business. The town of Houston had grown rapidly in the few years of its existence, in large measure because of its position as capital of the republic. Those who, like Cruger, held vested interest in the locale feared that removal of the capital would cause the town to decline as quickly as it had grown. The *Star* spoke for them, campaigning throughout the spring and summer against relocation. Austin, Cruger's editor submitted, lay too far from the settled portions of the republic and exposed to Indian attack; the area afforded poor water and little timber; and transportation costs, already high, would rise in direct proportion to the number of miles of freighting to the new capital.

These arguments, although valid, availed nothing. Advocates of the move hailed it as the opening of a new era, for it placed the capital nearer the center of the vast territory claimed by the republic, a territory that stretched across an uncharted expanse to include the town of Santa Fe. The location stood at the crossroads of two potential trade routes—one from the Red River to the Rio Grande, and, more importantly, one from Santa Fe to the Gulf of Mexico. The diversion of the profitable Santa Fe trade from the United States through Texas would bring prosperity, hasten the settlement of the western lands, and perhaps open the way for further territorial claims. The vision inspired a number of Texans, and the prospect of starting over again appealed to still others. By the end of the summer, the *Star* conceded at least temporary defeat, and the editor consoled himself by observing that the move would not hurt Houston, for the best route to the new capital lay through the old one. "If they don't behave very well up there in Austin, we will *cut off* their supplies and throw them upon cornbread and beef," he commented. As he watched thirty wagons loaded with the national archives leave Houston for Austin in the fall, he even glimpsed the course of empire. "Many citizens will remember," he reflected, "when the archives moved in a pair of saddle bags."[20]

The building of Austin proceeded while the controversy raged,

[20] Ibid., August 13 and September 10, 1839.

with workmen taking turns at carpentering and standing guard against
Indians. Hopeful journalists also began planning newspapers for the
new capital. The *Morning Star* of May 24, 1839, carried the prospectus of the *Epitomist*, a literary paper, which James Burke, one of Whiting's former editors, planned to edit and publish at Austin. By summer,
rumors circulated that James Decatur Cocke planned another paper
for the new town, but Cocke, who had broken with his old friend
Lamar on the issue of relocation, promptly denied them. He did intend to establish a paper, he informed the public through the *Star*, but
most emphatically not at Austin.[21] Nor did Burke's plans materialize.
The *Star* carried the prospectus of the *Epitomist* throughout the summer, but the paper never appeared.

In the end, the old rivals for public printing, Cruger and Whiting,
established the first two papers in the new town and continued their
jousting for government contracts there. Whiting won the initial advantage. A prospectus dated September 19 announced his plans to establish the weekly *Austin City Gazette*, to be printed on an imperial
sheet, with Joel Miner as head of the typographical department. The
prospectus announced further that the paper would support President
Lamar, but Whiting switched sides shortly thereafter. "General Houston arrived and from that time Whiting was for him," observed a rival
newsman.[22]

At about the same time that the government archives left Houston,
Whiting dispatched one of the presses from the *Intelligencer* office
westward. His other equipment remained in Houston for another five
years, giving Moore and Cruger indifferent competition as it passed
through the hands of a series of owners, publishers, and editors.

In Austin Sam Whiting met the greatest success and the worst
failure of his publishing career. His *Austin City Gazette* made its appearance on October 30, 1839, and even the *Morning Star*, upon receiving the first exchange copy, admitted that it was "got up in a very
creditable manner." The *Star* complained that the *Gazette*'s editor "as
that of its prototype the *Intelligencer*" was "behind the curtain" and
then extended a backhanded greeting: "We wish the *Austin City Ga-*

---

[21] Ibid., August 15, 1839.

[22] Austin *Texas Sentinel*, October 24, 1840. See also *Austin City Gazette*, November 13, 1839.

zette success in everything except the cause which it has espoused."[23]

For those who did not know, the cause soon became clear. The *Gazette* reminded members of the recently convened Congress of the heavy expenses Whiting had incurred in establishing the press and of his expectations. "The proprietor of this paper is a candidate for Public Printer. . . . He trusts that the members will not be influenced by the representations of his enemies, who do not like him, because they envy his success in life."[24]

By the time Whiting submitted his bid for public printing, competition had arrived in the person of George W. Bonnell, Jacob Cruger's newest partner. Cruger joined the enterprise, not only "to occupy the field," but also for the sake of expediency. He opposed the removal of the capital; the prolonged absence of Francis Moore thrust responsibility for the *Telegraph* on him; his new daily remained a "rash experiment," and death hung over his colleagues on the *Star*. But Bonnell held an interest in the power press that graced the *Telegraph* printing plant. A claim to some sixty thousand acres of western land enrolled him among the most ardent advocates of the frontier capital, and he determined to move the press there and establish a newspaper.[25] Cruger somewhat reluctantly joined him.

Bonnell, traveling far ahead of the printing press, presented a bid offering to print the laws and journals of the congress for 30 percent less than the sum allowed Whiting by the previous congress. He and his partner could afford the lesser figure, he explained, because they had a large machine-power press that reduced the expense. When the matter of public printing came before the congress on the morning of December 6, however, the speaker of the house of representatives, David S. Kaufman, for some reason did not present Bonnell's bid. Thus the combined votes of the house and senate gave the contract to Whiting.

By afternoon, friends of Cruger and Bonnell discovered the irregularity and forced congress to reconsider. The debate grew warm as Whiting's break with Lamar and his sale of land script in the United States figured into the arguments. But he also had his defenders.

[23] *Morning Star*, November 12, 1839.
[24] *Austin City Gazette*, November 13, 1839.
[25] Gifford White, ed., *The 1840 Census of the Republic of Texas*, p. 190.

"Much base calumniation and false detraction" had been wantonly showered upon his "innocent and devoted head," said one. "Mr. Whiting is envied for his prosperity; and often slandered and branded by men, at whose iniquities an honest man would blush."[26]

The final vote gave the contract to Cruger and Bonnell, but, to Whiting's embarrassment, his paper had gone to press carrying only the news of the morning election. The *Morning Star* made much merriment at his expense, writing in one issue: "Amusing—Sam Whiting's announcement in the last Austin *Gazette* of his election . . . as Public Printer to Congress for 1840. The Major came away before the reconsideration of the election took place the same day and resulted in the election of Bonnell and Cruger." Another issue also took up the matter: "We do not like to triumph over the disappointment even of a man who has tried every way to injure us; but we should like to know 'how you feel now,' Major."[27]

The triumph marked the high point for the Cruger-Bonnell partnership. The *Texas Centinel*, which appeared on January 15, 1840, proved the least successful and most troublesome of Cruger's publishing ventures. Indeed, Whiting's *Gazette* not only won the initial advantage in Austin, but held it until the disasters of 1842 interrupted the printing of newspapers there.

The relative success and failure of the two publishers hinged on their editors. Whiting at last found an editor with staying power, an eccentric Englishman named George Knight Teulon, who turned the *Gazette* into a respectable frontier journal. Cruger, on the other hand, left the editing and management of the *Centinel* to Bonnell, who had trouble deciding whether to be a journalist or soldier and who, when the choices narrowed, invariably chose soldiering.

The town of Austin grew rapidly in early 1840, with the two editors playing roles of consequence in the developing society. Both belonged to the Masonic Lodge. Teulon served as alderman in the city government, and Bonnell organized the Travis Guards. In recognition of their services, the citizens named two nearby mountain peaks for them—Mount Teulon and Mount Bonnell. "The editors, like their

[26] Republic of Texas, *Journals of the Fourth Congress of the Republic of Texas, 1839–1840*, ed. Harriet Smither, Senate Journal, III, 97. See also *Austin City Gazette*, January 29, 1840.

[27] *Morning Star*, December 13, 1839, and January 6, 1840.

readers, helped to decorate the old Capitol with wild flowers and then danced under their own decorations," recalled one resident. Julia Lee Sinks, who grew up with the city, waxed poetic about that early period. "Happy, lightsome days; only one who enjoyed the gladness of them can know how fresh and free they were, and yet how wit and refinement mingled with their joys," she reflected a generation later. "As a proof of their enlightenment, at this outpost of civilization . . . newspapers were read with avidity and their editors honored above the heroes of the swords. They measured that honor by the mountain tops . . . their monuments are the 'everlasting hills.'"[28]

Editors of another variety vied for honor with Teulon and Bonnell in early Austin. Sheets a later generation called underground newspapers appeared from time to time on the rough log benches outside Bullock's Hotel, sheets with names such as *Austin Spy, Wasp, Six-Pounder, Loafer's Advocate,* or *Ring Tail Roarer.* Young men about town congregated at "Bullock's Logs" in the late afternoon to make merry over the little papers they found there. Popular sentiment associated the papers, especially the *Spy,* with Dr. Richard F. Brenham, a Kentuckian who came to Texas in the summer of 1836 to fight in the revolution and remained to practice medicine. The *Spy,* Julia Lee Sinks remembered, sparkled with wit and humor, especially when enhanced by Brenham's "deep-toned reading." His humor "was inconceivable to one who never saw him; and was far past description by one who knew him well," she wrote. "Even the memory of his bright scintillations bring a thrill of pleasure."[29]

At the same time that citizens speculated as to the editors of the Bullock's Logs papers, they also speculated as to the past of Editor Teulon. Circumstantial evidence suggested a sub-rosa link between him and the British government. One man appeared who claimed to have served as game keeper for Teulon's father at Tanchley manor in England. Another rumor reported that Teulon had once been employed as a spy in a London printing office for the purpose of betraying secrets of the office to certain officers of the government. Discovered, said the rumor, he fled to Canada, where he pretended to be a patriot in the rebellion in progress and betrayed the patriots to the Tories.

[28] Julia Lee Sinks, "Journalists of Austin in 1840," *Dallas Morning News,* May 7, 1876.

[29] Ibid.

Again he fled, this time to the United States, where he lived for a time
in a garret in New York, subsisting on six cents a day. Teulon told little
of himself except that he owed allegiance to England—"My own, my
dear, my native land"—and that he had spent seven years in Canada
and then three years in the West Indies and southern United States. In
the summer of 1839 he wrote President Lamar pleading poverty and
asking for a job as a clerk. Lamar referred the letter to Whiting, and
within weeks Teulon—"a mite of a man"—arrived in Texas to become
Whiting's right-hand man.[30] The next February he emerged as editor of
the *Austin City Gazette*. About the same time Whiting left Austin because of family problems—his wife's mortal illness and his brother's
death—and appointed Teulon his agent. The editor was "an odd little
man, short, very short," remembered Julia Lee Sinks, "and wore,
when I saw him in the summer of 1840, a black cap, which made him
look still shorter." His contemporaries considered him a better writer
than Bonnell, she remembered further, "and he had beside the advantage . . . of being considered eccentric."[31]

As an editor, Teulon defended Whiting against all comers and supported his political leanings of the moment. Consequently fellow editors accused him of being a "cat's paw" and played on his name, writing
that "nobody can edit a paper for Sam Whiting without being made a
"tool-on." Even so, Teulon raised the *Gazette* above the other Whiting
journals and took advantage of his publisher's prolonged absences to
improve relations with other newsmen. Only a few months after as-
suming the editor's chair, he suggested a convention of newspaper proprietors for the purpose of setting uniform rates of charges, establishing the cash system, and creating "harmony and good feeling toward
each other." Nothing came of that suggestion, but papers to the east
came to rely on Teulon for news from the west, and even the Cruger
papers in Houston reprinted his accounts of Indian battles, including
those of the Council House fight at San Antonio and the Comanche
raid on Linnville.[32]

---

[30] *Texas Sentinel*, April 15, 1840; *Morning Star*, August 26, 1841; Gulick, *Papers of Lamar*, V, 288, 301; *Austin City Gazette*, May 13 and June 17, 1840; "George K. Teu-lon," Civil Service Claims, Archives, Texas State Library.

[31] *Austin City Gazette*, February 12 and 19 and March 4, 1840; Sinks, "Journalists of Austin."

[32] *Morning Star*, February 13 and March 5 and 30, 1840; *Telegraph and Texas Reg-ister*, July 1 and September 3, 1840.

Indeed, Teulon eventually received scarcely less critical comment from Cruger's *Morning Star* than did Cruger's own editor in Austin. "The Major of the *Sentinel* snaps at friend and foe alike," the *Star* complained of Bonnell on one occasion, and on another it quipped, "Geniuses die young. . . . Bonnell will rival Methuselah." The *Star* accused the *Sentinel* of reprinting material without giving proper credit, and the *Sentinel* charged that "the *Morning Star* for the last month has been nothing but a tissue of misstatements and corrections." When a feud developed between Bonnell and Augustus M. Tomkins of the Houston *Times*, the editor of the *Star* obviously enjoyed the fray. Tomkins called Bonnell a coward, and Bonnell in turn called Tomkins a liar and "no Gentleman," whereupon the *Star* commented, "Gentlemen . . . you may both be right."[33]

As these exchanges suggest, the partnership of Cruger and Bonnell fell early on troubled times. The power press promised by Bonnell in the bid for public printing never reached Austin. Nor did the Fourth Congress ever make an appropriation for the printing of its journals. Instead of the power press, the small press it had replaced in the *Telegraph* office, the one Gail Borden had purchased in Cincinnati, traveled to Austin to print the *Sentinel*. Because of the chronic shortage of paper at the frontier capital, the high price of that paper caused by added transportation costs, and the ruinous decline in Texas currency, the small press adequately filled the need. Even so, the absence of the power press embarrassed Bonnell and brought jibes from his rival. "The Power Press, the Power Press—where is the Power Press?" jeered Teulon. "Where, oh where, illustrious Mister Bonnell, is your far-famed 'Power Press?'"[34]

Bonnell, no novice newsman, had previously edited the *Southern Argus* at Selma, Alabama, and the *Alabama Times* and *Mobile Jeffersonian* at Mobile, Alabama. From his arrival in Texas, he had yearned to resume his profession. After ordering the power press early in 1838, however, he accepted an appointment as commissioner of Indian affairs from President Sam Houston and, leaving the press with Cruger and Moore, departed for the frontier to fight Indians. "Major Bonnell was a young man of more than ordinary ability and information," said a sol-

[33] *Morning Star*, March 7 and 10, May 2, and October 11, 1840.
[34] Streeter, *Bibliography of Texas*, pt. 1, vol. I, lii; *Austin City Gazette*, March 4, 1840.

dier who served with him then. "He was of medium height, with red
hair and freckled face under a slouched hat, and he came into camp in a
very long coat reaching nearly to his ankles, making quite a priestly
appearance."[35]

The uncharted country Bonnell saw during his Indian campaigns
fascinated him. He acquired a claim to vast tracts beyond the edge of
settlement and wrote a small book, *A Topographical Description of
Texas* . . . , which he printed in the *Sentinel* office in the spring of 1840.
His book gave a pedestrian description of the country for prospective
emigrants, but one who knew him at the time recalled the "twinkling
eagerness" of his eyes when he talked of the land and how he wove
marvelous tales of it, tales that included a fountain of youth, an El-
dorado, a mountain of light, and a petrified forest. The most noticeable
thing about Bonnell, remembered Julia Lee Sinks, was his ugliness,
"an ugliness so pronounced that it was unique." "He was extremely ill-
favored," she wrote. "A shock of rosy hair lifted itself above his light
blue eyes and a face that seemed to be trying to outdo in color the rosy
color of his crown."[36]

Bonnell gathered an interesting group of young men around him
at the *Sentinel* office, among them Joseph Addison Clark, John Henry
Brown, and Martin Carroll Wing, whose names appeared as publishers
of his book. Both Clark and Brown had long and varied careers ahead
of them, while Wing, a practical printer, would die like Bonnell in the
Mier Expedition.

Despite the array of talent, the course of the *Sentinel* did not run
smoothly, in part because of the inherent difficulties of the time and
place and in part because of the penchant of Bonnell and his staff to
pursue adventure. Caustic comments in the *Morning Star* indicated
Cruger's growing displeasure with his Austin partner, and on July 28,
1840, the partnership ended. Bonnell continued the *Sentinel* with indifferent success until late in the year, when plans for the Santa Fe Expedition preoccupied him. He then turned the press back to Cruger,
who resumed ownership with a new partner, Martin Carroll Wing.

[35] Francis Richard Lubbock, *Six Decades in Texas; or, Memoirs of Francis Richard
Lubbock*, ed. C. W. Raines, p. 85. For Bonnell's early career, see Joseph Lynn Clark,
Thank God We Made It!, pp. 68–82; and John M. Wallace, "George W. Bonnell, Frontier Journalist in the Republic of Texas" (M.A. thesis, University of Texas, Austin, 1966).
[36] Sinks, "Journalists of Austin."

"Mr. Cruger will be able to make the paper far more useful than it could be in our hands," commented Bonnell as he removed himself from Texas newspapering.[37]

Cruger and Wing promptly submitted a bid for public printing, winning the contract over Whiting. Then, motivated at least in part by the approaching presidential election, Cruger assumed editorial charge of the *Sentinel*, leaving his brother Joseph as publisher and Fitch as editor of the *Morning Star*.[38]

By early 1841, the Lamar administration had fallen on severe hard times, its popularity reflected in the value of Texas bonds—from six to eight cents on the dollar in New Orleans. In large measure, the prevailing depression in the United States accounted for the economic debacle in Texas and the failure of Lamar's grand plans, but the general public found a ready scapegoat in the president, and Lamar, dreamer, poet, and visionary, found himself unable to cope with the realities of frontier politics. By November, 1840, the *Telegraph* reported his desperate illness, and the following month he turned over the duties of his office to Vice-President Burnet and retired to the United States to recuperate. Lamar returned to assume his title again in the spring of 1841 and to promote the Santa Fe Expedition, but he never regained substantial influence. As the presidential campaign grew heated, Sam Houston and David G. Burnet emerged as the major contenders, and Lamar, a lame duck, played only a negative role. Houston, from the time he left the executive office, had run for reelection against the Lamar administration; Burnet, for reasons of expediency, dissociated himself from it, using the position of vice-president and acting president to further his own ambitions.

The Texas press divided more evenly during the presidential campaign of 1841 than in that of 1838. Burnet received his most substantial support from the *Sentinel, Telegraph,* and *Morning Star,* the papers controlled by his old friends Jacob Cruger and Francis Moore. During the campaign, other supporters founded the *National Intelligencer* at Galveston, with A. J. Cody as editor, a paper that after the campaign became the *Daily Advertiser*, Andrew Janeway Yates, editor.

Sam Houston's support came from presses more diverse in ownership and geography—the *Austin City Gazette*, the *Galveston Civil-*

[37] *Morning Star*, January 9, 1841.
[38] Ibid.

ian, the *Red-Lander* at San Augustine, and the *Colorado Gazette and Advertiser*, the successor to the *Bulletin* at Matagorda. In addition, at least two sheets appeared in March, 1841, for the primary purpose of furthering his interests—the *Houstonian* from the old *Intelligencer* office and the *Galvestonian*, the second paper of that name to appear on the island and one issued by Samuel Bangs and George French.

The campaign sank to a low level, with both sides indulging in personalities rather than debating issues. Each candidate wrote letters for the press under pseudonyms, letters that reviewed his own career in the best possible light while insulting his opponent. Burnet's letters, under the name of Publius or Texian, appeared first in the *Telegraph*; while Houston's, under the name of Truth, appeared in the *Houstonian*.[39]

As the campaign waxed acrimonious, the rival editors hurled epithets at each other as well as the candidates. Moore charged Hamilton Stuart with being a puppet that jerked to the commands of Samuel May Williams and Thomas McKinney; Stuart accused Moore of drunkenness. The *Morning Star* referred to W. D. Wallach of the *Colorado Gazette* as the "Fat Boy" and to Joseph Baker as "Don Jose" or "Lazy Joe"; the rival editors derided the military service of Moore and Cruger, calling the first a mere "warden" of a hospital and the other a "drummer" during the revolution. Rumors circulated and appeared in rival papers that the *Telegraph* had lost "upwards" of a thousand subscribers because of Moore's support of Burnet. "What a pity it is that Dr. Moore has not a better cause to support," commented the *Galvestonian*. Moore promptly set the record straight. Only nine subscribers had quit the *Telegraph*; seven of those were in arrears in dues, and the eighth, Thomas McKinney, had paid his back dues before cancelling his subscription. If any others wished to cancel, Moore invited them to follow McKinney's example.[40]

Even if Moore lost only a few subscribers, he did not represent his readers. Sam Houston defeated Burnet by a vote of almost two to one. Sam Whiting took credit for the results but without justification. As in 1838, the press reflected the temper of the time without determining the outcome of the election.

[39] Eugene C. Barker and Amelia W. Williams, eds., *The Writings of Sam Houston*, II, 386.

[40] *Telegraph and Texas Register*, July 14 and 28, and August 4, 17, and 18, 1841; *Morning Star*, May 4 and June 20, 22, and 24, 1841.

Jacob Cruger, whose *Sentinel* had given even more partisan support to Burnet than the *Telegraph*, accepted the defeat philosophically, announcing that he would support the president-elect and that much of the criticism of Sam Houston had come during his, Cruger's, absence from the editorial chair. At the same time, he accepted the failure of his Austin printing venture. Obviously, with Sam Houston as chief executive and his cohorts in control of congress, the *Sentinel* office could hope for no government patronage. Moreover, Cruger had always harbored misgivings about the future of Austin and those misgivings seemed more justified than ever after Houston's election. Houston had opposed the relocation of the capital and during the campaign had been quoted (although he later denied it) as saying that he would see grass growing in the streets of Austin. With these factors in mind, Cruger and Wing sold the *Sentinel* to General Greenberry Horras Harrison in late 1841.

Harrison, founder of the paper town of Alabama on the Trinity River and veteran of several Indian campaigns, initially proved a worthy rival of Whiting. In the competition for the public printing, Harrison entered as a spoiler rather than a serious contender. Whiting's support of Sam Houston virtually assured him the contract, so he resorted to a ploy he had used on a few prior occasions. Instead of setting a price in his bid, he simply offered to meet the price submitted by any other bidder. Harrison, suspecting Whiting's approach, submitted an extremely low bid and then withdrew it on the eve of the decision, leaving Whiting yet another time the winner of a contract he could not afford to fulfill. Whiting furiously protested when he discovered the trap, but Harrison coolly insisted that the price was a fair one while Moore and Cruger watched in amusement from Houston.[41]

At the same time, Harrison took steps to remove the stigma attached to the *Sentinel* office because of its previous editorial policy. Announcing his support of Sam Houston, he discontinued the *Sentinel* and in its place issued the *Weekly Texian*. In addition he launched another paper, the *Daily Texian*, "designed to communicate daily intelligence of the two houses of Congress" by printing transcripts of the journals of the senate and house of representatives.

Not to be outdone, Whiting began his own daily, the *Bulletin*, on November 24, 1841, about two weeks after the appearance of the *Daily*

---

[41] *Telegraph and Texas Register*, December 1, 1841.

Texian. Thus, at the opening of the new year, the town of Austin could boast of four newspapers, two of them dailies. Again Whiting proved his own worst enemy. "Vulgar abuse," the *Telegraph* noted, characterized some of the early numbers of the *Bulletin.* This antagonized the senate, which passed a resolution ending its subscription on December 30 and subscribing instead to the *Daily Texian.* The tone of the *Bulletin* improved when Charles DeMorse served a stint as editor, beginning there his important career as a Texas newsman, but both the *Bulletin* and *Daily Texian* suspended publication early in 1842 in anticipation of the adjournment of congress.[42]

Within a few months, events of a more ominous nature brought an end to the other two papers in Austin and proved Jacob Cruger's wisdom in removing himself from the scene. Even as the presidential campaign raged, President Lamar set in motion the Santa Fe Expedition, one last project designed to redeem his administration by establishing Texan jurisdiction in New Mexico and turning a valuable trade through Austin toward the Gulf of Mexico. Had the expedition succeeded, it would have assured Lamar a high place in the history of the republic. But it proved a miserable failure that blighted his reputation and at the same time gave him his revenge against the incoming president. The expedition stirred Mexico to fresh efforts against Texas, and the newspaper industry, like the rest of the republic, suffered the consequences. In the aftermath of the Santa Fe Expedition, several Texas newsmen met tragic deaths, newspapers in Austin suspended publication, and Samuel Whiting fell into financial ruin. On a more positive note, the expedition brought to Texas the newsman George Wilkins Kendall, who gave a new dimension to reporting in the southwest and who later became "the first modern war correspondent and the most widely known reporter in America in his day."[43]

The Santa Fe Expedition loomed large in Lamar's considerations from the beginning of his administration. As early as February, 1839, William Jefferson Jones outlined plans for it, winning for himself dubious distinction as "Father of the Santa Fe Expedition," and a few months later Jones lingered on the frontier with a group of soldiers waiting "to form a junction with the residue of the men designed for

---

[42] Streeter, *Bibliography of Texas,* pt. 1, vol. II, 505–506, 508–509; *Morning Star,* November 17, 1841.

[43] Fayette Copeland, *Kendall of the Picayune,* p. 150.

the Santa Fe expedition."[44] Visions of Santa Fe fired the imaginations of a number of Texans and inspired the location of the capital city. Still, when Lamar returned from sick leave in the spring of 1841, he found his cherished project no nearer a reality than it had been two years earlier. The Texan Congress endorsed the expedition in late 1840 but adjourned without appropriating money for it.

Lamar, his administration drawing to a close and public attention already focusing on the choice of his successor, took matters in his own hands. Declaring the expedition a private commercial venture rather than an official one, he called for volunteers. At the same time he arranged to channel public funds to it, a circumstance that brought irate calls for his impeachment from the *Morning Star*.

A more favorable response came from George Fisher, who wrote from Houston offering a printing press. "Should the Government be disposed to patronize a Press at Santa Fe . . . I would be willing to venture with one, on the same terms as you proposed to me last year to go to San Antonio," he wrote. "I can, with the assistance of the Executive, and with his Sanction obtain a Press &c.: in this place, & be ready to join the Expedition immediately, if authorized to that effect."[45]

A similar response came from Reuben M. Potter at San Antonio, who suggested that the expedition carry "a cheap and portable substitute" for a press—"a few lbs of type & one or two small forms with an ink ball, stick and a suitable quantity of printers ink." "With these articles, which would weigh but little," wrote Potter, "hand bills and other small impressions could be struck off by a process which I think is technically called planing, the same by which small proofs are taken; for among 400 volunteers I suppose there must be some printers."[46]

Among the 321 men who set out for Santa Fe on June 21, 1841, there were indeed newsmen of several varieties. George W. Bonnell, an ardent supporter of the expedition, joined as a private; Hugh McLeod, later editor of the *Republic of the Rio Grande*, accepted an appointment as military commander; Richard F. Brenham, of the Bullock's Logs sheets, served as commissioner. Eventually, the expedition produced its own "newspaper," though not one printed on even "a cheap and portable substitute" press. George W. Grover while in

[44] Gulick, *Papers of Lamar*, II, 437, 529.
[45] Ibid., III, 505.
[46] Ibid., III, 532.

prison in Mexico City edited a weekly handwritten sheet called the *True Blue*, which reported on prison happenings. "In newspaper parlance," George Wilkins Kendall said of the *True Blue*, "the whole affair was exceedingly well got up."[47]

Kendall proved the newsman-chronicler par excellence of the expedition. Born in New Hampshire on August 22, 1809, he worked as a printer in Boston, New York, and various other cities before settling in New Orleans. In January, 1837, he joined with a friend in the founding of a small paper, the *Picayune*, that represented something new in the South—a low-priced paper aimed at the mass market and patterned after the so-called penny press of the northeastern cities. Enlivened by Kendall's wit and eye for human-interest stories, the *Picayune* proved an instant success. A series recounting a trip to Santa Fe in 1839 attracted particular attention from readers and especially impressed Kendall. Inspired by the series, he planned his own trip across the western prairies for the double purpose of gathering material for the *Picayune* and satisfying his craving for adventure. To this end, he attached himself to the Texan–Santa Fe Expedition in the summer of 1841.[48]

Kendall found more material than he expected. His sketches for the *Picayune* grew into one of the best and most popular adventure books to come from the American West. Originally published as *Narrative of the Texan Santa Fe Expedition . . .* , the book brought him fame and went through seven editions before 1856. Just as he did not anticipate its success, he did not anticipate the trials he recorded in it. Indeed, he found considerably more adventure than he wanted. Contrary to George W. Bonnell's theory, the land between Austin and Santa Fe did not consist of a series of grassy, rolling hills. The men, uncertain of the route and unprepared for its hazards, made their way across a rough terrain, eventually straggling over the formidable Llano Estacado into New Mexico. If they entertained thoughts of conquest, as all of them denied, geography defeated them before they reached their destination. Nor did they receive the welcome they expected. Contrary to popular belief in Texas, the citizens of Santa Fe harbored no yearning to come under the jurisdiction of the republic. Mexican

---

[47] George Wilkins Kendall, *Narrative of an Expedition. . .* , II, 357; Gray, "History of the Texas Press," pp. 380–81.

[48] For biographical information, see Copeland, *Kendall*.

officials considered the expedition a hostile force and, taking the men prisoner, marched them toward Mexico City. The men surrendered without firing a shot in their defense, a circumstance that occasioned some embarrassment when the news reached home. "Thus the big expedition ended in smoke but not the smoke of gunpowder," commented the *Morning Star*, which had never supported the venture.[49] Kendall and his fellows suffered imprisonment until diplomatic negotiations brought their release in the spring of 1842.

Kendall's deliberate quest for news for the *Picayune* introduced a new element to Texas reporting, and a few years later during the Mexican War he returned to the border country to gain renown as the first modern war correspondent. His dispatches made the *Picayune* an authority on Texan and Mexican affairs, and eventually he settled his family on a sheep ranch near San Antonio. He considered himself a Texan and stands as the most celebrated resident journalist before the Civil War. Yet he does not qualify as a Texas newsman, for he maintained his connection with the *Picayune* and never attached his name to a Texas newspaper. Nor did his example perceptibly change the local methods of gathering news. Texas newspapers continued as before to rely for information on other papers, travelers' accounts, and citizens near the scene of action.

Even as the diplomats worked to free Kendall and the other Santa Fe prisoners, Texas felt the repercussions of the expedition. In retaliation for what seemed a hostile action, Mexico launched a series of raids across the border in 1842. Early in the year Spanish-speaking citizens of San Antonio received warning of incursions and relayed the message eastward. In February the *Morning Star* received along with its exchange papers from Austin a new paper with the "startling title" *Alarm Bell of the West*. "It is dated San Antonio, Jan. 22nd, and has for its motto the memorable words 'remember the Alamo!'" commented the *Star*. "It is a spirited sheet, and breathes nothing but war and vengeance, and as usual this theme has rendered it truly eloquent and even poetic. We can only say if it never sounds a false alarm, we bid it 'God speed.'"[50]

The little sheet sounded no false alarm. A few weeks after its appearance, a Mexican army under Rafael Vásquez seized San Antonio

[49] *Morning Star*, December 30, 1841.
[50] Ibid., February 3, 1842; Streeter, *Bibliography of Texas*, pt. 1, vol. II, 505.

and held the city a few days before retiring. Panic gripped the western parts of the republic as some citizens prepared to flee and others to fight. Again the message went eastward by way of a small new paper, this one called the *Anti-Quaker* in an obvious slap at the pacifist convictions of the Society of Friends. The *Star* received the "first and last number" of the *Anti-Quaker*, published at Austin, March 12, 1842, with the comment that it seemed to be "a new edition of the 'Alarm Bell.'"[51]

In the face of the crisis, President Houston called congress into special session, taking advantage of the circumstances to shift the capital eastward. Citing the exposed location of Austin, he directed the congressmen to meet at the city of Houston. At the same time, also in the interest of safety, he ordered the national archives removed from Austin.

As in 1836, Houston's retreat eastward before the enemy brought a howl of protest. Hardy citizens of Austin, suspecting correctly that the president intended to relocate the capital permanently, banded together to prevent the removal of the archives. Sam Whiting stood among the most vehement of them. As a speculative landholder in the area as well as a newspaper publisher and public printer, he faced ruin. Moreover, the *Gazette* had given Sam Houston vigorous support, and early in 1842, at Houston's behest, George Knight Teulon had taken a leave of absence from his editorial duties to carry diplomatic missives to England. Under the circumstances, Whiting felt betrayed and did another of the about-faces that characterized him politically. Lambasting Houston in his paper, he turned to former President Lamar for sympathy, complaining that "Old Sam Burnet & David G. Houston have played the very devil here."[52]

The *Gazette* appeared only erratically after the removal of the capital and in Teulon's absence. Eventually Whiting suspended publication in the late summer, at the same time vowing to even scores with Houston. "As we have expended some thousands in puffing Sam Houston into office under false promises, and the only reward we have yet received from him has been his curses, we will expend what spare

[51] *Morning Star*, March 22, 1842.
[52] George P. Garrison, *Diplomatic Correspondence of the Republic of Texas*, III, 956, 971, 978; Feris A. Bass, Jr., and B. R. Brunson, eds., *Fragile Empires: The Texas Correspondence of Samuel Swartwout and James Morgan: 1836–1856*, p. 165; Gulick, *Papers of Lamar*, pt. 1, vol. IV, 5.

means we have to give the public his character in its true light," he said in one of the last issues.[53]

As panic from the Vásquez raid subsided and westerners still continued their complaints, Sam Houston attempted to compromise by moving the capital westerly, but only as far as Washington on the Brazos. Greenberry Horras Harrison moved his press there and began publishing the *Texian and Brazos Farmer* in June, 1842. In the fall he sold the paper to Tom Johnson, called "Ramrod Johnson" because of his unwavering support of Sam Houston. In Johnson's hands the *Brazos Farmer* became known as the organ of the Houston administration, and in the summer of 1843 he changed the name of the paper to the *National Vindicator*.[54]

Sam Whiting and some other Austinians did not accept the capital's removal to Washington with as much grace as Harrison. Instead, they empaneled a grand jury that, with Whiting as foreman, presented an indictment against the president, calling him guilty of "MORAL TREASON."[55] When Houston sent men to remove the archives, they resisted with a show of force, and the archives remained in Austin.

While Whiting and his fellow townsmen engaged in the so-called Archives War, yet another threat came from Mexico. In September, 1842, a second Mexican army, this one under General Adrian Woll invaded San Antonio. Again panic gripped the republic, and again citizens pressured Sam Houston to take action. In response, he reluctantly ordered Alexander Somervell to raise troops and follow Woll toward the Rio Grande.

Some seven hundred men gathered near San Antonio to join the Somervell Expedition in the fall of 1842. Among them, recalled Big-Foot Wallace, were "brokendown politicians from the 'Old States,' . . . renegades and refugees from justice that had 'left their country for their country's good,' and adventurers of all sorts, ready for anything or any enterprise that afforded a reasonable prospect of excitement and plunder."[56] But included were a number of greats or future greats of the Texas Rangers: Wallace himself, John C. Hays, Ben McCulloch, and Samuel H. Walker.

---

[53] *Telegraph and Texas Register*, September 14, 1842.
[54] Streeter, *Bibliography of Texas*, pt. 1, vol. II, 547–48; *Telegraph and Texas Register*, December 7, 1842.
[55] *Telegraph and Texas Register*, October 19, 1842.
[56] John C. Duval, *The Adventures of Big-Foot Wallace*, p. 167.

Included, too, were a number of newsmen. George W. Bonnell and Richard F. Brenham, only recently returned home from their Santa Fe misadventure, joined for another swing at Mexico; James Decatur Cocke came from Houston to lend his services, and Martin Carroll Wing interrupted his plans to join Charles DeMorse in establishing the *Northern Standard* at Clarksville. Gideon, or Legs, Lewis and Michael Cronican, both later of the *Galveston News*, volunteered, as did other newsmen, Andrew Janeway Yates, Sidney Smith Callender, James A. Glasscock, Fenton M. Gibson, and John Henry Brown. John N. O. Smith started from Houston but fell ill at Gonzales and missed the action.

After marching to the Rio Grande and engaging in a few desultory actions, Somervell ordered the men to return home, whereupon some three hundred of them, including all of the newsmen except Brown, protested. Organizing a rump expedition under the command of William S. Fisher, they attacked the Mexican town of Mier. Defeated and captured, the survivors marched as prisoners toward Mexico City.

Of the newsmen who joined the Mier Expedition, Bonnell, Brenham, Cocke, and Wing did not return. George W. Bonnell died first—in the immediate aftermath of the battle. Separated by chance from the main body of men, Bonnell waited out the battle on the east bank of the river with a camp guard of some forty men. As the outcome of the battle became evident, others of the guard beat a retreat, but Bonnell and a man named Hicks lingered behind too long and fell into the hands of a Mexican force. Hicks managed to escape and "without so much as a pocketknife for a weapon, walked all the way to Victoria." He brought the last news heard of Bonnell. "It is supposed the Mexican guard, exasperated at Hicks' escape, shot Bonnell in cold blood," said one chronicler of the episode. Another wrote: "Thus fell a brave man and a pure patriot, without the last sad rites of burial. His bones now lie bleaching upon the banks of Rio del Norte."[57]

Richard F. Brenham died next, at the Mexican village of Salado, when the Texans attacked their captors and escaped. "Poor Brenham!" wrote George Wilkins Kendall upon hearing the fate of his comrade of the Santa Fe Expedition. "He led the attack upon the guards, had al-

[57] George Bernard Erath, "Memoirs of Major George Bernard Erath," *Southwestern Historical Quarterly* 27 (July, 1923): 49; Thomas J. Green, *Journal of the Texian Expedition against Mier*, pp. 114–15.

ready killed two of them, and severely wounded a third, when he stumbled and fell directly upon the bayonet of his falling enemy. Thus died Brenham, and in him Texas lost one of her bravest and most generous spirits."[58]

Shortly after Brenham's death, Martin Carroll Wing and James Decatur Cocke also died at Salado, but under even more dramatic circumstances. Along with almost two hundred of their fellows, they effected the escape, only to endure great suffering in the rough country, to surrender again to Mexican troops, and to come again in chains to Salado. As punishment for the escape, Santa Anna, again dictator of Mexico, ordered the execution of one-tenth—seventeen—of those recaptured. A lottery determined the victims. Mexican officials placed 17 black beans and 159 white ones in an earthen jar. The prisoners then drew lots, with a black bean meaning death and a white bean life. Both Cocke and Wing drew black beans, Cocke the first and Wing the last.[59]

Cocke met his fate with bravado. Upon drawing the black bean, he held it up between his fingers and with a contemptuous smile said, "Boys, I told you so; I never failed in my life to draw a prize." Turning to a comrade, he commented, "They only rob me of forty years," and asked that his friends be told that he died in grace. Cocke wrote a "sensible and dignified letter of remonstrance" to the United States minister in Mexico. Then, believing that the Mexican soldiers would strip his body after his death, he removed his trousers, gave them to a surviving comrade, and died in his underclothing.[60]

Wing, by contrast, was "perceptibly affected" upon drawing his black bean. "He had been very religious when at home," explained Big-Foot Wallace, who drew a white bean, "but had left the beaten track of Christianity and had gone sadly astray and that seemed to trouble him a great deal." After news of his death reached Texas, the *La Grange Intelligencer*, a newspaper founded in early 1844, printed an appropriate and classic requiem for him: "Technically speaking, his *form* now lies in *pi*. A perfect gentleman, a scholar, and a master in the art of printing."[61]

[58] Kendall, *Narrative of an Expedition*, I, 27.

[59] Marilyn McAdams Sibley, ed. *Samuel H. Walker's Account of the Mier Expedition*, p. 59.

[60] Green, *Texian Expedition against Mier*, pp. 114–15.

[61] A. J. Sowell, *The Life of Big-Foot Wallace*, p. 24; *La Grange Intelligencer*, October 17, 1844.

The Mier men went into Mexico without orders from their government, thus placing themselves, as President Houston noted, outside the protection of their government. Even so, their martyrdom excited much sympathy in Texas. Houston's attitude outraged the friends and relatives of the victims, and the press, having contributed several martyrs to the cause, generally criticized him.

Sympathy for the Mier men ran particularly high in La Grange. During the Mexican War an American force directed by Walter P. Lane collected the remains of the black-bean martyrs and returned them there for burial on a high bluff nearby, and in 1850 a group of sympathizers founded there a newspaper for the purpose of collecting money to build a suitable monument. Entitled the *Texas Monument*, the paper appeared weekly between July 20, 1850, and February 24, 1855, with five men serving in turn as editor—John W. Dancy, J. K. Kuykendall, William P. Smith, Albert P. Posey, and A. R. Gates. The paper merged with the *La Grange Paper*, edited by William B. Mc-Clellan in 1855.[62]

The events of 1842 ended Sam Whiting's newspaper career almost as decisively as those of erstwhile rivals, George W. Bonnell and Martin Carroll Wing. By the end of the year, Whiting faced the fact that Sam Houston would not return the capital to Austin and packed his belongings to leave. As the government had not paid him the amount due for public printing, he appealed to Secretary of State Anson Jones in that regard. "I have nearly had my life teased and fretted out by duns of printers . . . and I must away, but where to go God only knows," he wrote. "I have some $7,000 stock, printing materials, &c., and they are safe here no longer, and me without a dollar to remove them. My last hope is to get my accounts that are approved audited, and I may be able, at a sacrifice, to pay transportation with them."[63]

Teulon, who had returned in September from his mission to England, also appealed to Jones on Whiting's behalf. "The Major is hard put to it here," Teulon wrote. "He depends altogether upon the pay-

[62] James M. Day, *Black Beans and Goose Quills*, pp. 146–52; Walter P. Lane, *The Adventures and Recollections of a San Jacinto Veteran*, pp. 59–60; Julia Lee Sinks, "Editors and Newspapers of Fayette County," *Quarterly of the Texas State Historical Association* 1 (July, 1897): 34–37.

[63] Anson Jones, *Memoranda and Official Correspondence Relating to the Republic of Texas*, pp. 180–82.

ment of his accounts due by the Government to enable him to move from here. What he will do, or where he will go, he cannot at present say—it is rather with him where he *can* go."[64]

Whiting did not receive payment in time to remove the press— through Sam Houston's spitefulness, Jones maintained—and reputedly lost nearly all of the $20,000 he had invested in buildings and other property at Austin. The county sheriff eventually foreclosed and transferred the printing establishment to James Webb. Other suits and judgments against Whiting lingered in the courts for years. He passed through Texas one last time in 1849, stopping long enough to assign all accounts due him from the Texas government to his son. Then he continued west to the gold fields of California, where he died a few years later.[65]

Teulon, with the backing of several Austin citizens, used Whiting's press to establish the *Western Advocate* in February, 1843. He continued the paper erratically for about a year before he too gave up. By then grass literally grew in the streets of Austin, and the capital still remained at Washington on the Brazos. Teulon wrote Anson Jones a sad farewell letter before leaving Texas forever. "I am attached to Austin,—I love its mountain seat, its beautiful scenery, and even its very atmosphere; it was my first abiding-place in Texas—it shall be my last. . . . When I quit here I quit Texas."[66]

Teulon visited New England in the summer of 1844 and then sailed for Calcutta, India. A few years later he died there of cholera, word of his death coming back to Texas through the Masonic Lodge: "Brother Teulon died on 28 April 1846 and his remains were interred in Masonic form by the Lodge 'Kilwinning in the East.'"[67]

With Teulon's departure the first period of newspapering in Austin ended—and the westward movement of the Texas press faltered. The printing press remained in Austin, but silently until July 23, 1845. Then Jacob Cruger, the most durable of the early publishers and editors, returned with Joel Miner, formerly printer of Whiting's *Gazette*,

[64] Ibid.

[65] Deed Records of Travis County, County Clerk's Office, Austin, vol. A, p. 567; Kenneth F. Neighbours, "The Expedition of Major Robert S. Neighbors to El Paso in 1849," *Southwestern Historical Quarterly* 58 (July, 1954): 56.

[66] Jones, *Memoranda and Correspondence*, p. 259.

[67] A. S. Ruthven, *Proceedings of the Grand Lodge of Texas . . .* , I, 151–52, 242–43.

and again put it into use. Cruger and Miner established a paper to publish the proceedings of the Convention of 1845, a meeting called to
consider accepting an offer of annexation by the United States. They
called their paper the *New Era*, and although the paper discontinued
with the adjournment of the convention on August 28, 1845, they
chose the name well. With annexation, the capital at last returned to
Austin, and with it a new beginning to journalism there.

CHAPTER 8

Eastward the Press—and Northward

In the wake of the crises of 1842, Francis Moore made an apt observation in the *Telegraph and Texas Register*. "While on the extreme western and northwestern frontier the settlements are either stationary or slowly decreasing; on the eastern and northeastern sections of the Republic emigration seems to have received a new impulse and the settlements are extending with astounding rapidity."[1]

Moore linked the decline of one section with the development of the other, and no doubt some prospective immigrants turned northeasterly rather than westerly because of the 1842 invasions. Still, those invasions alone did not account for the rapid growth of the northeast in the early 1840s. Nor did they account for the relocation of Charles DeMorse from Austin to Clarksville to found the newspaper that became both the spokesman and the sounding board of the section for almost half a century. Rather, the increase in population stemmed from the opening of a new transportation artery and the availability of new lands for settlement; DeMorse's relocation, from the consequent need for a newspaper and his personal circumstances.

During the 1830s Captain Henry Shreve removed the notorious Red River raft, or log jam, making the river navigable above Shreveport, Louisiana, and making possible the development of its upper reaches. The removal of the Cherokee Indians from east Texas during Lamar's administration opened other choice lands for settlement, and empresario grants to W. S. Peters and associates from the Republic of Texas in 1841 and 1842 hastened the settlement of the northern boundary. Hard times in the United States gave impetus to immigration,

[1] Houston *Telegraph and Texas Register*, February 15, 1843.

making northeastern Texas a relatively bright spot in a generally gloomy economic picture in the early 1840s. This circumstance caused leading citizens of the Clarksville area to feel the need of a newspaper and to seek an editor. "Major J. B. Ransom . . . told me that he had never seen people more anxious to have a press established than the population of this section, and they had offered to furnish him an office if he would take charge of it," DeMorse later wrote.[2] Upon Ransom's refusal, the Red River delegation to the Texas Congress in 1841–42— Robert Potter, senator, and Albert Hamilton Latimer, representative —approached DeMorse.

The offer came at an opportune time for DeMorse. Born Charles Denny Morse on January 31, 1816, at Leicester, Massachusetts, he received a good academic education at New Haven, Connecticut, and studied law in New York. Upon the outbreak of the Texan Revolution, he joined the battalion of Major Edwin Morehouse, a battalion that included several others whose names figure in the newspaper history of Texas—Martin Carroll Wing, Algernon P. Thompson, and Charles A. Ogsbury. The battalion, 174 strong, sailed on the brig *Matawomkeag* on November 21, 1835, but encountered adventure before reaching Texas. The British brig-of-war *Serpent* captured the *Matawomkeag* and carried it to Nassau, where the government held the men on suspicion of piracy until a court acquitted them of the charges on January 15, 1836. Charles D. Morse acquired the name he bore thereafter when a British officer misunderstood his name and rendered it Charles DeMorse on the records. His friends suggested that the new name sounded better than the old one, so he adopted it. On the eve of his departure for Clarksville in early 1842, the Texas Congress made the name change official.[3]

Morehouse's battalion sailed from the Bahamas for Texas on February 16, 1836, on the steamer *Shark* but was detained at the mouth of the Mississippi River. DeMorse and several others left the main group there, and DeMorse fought a duel with a young man named Tileston at New Orleans before finally landing in Texas about March 2. He accepted a commission in the Texas navy and was at Galveston with the Texas government when news came of the victory of San Jacinto. De-

[2] Clarksville *Northern Standard*, September 23, 1848.
[3] Ernest Wallace, *Charles DeMorse, Pioneer Editor and Statesman*, p. 12. Where not otherwise noted, biographical information on DeMorse is derived from this book.

Morse guarded Santa Anna during the summer of 1836, when elements of the army demanded his execution. Later DeMorse served in the Texas army as aide to Albert Sidney Johnston. Discharged in the summer of 1837, he practiced law at Matagorda, where he met and married Lodiska C. Woolridge.

An ardent supporter of Mirabeau B. Lamar, DeMorse held the office of stock commissioner, a clerical position in the treasury department, during the Lamar administration and moved to Austin upon the founding of the new capital. When Lamar left office in late 1841, DeMorse also found himself unemployed. While he pondered his future, he edited the latter numbers of Sam Whiting's *Daily Bulletin* and discovered a natural talent for journalism. The improvement of the paper in his hands attracted favorable attention, not only from Francis Moore, but also from Whiting and others. When George Knight Teulon relinquished the editorship of the *Austin City Gazette* to go to England, Whiting offered DeMorse that position. About the same time, he received another offer to establish a newspaper in San Antonio, and Potter and Latimer presented the Clarksville offer. "Some friends who were in Austin at the time advised me upon comparison of the offers to accept this, which accorded with my own judgment," DeMorse said later. "I accordingly came."[4]

Time proved the wisdom of his decision. Within a few months the Mexican invasions paralyzed the west, and by the time the press resumed the westward movement, he had entrenched himself at Clarksville and established the *Standard*. "We shall endeavor to make our newspaper such a complete record of the progress of affairs in the country that foreign subscribers will be as fully advised of its condition as resident citizens," he told his readers in the first issue. No editor ever more fully achieved his purpose. For forty-five years, until his death in 1887, he kept his readers informed of events—local, national, international, economic, political, military, and social. From his vantage point he watched the annexation of Texas, the Mexican War, and the development of the sectional crisis. He interrupted publication briefly to take up arms himself during the Civil War and returned to aid in the rebuilding of his section. "From the date of its first issue the *Standard* constitutes the most fertile source for the study of the eco-

[4] *Northern Standard*, September 23, 1848.

nomic, social and political life in Northeast Texas," says his biographer. "The paper wielded an influence in Texas that has been the privilege of few newspapers to exert either before or since."[5] When he died, his fellow editors hailed him as the "Nestor," the Grand Old Man, of Texas journalism.

Initially Martin Carroll Wing, having recently sold his interest in the *Sentinel*, joined DeMorse in plans for the *Northern Standard*. The two issued a prospectus for the paper in mid-January, 1842, but shortly thereafter rumors of the Mexican invasion of south Texas reached Austin. The prospect of military adventure diverted Wing's interest, and he remained behind in February, when DeMorse set out for Clarksville in company with Robert Potter and Thomas F. Smith, representative from Fannin County.

DeMorse met with high adventure sooner than his friend Wing, for, if he rode away from one battlefront, he rode toward another, and he rode in dangerous company. At the same time that Texas geared to face the Mexican invasions, two factions, the Moderators and Regulators, waged a private war in the extreme eastern border. Robert Potter, a controversial man charged variously with maiming his enemies and stealing another man's wife, belonged to the Moderator faction, and he had not long to live. At his behest the previous fall, President Lamar had placed a reward on the head of William Pinkney Rose, a leading Regulator, and Potter rode eastward to see his rival face judgment.

The party stopped in Nacogdoches at the house of Adolphus Sterne, merchant, postmaster, and diarist, where DeMorse made a favorable impression. "Mr DeMorse is going to publish a Paper at Clarksville Red River County," Sterne wrote in his diary, "judging of the man as I have heard those who know him well speak of him, I am satisfied the Paper, will be a very respectable one." On February 23, 1842, DeMorse, Potter, and Smith took the road north to Clarksville. Potter left his companions to visit his home and confront Rose, and a few days later, on March 2, his enemies killed him as he tried to escape them by diving into Caddo Lake, then known as Ferry or Soda Lake.[6]

[5] Ibid., August 20, 1842; Wallace, *DeMorse*, pp. 24–25.

[6] Archie P. McDonald, ed., *Hurrah for Texas: The Diary of Adolphus Sterne, 1838–1851*, pp. 81, 84, 85; John H. McLean, *Reminiscences*, pp. 12–21; C. L. Sonnichsen, *Ten Texas Feuds*, pp. 58–66; L. W. Kemp, *The Signers of the Texas Declaration of Independence*, pp. 258–77.

The murder gave DeMorse a rude introduction to the section and suggested the pitfalls that awaited an unwary editor there.

Clarksville stood to the north of the Regulator-Moderator war zone, however, and attracted a different type of settler. The country to the south and east, long an international boundary, had drawn lawless elements from both countries, elements that either terrorized more law-abiding citizens or provoked them to retaliation. By contrast, the Red River country when it opened up attracted sturdy yeoman farmers, intent on acquiring rich lands and rearing their families.

Clarksville citizens gave DeMorse the warm welcome their congressmen promised. Indeed, no other early Texan editor received such wholehearted community support, or support that accounted in so large a measure for his success. For the financing of the paper, DeMorse found awaiting him a letter of credit for $2,500, drawn on the three major mercantile establishments of the town and signed by some twelve or fifteen of the leading citizens.[7]

He set off immediately for New Orleans to obtain equipment and experienced for the first time the vagaries of the stream that dominated life in his area and that would be a running topic of discussion in his newspaper. Although Captain Shreve had cleared the raft, it did not stay cleared, and the struggle against it continued for a generation. Moreover, navigation on the river depended on the amount of rain that fell upstream. "One month we were upon the river and at the little towns upon its banks," DeMorse wrote of his first attempt to navigate Red River. Nor was the river the only unforeseen problem that he faced. While he waited on the stream above Shreveport, he met returning from New Orleans the three merchants on whom his letter of credit was drawn. The market being bad, they had not sold their cotton, and they requested that he not use the letter. Instead, they suggested that he return to Clarksville and raise the money by public subscription. DeMorse followed this suggestion, and the citizens rallied to his support, subscribing between $700 and $800, about $450 of it in cash. "With this I went below, procured a press and type, forty reams of paper, and fixtures," he said. He secured the items only with the assistance of New Orleans printers and from three different offices, for no one establishment had them.[8]

[7] *Northern Standard*, August 20, 1842.
[8] Ibid., September 23, 1848.

The first issue, long delayed, at last appeared on August 20, 1842. Two weeks later a copy reached Nacogdoches, where Adolphus Sterne gave it his approval. It was in appearance, he declared, much better looking than the *Friend of the Laws* printed in New Orleans when he first arrived there in 1821 and "a far better looking Sheet than half the Country Papers" of the United States. "Success attend the *Standard*, and its Editor, as good a fellow as ever lived," he wrote in his diary.[9]

By September 29, almost six weeks after publication, a copy reached Houston, where Francis Moore gave it the courteous welcome he reserved for new papers. The time lag between publication and delivery pointed up the problem of which all Texas editors complained and which affected DeMorse even more acutely than most others—the slowness of the mails. By 1844 the *Standard* generally took from three to four weeks to reach Houston and as long as another four to reach Washington on the Brazos. Moreover, the paper arrived in clusters rather than regularly at distant points. "Eastern mail arrived brought . . . a lot of *Back* issues of the *Northern Standard*," commented Sterne, voicing the complaint of many of DeMorse's subscribers. As a result, DeMorse kept up a running battle for better mail service. "This irregularity seriously affects the interest of newspaper publishers who lose and fail to get subscribers in consequence of it," he wrote, "and it seems to us clear that it results from culpable negligence or something worse on the part of Post masters."[10]

Because of his remote location and dependence on the Red River, DeMorse felt even more keenly than most early editors the shortage of paper. During the spring of 1845 he suspended publication for nine weeks for lack of paper, and on several other occasions he suspended for a few weeks at a time or reduced the size of the *Standard*, in each instance taking the loss himself and giving his subscribers a full volume. Finding New Orleans an undependable source, he turned to Boston and then Philadelphia for paper. At one point in the 1850s, when the river ran unusually low, he had a shipment of paper freighted from Alexandria to Shreveport at the almost prohibitive cost of $3.50 a barrel and then sent ox wagons to haul it from Shreveport to Clarksville.[11]

During his early years in the northeast, DeMorse sometimes felt

[9] McDonald, *Hurrah for Texas*, p. 112.
[10] Ibid., p. 201; *Northern Standard*, October 14, 1843.
[11] Wallace, *DeMorse*, p. 46.

lonely and isolated. "We are tired of plodding at our daily labor and would draw inspiration from associating with great men," he once wrote. "We want to see Houston and Galveston, Velasco, Matagorda, Texana, Victoria, and San Antonio, and then passing over to Austin, thence to Washington, if Congress sits there." But his chosen life did not permit indulgence. "Even as we write our foreman informs us that our devil has a chill," he concluded, "and that we must sink the majesty of our editorial plural, and take hold of the roller, otherwise we cannot get the paper out in time."[12]

DeMorse did indeed travel a great deal, but mostly in the northeastern area served by the *Standard*. He did not depend entirely on the paper for a livelihood but continued the practice of law, a profession that complemented his editing. When he traveled to various county seats on legal business, he sold and collected for subscriptions and advertisements. Initially he set the subscription at five dollars per year, the customary rate. In order to meet community needs, he accepted produce—corn, hogs, and other produce—in payment, but dropped the cash subscription price to four dollars. Again to meet the needs of the section, he established a branch office of the *Standard* at Bonham in 1846, printing an edition there at the same time as in Clarksville. This experiment proved a failure, and he discontinued it after eight months.[13]

To compensate for the lack of timely news from "below"—a word that to Red River people meant either downstream or the more southern regions of Texas—DeMorse kept his readers apprised of the condition of the river, the state of crops, and other local matters that affected them. He followed an anti–Sam Houston line during the early years of the paper, worked for annexation to the United States, and then became an ardent partisan of the Democratic party. Throughout, the responsibility of educating his readers and improving the community weighed heavily on him, and he showed a discriminating literary taste. His style emerged in his early issues when he carried George Wilkins Kendall's columns on the Santa Fe Expedition, columns that were at the same time news to his readers, entertainment, and literature.

From his outpost, DeMorse avidly read the exchange papers that

---

[12] *Northern Standard*, October 28, 1843.
[13] Wallace, *DeMorse*, p. 48.

arrived from "below" and occasionally gave objective views of them. In late 1843 he found the *Telegraph* and *Civilian* exchanging "light shot from their small guns" and the *National Vindicator*, after a period of lethargy, rebuking the *News* and beginning a controversy with the *Telegraph* about the Indian treaty. The *Planter*, published at Columbia by Samuel J. Durnett, was "as interesting and quiet as usual, wending its way through romances and agriculture," while the *Western Advocate* had come alive again to hint at conspiracies against the interest of the country. At that time the papers lined up for or against President Houston and quarreled about the sale of the navy, the armistice with Mexico, and the Indian treaty. "Altogether they seem to have got into a snarl down below if the public journals are any indication," he commented. "There seems to be too much party spirit, too much personal controversy. . . . So far as public feeling is concerned, they are far behind us in these Northern regions where, feeling an equal interest in public interest, we have no bitterness of party spirit and busy ourselves in making crops and paying debts."[14]

DeMorse possibly spoke with tongue in cheek, for his section had its own particular problems and its editors their own squabbles. When he first planned the *Standard*, the whole of Texas north and east of Galveston could boast of only one newspaper—the *Red-Lander* at San Augustine, some one hundred fifty miles distant from Clarksville. But before he began publication, another press arrived in east Texas to become the organ of several ephemeral newspapers, known only by reference.

On May 25, 1842, Francis Moore welcomed a new paper, the *Sabine Advocate*, "published weekly at Pulaski, Harrison County, by S. P. January & Co." and edited by a man named Shelton. Both town and paper proved sometime things and vanished, leaving few signs. The founders of Pulaski, located at a crossing of the Sabine River east of present-day Carthage, envisioned the town as a river port, but the river rarely cooperated. Pulaski served as the seat of Harrison County until 1846 and briefly as the seat of Panola County before disappearing from the map and almost from memory.[15] The *Sabine Advocate* lasted only until the late summer or fall of 1842.

[14] *Northern Standard*, December 16, 1843.

[15] *Telegraph and Texas Register*, May 24, 1842; San Augustine *Red-Lander*, May 26, 1842; Lawrence R. Sharp, "A History of Panola County" (M.A. thesis, University of Texas, 1940), p. 143.

By early 1843 the press had moved to Marshall, where L. A. W. Laird launched the *Marshall Review*, a continuation of the *Sabine Advocate*, with Shelton—"a very clever gentleman"—as "senior editor" and one Stinson as his assistant. The *Review* lapsed into silence in the fall of 1843, to be succeeded the following February by the *Harrison Times*, which Anson Jones described in 1844 as "a well-conducted paper, with a circulation of some four or five hundred." The *Times* continued publication until the fall of 1845, when the press again changed hands. A prospectus dated October 16, 1845, announced its successor, the *Soda Lake Herald*, with E. C. Beazley as editor and T. A. Harris and Zach. Wills, publishers. The *Herald* continued until at least late 1847.[16]

DeMorse occasionally exchanged salvos with the various editors of the Harrison County press, but his editorial battle royal developed with Alanson Wyllys Canfield of the *Red-Lander*. Canfield could boast of presiding over the most venerable press in Texas, it being the one Milton Slocum had introduced to Nacogdoches in 1829 and on which he had opened the era of the permanent press by printing the *Mexican Advocate*. On it David Lawhon had printed the *Texean and Emigrant's Guide* during the revolution, and Isaac Watts Burton had printed the *Texas Chronicle* during the presidential election of 1838.

W. W. Parker purchased the press from Burton in the summer of 1838 and moved it to San Augustine, where he published the *Red-Lander* until declining health prompted him to discontinue the paper in late 1839. He sold the press to Canfield, who in May, 1840, launched the *Journal and Advertiser*, with Parker assisting in the publication until his death the following October. Upon the completion of a full volume of the *Journal and Advertiser*, Canfield changed the name of the paper to that of its immediate predecessor. With J. A. Whittlesey and Henry Sublett as assistant editors and George W. Morris as printer, Canfield made the second *Red-Lander* the most influential paper to come from the Slocum press. He usually spoke for east Texas, giving Sam Houston loyal support and agitating for the repeal of the tariff. Francis Moore called the *Red-Lander* "one of the best" newspapers in the republic in early 1846, and in the summer of 1844 Anson Jones estimated that it

---

[16] *Northern Standard*, January 14, 1843; Anson Jones, *Memoranda and Official Correspondence Relating to the Republic of Texas*, pp. 360–61; Thomas W. Streeter, *Bibliography of Texas*, 1795–1845, pt. 1, vol. II, 535–36, 539.

had a greater circulation than the *Telegraph,* the *News,* and the *Intelligencer* combined.[17]

Jones probably exaggerated, for he was running for president at the time, and the *Red-Lander* supported him while the other papers opposed him. Even so, before 1842 the *Red-Lander* press held a monopoly on printing over a vast area of the republic. It stood astride an ancient thoroughfare, the Old San Antonio Road, and was the first—sometimes the only—newspaper seen by immigrants and visitors traveling that route. Canfield, moreover, proved a competent editor.

Born in Connecticut about 1808, Canfield married Elizabeth A. Russell, also Connecticut-born, and came to Texas with her brother Robert B. Russell in time to enroll in a company of Sabine volunteers in July, 1836. The Canfields and Russells resided for a time in Sabine County and then moved to San Augustine, where Canfield succeeded in business. Noted for his artistic taste, he built a home that became a local showplace because of its landscaping, and he and his wife played an active role in the social life of the area.[18]

Canfield gave DeMorse a frigid welcome to the journalistic world, launching the editorial feud even before the *Northern Standard* appeared. He declined to print DeMorse's prospectus, explaining in an editorial about twice as long as the prospectus that he did not have the space. His hostility stemmed in part from the monopolist's natural jealousy of any infringement on his territory, but sheer distance ruled out real competition between the two papers, and the *Standard,* located on a different transportation route, served a different clientele.

Canfield's real grievance, as he made clear after the feud grew heated, stemmed from political differences. He saw the founding of the *Standard* as part of a grand conspiracy to undermine his hero, Sam Houston. The "broken down politicians" of the Lamar-Burnet faction, he believed, resolved on a plan of revenge after Burnet's defeat. "The plan of campaign was no other than to open upon the good people of Texas a full charged battery of Presses which were to be manned and worked entirely by the phalanx of retired secretaries, newly-elected

[17] Streeter, *Bibliography of Texas,* pt. 1, vol. II, 542–43; Jones, *Memoranda and Correspondence,* pp. 360–61.
[18] Muster Roll, General Land Office, Austin, Texas, Book I, p. 59; George Louis Crocket, *Two Centuries in East Texas,* pp. 245–46; United States, "Census of Jefferson County, Texas. Population Schedule," microfilm copy in Clayton Library, Houston Public Library, Houston.

judicial officials, ex-stock commissioners etc. etc." he charged. "The most prominent points in the Republic were to be forthwith occupied and offensive operations were to commence simultaneously at Clarksville, Nacogdoches, Montgomery, Galveston, Crockett, Austin, and Matagorda."[19] Francis Moore, presumably one of the clique, called Canfield's theory as "false as it is silly," and certainly Lamar and Burnet had not the financing for such a conspiracy had they been so inclined. Even so, Canfield continued his vendetta against DeMorse.

DeMorse, taken aback by the attack at first, returned in kind, threatening at one point to "settle the matter with cowhide." The feud raged through the winter and spring of 1842 and 1843, with the two editors eventually refusing to exchange papers, a clear indication that their feud was no cosmetic thing designed to titillate their readers. Their duel of words came to a climax in the fall of 1843, when DeMorse published a letter from an unnamed writer making grave charges against Canfield. Ridiculing Canfield's claim that he had chartered the cabin of a vessel in New York exclusively for himself and his family when he set out for Texas, the writer said Canfield had worked as a day laborer in Sabine County upon first arriving in Texas with his family. The writer then accused Canfield of returning to the United States and having spurious bank bills engraved, which he passed off in Texas, "buying anything that was for sale." In addition, charged the writer, "Canfield dare not go to the States, if it is known, for he stole a large quantity of jewelry from a ship at New York which he has here now."[20]

The letter had the strange effect of clearing the air between the two editors. They dropped their venomous name-calling and within a few months resumed the exchange of newspapers. Nor was anything further said about the charges against Canfield by either DeMorse or other editors. Francis Moore, usually the keeper of public morals, always treated Canfield with respect, even when vigorously disagreeing with him on issues. When Canfield sold the *Red-Lander* to James Russell and H. M. Kinsey in early 1846 in order to join Zachary Taylor at Corpus Christi, Moore bid him a fond farewell, writing that "this gentleman during the long period that he conducted the Red Lander was endeared to his contemporaries by his candor and courteous deportment."[21]

[19] As quoted in the *Telegraph and Texas Register*, October 5, 1842.
[20] *Northern Standard*, September 21, 1843.
[21] *Telegraph and Texas Register*, February 11, 1846.

DeMorse and Canfield in fact agreed on many points and in representing their section found themselves on the same side of several issues. Both advocated the reform or abolition of the tariff; both faced
the delicate problem of handling news of the private warfare that
wracked the border; and both ardently supported annexation to the
United States.

The issue of the tariff divided the republic along sectional lines,
pitting editors and citizens of the east and north against those of the
south and west. Generally, Texans who received goods by sea routes
favored the tariff, while those who relied on land routes opposed it. As
advocates of the duty pointed out, the republic depended on income
from the tariff to operate the government, but, as those citizens who
paid it protested, the tariff fell unevenly on the sections. Customs
houses at each port of entry along the Gulf coast duly collected the tax,
but only one custom house, that at San Augustine, served the entire
eastern boundary, and it did minimal business. The east not only favored free trade, but usually practiced it. Smuggling had been a time-
honored tradition of the border from the time Spanish soldiers bought
goods from French Louisiana, and few indeed were the Texans who
chose to declare goods and pay taxes. Merchants who kept the law
found themselves unable to compete with those who did not.[22]

Canfield campaigned in the *Red-Lander* for the repeal or at least
the reform of the tariff on the grounds that it could not be enforced. In
late 1842 he reported the custom house closed and no duties being collected from the Red River to the mouth of the Sabine. The populace
openly defied the collectors and brought goods from the United States
as freely as they carried them from one county to another. A few years
later he explained how the firm of Austin and Clapp avoided the tax.
The merchants simply moved to the United States side of the Sabine,
established a free ferry for their Texan customers, and sold their goods
at 25 percent less.[23] DeMorse called Canfield "rabid" on the subject
but at length supported a similar position.

Editors along the Gulf coast argued that the uneven enforcement
of the law penalized their section, and a definite sectionalism developed. Once, for example, when easterners suffered from the closing of

²²Asa Kyrus Christian, "The Tariff History of the Republic of Texas," *Southwestern
Historical Quarterly* 20 (April, 1917): 317–40.
²³*Telegraph and Texas Register*, December 14, 1842, and March 12, 1845.

the Red River, the *Civilian* at Galveston noted the consequent benefit "to our own parts" and pointed out that the river did the republic as a whole a disservice by identifying Texans of that area with the United States. Again when congressmen of the Red River and southeastern counties joined forces "to carry out the great measures dear to the Eastern people," Francis Moore expressed hope that those measures would be equally dear to the whole republic.[24] The argument over the tariff and the problems of its collection raged until annexation. Then, of course, the issue vanished instantly as the Texas-Louisiana border for the first time since 1800 lost its position as an international boundary.

The matter of the civil war in the eastern counties did not vanish so quickly, much to the discomfort of Texan newsmen. A later generation of editors might seek sensationalism, but self-interest and public interest advised those of early Texas to avoid it. The editor who incautiously reported local broils risked angering all parties and endangering his business and even his life. The publicizing of violence, moreover, did little to encourage immigration, and the editor tied the appreciation in value of his land and business to the continued growth of the republic. Texan editors subscribed wholeheartedly not only to the unwritten rule of printing nothing that would hurt the country but also to the corollary of that rule, that what would hurt the country would also hurt them. They cringed when their counterparts in the United States pictured the republic as the haven of renegades and rebuked their Texan colleagues who wrote anything that failed to improve the image of Texas. "To read the Colorado Gazette one would never suppose the paper to be published in Texas by a Texian," sniffed one editor.[25] Only with reluctance did they print news that reinforced the negative image.

Thus, they gave but brief attention to one of the few editorial feuds in Texas before 1860 that culminated in the slaying of one of the editors—even though that feud spelled the end of San Augustine University and hastened the decline of the *Red-Lander*.

The feud, to be sure, blew up quickly over a private matter and within the confines of a single town. The principals, moreover, were relative newcomers to the state and the profession. The victim, James Russell, Canfield's successor as editor of the *Red-Lander*, arrived at

[24] Ibid., November 12, 1842, and October 24, 1843.
[25] Houston *Morning Star*, October 28, 1841.

San Augustine about 1843, first to teach and then to serve as president at San Augustine University. A Scottish-born Presbyterian minister, he could boast of more scholarly accomplishments than most of his contemporaries. He held the Master of Arts degree from Edinburgh University, and he brought with him to Texas a personal library of some five hundred choice books. Russell won a reputation as "a trenchant writer and an accomplished lecturer," but, as a later historian of San Augustine put it, he was also "a man of irascible, impetuous temperament and domineering personality, and was constantly in trouble one way or another. He was perfectly fearless and did not hesitate to meet an antagonist in a personal encounter. He possessed a biting tongue and expressed his opinions regardless of possible consequences."[26]

Russell became involved in various theological disputes that divided the townspeople, and, after acquiring the *Red-Lander*, incurred the wrath of a young printer, Henry A. Kendall, who founded a rival paper, the *Shield*, in the summer of 1846. A few lines in the *Northern Standard* the following summer reported in typical fashion the culmination of their differences:

> We learn from a reliable source that the Rev. James Russell, editor of the *Red Lander*, was killed in San Augustine some days since by Mr. Kendall, publisher of the *Shield*.
>
> This deplorable result grew out of some bitter controversy which had been going on between the two persons for some weeks past. The parties are said to have met the day before the killing and exchanged two shots each, ineffectually. On the day of the occurrence, Kendall, it is said, waylaid Russell as he left his office, and shot him dead. . . . We missed the *Red Lander* last mail, but little thought to have heard so unfortunate a reason for the failure.[27]

The news reached Houston by way of the *Natchitoches Chronicle* almost as soon as it reached Clarksville. Francis Moore carried a similar account, concluding with a sentence that revealed the usual embarrassment of the editors in reporting such news: "We have received no direct information of the event and we still hope for the credit of the *Texian* press that the horrid report is not correct."[28]

An obituary in a later issue of the *Telegraph* settled any doubts

---

[26] Crocket, *Two Centuries*, pp. 305–306.
[27] *Northern Standard*, August 28, 1847.
[28] *Telegraph and Texas Register*, August 30, 1847.

about Russell's demise without explaining the circumstances and, presumably, without reflecting discredit to the Texas press. The obituary lauded Russell's intellectual and scholarly attainments and spoke of him as a man of "many years," whose exact age was unknown. One sentence only suggested his problems: "His course as an editor involved him in many distressing and lamentable broils in all of which he displayed a firmness evincive of cool and unquestionable courage." The obituary ended with the comment: "The victim bowed in death to the inscrutable will of his God! Peace to his ashes!"[29] The reader who had missed the previous notice might well have inferred that Russell died a natural death of ripe old age.

The *Northern Standard* carried no further direct mention of the matter, but a few months later DeMorse indirectly informed his readers of the ending. The *Standard* picked up from the *Picayune* a notice telling of the death of Henry A. Kendall of yellow fever in New Orleans, where he worked as a printer in the *Picayune* office: "Mr. Kendall was unfortunately engaged in a personal rencontre with a Mr. Russell, editor of the *Red Lander* of San Augustine in which Mr. Russell lost his life." Most citizens of San Augustine knew the reason for the embroglio, but not until 1932 did a local historian enlighten the general public. Russell had printed in the *Red-Lander* an article that defamed Kendall's sister. Even then, more than eighty years later, the historian omitted the lady's name.[30]

The coverage of the Potter-Rose feud further illustrates the press handling of such matters. Primarily because of Potter's character and the circumstances of his personal life, his murder created a stir of excitement then and later. Charles Dickens, visiting in the United States at the time, took notice of it in his *American Notes*; the woman who considered herself Potter's wife wrote her account of it; and a twentieth-century writer wrote a novel featuring it. Contemporary Texan newspapers gave fuller coverage to it than to any similar story of the era, but they confined themselves to an account of the murder and avoided the sensational aspects of Potter's personal life.[31]

[29] Ibid., September 13, 1847.
[30] *Northern Standard*, October 30, 1847; Crocket, *Two Centuries*, p. 306.
[31] Charles Dickens, *American Notes and Pictures from Italy* (London: Oxford University Press, 1957), pp. 237–38; Elithe Hamilton Kirkland, *Love Is a Wild Assault* (Garden City, N.Y.: Doubleday, 1959); *Morning Star*, March 30, 1842.

Charles DeMorse, who had traveled with the victim only days before the tragedy and who came close to being an eye witness, eventually gave more space and editorial comment to the tragedy than any other editor. His contemporaries considered his coverage daring, but by the standards of a later generation it was timid in the extreme. He, of course, did not begin printing the *Standard* until almost six months after the event, but another two months passed before any mention of it appeared. Then, boldly for the time and place, he printed on the front page an account of the court proceedings that eventually freed Rose for lack of evidence. DeMorse carefully disclaimed any criticism of the court and confined his editorial comment to a regret at the "premature loss of a valuable citizen and a most excellent and efficient Senator."[32]

Although William Pinkney Rose and Robert Potter carried the label of Regulator and Moderator, their feud developed independently of the real war. Strictly speaking, the Regulators and Moderators belonged to Shelby County, but the violence overflowed into the adjoining counties, especially Harrison, and the name sometimes covered personal vendettas, private acts of vengeance, or common criminality.

The Regulator-Moderator war roared to a climax at a time when annexation hung in the balance, thus causing Texan newsmen extreme embarrassment. They supported annexation almost to a man, but a vocal group in the United States opposed it, in part because of the reputation of the inhabitants. The Texans could scarcely report the bare facts of their civil war without giving fuel to the enemies of the cause in the United States—Whigs, abolitionists, and New Englanders in general. Indeed, had full accounts of the affray appeared in the papers, annexation might well have been delayed, for the border country harbored some characters—assassins, horse thieves, counterfeiters, and land pirates—even more unsavory than the New Englanders imagined. Some of those characters, moreover, had entrenched themselves in the area before the Republic of Texas came into existence. In 1806 when the United States and Spain disagreed over the boundary line between Texas and Louisiana, they established along the Sabine River a neutral ground, or no-man's-land, that attracted the dregs of both countries. Even after a treaty abolished the neutral ground in 1819,

[32] *Northern Standard*, October 22, 1842.

the international boundary continued to draw the criminal elements. Many of the old outlaws remained there, and new recruits of similar character joined them.

Both the Regulators and the Moderators claimed to be warring against outlaws, but both contained criminal elements and both committed outrages—ambushes, lynchings, and house-burnings. The local government and courts, either intimidated or otherwise controlled by one faction or the other, declined to intervene, and the conflict developed into gang warfare, complete with hired killers. Each side eventually mustered at least one hundred fifty armed men, and in the latter stages they fortified military camps and engaged in pitched battles.[33]

Throughout 1842 and early 1843 both the central government and the press tried to ignore the violence in the eastern counties. The *Morning Star* mentioned "the reign of terror" in Shelby County in late 1842, and other reports appeared. But in the summer of 1843 DeMorse again showed himself bolder than his fellows and reported the killing of four men in Harrison County. By that time Francis Moore too found silence in the matter intolerable. When critics questioned DeMorse's judgment in mentioning the murders, Moore came to his defense. "We know that many believe the accounts of murder that occur should not be published," he admitted. Then he suggested that publishing them might have a salutary effect. "One of the representatives from Harrison County informed us some time since that in the early settlement of that county, twenty-five men were killed in one year and not one of the murderers hung."[34]

With the murder of Judge John M. Hansford late in 1843, neither the government nor the press could ignore the war. Earlier Hansford had angered the Regulators by dismissing a court trial of one of their number because he found himself "surrounded by bravos and hired assassins, and no longer left free to preside as an impartial Judge." "We are told," reported DeMorse, "that Judge Hansford was shot down like a dog in the presence of his wife by half a dozen men without threat of provocation on his part." DeMorse no longer tried to contain his indignation. "Harrison is making decided improvements upon the old dull systems of law, order, and morality, and almost every week they slay somebody down there, occasionally two at a time to show that they do

---

[33] Sonnichsen, *Ten Texas Feuds*, pp. 44–51; Crocket, *Two Centuries*, pp. 199–200.
[34] *Telegraph and Texas Register*, August 9, 1843.

not halt in the good work," he wrote. "It must be a glorious field for a newspaper; it can get such quantities of advertising in the way of probate notices."[35]

The newspaper on the scene, the *Harrison Times*, took a bright view of the affair. The defendants promptly submitted themselves to the law, the *Times* reported cheerfully, in a manner that spoke "well for them and for the law abiding character of the citizens of our county." Francis Moore quoted the *Times* in the *Morning Star* and added his own view: "It would have been spoken better for the citizens of the county if the parties had submitted their cause to the legal tribunals before the murder of Judge Hansford."[36]

Hansford's murder and that of Captain John M. Bradley as he left church a few months later precipitated open warfare, with each side bringing in reinforcements from adjoining areas. At that point President Sam Houston intervened. He journeyed to east Texas, where he enjoyed immense popularity despite his stand for the tariff, and personally supervised the dismantling of the war. He ordered all parties involved to lay down their arms and to retire to their homes, at the same time calling in the militia. Houston then arranged for the surrender of the leaders and convened a court to devise a peace plan. The leaders of both factions signed the plan, and the *Telegraph* declared the Regulator-Moderator war at an end.[37]

The *Telegraph* spoke somewhat prematurely and possibly with an eye on the election in progress in the United States and the prospects of annexation. More than a year later with annexation assured and the Regulator-Moderator affair still simmering, Francis Moore again took notice of the troublemakers. Immigrants shunned Shelby County as they would Sodom, he commented, for "its soil has been polluted with human blood unlawfully shed in broils and by private assassinations."[38]

At the same time he and A. W. Canfield engaged in an editorial debate about the ethics of printing handbills for the warring parties. Both editors agreed on the immorality of carrying in their newspapers personal advertisements attacking other individuals, but Canfield printed handbills carrying such attacks and defended his action. "Our

[35] *Red-Lander*, July 22, 1841; DeMorse, quoted in *Morning Star*, February 29, 1844.
    [36] *Morning Star*, February 29, 1844.
    [37] *Telegraph and Texas Register*, September 18, 1844.
    [38] *Northern Standard*, May 26, 1847; *Telegraph and Texas Register*, May 17, 1847.

business is printing. We cannot refuse to print jobs for any person," he insisted.

Moore, by contrast, deplored Canfield's printing of the handbills, "as it is quite probable that by this means he has inadvertently increased the evil. The same reasons that should prevent an editor from publishing personal advertisements in a newspaper should prevent him from publishing such advertisements in a handbill."[39]

Later, all Texas newspapers studiously avoided sensationalizing an episode that some observers considered the last atrocity of the Regulator-Moderator war. Charles DeMorse gave typical coverage to the story, carrying at the bottom of the last page of the *Standard* an account that he excerpted from the *Red-Lander*: "A youthful couple married at the home of John Wilkinson in the neighborhood of Hamilton on the Sabine River, Shelby. It appears that of the party, seventy-two individuals have been suddenly seized with violent sickness, twelve of whom have since died exhibiting every symptom of the effects of poison. Whether the arsenic was mixed with the cake by accident, reckless carelessness, or diabolic design has not yet been satisfactorily discovered."[40]

The *Telegraph* mentioned that the San Augustine *Shield* reported ten people dead after being poisoned at a wedding party, and the Galveston *Civilian* later refuted rumors that John Wilkinson had been lynched and reported instead that he had been cleared of charges but that his wife remained in custody.[41] No doubt the details circulated among the citizenry along with other rumors, but the editors dropped the story at that, leaving curious historians to sift through old court records for the outcome.

By the time of the Great Arsenic Poisoning, as the affair became known in east Texas lore, the Mexican War had begun, bringing to a final end the private east-Texas war. One company of Regulators and one of Moderators marched off to the Rio Grande and in fighting a common enemy reportedly forgot their old grievances. Feelings ran high in the east for at least half a century, however, and descendants for several generations told accounts—usually partisan—that enlarged considerably on the newspaper accounts of the Regulators and Moderators.

[39] *Telegraph and Texas Register*, October 1, 1845.
[40] *Northern Standard*, May 26, 1847.
[41] *Telegraph and Texas Register*, May 17, 1847; Galveston *Civilian*, June 26, 1847.

CHAPTER 9

The Old Lady by the Sea

In the summer of 1842, while western Texas reeled under the shock of the Vásquez raid and while Charles DeMorse collected equipment for his printing office in the northeast, Hamilton Stuart found himself in a unique position. He published the only newspaper in Galveston, a circumstance so unusual that he called it to his readers' attention. No less than seven newspapers involving eighteen publishers had failed in the previous four years. "The following is a list of the newspapers which have been published here," he wrote in the *Civilian* of June 12, 1842: "the *Commercial Intelligencer*, the *Galvestonian*, the *Morning Herald*, the *Peoples Advocate*, the *Commercial Chronicle*, the *Croaker*, and the *Daily News*." [1]

Stuart possibly understated the case, for a century later the definitive bibliographer Thomas W. Streeter counted several additional defunct papers for the period, and a visiting Englishman wrote from Galveston on August 4, 1842, that "within 4 years there have been a dozen newspapers started here. There is one now—the Civilian—quite enough at this time of the year." [2] Anyone's count confirmed the impression of contemporary Texans that Galveston was a graveyard for newspapers, and before annexation at least five other papers had come and gone to reinforce that impression.

But the number of failures in no way reflected the state of newspapering on the island. A wealthy English lady who visited on the eve of annexation commented favorably: "There are three newspapers

[1] Ben C. Stuart, "History of Newspapers in Texas" (manuscript, Houston Public Library), p. [33].
[2] Thomas W. Streeter, *Bibliography of Texas 1795–1845*, pt. 1, vol. II, 516–25; W. Eugene Hollon and Ruth Lapham Butler, eds., *William Bollaert's Texas*, p. 128.

printed and circulated at Galveston. These have a considerable sale, and as entire liberty of the press is, of course, allowed, their contents are often amusing enough."[3] All of the defunct papers, moreover, emanated from only two presses, all except the *Herald* and the second *Galvestonian* from the old Niles and Company press, and, after the long string of failures that same press finally produced the most long-lived of all Texas newspapers. The year after Hamilton Stuart took note of the lonely position of the *Civilian*, a group of printers headed by Michael Cronican founded the *Galveston News*, "the Old Lady by the Sea," which Willard Richardson nursed to greatness. The *News* and the *Civilian* were among the four papers founded during the era of the republic that survived the Civil War, and of those four only the *News* continued into the twentieth century. Indeed, it not only continued but did so in considerable style, becoming the parent paper of the mighty *Dallas News*.[4]

Galveston became a two-press town in the fall of 1838, when Hamilton Stuart established the *Civilian* office in competition with the *Commercial Intelligencer* office of Niles and Company. But not until the mid-1840s did the town generate enough business to support adequately two newspapers. In the early years, while the rival press struggled to survive, the *Civilian* thrived due to two important advantages—a competent editor and substantial financial backing from the founders of the city.

Hamilton Stuart set the course of his career when he broke step with the Niles and Company crowd in the summer of 1838. In switching to the *Telegraph* office to edit the first pro–Sam Houston organ, he came under the patronage of Dr. Levi Jones, agent for the Galveston City Company, an enterprise that counted merchant-entrepreneurs Samuel May Williams and Thomas McKinney prominently among its stockholders. The election, of course, spelled the end of Stuart's little campaign sheet, the *Civilian*, and about the same time Francis Moore and Jacob W. Cruger acquired the handsome new power press that freed their older press for other purposes. By then the Island City had begun its mushroom growth, and the founders felt the need of a print-

[3] Mrs. [M. F. C.] Houstoun, *Texas and the Gulf of Mexico or Yachting in the New World*, p. 126.
[4] See Sam Acheson, *35,000 Days in Texas: A History of the Dallas News and Its Forebears*.

ing office to advertise their wares and print the various forms needed for a developing port city. They initially planned a newspaper entitled the *Galveston City Gazette*, but instead they consolidated their efforts with Stuart's. He transferred to the island to establish the *Civilian and Galveston City Gazette*—"a combination of the 'Civilian,' recently published at Houston, with the 'Gazette,' a new paper which was about to be established at this place." The second *Civilian* supported Sam Houston as faithfully as the first, even after Dr. Levi Jones, Samuel May Williams, and some others among the original sponsors abandoned him. Just as faithfully, it promoted the economic development of Galveston. "To the people of the United States we look for an increased patronage; and we promise them to give no accounts of this country which will not be sustained by their own sober inspection," Stuart said in the prospectus. "We are certain that the real character of Texas is but imperfectly understood even in that country; and we shall aim to correct some of those errors which operate to the prejudice of our country; and frequently prove injurious to the immigrants."[5]

Advertisements for McKinney and Williams and the Galveston City Company assured the success of the *Civilian* during its first year, while job work for the company and later printing for the city added to Stuart's income. But the patronage brought with it certain disadvantages. "Our friends frequently give work to others under the impression that we do not need it," Stuart once complained.[6] His rivals for their part complained on occasion that he operated a subsidized newspaper. "The editor of the *Civilian* is well known to be owned, occupied, and used by a certain gentleman of Galveston whose will he does and to whose beck and nod he is subservient," said D. H. Fitch of the *Morning Star*. "We have much respect for Mr. Williams, the owner of the editor."[7]

The charges flew especially fast and furiously during the heat of the campaign of 1841, when the *Civilian* supported Sam Houston and the Moore-Cruger papers, David G. Burnet. The *Telegraph*, commenting that "proprietors of a paper control it," suggested that Jones and McKinney had promised Stuart a job before he left the *National Banner*. Stuart denied as much, whereupon the *Telegraph* made a cor-

[5] Galveston *Civilian*, January 11, 1839.
[6] Houston *Morning Star*, August 17, 1841.
[7] Ibid., June 20, 1840.

Aaron Mower, a Philadelphia printer, set type for the *Gaçeta de Texas* at Nacogdoches, but printed the paper in Louisiana. Courtesy, National Archives

Although entitled *El Mexicano*, this sheet is numbered as a second issue of *Gaceta de Texas* and carries the same motto. Courtesy, National Archives

PROSPECTO.

A LOS AMANTES
de las
LUZES. DE LA RAZON,
Del bien de la Provincia de Texas, y del todo
DEL YMPERIO MEXICANO.

La tortuósa política de un gobiérno oprési-vo tuvo, por mas de tres siglos, desiérta y des-conocida al résto del mundo, la fértil y hermosa provincia de Texas; descuidada en ella la .du-cacion pública; sufocadas las ártes y la indús-tria, y para cólmo de desdichas, á sus candoro-sos y desgraciados habitantes, reducidos á una misérable y précaria existencia. Males tan grandes no podian ser eternos...La época de la *razon y de las luces*, rompiendo para siem-pre, las pesadas y degradántes cadénas que oprimian el nuevo hemisferio; elevando al hombre á su verdadera dignidad y restable-ciendole en el goce de sus sagrados é impres-criptibles derechos, habia de extender, hasta en los ángulos mas rémotos de éstas vástas regiones, su saludable y benéfica influencia; para que la Ciudad de Béxar que, no mereció de la culpable indiferencia de sus antiguos mandarines, ni aun el establecimiento de una escuéla de priméras letras, tuviese hoy, por beneficio de su Governador, en el de una buena imprénta, el único organo capaz de informarnos sobre nuestros mas caros é íntimos interes...

Si fué de la incumbéncia del sistéma despó-tico que nos tiranizába, el tener los pueblos aislados, y sin la menor idéa de los aconteci-miéntos politicos de los otros paises, de la nuestra es, y debe ser, el de comunicarles, con la mayor puntualidad, todas las noticias que puedan interesarles, y que se encuentren en la correspondencia y gacetas que se reciban de las naciones extrangeras y delas otras provin-cias del império; y además, de todo lo que concierna á la seguridad y adelanto de esta provincia y al bien general del estado.

Este impreso se denominará

Correo de Texas,

y saldrá el Miércoles de cada semana en Cas-tellano é Yngles. Se admiten subscripciones en la Ymprenta: para ésta ciudad pagarán los subscriptores al año, seis y medio pesos y para fuera diez, libres de portes: seis meses se han-de pagar adelantados: la primera publicacion será el Miércoles proximo.

EL EDICTOR.

TO THE ADVOCATES
of
LIGHT & REASON,
THE FRIENDS TO THE
Province of Texas,
and the
Mexican Empire.

The changeable and vicious policy of an oppressive tyrannical government had kept for more than three centuries, unknown to the world the rich and beautiful Province of Texas. Public education has been neglected, the arts stifled, industry discouraged; thus, by encreas-ing the misfortunes of its unhappy inhabitants, had reduced them to a scanty and precarious existence. Evils of such magnitude could not be everlasting. The epoch of reason and light, breaking forever the degrading chains which oppressed the new hemisphere; raising man to his true dignity, and establishing him in the enjoyment of his unalienable rights, was desti-ned to extend to the most remote angle of this wide and fertile region its salutary influence. The town of Bexar, which, by its ancient ru-lers, was not thought deserving of a primary school, is now in possession of a Printing Press, the best organ of information, and guardian of our dearest interests.

If then it was a favorite point in the former despotic system to deprive us of all knowledge, and keep us in ignorance of the political events in other countries, under the present free go-vernment our greatest care will be to instruct the public in every thing that may have a connection with its prosperity. To this end all the foreign papers that can conveniently be procured will be consulted, together with those of the other provinces of the empire.

This Gazette shall be called the

TEXAS COURIER,

and shall be published every *WEDNESDAY MORNING*, in Spanish and English. The subscription in town will be six dollars and a half per annum, payable half in advance—the other half at the expiration of the year. Those of the other Provinces and Cities of the Em-pire will pay ten dollars per annum, half in advance—free of postage.

Ymprenta del Govierno de Texas, en San Antonio de Bexar.   Abril 9 de 1823.

This prospectus of the *Correo de Texas*, or *Texas Courier*, printed at San An-tonio and dated April 9, 1823, is the earliest extant Texas imprint. The only known copy is in the Bancroft Library. The newspaper probably never ap-peared. Courtesy, Bancroft Library, University of California, Berkeley

Left: Anderson Buffington, a Baptist minister, fought at the Battle of San Jacinto and established the *Tarantula* at Washington-on-the-Brazos in 1841. He suspended the paper to go on the Texan–Santa Fe Expedition. Courtesy, San Jacinto Museum of History Association. *Right:* Robert W. Loughery made his Marshall *Texas Republican* a strong voice for the South. Courtesy, Barker Texas History Center, University of Texas at Austin

Left: Gail Borden made the *Telegraph and Texas Register* the voice of the Texan Revolution. Later he established the Borden Milk Company. Courtesy, Texas State Library. *Right:* David E. Lawhon, a Tennessee printer en route to join the Texas army in 1835, stopped at Nacogdoches to issue the *Texean and Emigrant's Guide.* Courtesy, John Murphy and Texas Daily Newspaper Association

Left: Francis Moore in partnership with Jacob Cruger continued the Houston *Telegraph and Texas Register* until the 1850s. Courtesy, Texas State Library. *Right:* Jacob Cruger not only held an interest in the Houston *Telegraph and Texas Register* but also established the Houston *Morning Star*, the first daily newspaper in Texas. Courtesy, Texas State Library

Left: Edward Hopkins Cushing edited the Houston *Telegraph* beginning in the mid-1850s. Courtesy, Texas State Library. *Right:* Charles DeMorse founded the Clarksville *Northern Standard* in 1842 and continued it until his death in 1887. Courtesy, Texas State Library

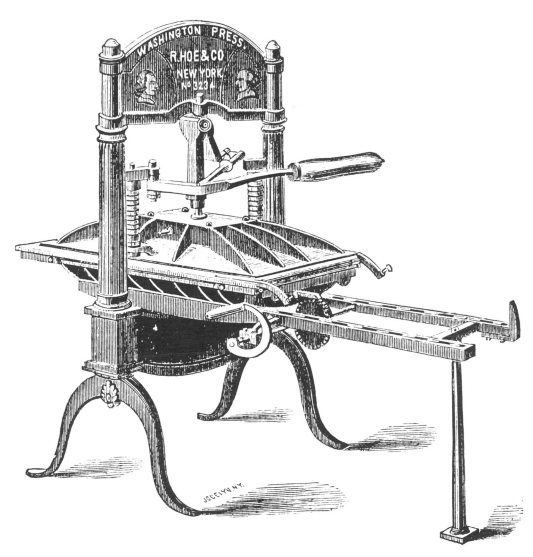

This **Washington press** is similar to one used by Samuel Bangs in Galveston.
From *100 Years of Progress of the United States* (Baltimore: O. H. Elliott,
1876), courtesy, Museum of Printing History, Houston.

Stephen F. Austin sponsored the establishment of the San Felipe *Texas Gazette* in 1829. Courtesy, Barker Texas History Center, University of Texas at Austin

TO THE AFFLICTED.

DR, HARDEMAN'S.

Vegetable Ointment.

A CERTAIN and sure cure for PILES, and is good for any old sores, eruptions on the skin. Take this ointment and anoint the part affected 3 times a day, and it will effect a sure cure of the piles in 8 or 10 days. Price 5 dollars. The following certificate has been here appended from among many others in my possession,

BLACKSTONE HARDEMAN.

NACOGDOCHES, May 13, 1841.

DR. BLACKSTONE HARDEMAN :—

DEAR SIR.—At your request, I very cheerfully furnish you with this statement. I had for several years been painfully afflicted with the piles, and had tried a great many medicines, all of which afforded me but temporary relief, until I tried your ointment. It effected a perfect cure on me in a very few days, and I can with great confidence recommend its use to all who are afflicted with that disease.

Very respectfully Yours,

THOMAS J. RUSK.

General Rusk's testimonial for this remedy foretells a later means of advertising. From the San Augustine *Red-Lander*, September 9, 1841

$300,00 REWARD.

RUNAWAY, or was Stolen from the subscriber on Saturday night the 7th Inst, a very likely Negro Boy, of dark complexion, medium size, good countenance, about 28 or 30 years of age, named Barney. Had on when he left, a pair coarse boots, and old white wool hat, white cotton goods for shirt, pants &c. It is thought that said boy was decoyed off by some white man, therefore the above reward will be given for the apprehension of both; fifty dollars for the negro alone, and confined in some jail in the Republic or delivered on my plantation, near Huntsville Montgomery County,

JOHN COTTON.

Montgomery, Aug. 18 1841 no 14 tf.

Advertisements for runaway or stolen slaves, such as this one from the San Augustine *Red-Lander*, appeared regularly.

FOR CALIFORNIA!

ALL persons who are desirous of emigrating to or visiting California, are informed that there is a company forming at Austin for the purpose of exploring Upper California, to organize at Austsn on the 1st of February, 1849, and to leave Austin on the 1st of March. Persons who intend going are requested to forward their names to the undersigned immediately, in order that they may be enrolled. The route we propose to travel is by way of Passo del Norte, on the Rio Grande, and from thence pursue the most direct route to the Pacific that is practicable. It is thought necessary that each mess of four men should have two pack mules and a good tent, and to be well armed and equipped.

JOHN H. MATTHEWS.

Austin, Jan. 1, 1849.

Some advertisements, like this one for a trip to California, told as much about the news of the time as the front pages. From the Houston *Democratic Telegraph and Texas Register*, January 18, 1849.

Left: George Wilkins Kendall, the "first modern war correspondent," blazed trails in reporting by looking for news. Courtesy, *Times-Picayune*, New Orleans. *Right:* Willard Richardson of the *Galveston News* was called "The Napoleon of the Texas Press" by his contemporaries. Courtesy, Texas State Library

Left: John Marshall Wade, a hero of the Battle of San Jacinto, helped found the typographical association in Texas and established the Montgomery *Patriot* in 1845. He later moved the paper to Huntsville. Courtesy, San Jacinto Museum of History Association. *Right:* Andrew Jackson McGown established the *Texas Presbyterian*, first at Victoria and then at Houston and Huntsville. Courtesy, San Jacinto Museum of History Association

Left: George Washington Baines, a Baptist minister, edited the Anderson *Texas Baptist* and later served as president of Baylor University. His great-grandson became president of the United States. Courtesy, Baptist Standard Publishing Company. *Right:* John Salmon (Rip) Ford, Texas Ranger, doctor, and journalist, made his Austin *Texas State Times* the voice of the American party in the mid-1850s. Courtesy, Texas State Library

Left: English-born Launcelot Abbotts printed the San Felipe *Telegraph and Texas Register* and several papers at Houston and La Grange. Courtesy, Barker Texas History Center, University of Texas at Austin. *Right:* John Henry Brown, later noted as a historian, published newspapers at Indianola, Galveston, and Belton. Courtesy, Barker Texas History Center, University of Texas at Austin

Sam Houston sits with a copy of the Austin *Texas State Gazette*, a newspaper that in large measure accounted for his defeat in the governor's race in 1857. Courtesy, Library of the Daughters of the Republic of Texas at the Alamo, San Antonio, Texas

Mastheads of the papers in the period before the Civil War often gave clues to their editorial slant or purpose. That of the 1852 La Grange *Texas Monument* (*top*) featured the monument to Texas heroes it was established to promote. The masthead of the 1857 Austin *State Gazette* (*center*) carried a wood cut of the capitol. That of the 1861 La Grange *State Rights Democrat* (*bottom*) bore the snakes of abolitionism, unionism, Whiggery, opposition, federalism, Americanism, and Know-Nothingism that led Opposition editors to call this ultra-Southern paper "Snakes."

rection: "We learn that he has purchased the interest of McKinney and Williams in the *Civilian*. He says he has purchased the interests of McKinney and Dr. Jones."[8]

Hamilton Stuart and the *Civilian* became institutions in Galveston. He served as mayor for four terms and as customs collector under two American presidents. As the years passed and he assumed other duties, various associates joined him in producing the paper— Samuel J. Durnett from 1847 to 1850 and again from 1853 to 1860; D. Ferguson and Abbey in 1855; James M. Conrad from 1853 to 1855; John Henry Brown from 1854 to 1858; Adolph Menard in 1860; and Eber W. Cave in 1861. Stuart suspended the *Civilian* during the Civil War but resumed publication in 1865 and continued for nine years, bringing in other associates, among them W. H. Pascoe and J. S. Thrasher of the *New York Herald*. Becoming dissatisfied with his last partner, Stuart sold his interest in the paper in 1874. Then he joined his erstwhile rival the *News* as an editorial writer, continuing there for twenty years, until his death in 1894 at the age of eighty-one years, two months, and eleven days. He told one youngster "that the reason he lived so long and had such good health was because of his very regular habits, because he did not smoke, didn't drink and because he took the very best care of his body, as well as of his mind." Stuart outlived by eight years the paper he founded. The *Civilian* under its new owners suspended publication permanently in 1886.[9]

During his prime Stuart commanded respect both at home and abroad. Situated at the primary gateway to Texas, he transmitted news to and from the interior. Fellow editors, even those who disagreed with him politically, depended on his exchange papers for news and complained when the *Civilian* did not arrive. D. H. Fitch, for example, in welcoming the second *Galvestonian*, took occasion to chide Stuart: "We trust the *Galvestonian* will not from being published in the office of the *Civilian* get into the same negligent habits with its exchange as characterize the latter paper."[10]

Because of Stuart's long connection with Sam Houston, citizens,

[8] Houston *Telegraph and Texas Register*, July 28 and August 4, 1841; *Morning Star*, August 17, 1841.
[9] Ben C. Stuart, "Hamilton Stuart: Pioneer Editor," *Southwestern Historical Quarterly* 21 (April, 1918): 381–88.
[10] *Morning Star*, March 28, 1840.

diplomats, businessmen, and government officials alike watched the *Civilian* for clues to Houston's policies and stands on issues. Rarely did it disappoint them. Stuart played Houston's game during the annexation negotiations and stood with him in regard to secession fifteen years later. Only in regard to Know-Nothingism did the two men disagree.

Stuart took seriously the role of the *Civilian* as the representative of Texas to the world at large and felt responsibility for showing the state—especially Galveston—in the best possible light. Time and again he rebuked other Texas editors who published matter that, in his opinion, hurt the country, and on occasion he took well-aimed swats at them. "Stuart of the *Civilian* is remarkably severe at times, and people that attack him generally get repaid with interest," the editor of the *Morning Star* once observed. But as a rule, Stuart disdained editorial feuds, saving his ammunition for weightier matters. He preferred long, reasoned discussions of diplomacy, economics, or government and at times waxed philosophical in his editorials. "He was a man of cheerful nature, philosophical and with a sense of humor," said a colleague. "Everyone who came in contact with him liked him."[11]

In the *Civilian* of June 24, 1843, Hamilton Stuart noted the founding of the paper that became his chief rival and on which he finished his journalistic career: "Messrs. M. Cronican & Co. have commenced, in this city, the publication of a small semi-weekly paper entitled *The News*." Francis Moore extended his courtesy welcome in the *Telegraph* of June 7, 1843, with the comment, "*The News* is the title of a new newspaper published at Galveston by M. Cronican and Co. on Tuesday and Friday." Charles DeMorse acknowledged the receipt of "six numbers of a neat little paper entitled 'The News' published at Galveston by M. Cronican and Co.," in the July 27, 1843, issue of the *Standard*.

These early statements by contemporary editors unmistakably date the *News* from June of 1843, but the precise date of its appearance remains unknown. During the Civil War a fire destroyed its office and files, and no issues survive before May 11, 1844. These circumstances led a few writers to pronounce the *News* a continuation of the paper of the same name that existed for a short while in the spring of 1842 and

[11] Ibid., October 15, 1839; Stuart, "Hamilton Stuart," p. 388.

to claim a single copy of it as the earliest surviving issue of the *News*. Hamilton Stuart specifically listed the earlier paper as defunct on June 21, 1842, however, and Ben C. Stuart, his son and also a Galveston newsman, declared the claim of continuity "without warrant." Even the *News* discredited the claim. "There was no connection between that paper and the present *Galveston News*," said a feature story in 1884, "June 1843 Michael Cronican and Wilbur Cherry, both printers, started a semi-weekly called *The News*, which was the real parent of the present publication." Yet the earlier date became firmly fixed in tradition, and the same issue that carried the feature story also carried on its masthead the legend "Established 1842."[12]

Regardless of the exact date, the story of the *Galveston News*, as Ben Stuart observed, began "before the real beginning." Indeed with just a little stretching, the *News* could trace its origins to the first newspaper on the island, for it shared with the *Commercial Intelligencer* and its defunct successors two important constants—the Niles printing press and Samuel Bangs.[13]

Bangs, to be sure, played his role reluctantly. He returned to Texas in 1838, not to establish a paper or operate a printing press, but to validate his claim to a large tract of land. He discovered, as had others of similar intent, that claiming the land and clearing title to it were two different matters, and, while he waited to reap the rewards from his landed estate, he turned back to his craft for a livelihood. Thus, he printed and "published for the proprietors" the *Commercial Intelligencer*.

Bangs's wife, née Caroline French, and her two brothers Henry and George, joined him in Galveston, and the extended family became well known in printing circles along the Texan coast. Mrs. Bangs wrote articles under the pen name "Cora"; her brothers printed, edited, or published several papers, usually in cooperation with Bangs; and George French's widow eventually married Wilbur H. Cherry, a founder of the *News*.[14]

Bangs acquired the Niles printing press in the same manner as he became publisher of the *Commercial Intelligencer*, not by design but by the turn of events. Moseley Baker lost interest in the paper once

---

[12] Stuart, "Newspapers in Texas," p. [36]; *Galveston News*, June 14, 1884.

[13] Stuart, "Newspapers in Texas," p. [35].

[14] Lota M. Spell, *Pioneer Printer: Samuel Bangs in Mexico and Texas*, pp. 93–116.

the campaign ended, and the disintegration of Niles and Company left the press in limbo. Thus, Baker transferred the printing establishment to Bangs on November 3, 1838, probably in settlement of wages due, and John S. Evans became the proprietor as well as editor of the *Intelligencer* on November 24. Evans continued the paper until early 1839, when he found himself unable to pay the printers and gave it up as a lost cause. Bangs, still holding the press, considered continuing the paper but decided against it and instead asked Francis Moore for a job as printer in Houston. When Moore had no opening, Bangs, assisted by the Frenches, turned again to operating the Galveston press. The *Galvestonian*, edited and published by "Plain" John Gladwin, "a fellow of infinite jest," appeared from the press in March, 1839, but Bangs still looked upon printing as a pursuit secondary to his land dealings. An advertisement in an early issue of the new paper offered the press for sale.[15]

John S. Evans announced the disposal of his interest in the *Intelligencer* in the same paper, but during the summer of 1839 he entertained hopes of starting a new paper on the island in support of President Lamar's administration. Explaining that he had exhausted his means on the *Commercial Intelligencer*, he contacted Lamar, offering the use of "my Printing Press" for the project, if other friends would underwrite it."[16] Nothing came of that effort, nor did any other buyer take the press off Bangs's hands.

Instead, Gladwin's death of yellow fever in October, 1839, brought fresh problems. Henry French, erratic and alcoholic, assumed Gladwin's role as editor of the paper, but other newsmen in Louisiana and Texas ridiculed his efforts, and the paper ceased publication in early 1840. About that time he broke with other members of the family and transferred his efforts to the *Civilian* office, where in March he founded another *Galvestonian*, the first daily paper on the island.[17]

Samuel Bangs and George French answered him a few weeks later by founding their own daily, the *Courier*, with Joel T. Case, a Yale

[15] Streeter, *Bibliography of Texas*, pt. 1, vol. II, 517–18; Harriet Smither, ed., "The Diary of Adolphus Sterne," *Southwestern Historical Quarterly* 30 (October, 1926): 223–24; Stuart, "Newspapers in Texas," p. [25]; *Galvestonian*, March 27, 1839.

[16] Charles A. Gulick et al., eds., *Papers of Mirabeau Buonaparte Lamar*, V, 297–98.

[17] Spell, *Pioneer Printer*, pp. 106–107; Streeter, *Bibliography of Texas*, pt. 1, vol. II, 519; *Morning Star*, March 28, 1840.

graduate and later a distinguished Presbyterian minister, as editor. The appearance of the two dailies within so short a time inspired considerable comment in the press community. "Galveston is perhaps the only city in the world which at two years old could boast of two daily papers and one semi-weekly paper," observed the *Texas Sentinel* from Austin, while Hamilton Stuart declared that the city did not afford patronage to support three newspaper publishers. Falling back on an old newspaper pun, Stuart predicted that both daily papers would soon become "weakly," and time proved him right.[18] Although Henry French enlisted David Davis as an associate, the second *Galvestonian* lasted only about four months.

The *Courier* persisted for over a year, until May, 1841, but not under the same management. Joel Case, in association with printer D. E. Smith, became publisher as well as editor in May, 1840. About the same time Samuel Bangs and George French left Galveston for Houston. There they ran Sam Whiting's printing office and on July 12, 1840, established on their own account the "witty and spirited" little *Musquito*, a triweekly that Bangs printed and French edited. "The *Musquito* buzzed about quite harmlessly on its first appearance," commented the *Telegraph*, "but if we are not mistaken in the animal it will show its sting before many weeks."[19]

A seemingly formidable new competitor inspired Bangs to seek employment in Houston. In the summer of 1840, the founders of the new city of San Luis introduced another printing press and newspaper to the coastal area. Observing the success of Galveston, the promoters envisioned a rival port city. They believed that San Luis Pass at the western end of Galveston Island afforded the best natural harbor on the Texas coast. Accordingly, they laid out the new town with great fanfare, promising that it would soon outdistance Galveston. The venture attracted a number of important investors, among them, David G. Burnet, Moses Austin Bryan, James F. Perry, W. H. Austin, Tod Robinson, Jacob W. Cruger, Ferdinand Pinckard, and Matthew Hopkins. The promoters thought big and initially secured ample financing. They planned a canal from San Luis to the Brazos River to divert

[18] Austin *Texas Sentinel*, May 9, 1840; *Civilian*, as quoted in *Morning Star*, March 26, 1840.

[19] *Telegraph and Texas Register*, July 15, 1840; Spell, *Pioneer Printer*, p. 108; Streeter, *Bibliography of Texas*, pt. 1, vol. II, 528.

trade from Galveston and projected roads to Brazoria and Houston. In addition, they formed a company to build a railroad connecting their new town with the cotton plantations of the Brazos valley. The *San Luis Advocate*, designed to promote the new city as the *Civilian* had Galveston, appeared under the date of August 31, 1840, with Samuel J. Durnett as editor and Tod Robinson and Company as publishers. As might be expected, the paper received considerable favorable attention from the press office of Houston investor Jacob W. Cruger. The *Morning Star* described it as "a very large weekly journal in the rising town of San Luis." Then business manager Cruger extended a welcome interspersed with a few helpful hints: "We wish the editor . . . all of the few joys that an editor can receive; we need wish the publishers nothing but an extensive subscription list, with *payments invariably in advance and advertisements* without number, always accompanied by *cash.*"[20]

Early issues of the paper suggested the hum of activity. The city company offered lots for sale; contractors advertised for bridge builders, wharf builders, and carpenters; the Brazos and Galveston Railroad Company explained its plans and listed its stockholders. A news item reported plans for a free school for the children of the city and proposed the founding of a military academy patterned after West Point. In addition, the editor carried a series recounting the Mina expedition that had first brought Samuel Bangs to the Texas coast. By fall the city, on paper at least, seemed thriving, and the *Advocate* announced plans for yet another sheet from its office, a medical and surgical journal edited by "Doct's Richardson and Smith."[21]

Such activity not only prompted Bangs to relocate but gave urgency to his efforts to sell his press. Finally on November 14, 1840, he sold the "Washington press standing . . . and everything belonging thereto as per invoice from J. W. J. Niles," which property he owned "by virtue of a bonafide purchase from J. W. J. Niles, John Belden and Mosely Baker."[22] But he sold to the errant Henry French, and he sold

[20] *Morning Star*, September 1, 1840; A. B. Norton, "A History of the Early Newspapers of Texas," in *A History of the Texas Press Association*, ed. Ferdinand B. Baillio, pp. 326–28.

[21] *San Luis Advocate*, October 20, 1840.

[22] Deed Records of Galveston County, County Clerk's Office, Galveston, Book A, p. 651; Spell, *Pioneer Printer*, p. 110.

on credit. Henry, running true to form, failed to make payments, and the press reverted to Bangs within a few months.

Other problems conspired to end Bangs's Houston interlude and send him back to operate the Galveston office. The *Musquito*, as predicted by the *Telegraph*, showed its sting, and it stung the wrong man. Both it and the *Courier* ran afoul of Judge Anthony B. Shelby, who presided over the district court of Galveston and Houston. Judge Shelby dealt harshly with those who offended his dignity, and the *Musquito* of January 6, 1841, published some barbs that particularly outraged him. The *Courier* followed suit, thereby bringing his wrath on its editor as well. Judge Shelby had George French arrested, sentenced him to a year in jail, and fined him a thousand dollars. The pro tem editor of the *Courier*, one Edmunds, received a fine of two hundred dollars and a sentence of ten days in jail. This blatant infringement on freedom of the press aroused the citizenry of both cities and brought the intervention of Judge Thomas Johnson. Through his efforts the editors purged themselves of contempt and had their sentences remanded. The affair precipitated a long contest between the two judges as to who held jurisdiction.[23] It also hastened the end of the *Musquito* and helped persuade Bangs and George French to leave Houston.

By late March, 1841, Bangs and George French had returned to the old stand in Galveston, where they began issuing the *Daily Galvestonian* with French as editor and Bangs as "Printer, Publisher, and Proprietor." The *Morning Star* noted "the first issue of the *Musquito* metamorphosed into the *Galvestonian*" on April 1 and commented with tongue in cheek, "By the way, they need another paper at Galveston—*only four there.*"[24]

Indeed, the new *Galvestonian* joined not only the *Civilian* and *Courier*, but also the *Morning Herald*, which in late 1840 appeared from the *Civilian* office, published by Sidney Smith Callender. Callender, "a deaf printer," joined the New Orleans Volunteer Greys on October 22, 1835, and came to Texas to fight in the revolution. He received an honorable discharge at Refugio on January 26, 1836, and later printed and published the *Richmond Telescope and Register*.

---

[23] Spell, *Pioneer Printer*, pp. 109–10; *Telegraph and Texas Register*, Janaury 15, 1841; *Picayune*, September 28 and October 5, 1840, and January 24, 1841.

[24] *Morning Star*, April 1, 1841.

John S. Evans returned to newspapering as "assistant editor of the *Herald*," but the issue of April 24, 1841, announced his death. Two weeks later yet another paper from Bangs's printing office, the *Weekly Galvestonian and Ladies' Saturday Evening Visiter* [*sic*], announced with regret the "death of the spicy little *Herald*." The *Courier* joined the list of defunct papers in May, 1841, when Joel T. Case left to join the Santa Fe Expedition.[25]

The presidential election of 1841 gave a decided boost to the printing business in Galveston. The *Civilian* of course gave steady support to Sam Houston, but Bangs, with businesslike objectivity, printed sheets for both sides. His *Galvestonian* supported Sam Houston, as did the immediate successor to the *Courier*, the *People's Advocate*, published by John O'Brian and edited by Charles W. Moore. But the *People's Advocate* lasted only from May until June or July, 1841, and then from its "ashes" came the *National Intelligencer*, an ardent supporter of David G. Burnet, edited first by A. J. Cody and then by Andrew Janeway Yates.[26]

Yates added a dash of spice to the campaign, for he had personal as well as political scores to settle with Sam Houston. Born in Hartford, Connecticut, on April 20, 1803, he graduated from Union College with Phi Beta Kappa honors. He accumulated a sizable fortune and won recognition as a lawyer, college professor, and author before coming to Texas in 1835. During the revolution he served first as a soldier and then as loan commissioner under Stephen F. Austin, Branch T. Archer, and William H. Wharton. A diplomat during the Lamar administration, Yates came into sharp disagreement with Sam Houston when both of them laid claim to a league of land at Cedar Point near Galveston. Their quarrel and Yates's private life kept tongues wagging along Galveston Bay in the early 1840s. Yates "has a lady living with him at Galveston whom he brought from N York (*Capt Hurds widow!*) which at first created whispering slanders but now no longer whispering! His wife is in the state of N.Y.," wrote one gossip. The same gossip, James Morgan, reported further that by the time Yates took up newspapering, he had lost his reputed fortune and was "so poor he could hardly keep soul & body together." Morgan also gave a succinct

[25] Stuart, "Newspapers in Texas," p. [33]; Walter Prescott Webb and H. Bailey Carroll, eds., *The Handbook of Texas*, I, 305; Streeter, *Bibliography of Texas*, pt. 1, vol. II, 520–21.

[26] Streeter, *Bibliography of Texas*, pt. 1, vol. II, 516, 521–22.

explanation of why Yates started the paper and evaluated its success: "He took charge of this paper to write Genl. Houston down in that quarter and was very bitter in his publications against him—publishing slanderous reports &c. His success will be seen in getting for Burnet in that County but of 545 votes 51 only!"[27]

When his efforts did not defeat Houston, Yates started in November, 1841, yet another paper on the Bangs press—the *Daily Advertiser*—and opened a reading room in Galveston. He continued both the *Intelligencer* and the *Advertiser* until about May, 1841, when panic over the Vásquez invasion brought business to a virtual standstill at Galveston. Then Yates ended his newspaper career and headed west to join the Somervell Expedition.[28]

In the meantime, other problems developed between Bangs and Henry French. Henry joined George French as editor of the *Galvestonian* in late 1841 but departed in a huff early in 1842, to open a sweet shop. He announced in an advertisement that he had "cut the business of catering for the literary tastes of his friends" and taken up the more agreeable one of providing for their appetites. As he held claim to the name "Galvestonian," his brother and brother-in-law suspended publication of that paper in March and on April 11, 1842, issued in its place the *Daily News*. The little paper carried news of the Mexican invasion and carried an advertisement "to Printers" in which Bangs offered for sale "a good screw press and an iron printing press with type and stands, all very little used."[29]

The *Daily News* lasted only a few weeks and then folded, whereupon Hamilton Stuart noted his lonely and unusual position as the publisher of the only newspaper in Galveston. He enjoyed that position, however, for only a few weeks. Before August 2, 1842, Samuel Bangs, outraged at President Houston's handling of the invasion crisis, issued the *Commercial Chronicle* to vent his wrath on the man he had so recently supported for president. "It is anti-Houston, all the time" commented A. W. Canfield upon receiving the first issues of the new paper, "and *bangs* away at every measure of 'Old Sam's.'"[30]

[27] Webb and Carroll, *Handbook of Texas*, II, 942; Feris A. Bass, Jr., and B. R. Brunson, eds., *Fragile Empires: The Texas Correspondence of Samuel Swartwout and James Morgan, 1836–1856*, pp. 105, 140.

[28] Streeter, *Bibliography of Texas*, pt. 1, vol. II, 522.

[29] *Galvestonian*, February 28, 1842; Spell, *Pioneer Printer*, p. 112.

[30] San Augustine *Red-Lander*, September 8, 1842; Streeter, *Bibliography of Texas*, pt. 1, vol. II, 517.

The Galveston newspaper scene became more normal in October, 1842, when the remnants of Bangs's once mighty competitor, the *San Luis Advocate*, came to rest in his office. Both paper and nascent city had fallen early on hard times. As early as June 26, 1841, the *Morning Star* wrote a requiem for the *Advocate*: "Not a number has come to hand for the last month," said the editor. "We regret the loss of that able sheet—it deserved a better fate. The plan on which it had its origin was too extensive to afford a prospect of long duration to its existence." But the next issue of the *Star* offered an embarrassed retraction and apologized for "apprehending" that the *Advocate* had "gone the way of all the earth." "We received a number yesterday which contained an excuse for its late non appearance—the cause is a *strike* for money among the printers! Who ever heard of printers wanting money?" Later in the year the paper again suspended publication. Then in December it resumed with Ferdinand Pinckard as editor. Described as "a nabob from Vicksburg during the flush times of Mississippi," Pinckard arrived in Texas about 1841 to promote San Luis and to announce himself in various local papers as a cotton factor. As the course of the paper suggested, the new town had trouble getting started. San Luis was already in peril, and the economic stagnation brought by the invasion further deterred it. Shortly after learning of the invasion, Ferdinand Pinckard explained to James F. Perry that he had "held out at San Luis" as long as he could and made plans to move to Galveston under the auspices of Thomas McKinney, James Love, and John S. Sydnor. An acquaintance explained further: "Mr. Pinckard was daily mortified for want of patronage and means to carry it on. He thought the whole Brazos Valley was interested in the prospects of this place. When he saw more than one half of his subscribers refusing to pay their subscription and at the same time sending their cotton by to Galveston, he became very much dissatisfied."[31]

Yet another disaster awaited the *San Luis Advocate*. The ship that carried its office to Galveston went down in the bay under fourteen feet of water. "Our friend Pinckard will hardly be deterred from a laudable enterprise by a *little cold water*," commented the *Morning Star*. Some of the materials were salvaged, and about October 11, 1842, the suc-

---

[31] *Morning Star*, June 26, 1841, and January 4, 1842; Ferdinand Pinckard to James F. Perry, March 29, 1842, and Edmund Andrews to James F. Perry, April 11, 1842, James F. Perry Papers, Archives, University of Texas, Austin.

cessor to the *Advocate* finally appeared from Bangs's office as the *Texas Times*. For a time Pinckard continued as editor; by November 6, David Davis published the paper "for the proprietors"; in late 1842 a tri-weekly edition of the paper appeared; and by March 11, 1843, George French and G. L. Hamlin assumed publication. At that time, accord-ing to one report, Pinckard "sailed for Yucatan," presumably with Commodore E. W. Moore of the Texas navy.[32]

Even with the new name, wretched luck still dogged the *San Luis Advocate*. George French had edited only a few issues when he died of yellow fever, thus bringing an end to the paper. The last will and testa-ment of the "dying 'Times,'" appearing in the May 16, 1843, issue of the triweekly edition, informed those who had paid in advance that they would receive the *Telegraph* in its place. W. Y. Allen, who wrote ten columns for the *San Luis Advocate*, later recalled that he never received "one *red*, not even a promissory note" for his labor.[33] A hur-ricane in the fall of 1842 completed the ruin of the paper city.

With the demise of the *Times*, Hamilton Stuart again presided over the only newspaper published at Galveston—again for only a short time. The next paper he welcomed was the one destined to grow into his great rival the *Galveston News*, but no prescience could have suggested as much to him. At its founding, nothing set the *Evening News* apart from the ephemeral sheets that had preceded it from the same office. Neither Stuart nor other editors who greeted it bothered to record the first date of issue, much less save the early copies. In-deed, the *Morning Star* saw it as merely a continuation of the *Times*, commenting that "the defunct *Times* seems to be embodied forth again in the form of the *News*." Cronican and Company paid Samuel Bangs four dollars per month for the use of his press and another eight dollars monthly rental on the building, but Bangs continued to print job work there and from time to time issued still other journals, among them the *Independent Chronicle*, the *Daily Globe and Galveston Commer-cial Chronicle*, and the *Texas State Paper*.[34]

[32] *Morning Star*, May 12, 1842; Streeter, *Bibliography of Texas*, pt. 1, vol. II, 524, 545–46; Stuart, "Newspapers in Texas," p. [34].

[33] Streeter, *Bibliography of Texas*, pt. 1, vol. II, 524–25; William Youel Allen, "Al-len's Reminiscences of Texas, 1838–1842," *Southwestern Historical Quarterly* 17 (April, 1914): 302.

[34] *Morning Star*, August 8, 1843; Stuart, "Newspapers in Texas," pp. [37–38].

Certainly, neither the publishers, Cronican and Wilbur H. Cherry, nor the first editor, Richard Drake Sebring, could take credit for the enduring success of the *News*, for within two years all were gone. Cronican remained long enough to issue on December 9, 1843, in conjunction with his two associates, a prospectus for a weekly edition of the paper. That edition, entitled at first the *Weekly News*, and later the *Galveston Weekly News*, made its appearance about February 17, 1844, and shortly thereafter Cronican sold his interest to Sebring.[35]

If Cronican did not stay long, he did leave with the *News* a tradition of survival. A native of Massachusetts, he joined the New Orleans Greys and arrived in Texas in late 1835 to participate in the siege of Bexar. Due to illness, he received a furlough after the battle and went to New Orleans to recuperate. Thus he missed the Goliad Massacre, in which most of his original company died, but he returned to Texas in time to fight in the Battle of San Jacinto and to share its glory. Afterward, Cronican worked variously as a printer and hotel keeper, and in the fall of 1842 he marched with the Somervell Expedition to the Rio Grande. He joined the men who broke away from the original command to form the Mier Expedition, but again he escaped the disaster that befell many of his comrades in arms. A member of the camp guard during the Battle of Mier, he escaped so expeditiously that rumors later accused him of cowardice. Returning to Galveston in January, 1843, he brought one of the first accounts of the battle, an account that appeared in the *Civilian*.[36]

After leaving the *News*, Cronican went westward. He joined John Salmon Ford in late 1845 to buy the *Texas National Register* and to move it from Washington on the Brazos to Austin. Later, he became owner and publisher of the *Western Texian* at San Antonio. There he died of cholera in 1849, prompting Charles DeMorse to eulogize him as "a warm hearted man, a printer, and, in his late years a sprightly editor."[37]

The other founding publisher of the *News*, Wilbur H. Cherry, remained with the paper for about two years. Born in New York in 1819, he too served in the Texan Revolution, having fought with Cronican at the siege of Bexar. Later he settled in Galveston, where he plied his

[35] Streeter, *Bibliography of Texas*, pt. 1, vol. II, 522–23.
[36] *Civilian*, January 21, 1843.
[37] Webb and Carroll, *Handbook of Texas*, I, 437.

trade, married George French's widow, and founded several other newspapers in addition to the *News*. One who knew Cherry called him "one of the old-time printers," who knew his trade "from the ground up" and who turned out proof so clean that it hardly required marking for errors.[38] Appropriately, when he died on June 12, 1874, he had returned to the *News* as a printer.

After Cronican's departure from the *News*, Cherry continued it in partnership with Richard Drake Sebring, "a talented young man from the Mohawk Valley, in New York State, a vigorous writer," and formerly editor of the paper at Matagorda. Their partnership lasted only a short while, until July, 1844, when Sebring died, probably of tuberculosis. Cherry then brought in Benjamin F. Neal, who had previously been associated with newspapers in Houston and Galveston, and they formed the firm of Cherry, Neal and Company. They persuaded Willard Richardson, pro tem editor of the *Telegraph*, to serve in the same capacity at the *News* in late 1844. Thus he, like Hamilton Stuart, left the *Telegraph* office to become one of the great editors at Galveston— the real father of the *News*.[39]

On the record, Richardson seemed an unlikely candidate for the role. Forty-two years old when he joined the *News*, he had never put down deep roots anywhere and had acquired neither fortune nor family. Described by one contemporary as "a genial, companionable fellow" and by another as "prudent, persevering, cool and indomitable, never caught by surprise nor unnerved by adversity," he was born at Marblehead, Massachusetts, on June 24, 1802. At sixteen years of age, he and a brother ran away from home, eventually arriving at Charleston, South Carolina, where the brother died of yellow fever. Richardson's efforts at educating himself attracted the attention of one Judge O'Neil, who helped him finish his education at the state college at Columbia. Richardson then went to Tuscaloosa, Alabama, with one of his professors and taught school to repay O'Neil for his assistance.

He emigrated to Texas in 1837 and spent several years on the frontier locating and surveying land. Then he established a school for young men at Houston, where he made the acquaintance of Francis Moore and found his true calling. In 1844, during the last presidential

---

[38] Ibid., I, 335; Stuart, "Newspapers in Texas," pp. [37–38].

[39] Stuart, "Newspapers in Texas," p. [37]; Streeter, *Bibliography of Texas*, pt. 1, vol. II, 522–23.

campaign of the republic, Moore went to Washington, D.C., to lobby for the cause he considered most crucial to Texas, annexation. He left Richardson as pro tem editor of the *Telegraph*, and Richardson filled the chair so admirably that he won the favorable notice of readers and the offer to edit the *News*.[40]

A man with a flair for the dramatic, Richardson enjoyed the theater and eventually built an opera house in Galveston to indulge his taste for the theatrical arts. The same taste for drama influenced his editorial style. He "exhibited a degree of energy, pluck, and enterprise which had never been dreamed of up to that time by the representatives of Southwestern journalism," said an early historian of the *News*. Upon joining the paper, he began employing able writers, engaging correspondents in different parts of the state, and otherwise introducing innovations that prompted critics to predict imminent ruin. Alarmed at the show of energy, Cherry and Neal sold their interest to him and printer Gideon K. Lewis within a year. By late 1845 Richardson and Lewis were publishing the *News*, and Neal was editing the rival *Daily Globe and Galveston Commercial Chronicle* for Samuel Bangs from the same press.[41]

Gideon K. Lewis, like Michael Cronican, brought a tradition of survival to the *News*, for he had just returned from misadventures in Mexico as a Mier man. He not only had drawn a white bean in the lottery of death, but also had won the nickname Legs for his ability to cover ground on foot. But, again like Cronican, he did not stay long at the *News*. Upon the outbreak of the Mexican War, he and Richardson dissolved their partnership, and Lewis departed for the scene of action to join Samuel Bangs in publishing a paper on the Rio Grande.[42]

Willard Richardson remained behind to build the *News* into the most widely circulated and most influential paper in Texas during the 1850s. From his South Carolina patron, he had imbibed the ideas of John C. Calhoun in regard to states' rights, and to those ideas he re-

[40] Noah Smithwick, *The Evolution of a State*, pp. 309–11; Acheson, *35,000 Days*, pp. 16–18.

[41] *Galveston News*, June 14, 1884; Earl Fornell, *The Galveston Era*, pp. 140–46; Streeter, *Bibliography of Texas*, pt. 1, vol. II, p. 520.

[42] Spell, *Pioneer Printer*, pp. 129–30; Marilyn McAdams Sibley, ed., *Samuel H. Walker's Account of the Mier Expedition*, p. 88; Tom Lea, *The King Ranch*, I, 99–110, 131–36.

mained true "through good and evil report . . . in war as in peace" until he died. His basic ideology made him a friend and staunch partisan
of Mirabeau B. Lamar during the era of the republic and an outspoken
critic of Sam Houston until 1861. Richardson crusaded for the annexation of Texas and later for a system of railroads fanning out from Galveston and channeling the trade of the state through that port. He defended the institution of slavery, advocated the reopening of the slave
trade, and eventually supported secession. In his hands, the *News* became not just a Galveston paper, but an all-Texas paper, with a circulation on the mainland larger than its city circulation and an extensive
circulation outside the state.[43]

[43] Acheson, *35,000 Days*, p. 16; Fornell, *Galveston Era*, p. 141.

CHAPTER 10

"Died . . . a Nation"

WILLARD RICHARDSON served his apprenticeship as editor during the closest presidential campaign the republic had witnessed, but a campaign to which the citizenry gave only perfunctory attention. The all-absorbing question of annexation overshadowed the election, and voters watched the corresponding election in the United States with more interest than their own, knowing full well that the fate of the republic hinged on results there rather than in Texas. Indeed, Richardson received his opportunity to edit the *Telegraph and Texas Register* because of the relative unimportance of the Texas election. Francis Moore departed for the United States in May of the election year, leaving Richardson in the editorial chair, and did not return until eight months later—after James Knox Polk had been elected president of the United States on an expansionist ticket and after John Tyler had introduced to Congress joint resolutions offering annexation to Texas. When critics accused Moore of abandoning the republic during a crucial period, he responded that he had been working in Washington for annexation by disspelling mistaken ideas about Texas and that he had considered the election in Texas "of secondary importance compared to that in the United States."[1]

In this instance Moore reflected the sentiment of his fellow citizens. In the first election held in the republic, Texans asked for annexation to the United States by a resounding vote. But the United States rejected their bid, and before the end of Sam Houston's first administration he withdrew it, explaining later that Texas had been left like a jilted bride standing on the doorsteps of the church. During Mira-

---

[1] Houston *Telegraph and Texas Register*, January 15, 1845.

beau B. Lamar's administration, the issue lay dormant. Reportedly, he had been among the few who voted against annexation in 1836, and certainly after becoming president he turned westward to pursue the dream of a big Texas stretching toward the Pacific. With the failure of his grand projects and the reelection of Houston in 1841, the issue of annexation came back to life, with the vast majority of citizens showing themselves no less eager for it than they had been in 1836.

Sam Houston opened the way for renewed negotiations almost immediately after beginning his second term, but he did so cautiously, wary of again putting Texas in the position of a jilted bride. Both he and his secretary of state, Anson Jones, recognized the vulnerability of the republic and the pressing need for either annexation to the United States or special protection from Great Britain. Unsure of whether they could obtain either, they worked for both at the same time, playing the two powers against each other. Britain wanted to block the westward expansion of the United States and saw other potential uses for the republic within the orbit of the empire, while the United States saw Britain as the traditional enemy, a trade rival, and the greatest threat to manifest destiny. Sam Houston and Anson Jones understood full well that an overture to one power whetted the interest of the other, and they played the game with skill, a skill often unappreciated by their fellows. Many editors and citizens failed to understand the intricacies of diplomacy and, thirsting for annexation, accused Houston and Jones of opposing the cause because of their gestures toward Britain.

President John Tyler gave ardent support to annexation, and by late 1843 his secretary of state, Abel Upshur, had begun serious negotiations with the Texas minister, Isaac Van Zandt. Word of the negotiations leaked to the press, raising hopes among the citizenry and bringing speculation that the republic would not need another president.

Under these circumstances the presidential campaign got off to a slow and halting start. Although the Houston and anti-Houston factions remained, both had difficulty settling on a candidate. Rumors circulated of support for Thomas J. Rusk, the perennial non-candidate in Texan presidential contests; the anti-Houston *Times* at Galveston endorsed James Hamilton early in 1843; somewhat later the equally anti-Houston *Northern Standard* came out for John Hemphill, and the *Galveston News* mentioned Lamar's name. The pro-Houston *Red-Lander* advocated Abner S. Lipscomb in September, 1843, while Houston himself maintained a silence in the matter, and Anson Jones, the obvious heir to Houston's mantle, conducted the negotiations that would obviate the need for the presidential election. Jones also waited long for Houston's endorsement and, in the interim, thoughtfully looked for press support.[2]

From the election of 1838, the Houston faction appreciated the potential, if not the demonstrated, power of the press and arranged for his views to appear in print. To this end, his administration sponsored a brief flowering of the press at Washington on the Brazos after the location of the government there. Washington had boasted a press since J. W. J. Niles had established the *Texas Emigrant*, but, according to John Lockhart, historian of the town, the type, press, and other materials had been dumped in an old house in the suburbs after the failure of the *Emigrant*. In the spring of 1841, two printers, Anderson Buffington and Alfred Brigance, salvaged enough of the material to set up the press and launch the *Tarantula*—"a small affair . . . twelve by fourteen or sixteen inches in size." Passing over the larger issues, Editor Buffington, a Baptist minister, declared war on grog shops at Washington and promoted the founding of a temperance society. The *Tarantula* was "published weakly" on "foolscap," observed the *Morning Star*, while John Lockhart remembered it as "a weak and delicate child" that "died in a short time, whether from inanition or its name no one could tell, most probably for the want of funds to buy paper . . . whenever old Man Buffington ran short of paper he went around town and collected all the blank leaves of the old blue back spellers and printed his paper on them."[3]

The *Tarantula* ceased publication early in 1842, and by fall, when the government removed to Washington, the press was in such condition that the administration made no effort to utilize it. Instead, friends of Houston acquired the press G. H. Harrison had brought to Washington from Austin in the summer of 1842, the same press that under Jacob Cruger's management had so bitterly fought Houston's election. Harrison had changed the name of his paper from the *Texian* to the

---

[2] Ibid., November 8 and 15, 1843; San Augustine *Red-Lander*, September 2, 1843; Galveston *Civilian*, September 2, 1843.

[3] Jonnie L. Wallis and Laurence L. Hill, eds., *Sixty Years on the Brazos: The Life and Letters of Dr. John Washington Lockhart, 1824–1900*, p. 47; Houston *Morning Star*, May 1, June 29, July 6 and 24, and August 10, 1841.

Texian and Brazos Farmer upon moving it and then sold it to Judge Thomas Johnson in November, 1842.[4]

Johnson gave a folksy touch to the paper, adopting the motto "He that by the plough would thrive—himself must either hold or drive" and offering copies of the paper to local citizens in exchange for produce delivered to his office. He also made the paper, known familiarly as the *Brazos Farmer*, frankly the organ of the administration. "Mr. Johnson was quite an able man," remembered John Lockhart, "but was assisted secretly by General Houston himself and his private secretary, Mr. Miller." Lockhart remembered further that Houston seldom read either books or newspapers but that Johnson's paper was his favorite.[5]

The *Brazos Farmer* took on all of Houston's press critics. It launched a feud with the *Western Advocate* at Austin, which still emanated occasionally from the old Whiting press, then owned by James Webb, to heap recrimination on Houston for moving the capital. Johnson then attacked Francis Moore, calling him a "pious maw-worm" and his paper the "Santa Anna Telegraph" on the ground that it abetted the cause of the Mexican dictator by criticizing Sam Houston. Moreover, charged Johnson, Moore had attempted to enrich himself as public printer and as a senator had franked copies of *Houston Displayed* under the guise of copies of the laws and journals and sent them to north Texas during the campaign of 1841.[6]

Anti-Houston editors replied in kind. Moore scorned the *Brazos Farmer* as a subsidized paper that depended entirely on monies received from the treasury and joined with others to call its editor "Ramrod" Johnson. "Among all the paper warriors that have appeared on the political arena in Texas from the organization of the government until the present period, we know none who so fully personates Don Quixote as the present editor of the *Texian and Brazos Farmer*," declared the *Morning Star*. "He has been jocularly styled the *ramrod* of the Executive, for he appears to be as passive an instrument in the hand of the Executive in conducting a paper warfare, as the ramrod in the hands of the soldier."[7]

Johnson renamed his paper the *National Vindicator* in June, 1843,

[4]Thomas W. Streeter, *Bibliography of Texas, 1794–1845*, pt. 1, vol. II, 549–50.

[5]Wallis and Hill, *Sixty Years*, p. 157; Washington *Texian and Brazos Farmer*, January 28, 1843.

[6]*Telegraph and Texas Register*, April 5 and 26, 1843.

[7]*Morning Star*, February 23, 1843.

choosing a name that more accurately described its role as defender of the administration and adopting a new motto: "Our Country—our whole Country—and nothing but our Country." Other editors watched Johnson's paper with interest, accepting it as the spokesman of the president, and Anson Jones estimated its circulation at nine hundred during the summer of 1843. But Johnson had scarcely changed the name of the paper before his health and fortunes began failing, and he wrote Attorney General G. W. Terrell that he would have to discontinue it. His move coincided with Anson Jones's first steps toward entering the presidential race and prompted Terrell, a supporter of Jones, to express dismay. "Johnson was doing a great deal of good; his paper was beginning to wield a powerful influence throughout this country, and was more sought after than any other in the Republic," Terrell wrote Jones. "Can it not be so arranged as to be purchased by some of our friends, and continue him in the editorial department? He would do a great deal in a close contest; for I assure you, you have no conception what a stand his paper was acquiring throughout the East."[8]

Johnson suspended the *Vindicator* in September, 1843, pleading ill health, but resumed publication about two months later, with help from Washington D. Miller and William H. Cushney.[9] He reported cheerfully in the issue of November 25 that his subscription list had grown from between three and four hundred to between six and seven hundred, figures that differed substantially from Jones's estimate during the summer. By then Jones's name had been officially entered in the list of presidential candidates, and the *Vindicator* gave him loyal support until it ceased publication in late 1844 after his election.

Anson Jones by no means depended solely on Thomas Johnson for press support. In the summer of 1843, at about the same time that Johnson changed the name of his paper, John N. O. Smith, a practical printer and Sam Houston loyalist, acquired the old Whiting printing office in Houston. He had previously been associated with the office, since he and his brother, D. E. Smith, had founded the *Houstonian* in support of Houston's candidacy in 1841. By May, 1843, S. E. Powers had replaced the Smiths and listed himself as editor, publisher, and

[8] Anson Jones, *Memoranda and Official Correspondence Relating to the Republic of Texas*, pp. 234–35.
[9] Streeter, *Bibliography of Texas*, pt. 1, vol. II, 547–48.

proprietor of the *Houstonian*, but shortly thereafter, according to the *Red-Lander*, Powers "absquatulated to Yucatan" with the mutinous Texas Navy, in effect abandoning the printing office. Smith, upon taking possession of the office, found it "in a most miserable condition" and reported that it took him several weeks to put it in order.[10]

Smith could claim to be the first labor leader in the republic. Not only had he organized the typographical association to improve the lot of printers, but later he also called a meeting of "Mechanics and Working Men" of Harris County to support annexation and still later a meeting of "Farmers, Mechanics and Working Class of Harris County" to choose a suitable candidate to represent them in the state legislature. "He was a man of note in his day," recalled one who knew him. "With a well-balanced and cultivated mind and more than average ability, he was qualified to fill almost any public position, and would doubtless have attained to more prominence than he did but for an unfortunate habit which rendered him unreliable."[11]

Anson Jones welcomed the news that Smith had acquired a press and promptly made plans to use it to counteract the opposition he expected from the Moore-Cruger papers at Houston in the coming election. He suggested a name for the new paper and offered the services of Milford Phillips Norton, his friend and campaign manager, as editorial writer. Smith politely explained that he already had a name, the *Citizen*, but he accepted the editorial writer and later in the fall accepted Anson Jones as a silent partner. Jones purchased a printing press for the *Citizen* office for $410 on October 15, 1843, on the eve of his formal entry into the race.[12]

Possibly because of Printer Smith's "unfortunate habit," Jones also arranged for Norton to move to Houston to oversee the printing office. Born in Readfield, Maine, in 1794, Norton had served in both houses of the Maine legislature while still a very young man. He arrived in Texas in 1838 to clear titles to land purchased by his father-in-law and, finding the country attractive, settled his family in Montgomery County, where he practiced law and aligned himself with the Sam Houston

[10] Jones, *Memoranda and Correspondence*, p. 229.

[11] A. C. Gray, "A History of the Texas Press," in *A Comprehensive History of Texas, 1685–1897*, ed. Dudley G. Wooten, II, 377; *Telegraph and Texas Register*, April 23 and November 19, 1845.

[12] Herbert Gambrell, *Anson Jones, the Last President of Texas*, pp. 290–91.

faction. Upon the announcement of Jones's candidacy, the president appointed Norton postmaster at Houston to facilitate his association with Smith's newspaper. Norton acquired an office adjoining the printing office, writing Jones that "my great anxiety is to get charge of the paper." Early in the year, the *Citizen* became the *Texian Democrat*, with John N. O. Smith, D. E. Smith, and John Benson officially listed as the publishers. Even so, the public recognized it as an administration paper, and Norton, in telling Jones of the name change, spoke of it as "our paper."[13]

The paper proved as much a liability as an asset to Jones. The prospects of annexation brightened about the time of its appearance, and, while most citizens and the Moore-Cruger papers waxed ecstatic, the *Texian Democrat* initially took an anti-annexation stand. This prompted rumors that President Houston and Anson Jones opposed annexation, a stance fatal to any political career at the time, and caused a sharp division between Smith, Norton, and an editorial writer, John Manson. Norton favored annexation, Manson opposed it, and Smith felt that for diplomatic reasons an organ linked to the administration should not appear too eager. After the early numbers appeared, Jones directed Norton to "quit piping against annexation, as that course will ruin us," and all three newsmen wrote Jones to explain or seek guidance—or perhaps to determine his position, for appropriately both he and Sam Houston maintained a discreet ambivalence in the matter. Smith wrote that he had declined to publish "a very elaborate article" by Manson and was "puzzled which course to pursue," as some advised him to continue showing the disadvantages of annexation while others pointed out the harmful effects on the administration. Manson assumed that Jones opposed annexation but granted that "a paper which supports the administration so strongly as the *Democrat*, might implicate you, and be prejudicial in the coming election." Thus, he proposed printing his editorial as a separate pamphlet. Norton, for his part, assured Jones that he had used "every effort to prevent Smith taking the course he has . . . but without effect. . . . The truth is that Smith must be *strongly* advised by you to admit nothing as editorial without consulting me." A few days later Norton complained that Smith had "mutilated" his editorial and remarked that "it is very annoying.

[13] Eugene C. Barker and Amelia W. Williams, eds., *The Writings of Sam Houston*, VI, 4–5; Jones, *Memoranda and Correspondence*, pp. 281, 296.

Has he any authority for giving your views, and those of the President?" When Jones addressed Norton as "Editor of the *Democrat*," Norton declined the title until he obtained "its political control."[14]

Soon thereafter, Norton obtained the control he desired. The *Democrat* changed its tune, and he promised that it would be the last paper to abandon the cause of annexation. But his discontent remained. "No one here is disposed to give one copper to help matters along—hardly to subscribe to the paper," he complained to Jones at one point, and on another occasion he threatened to abandon the *Democrat* before the election. Becoming thoroughly discouraged about Jones's chances for victory, Norton advised him to withdraw in favor of a more promising candidate.[15]

Jones indeed inspired no great enthusiasm among the voters. As expected, the Moore-Cruger papers took a strong stand against him, seeing him as Sam Houston's stand-in. "He is nothing but a mere tuft of political mistletoe, having no root of his own, adhering to and supported by the limb of a distant trunk altogether," declared the *Morning Star*, citing a comment about Martin Van Buren's relation to Andrew Jackson.[16]

But Francis Moore, like Sam Houston and no doubt for the same reasons, delayed endorsing a candidate. Instead, he and Houston ignored the forthcoming election to engage in another round of their running battle with each other. At a meeting in the Presbyterian Church at Houston with Moore sitting in the audience, the president lambasted the opposition newspapers—"his clenched hands and the gnashing of his teeth" indicating the "wounds that rankle in his bosom." Moore responded with a scorching editorial in the *Telegraph* in which he charged Houston with attempting to stifle freedom of the press. "He has the right to assail us with his tongue and we have the right to assail him with our pen or tongue as the circumstances may require," said Moore. "We would say to Houston: Rejoice that Texans are so truly free that they dare to reprove you and if they err, truth ere long will triumph over their errors."[17]

The two continued their feud intermittently throughout the spring

[14] Jones, *Memoranda and Correspondence*, pp. 312, 314, 317, 321.
[15] Ibid., pp. 352, 355.
[16] *Morning Star*, November 16, 1843.
[17] *Telegraph and Texas Register*, November 15 and 22, 1843.

while both watched the progress of the annexation treaty in the United
States and stalled about endorsing a presidential candidate in Texas. At
one point Houston charged that newspapers opposed to his administration had defeated his main plans of policy, with the exception of his
peace policy with the Indians, to which Moore retorted, "If the Indians could read newspapers we suppose he would have ascribed the ill
success of the negotiations with the Comanches and their recent depredations to newspaper paragraphs."[18]

Early in 1844 annexation seemed imminent. Reports arrived that
set the press atwitter with excitement—reports that President Tyler
yearned for annexation, that Upshur had reached terms with Van
Zandt, that votes for ratification waited in the Senate. At the height
of the excitement, Francis Moore put out an extra announcing the
"Glorious News of Annexation."[19] The announcement proved premature, but Moore showed little embarrassment and in the euphoria of
the moment temporarily suspended his feud with Sam Houston. The
president, Moore reported, was a "zealous advocate of the measure"
and had said that "we should need no more president." Moreover, all
journals in the confidence of the government—"with exception perhaps of the *Civilian*"—advocated annexation; the editor of the *Brazos
Planter* reported that Secretary of State Jones had said that in less than
ninety days Texas should form a part of the United States, and a gentleman who resided in San Felipe said that Secretary Jones had told
friends there that Texas would be annexed within fifty days.[20]

As negotiations neared completion, Sam Houston detached his
secretary and troubleshooter, Washington D. Miller, from the *Vindicator* at Washington on the Brazos and sent him to Washington on the
Potomac to expedite matters. Miller carried with him a letter to Andrew Jackson that expressed both Houston's hopes and his misgivings.
"Texas is presented to the United States, and this is the third time she
has consented. Were she now to be spurned, it would forever termi-
nate expectation on her part."[21]

A tragic accident intervened to justify Houston's misgivings. Just
when the completion of the treaty seemed assured, Secretary Upshur,

[18] *Morning Star*, April 11, 1844.
[19] *Telegraph and Texas Register*, February 14, 1844.
[20] *Telegraph and Texas Register*, March 20, 1844.
[21] Barker and Williams, *Writings of Houston*, IV, 265.

President Tyler, and a host of dignitaries boarded the war steamer *Princeton* for an excursion down the Potomac. A gun exploded during a demonstration, killing Upshur, Secretary of Navy Gilmer, and three others. Van Zandt, who was also in the party, escaped injury and promptly informed his government of the "awful calamity," observing that "the occurrence will have, I fear, an unfavorable influence on our affairs here. Texas has lost two of her best friends in this country."[22]

Upshur's death did indeed set back the cause of annexation. As the *Civilian* noted in a tasteless pun, the bubble had "exploded."[23] John C. Calhoun, who replaced Upshur as secretary of state, tied the issue to the perpetuation of slavery, and the treaty suffered defeat in the Senate in July, 1844. Yet again the bride stood waiting on the church steps. But the romance had not yet ended. As soon as the treaty of annexation went down in defeat, the matter became a major issue in the presidential contest in the United States. The Whigs nominated Henry Clay, an opponent, while the Democrats passed over Martin Van Buren, also an opponent, to choose a dark-horse candidate, James Knox Polk, an advocate. Then the Democrats adopted an expansionist platform calling not only for the "Reannexation of Texas," but also for the "Reoccupation of Oregon."

Texans turned back to their own election as hopes for the treaty faded, with Jones emerging as the Houston candidate and Vice-President Edward Burleson as the anti-Houston. Texan editors accepted the turn of events with what grace they could muster. Hamilton Stuart accepted the failure of the treaty with more aplomb than most, for, while he denied opposing annexation, he had never supported the treaty editorially. Instead, throughout the negotiations, the *Civilian* had continued to point out the advantages of an independent Texas. Stuart's approach reflected his close association with Sam Houston and the knowledge that readers abroad looked upon the *Civilian* as an administration organ. To appear too eager could hurt the cause of annexation and at the same time close some of the options that remained if it failed. Moreover, a number of prominent Galvestonians genuinely opposed annexation, and British and French ministers clustered on the island actively worked against it. Stuart thus avoided taking a stand and, when the treaty failed, professed to be pleased. "The annexation

[22] Jones, *Memoranda and Correspondence*, p. 323.
[23] *Telegraph and Texas Register*, March 20, 1844; *Civilian*, May 14, 1844.

fever is, we are happy to state, now confined principally to the other side of the Sabine," he wrote. "It passed off sooner in Texas than in the United States and we find a growing aversion to it here."[24]

He also commended "the tone" of those papers that had favored the treaty. "With frankness and consistency they acknowledge that the failure of the treaty is the end of the scheme and look upon further negotiations as merely trifling and degrading to the intelligence and character of Texas," he wrote. "They say that the time has gone by when annexation would have been a benefit to Texas."[25]

Stuart misstated the case, possibly for consumption of readers in the United States, for some editors had difficulty in concealing their disappointment. Sam Durnett of the Columbia *Planter* expressed such dismay that Stuart dismissed that paper as "an excitable little sheet." Charles DeMorse began working for Polk's election as if the voters in north Texas had a say in the matter, and Francis Moore and Jacob Cruger abandoned their press and headed for the United States to influence opinion there.

As late as April 10, Moore had not endorsed a candidate in the Texas presidential election, confessing "that we yet entertain a faint hope that no other president will be needed in Texas." But two weeks later he conceded that the republic would see at least one other president and gave Edward Burleson an endorsement only slightly less detrimental than no endorsement at all. "It has been objected to him that he is ignorant," Moore said of Burleson. "But however deficient he may be in the abstruse mysteries of science and classic lore, he is by no means so deficient in that learning which is most essential to advance the true interests of his country."[26]

Burleson could take as little satisfaction in the comments of other friendly editors. James Attwell, editor of the Matagorda *Weekly Despatch*, which first appeared in later 1843, endorsed him with the comment, "We do not claim for him exalted talents . . . but we claim for him an honesty of purpose, a singleness of heart, a devotedness to country which no talent can supply the want of." Charles DeMorse gave wavering support that was even more damaging. After conceding that his first choice, John Hemphill, had no chance, DeMorse en-

[24] *Civilian*, June 15, 1844.
[25] Ibid., July 20, 1844.
[26] *Telegraph and Texas Register*, April 24, 1844.

dorsed Burleson in early March, commenting that "there are some who object to General Burleson as not sufficiently qualified . . . and to a certain extent we shall admit its justness. But then his opponent is not qualified either." A month later DeMorse withdrew the endorsement, saying that he had not changed his personal views but that he would not participate actively in the campaign.[27]

Burleson received his most enthusiastic press support from the *La Grange Intelligencer*, a new paper, "about the size of the *Civilian* and *Vindicator*," that appeared in January, 1844. James P. Longley, proprietor, and William P. Bradburn, publisher and editor, adopted the motto "Westward the Star of Empire takes its way," and the *Morning Star* hailed the *Intelligencer* as with one exception the "most western paper published in the English language on the American continent." That exception, the *Western Advocate* at Austin, ceased publication within a few weeks, when George K. Teulon departed Texas, leaving the *Intelligencer* to give voice to the grievances of the western citizenry. The new paper steadfastly supported vice-president and fellow westerner Burleson for the presidency, but it underwent several changes in management before the election took place. Bradburn, a nephew and protégé of John Davis Bradburn, whose activities as Mexican commander at Anahuac had fomented discontent before the Texan Revolution, served as editor only a few weeks. A native of Tennessee, the younger Bradburn had received an appointment as midshipman in the United States Navy through the influence of James K. Polk. At the behest of his uncle, he resigned his commission to join the uncle in Mexico and accept adoption as his son and heir, but the uncle died before completing the proper legal work. William P. Bradburn then sojourned for a time in La Grange, where Longley, says a historian of the town, established the *Intelligencer* "in part to give him business, and in part to support General Burleson for the Presidency."

After Bradburn's brief stint as editor of the *Intelligencer*, he moved to Louisiana, where he gained more editorial experience on the New Orleans *Tropic*, *Picayune*, and *Bulletin* and where he achieved considerable success after 1848 as editor of the *Southern Sentinel*.

W. B. McClellan replaced Bradburn as editor of the La Grange paper with the issue of February 15, 1844, and Smallwood S. B.

[27] Matagorda *Weekly Despatch*, January 6, 1844; Clarksville *Northern Standard*, March 2, April 3, and July 15, 1844.

Fields, "a legal gentleman" with "very little editorial acumen," became editor and proprietor with the issue of May 30. An early settler in Fayette County, Fields campaigned with John H. Moore against the Comanches in 1839 and represented the county in the Seventh Congress of the republic. He gained a reputation as a buffoon in La Grange. "This editor of ours had hardly found his place in life," a local historian said of him.

> It was told of him that in the San Saba fight under Colonel Moore he stood behind a tree to shoot, and the tree was too small for the man or the man was too large for the tree. In turning to load his gun, an unlucky shot hit him in the back. Enraged by this irony of fate, he lost all fear, and in stamping and cursing he ended this day of martial achievement. As an editor, extracts from other papers were the tree he hid behind to load his gun, his own ammunition falling short often . . . our editor was a brave but unfortunate warrior, the fates being against him; an editor whose chair of office like the tree, could not screen him; a lawyer whose feats as a legal knight might rival Don Quixote in assumption, and whose wisdom as a legislator the archives of the Republic alone can tell.[28]

The *Galveston News* joined other anti-Houston papers in support of Burleson, while the *Civilian, Red-Lander, Planters' Gazette*, and newly founded *Harrison Times* joined the *Vindicator* and *Democrat* to support Jones. But over all, the press support of both candidates ran lukewarm. Certainly, the election lacked the intense partisanship that characterized that of 1841. The Burleson press repeated charges that Jones danced to Sam Houston's tune and opposed annexation; the Jones papers wisely avoided attacking the popular but semiliterate Indian fighter and simply bore down on his shortcomings as conceded by his partisans. "If General Burleson is capable of rendering services to the country on the frontier by driving off small parties of Indians, in the name of all that is politic, keep him in the public service," said the *Red-Lander*. "Give him the command of the Rangers, and award him such honors as he may deserve. Elect him President and you deprive the country at once and effectually of his aid in killing the savages and bring him into a sphere of action which he frankly acknowledged he is unqualified to fill."[29]

---

[28] Julia Sinks, "Editors and Newspapers of Fayette County," *Quarterly of the Texas State Historical Association* 1 (July, 1897): 34–35.

[29] Houston *Texian Democrat*, June 16, 1844.

Late in the campaign Sam Houston endorsed Jones, and on election day in early September the voters by a relatively narrow margin decided to keep Burleson on the frontier fighting Indians. Two months later, voters in the United States opted for Polk and the "Reannexation of Texas," and Tyler, the lame-duck president, began pushing through Congress the joint resolutions that invited Texas into the Union.

Texan editors greeted the news from the United States with a near-unanimous jubilation that the administration, strangely enough, found disturbing. Until Polk's election, Sam Houston and Anson Jones worked directly or indirectly for annexation, but, once that seemed assured, they changed tactics to work for the best terms possible. Their constituency again failed to appreciate their maneuvers, and the unrestrained elation of the press threatened to undermine their "more coy than forward" diplomacy.[30] Thus, they sponsored a new paper that represented an amalgamation of the Washington *Vindicator* and Houston *Democrat*, both of which discontinued publication shortly after Jones's election.

Washington D. Miller and William H. Cushney, both recently associated with the *Vindicator*, acquired the press of the *Democrat* and moved it to Washington on the Brazos, where they established the *Texas National Register* on December 1, 1844. Miller had just turned thirty years old when he undertook the task. Born on December 4, 1814, at Charleston, South Carolina, he graduated from the University of Alabama as an engineer in 1836 and arrived in Texas in the fall of the following year. After filling several clerical positions in the government, he won Sam Houston's favor, becoming his private secretary in 1841. The following year Miller helped repel the Vásquez invasion, and the next, as secretary to the senate of the Seventh Congress, he copied the senate journals of that congress. Possessed of a brilliant mind, Miller never realized the potential that his associates saw in him. "Throughout his life," says a biographer, "his unsteady habits were a drag on his career."[31]

William H. Cushney, twenty-five years old and a native of New York, assisted Miller in the founding of the *National Register*, and the paper began in a prosaic manner by publishing the records of the

[30] See Llerena Friend, *Sam Houston, The Great Designer*, pp. 115–61.
[31] Barker and Williams, *Writings of Houston*, IV, 256.

Texan Congress then in session.[32] Only as the United States Congress
opened debates on the joint resolutions for the admission of Texas did
the true nature of the paper emerge. Calling the conditions of the resolutions "ruinous" and "humiliating," the *Register* extolled the advantages of an independent republic. Throughout the late winter and early
spring, the editors hammered away on the theme, maintaining that annexation was rich in benefits to the United States in the same proportion that it was prejudicial to Texas and that it amounted on the part of
Texas to "giving them the marrow on condition we retain the BONE."
The *Register* especially deplored the condition that gave the United
States the right to settle the boundaries of the State and pointed out, in
addition, that even the passing of the resolutions did not guarantee
that Texas would actually be admitted and not yet again be humiliated
by rejection. Chiding citizens who would accept "anything labeled annexation," the editors submitted that "we have always been a warm
and hearty advocate for the cause of annexation, but never did we
dream that the approval of the people of Texas would be required to a
proposal so absurd."[33]

The *Civilian* echoed the sentiments of the *Register*, and both excited antagonism among the citizens, who viewed them as voices of the
administration. All other newspapers in the republic, including the *Patriot*, newly founded at Huntsville by J. M. Wade, advocated the resolutions and heaped criticism on the dissenters, with the *Register*
attracting most of the fire. Francis Moore headed the attack, calling
the *Register* an organ of the English party. Miller responded by calling
the *Telegraph* the textbook of the abolitionists and charging that John
Quincy Adams, the bête noir of the pro-annexationists, subscribed to
the *Telegraph*. A correspondent for the *Telegraph* countered the *Register's* rosy view of independence by writing that "self interest," "self
preservation," and "dire *necessity*" inclined the citizens toward annexation. "The sad experience of nine years of independent sovereignty
has given us a foretaste of what we must assuredly undergo as an independent state," he wrote. "It has convinced the people that we are too
weak to hold anything but a subordinate and insignificant rank among
other nations." He then mocked the *Register's* grandiose projections of

[32] For information about Cushney see his obituary, Austin *Texas State Gazette*, December 4, 1852.
[33] Washington *Texas National Register*, February 22 and March 1 and 8, 1845.

the future by noting that "the 'Lone Star' is a pretty theme for a senti-
mental sonnet, but unfortunately sense and rhyme are not always con-
vertible. The Polar Star and all other stars are 'small potatoes' compared with this 'Lone Star.' Its orbit is too large, its brilliance too
overpowering to admit the fellowship of twenty-six small satellites."[34]

When Jones did not act promptly after news reached Texas of the
passage of the joint resolutions, irate citizens revived the charge that
he opposed annexation. The *Telegraph's* correspondent reported that
Washington on the Brazos received news of the offer with "most frigid
coldness and disdain. I even thought I could discern a curl of contempt
for American institutions upon the lip of every officer of government as
the news was announced. . . . They declared the people of Texas
would be stupid dolts to accept terms so humiliating and base."[35]

Throughout the republic alarmed citizens held public meetings
advocating acceptance and arranged for the resolutions they passed to
be printed in the newspapers. As the furor grew, Jones's former editor,
M. P. Norton, wrote a letter warning him of the "strong feeling" growing from "the course taken by the *Register*." To it Jones attached an
endorsement disclaiming responsibility for the paper. "A few months
since I persuaded Judge Norton to 'quit piping against annexation,'" he
noted. "I have *tried* to persuade Miller to do the same, but cannot succeed. The *Register* is Gen. Houston's organ, not mine."[36]

Later Houston and Jones each claimed exclusive credit for the policy that guided Texas into the Union, and Jones grew bitter when the
public honored Houston while still charging him, Jones, with attempts
to defeat annexation. "Gen. Houston wrote to his private secretary,
Wm. D. Miller, editor of the Washington newspaper, to urge upon
him to use all his influence and power in opposing annexation," Jones
wrote in his journal. "He (Houston) approved every word which had
appeared in his (Miller's) paper opposing it; promising to sustain him
with all his means in doing so."[37]

In truth, Houston and Jones acted as one in regard to annexation,
and their break came not over the policy, but over who conceived it.

[34] *Telegraph and Texas Register*, March 12 and 26 and April 2 and 16, 1845; *Texas
National Register*, March 8, 1845.
[35] *Telegraph and Texas Register*, April 9, 1845.
[36] Jones, *Memoranda and Correspondence*, pp. 444–45.
[37] Ibid., p. 103.

Jones as president carried to a conclusion the policy he as secretary and Houston as president had formulated. They worked so closely that neither could claim exclusive credit for the ultimate results. Nor could either disclaim the *Texas National Register*. It appeared from a press owned, at least in part, by Jones, and from a town that served as his capital. The public, moreover, generally accepted the paper as the voice of the administration. But Washington D. Miller, one of the few men Sam Houston trusted completely, presided over the *Register*. "He knows all my actions and understands all my motives," Houston once wrote Andrew Jackson of Miller. "I have concealed nothing from him."[38]

The *Register* circulated widely in the United States, creating the impression of widespread Texan opposition to annexation and insulating the republic against further humiliation if another "explosion" snatched away the prize just as it seemed once more in hand.[39] But even as Washington D. Miller voiced his editorial opposition, Andrew J. Donelson, special agent to Texas and Andrew Jackson's nephew, recommended him to Jackson for a federal job. Miller, said Donelson, was "a meritorious friend" of General Houston, whose "prudence and patriotism" had saved the annexation measure.[40] Thus Miller could later claim to have been a part of Houston's and Jones's "coy" diplomacy, which pretended disinterest in order to whet interest, a policy that worked for the measure by circumvention.

Given less public enthusiasm for the resolutions, the policy of the administration as voiced by the *Register* and *Civilian* might have secured better terms of annexation. As it was, the vote of the Texas Congress, when it met at Jones's belated call, laid to rest any questions about public sentiment. By then the Jones-Houston strategy had not only produced the offer from the United States but also an offer of recognition from Mexico provided Texas refuse annexation. Although English and French diplomats had arranged and underwritten the Mexican offer, the Texas congressmen, meeting at Washington on the Brazos, gave it not even a courtesy hearing. Instead, they voted unanimously to accept the offer of the United States. A few weeks later a

[38] Barker and Williams, *Writings of Houston*, II, 389.
[39] See Justin H. Smith, *The Annexation of Texas*, pp. 380–81.
[40] Quoted in Friend, *Sam Houston*, p. 150.

special convention at Austin affirmed the decision of the congress with only one dissenting vote.

The convening of the special convention heralded the return of the Texas government to Austin and a new beginning for newspapering there. Jacob W. Cruger and Joel Miner, veterans of earlier Austin papers, acquired the use of the old Whiting press and won a contract to print the proceedings of the convention as it drew a constitution for the new state. They also launched a newspaper appropriately named the *New Era.* "This place has doffed her weeds (or a portion of them) and once more appears gay and lively," the paper reported. "Her prospects are at this time as bright and flattering as those of any inland towns in the Republic."[41]

After the actions of the congress and convention, the *National Register* and *Civilian* ceased their opposition, and, when the government shifted to Austin, the *National Register* ceased altogether. Miller and Cushney announced with the issue of October 9, 1845, the removal of their press to Austin, and with the issue of November 15 the sale of the press to John Salmon Ford and Michael Cronican. Ford and Cronican promptly disassociated themselves from the unpopular editorial policy of the *Register* by discontinuing it and founding in its stead on January 3, 1846, the *Texas Democrat.*

The voters approved the state constitution, as did the Congress of the United States, and Texas officially entered the Union on December 29, 1845. The following February 20 an extra of Ford and Cronican's paper gave a matter-of-fact account of the ceremony by which the last president of the republic handed the reins of government to the first governor of the state:

> Preparations were made for this event by decorating the Capitol with flags, etc. Their excellencies, the President and the Governor-elect, made their appearance, attended by a joint committee of both Houses, and escorted by the United States officers of this station. After being introduced, seated, etc., a prayer rich with the fervor of the Christian patriot was made by the Hon. R. E. B. Baylor. He was loudly applauded. The President then arose and delivered his valedictory. He was loudly applauded. The oath of office was administered to the governor by the speaker of the House and the inaugural followed.

[41] Austin *New Era,* July 30, 1845.

At San Augustine A. W. Canfield printed an appropriate requiem, which caught in a few words the delight tinged with sadness felt by most of the citizens. The *Red-Lander* carried in a black-bordered column the notice: "Died, without a pain, on the 15th instant, A NATION, aged 9 years, 11 months, and 13 days."

CHAPTER 11

To the Rio Grande

ONCE Texas had entered the Union, the newspapers focused attention on the development of the state. With a single voice the editors endorsed the building of railroads, recognizing correctly that the prosperity and growth of the state depended on improved transportation and communication. But, while they agreed on the necessity of the roads, they disagreed on the particulars of building them. Each editor pushed the plan that most benefited his town or area. Willard Richardson, for example, gave vigorous support to a system of roads that spread "fan-like" from Galveston, funneling the commerce of the state through the island port. Edward Hopkins Cushing, who replaced Francis Moore as the leading editor of Houston during the 1850s, designed a plan that connected his town with the transcontinental line and, as one fellow editor put it, "made Houston the commercial center of the universe."[1] Robert W. Loughery at Marshall drummed up support for a line that led to his town, while editors at San Antonio boosted a line from Matagorda Bay to Victoria and thence to San Antonio. Allied to the routing of the rails was the question of financing. Some editors opted for state-owned lines, others for state loans to builders, and still others for private enterprise. As a result the matter became a volatile political issue in the 1850s.

With only slightly less unanimity than in their support for the principle of railroads, the editors favored "southern causes," which translated as "slavery." Any editor who voiced abolitionist views found himself quickly silenced; northern-born editors had to prove themselves; and feuding editors often accused each other of lack of devotion

[1] *Dallas Herald*, December 8, 1858.

to the South. But, as in the matter of railroads, they did not always agree in particulars. Some advocated acceptance of compromise on the issue of slavery in the territories in order to preserve the Union, while others took a hard line. Some enthusiastically supported filibustering expeditions into Cuba and Nicaragua with the implied expansion of slave territory, while others viewed such adventures with indifference or even negatively. Some advocated the reopening of the slave trade as the solution to the state's labor shortages, while others looked upon it as unrealistic at best.

Interwoven with southern causes was the personality of Sam Houston, who dominated politics and divided editors in the early statehood period as he had done in the preceding era. Houston did not question the legitimacy of the peculiar institution, but, when faced with a choice of protecting it or seeing the Union fall apart, he invariably came down on the side of the Union. The most powerful editorial voices in the state lined up against him in the late 1850s. Newspapers then exerted a greater influence over the direction of events than previously, and as a result Houston suffered his only electoral defeat at the hands of Texans. Largely because of editorial opposition, he lost his campaign for governor in 1857 and later was pressured into resigning the office after secession.

Newspapers wielded greater influence in part because of improved methods of gathering and distributing news. Indeed, the building of railroads and the introduction of the telegraph revolutionized journalism. By the Civil War some 450 miles of rail—350 of them leading to Houston—carried fresh news and materials for printing it to the hinterland. The same roads hastened the printed pages to subscribers.

The telegraph lagged behind the rail but not because of lack of vision or effort on the part of the citizenry. In the early 1850s two lines —one through the Mississippi Valley and the other from the Atlantic Coast—reached New Orleans. Two local lines connected Shreveport, Louisiana, with the Mississippi Valley line on November 28, 1853, and thirty-eight days later the Texas Telegraph Company obtained a charter to link Texas to Shreveport. In forty days the company strung wire along trees and poles from Shreveport to Marshall, and on February 18, 1854, the *Texas Republican* carried the first direct telegraphic news report in the state. "The Magnetic telegraph is at length in operation between Marshall and New Orleans," exulted Robert W. Lough-ery. "We are no longer cut off from the balance of the world by low water and slow mails. But in the twinkling of an eye—in less time than it takes to talk about it—a dispatch can be sent and received from the most distant portions of the Union where this wonder-working machine is in operation."

Loughery's exultation proved premature for reasons suggested by another item in the same issue of his paper. "Owing to the wires being down between Harrisonburg and Natchez, we are unable this week to get intelligence direct from New Orleans."

By June, 1854, telegraph wires stretched from Marshall through Henderson, Rusk, Palestine, Crockett, Huntsville, and Montgomery to Houston, and by December a specially covered cable under Galveston Bay linked Houston with Galveston. But the first excitement over the telegraph soon turned to disillusionment. The cable under Galveston Bay proved a failure; wires quickly attached to trees just as quickly broke loose; and, reportedly, wagoners pulled up poles on occasion to use as pry poles or firewood. L. K. Preston, general manager of the company and later on the staff of the *Galveston News*, tried valiantly to maintain the lines and operate the offices, but without success and under a barrage of criticism. "We have to forebear saying much about the telegraph company at this time," wrote one editor. "But we are constrained to say that the community has been greatly imposed upon and none more so than this newspaper editor. We think Mr. Preston the prince of humbugs." The operators seized the line for back wages late in 1855, and wire communication fell into limbo for several years.[2]

Late in 1859, E. H. Cushing revived the Texas Telegraph Company and promoted the building of the first permanent telegraph line in the state—a line between Houston and Galveston. Cushing's group, working with the Galveston, Houston and Henderson Railroad, strung a line across the new railroad bridge to Galveston, completing the line on January 24, 1860. Even without lines in Texas proper, however, news reached the state days and weeks sooner after the wire reached New Orleans. From the mid-1850s some papers carried columns

[2] See Charles H. Dillon, "The Arrival of the Telegraph in Texas," *Southwestern Historical Quarterly* 64 (October, 1960): 200–11, and Huntsville *Texas Presbyterian*, October 5, 1854.

headed "By Telegraph," meaning not that they had received the news directly that way but rather that the news had been transmitted to New Orleans by that means and then to Texas by older methods.

Printing presses and newspapers proliferated during the period. Texas boasted nine papers on the eve of annexation, and the census of the United States counted eighty-nine newspapers and periodicals in 1860. Nor do these figures tell the full story. More than three hundred newspapers appeared during the period, but, as during the earlier era, most of them vanished quietly, leaving little evidence of their existence.

A number of factors account for their founding. The Mexican War carried the press to the Rio Grande and beyond and gave impetus to the westward movement; a rapid increase in population brought a demand for general newspaper services and created a market for religious and special-interest sheets; German immigrants and Spanish-speaking citizens inspired the founding of papers in their languages; and emerging political parties established organs to further their interests.

The movement of the press into south Texas began even before formal annexation. As the convention at Austin hammered out a state constitution during the summer of 1845, an army under Zachary Taylor moved to Corpus Christi to occupy the territory still claimed by Mexico. Hard on the heels of the army came newsmen to establish papers for the soldiers, to report on events to the homefolks, and in the process to carry the pioneer press to new frontiers.

George Wilkins Kendall was hunting buffalo in western Texas when he learned of the first action to the south, and he hastened there to begin earning his title as the first modern war correspondent. Eventually, he set up a courier system that conveyed news from the front to the *Picayune* in record time, making that paper a primary distributor of war news. A. W. Canfield sold the *Red-Lander* and repaired to the front, while Samuel Bangs and Legs Lewis shifted their journalistic efforts from Galveston to south Texas. John Salmon Ford waited only until the death of his ailing wife before he left the *Texas Democrat* to join the Texas Rangers on the field. Other printers and newsmen arrived from outside Texas, among them a group of printers who made up almost an entire company of the Louisiana Volunteers. Their six-month enlistment expired before Taylor reached the Rio Grande, and a number of them chose neither to reenlist nor return home but to practice their craft with the army or in its wake. "The story of the Anglo-

Saxon press in Mexico during the Mexican War not only recalls the military steps by which the southwestern boundary of the United States was pushed to the Rio Grande and the Pacific Ocean," observes the historian of the Mexican War newspapers, "but serves as an introduction to the history of the press in the Southwest in the subsequent decade."[3]

Appropriately, the first to establish a war newspaper was that harbinger of the Anglo-American press, Samuel Bangs. He followed Taylor's troops to Corpus Christi in the summer of 1845 and, struck by the prosperity the army brought to that trading outpost, determined to found a weekly newspaper there. Feeling the need for local involvement, he planned a paper in partnership with George W. Fletcher, a Corpus Christi physician, and the two enlisted as editor José de Alba, a prominent member of the Spanish-speaking community. Eventually, Isaac Neville Fleeson, a printer who arrived in Texas in 1842 with the Mobile Grays, joined the staff. The prospectus of the paper, the *Corpus Christi Gazette*, promised to promote the interests of the army in the area.[4]

Returning briefly to Galveston, Bangs placed his journal there under the direction of B. F. Neal and acquired a new press and equipment, which he shipped to Corpus Christi. The new paper appeared on January 1, 1846, to be hailed by Francis Moore as the "most western journal in the English language on the American continent," and by the New Orleans *Picayune* as a "new and spirited paper." Bangs and Fletcher adopted Davy Crockett's motto—"Be sure you are right, then go ahead"—and for a time their paper served as the principal medium of information between Taylor's army and the American public. Excerpts from other newspapers transmitted news from the outside world, while the *Gazette* sent out reports on developments in south Texas. In addition, advertisements, some of them illustrated by woodcuts, reflected the life of the soldiers there: two theaters, the Army and the Union, offered entertainment; the Kinney House, accommodations; the Kilgore Oyster Parlor, pleasures of the palate; and mer-

---

[3] Lota M. Spell, "The Anglo-Saxon Press in Mexico: 1846–1865," *American Historical Review* 38 (October, 1932): 20.

[4] Ibid., 21–22; Lota M. Spell, *Pioneer Printer: Samuel Bangs in Mexico and Texas,* pp. 124–26; Walter Prescott Webb and H. Bailey Carroll, eds. *The Handbook of Texas,* I, 610.

chants, an array of merchandise ranging from music boxes to shoe-strings. Bangs and Fletcher also did job printing for both the army and civilians.[5]

For about two months their office prospered. Then the army moved toward the Rio Grande, taking with it the wartime prosperity. Bangs and Fletcher printed as an extra of the *Gazette* Taylor's order number thirty, instructing the soldiers not to molest civilians or property during the advance. At the same time, the printers adjusted their own affairs to the change in circumstances. Bangs and Fletcher dissolved their partnership, and Bangs planned a new paper, the *Rio Grande Herald*, to be published at Matamoros in partnership with Legs Lewis of the *Galveston News*.[6]

Before Bangs could establish the new printing office, Isaac Neville Fleeson, his erstwhile associate on the *Corpus Christi Gazette*, published the first war newspaper at Matamoros. Fleeson obtained the use of a Mexican press and joined with Hugh McLeod and William G. Dryden to issue the *Republic of the Rio Grande* on June 1, 1846. Both McLeod and Dryden had long records as expansionists, McLeod having been commander of the ill-fated Texan–Santa Fe Expedition and Dryden its advance agent. The paper, a semiweekly published in both English and Spanish, reflected their ideas, and its title revived memories of an earlier Mexican Federalist movement that had proposed to establish a separate nation, the Republic of the Rio Grande, in northern Mexico. McLeod, the editor, suggested the creation of such a republic and implied its eventual annexation to the United States. His editorial created consternation in high circles in the United States and brought an abrupt end to the paper. McLeod and Dryden broke their connection with the printing office, while Fleeson resorted to the usual ploy of printers who found themselves burdened with an untenable journal. He discontinued it and began another, the new one titled the *American Flag*. First John H. Peoples and then J. R. Palmer, both Louisiana printers, joined Fleeson to establish the *Flag* as one of the more important and long-lasting of the war newspapers.

In the meantime, Bangs and Lewis issued on June 24 the first

[5] Spell, "Anglo-Saxon Press in Mexico," p. 23; Spell, *Pioneer Printer*, pp. 126–28; Houston *Telegraph and Texas Register*, January 7, 1846.

[6] Spell, *Pioneer Printer*, p. 129; Ernest W. Winkler, *Check List of Texas Imprints*, p. 8.

number of their new paper. Entitled the *Reveille* rather than the *Herald* as originally announced, it ended as abruptly and in even greater controversy than the *Republic of the Rio Grande*. The *Reveille* initially appeared semiweekly in both English and Spanish, the Spanish section being entitled *La Diana de Matamoros*. Bangs and Lewis soon dropped *La Diana*, however, and, following the customary practice in Galveston, rented their press to a Mexican publisher, who printed a separate Spanish-language paper, *El Liberal*. This paper gave eloquent voice to the Mexican side of the war, prompting the *Picayune* to comment that its very existence gave evidence of the American respect for freedom of the press. But General Taylor's tolerance soon ended. He ordered the *Reveille* office closed and the printers jailed—"on account," said the *Northern Standard*, "of the publication of an article in the Spanish paper issued from that office, sustaining the pretensions of Mexico in the present war." The article, the *Standard* reported further, said that "if Mexico wished to fight, she could easily raise an army of 100,000 men, all of whom would make good soldiers. . . . If she does fall, the conquering army will find nothing but the vengeance of a valiant people." In face of official wrath, Legs Lewis departed in haste to join the Texas Rangers, leaving Bangs to explain that he had no part in the editorial policy of *El Liberal* and had merely rented his press for its publication. He convinced authorities of his innocence and obtained permission to resume the *Reveille*, but he never did so. Instead, he joined forces with his competitors at the *American Flag*, selling his printing materials and press to them and becoming a printer at their office.[7]

Bangs continued with the *Flag* until February 17, 1847, when the lack of paper forced its temporary suspension. Then, convinced by Simon Mussina, land speculator and entrepreneur, of the potential of Point Isabel, he decided to remove there to operate a hotel and establish a newspaper.

Returning to Galveston, Bangs liquidated his business and arranged for the shipment of his household effects and printing office. All of these possessions went down in a wreck at sea, thus ruining his plans for a paper.

For a time, Bangs and his wife operated a hotel at Point Isabel

[7]Spell, *Pioneer Printer*, pp. 130–33; Spell, "Anglo-Saxon Press," pp. 22–23; Clarksville *Northern Standard*, September 5, 1846.

with indifferent success, and in the late summer of 1848 he made one last attempt to establish a newspaper there. With R. A. DeVilliers, another of the printers from the Louisiana Volunteers, he planned the *Texas Ranger*. DeVilliers, as editor of a war paper, the *Free American*, at Vera Cruz, had run into trouble with authorities, and, reportedly, he and Bangs planned to support a variation of the old and controversial idea of the Republic of the Rio Grande. Rumors circulated that their new paper would advocate the formation of a new government, called the Sierra Madre, in northern Mexico. The scheme generated considerable excitement along the border, but Indian depredations and then gold in California diverted the attention of Bangs and DeVilliers, and their *Texas Ranger* never appeared.[8]

The following year Bangs made news himself. Indians captured him between Point Isabel and Brownsville. The *Corpus Christi Star* reported that "the stage from Point Isabel had been intercepted and the proprietor Mr. Bangs and Mr. Lombardo, a passenger, were taken prisoner. . . . We are rejoiced to learn of the escape of Mr. Bangs and his companion from captivity. They were, however, reduced to a state of nudity."[9]

Shortly thereafter, Bangs abandoned his south Texas venture as a failure and returned east. He died in Kentucky on May 21, 1854, with little in the way of material goods to show for his pioneer printing efforts in the southwest.

By contrast, his sometime partner, Legs Lewis, he of the white bean, accumulated so promising a fortune in south Texas that after his death in 1855, his estate lingered in probate for two decades. Lewis, while captain of a Ranger company, had met Richard King at a fair in Corpus Christi in 1852, and the two had formed a ranching partnership. During the next few years they acquired vast acreage in the area, laid the foundations for the King Ranch empire, and dreamed of developing a port at Corpus Christi.[10]

Nor did Lewis forsake newspapering. He and other veterans of various war papers—John H. Peoples, Charles Callahan, and James R. Barnard—left their mark on the press at Corpus Christi. Peoples left the *American Flag* in the spring of 1847 to follow the army into Mexico

[8] Spell, *Pioneer Printer*, pp. 137–39.
[9] Ibid., p. 140; *Corpus Christi Star*, May 26, 1849.
[10] Tom Lea, *The King Ranch*, I, 132–34, 435.

and to print several papers. He founded the Vera Cruz *Eagle* on April 2, 1847, and printed the *American Star*, first at Jalapa, then at Pueblo, and finally in Mexico City. In 1848, after the war, he returned to south Texas and, with backing from H. L. Kinney, established the *Corpus Christi Star*. Like some of the earlier journals in south Texas, the *Star* appeared in both English and Spanish, the Spanish section entitled *La Estrella*. Rumor had it that the paper would advocate the Sierra Madre scheme, but instead it took the opposite stand and also announced its neutrality in United States politics.[11]

Early in 1849, Peoples departed for the California goldfields, leaving the paper in the hands of Charles Callahan. Callahan, in turn, caught California fever in the summer and turned the *Star* over to James R. Barnard. Barnard continued the *Star* until, later in the year, it gave way to the *Nueces Valley*, initially published by Charles C. Bryant and one Scott and edited by James A. Beveridge.[12]

The *Nueces Valley* continued for almost a decade, its course interrupted by the adventures and misadventures of the men associated with it, among them H. L. and Somers Kinney, B. F. Neal, and Legs Lewis. Lewis purchased H. L. Kinney's interest in the office on June 5, 1852, and for a time served as editor and publisher. News of his various escapades drifted northward to his friends in other editorial offices. Once they heard erroneously that he had died in a border fracas; again, that he had been arrested for assisting an accused murderer escape from Mexican officials; and again, of his involvement in border intrigue. "The Nueces Valley says Legs Lewis proposed to the *Hombres* on the other side of the Rio Grande who want another revolution to lead them to certain victory and put them in possession of the Sierra Madre Republic for the sum of $175,000, paid in advance—as all printers' bills should be," reported the *Texas State Gazette*.[13]

About the time he acquired the *Nueces Valley*, Legs Lewis turned his attention from Mexican to American politics. Dashing, popular, and noted for his "wit, pleasantry," and "fine spirits," he ran for Congress, visiting many of his fellow editors to the north as he campaigned. They never failed to say a kind word for him. "We do not entertain, so far as we know, a political sentiment in common with him in

[11]Spell, "Anglo-Saxon Press," pp. 30–31.
[12]San Antonio *Western Texan*, July 17, 1851.
[13]Austin *Texas State Gazette*, October 4, 1851, June 26, 1852, and May 7, 1853.

reference to national affairs," commented an old friend at Galveston, "but he is a typo whom we have known at the case, and an editor of older date than ourselves, and, while we regret to see one of the fraternity fallen from so high a position as to run for Congress, he has our sympathies nevertheless. We might add also that printers and editors are hard to beat."[14]

Captain Lewis's luck finally ran out in 1855. Reputedly a devil with ladies, he met death at the hands of a wronged husband. The Texas press gave fuller coverage to the affair than customary in such delicate matters. "It appears that Dr. Yarrington suspected Capt. Lewis of improper and familiar freedom with his (Yarrington's) wife," explained the *Galveston Journal*. "Yarrington told him that 'if he came again it would be the last time.' He called again, and prepared with a double-barrelled shot gun, Yarrington shot him down."[15]

The aggrieved husband himself explained to the *Gonzales Inquirer* "that I had the misfortune to kill Capt. G. K. Lewis at Corpus Christi on the 14th inst. The reason was, he seduced Mrs. Yarrington from me and my children, then added insult to injury by continually coming to my house, and also trying to steal my children from me."[16]

The *San Antonio Herald* wrote an appropriate eulogy for the captain: "Few braver men could be found where all were daring, than G. K. Lewis. . . . While the mantle of charity is thrown over his errors, let us drop a tear to the memory of the boy-prisoner of Mier."[17]

About a year before Lewis's death, Henry L. Kinney, once owner of the press at Corpus Christi, had headed a filibustering expedition into Nicaragua. A number of the Corpus Christi journalistic fraternity joined him, among them, James R. Barnard, Charles C. Bryant, Charles Callahan, and Henry A. Maltby, who resigned as mayor to join Kinney. Callahan died in Nicaragua, but Barnard returned to revive the *Nueces Valley* in 1857, in company with George W. Kinney. The two announced their intention of keeping the paper going for one year, and at the end of the year they bade a firm *adiós* to newspapering. Henry A. Maltby began the *Ranchero* on the same press the following year, and,

[14] *Galveston Journal*, June 24, 1851.
[15] Quoted in Lea, *King Ranch*, I, 132–34.
[16] Ibid.
[17] Ibid.

in association with his brother, William H. Maltby, continued the paper intermittently during the Civil War.[18]

At Brownsville, as at Corpus Christi, the wartime printers left a permanent impression. Isaac N. Fleeson and J. R. Palmer continued the *American Flag* at Matamoros until the end of the war. Fleeson died of tuberculosis on July 26, 1848, and Palmer announced in the issue of October 9 the removal of the paper across the river to Brownsville. Edwin B. Scarborough acquired the paper in 1849 and held the "little pet," as he called it, for ten years. The *Flag* stirred up a controversy in 1850 by denying the authority of Texas in the area between the Nueces and the Rio Grande and advocating the establishment of a territorial government there. By 1855, it carried the slogan, "Devoted to the interest of no party or clique; Independent in all things; Neutral in None," but Scarborough, upon becoming a member of the state legislature, counted himself a loyal Democrat and, by the Civil War, a Southern Democrat.[19]

[18] *Washington* (Texas) *American*, November 26, 1856; Austin *Texas State Times*, March 7, 1856; Corpus Christi *Nueces Valley*, October 3, 1857, and September 23, 1858; Corpus Christi *Ranchero*, October 22, 1857, February 2, 1861, August 27, 1863, and November 7, 1864.

[19] Brownsville *American Flag*, May 19, 1855, and March 16, 1859; *Texas State Gazette*, April 25 and August 29, 1857.

CHAPTER 12

Beyond the Colorado

ANNEXATION and the Mexican War not only pushed the Anglo-American press to the Rio Grande and beyond but also hastened the establishment of newspapers west of the Colorado River and stimulated their establishment throughout Texas. In the same issue of the *Telegraph and Texas Register* in which Francis Moore noted Bangs's proposal to found a paper on the Rio Grande, he noted the movement westward. "The proprietors of the Frontier Whig that has been publishing for some time at Van Buren, Arkansas, intend to remove their printing office to Victoria early this spring and establish a neutral paper which will be called the Texan Advocate," he wrote. "We learn that a new paper also soon will be established at Bexar."[1]

The report of a paper at Bexar proved premature by more than two years, but on May 8, 1846, the same day as the Battle of Palo Alto, John D. Logan and Thomas Sterne, recently from Arkansas, began printing the *Texan Advocate*, a paper destined to become the second most durable in the state. Both men brought experience to the task. Sterne, born in Bedford, Pennsylvania, in February, 1818, became an apprentice printer at the age of twelve. He drifted south and west, practicing his trade on the *City Gazette* at Louisville, Kentucky, and then founding the *Intelligencer* at Van Buren, Arkansas. He sold the *Intelligencer* to George V. Clark and then in 1844 in partnership with Logan, a native of Kentucky, founded a competing paper, the *Western Frontier Whig*. The town proved too small for two newspapers. Bitterness developed between the editors, with Clark calling Logan "Big Mush" and Logan labeling his rival "Toady Clark." Their animosity cul-

[1] Houston *Telegraph and Texas Register*, March 4, 1846.

minated in a duel fought on the banks of the Arkansas River in 1845. Accounts of the encounter differ. One report says that Clark suffered a slight wound; another, that Logan received a leg wound that crippled him for life; and yet another, that the two men, having satisfied their honor, became reconciled. But territorial rights went to Clark of the *Intelligencer*. Shortly after the duel, Logan and Sterne decided to relocate their press.[2] The annexation of Texas had stimulated immigration there, and news seemed in the making along the Rio Grande. The new state, moreover, afforded a ripe mission field for two Whig editors, for their party had opposed annexation while the Democrats had favored it, thus establishing political prejudices in the state.

Logan and Sterne took a horseback trip to Texas and after visiting several towns determined to settle at Victoria. As Sterne recalled years later, only a few people lived south and west of the Colorado River at the time, and those clustered as near towns as possible for protection against Indians and Mexicans. But Victoria lay along the route from San Antonio to the Gulf of Mexico, and the arrival of immigrants and soldiers was already stimulating growth.

Returning to Van Buren, Logan and Sterne transported their press and materials by flatboat to New Orleans, by ship to Port Lavaca, and thence by ox cart to Victoria. Francis Moore welcomed the first issue of their paper in the *Telegraph* of May 13, only five days after it appeared. It was, he commented, about as large as the *Red-Lander* and printed in beautiful type. Its columns were filled with "well selected" miscellaneous material, and the editorial department evinced "much talent and literary taste." In addition, its central position enabled it to obtain news from the army and the Mexican border.[3]

The Mexican War gave the *Advocate* an initial boost toward permanency. Only four days after the first issue appeared, news arrived of the Battle of Palo Alto, and the editor put out an extra giving the details available. As other actions took place along the Rio Grande, the *Advocate* became a prime distributor of news for an important section

[2] Unless otherwise noted, information about the *Victoria Advocate* is derived from Geraldine Talley, "The Story of the *Advocate*," pp. 222–29, in *300 years in Victoria County*, ed. Roy Grimes, and Geraldine Talley, "The *Victoria Advocate*: A History of Texas' Second Oldest Continuous Newspaper, 1846–1888" (M.S. thesis, Trinity University, 1967).

[3] *Telegraph and Texas Register*, May 13, 1846.

of the state and forwarded news to other journals. Eventually, as Zachary Taylor emerged as the military hero of the war, the two Whig newsmen in Victoria claimed to be the first to raise his name for president of the United States and took personal pride in his election. Logan left Victoria for the nation's capital during Taylor's years in the White House but retained his partnership in the *Advocate* and continued to write for it.

Early in the history of the *Advocate*, John Henry Brown joined the staff, first as printer and then as editor. Later renowned as a historian and public servant and already renowned as a soldier, Brown, like the proprietors, brought considerable experience to the task. Born in Pike County, Missouri, on October 29, 1820, he had been apprenticed to the *Salt River Journal* printing office at Bowling Green, Missouri, when he was thirteen years old. He was, he recalled, "the first printer boy or printer's devil, on the Mississippi river above St. Louis." Brown worked for the same publishers after they purchased the *Republican* at Saint Louis, and in 1839 left that paper to join members of his family in Texas. After visiting his uncle, James Kerr, a pioneer settler in the vicinity of Victoria, Brown served as "assistant" to George W. Bonnell and Jacob W. Cruger in the *Texas Sentinel* office at Austin. During the frontier troubles of the early 1840s, Brown, in his own words, "went on divers campaigns—was in the battles of Plum Creek, Salado, Woll's retreat from San Antonio (March, 1842), and in Somervell's expedition to the Rio Grande."[4]

Returning to Missouri in the spring of 1843, he met and married Mary Mitchel and briefly held an interest in the *Missouri Journal* at Bowling Green. By mid-1845 Brown and his bride had returned to Texas, and by October, 1846, they had settled in Victoria, where he associated himself with Sterne and Logan. As he recalled, he remained with the *Advocate* only "some 7 or 8 months," during which time he began collecting and publishing the Indian War stories that later won him acclaim.

Characteristically restless, Brown moved to the new town of Indianola, where in 1852 he launched the *Indianola Bulletin*, and then to Galveston, where in September, 1854, he became part-owner with Hamilton Stuart and Samuel Durnett of the *Civilian*. The voters sent

[4]Lawrence E. Honig, *John Henry Brown, Texian Journalist, 1820–1895*, pp. 5, 8.

him to the state legislature in 1855 and then elected him mayor of Galveston.

Of Whig predilections in his younger days, Brown became a staunch Democrat, an opponent of the Know-Nothings, and a secessionist during the 1850s. Not all of those stands coincided with Hamilton Stuart's, so in 1858 Brown moved to Belton. By 1860 he was editing the *Belton Democrat*, an anti–Sam Houston, pro-slavery, and eventually, a secessionist paper. A member of the Secession Convention in 1861, Brown chaired the committee that wrote the articles of secession. Upon the outbreak of war, he entered the army, becoming a major, and for a time publishing a small newspaper entitled *War Bulletin* for the Confederate troops in Arkansas. At war's end he established a colony of ex-Confederates in Mexico.

Brown returned to Texas in 1870 and for a time again held interest in the *Indianola Bulletin*. In 1871, he resettled his family for the last time—moving to Dallas, where he entered business, served as mayor and legislator, and wrote the works that gave him his most enduring fame, *The Indian Wars and Pioneers of Texas* and *History of Texas*.[5]

John Henry Brown always remembered fondly his stint on the *Advocate* at Victoria and recalled with amusement how his uncle, James Kerr, and other old-timers had pressured Logan and Sterne into changing the spelling of "Texan." Originally the *Texan Advocate*, the paper became at the pioneers' behest, the *Texian Advocate*. Later, another owner changed the name to the *Victoria Advocate*.

Sterne and Logan retained ownership of the *Advocate* until 1853, when Sterne sold to George W. Palmer, and Logan to John J. Jamieson. Palmer and Jamieson dissolved their partnership in 1858, with Palmer continuing the paper alone, until he sold to Samuel Addison White in 1859. A native of Tennessee, White had come to Texas and settled on the Navidad River in 1830. He studied law with William H. and John A. Wharton, fought in the battle of Velasco in 1832, and served as a captain in the revolutionary army of 1835–36. Later, in 1840, he fought in the Plum Creek battle. He served in the First Congress of the Republic of Texas, in the sixth and tenth state legislatures, and as mayor of Victoria. Under his direction, the *Advocate* became a

---

[5] For a sketch of Brown, see Honig, *John Henry Brown*. Brown is best known for his *Indian Wars and Pioneers of Texas* (Austin: L. E. Daniell, [189-]) and *History of Texas from 1685 to 1892*, 2 vols. (Austin: L. E. Daniell, 1892).

Democratic organ, and largely because of his tenacity it weathered the hazards of the Civil War era.

Thomas Sterne, after selling the *Advocate*, retired to a ranch north of Victoria but continued his interest in local affairs until his death November 29, 1906, at eighty-nine years of age. John D. Logan also retired to a ranch, but only for a time.[6] He and a neighboring rancher in Refugio County, S. C. Thompson, purchased the *San Antonio Herald* from James P. Newcomb in the mid-1850s, and Logan was in and out of the publishing business in the San Antonio area until shortly before his death on February 10, 1878.

The permanent press preceded Logan to San Antonio by several years, established there by that veteran of Texian affairs and Texian journalism, Michael Cronican. Cronican and John Salmon Ford broke their association in the *Texas Democrat* at Austin in the summer of 1847 with the announcement that: "Dr. J. S. Ford, having received the appointment of Adjutant of the new twelve months regiment, under Col. Jack Hays, has given up his connection in the editorial management of the 'Democrat,' for the present, at least. . . . Dr. Ford will therefore be held blameless of all sins . . . of which the 'Democrat' may be guilty during his absence."[7]

The announcement suggests only a temporary dissociation, but it became permanent after Cronican neglected to print communications Ford sent from the battlefront. When Ford protested, Cronican explained the accounts were "too long," and he had tossed them into the wastebasket. "Truth requires the admission," Ford recalled in his memoirs, "that this information caused an uncommon emission of profanity."[8]

Joel Miner and Samuel Cummings replaced Ford at the *Democrat* office on December 15, 1847, but they too broke with Cronican in less than a year. In the fall of 1848, he took the printing press and equipment to San Antonio, leaving Miner and Cummings as proprietors of the *Democrat*. For a time they printed the paper on the old Niles press that Samuel Whiting had introduced to Austin and on which Dr. Chalmers had more recently printed the *New Era*. Then they sold the *Democrat* to William Cushney, who won the public printing contract,

[6]Talley, "The *Victoria Advocate*," pp. 32–34.
[7]Austin *Texas Democrat*, July 24, 1847.
[8]John Salmon Ford, *Rip Ford's Texas*, ed. Stephen B. Oates, p. 109.

ordered a new press, and changed the name to the *Texas State Gazette*. Within a few years, the *Gazette* became one of the most important papers in the state.[9]

In the meantime, Michael Cronican joined with James Abner Glasscock, a compadre of the Mier Expedition, to found his last paper, the *Western Texian*. The old town of San Antonio had not boasted a printing press since the departure of the one Félix Trespalacios had imported in 1821, the one on which George Asbridge had printed the prospectus of *Correo de Texas*. That paper probably never appeared; nothing came of Mirabeau B. Lamar's plans for a paper in the town in 1841; and the *Alarm Bell of the West* in 1842, although it carried a San Antonio dateline, probably came from one of the presses at Austin. Thus, the *Western Texian*, first issued about October 20, 1848, stands as the first newspaper of record for San Antonio.

The tenure of the founders did not last long. A cholera epidemic ravaged the town only a few months after the paper appeared, claiming Michael Cronican as one of its victims. The issue of May 3, 1849, carried his obituary. Glasscock had neither the experience nor the desire to continue the paper alone. Born in Kentucky in 1816 to Thomas and Elizabeth Glasscock, he followed an older brother to Texas, arriving in time to join the Somervell and Mier expeditions in 1842. Unlike Cronican, Glasscock was among those captured in battle. He participated in the escape and drawing of the beans of Salado, and, being among the lucky ones, received freedom in the general release of the Mier prisoners in 1844. He kept a diary of his ordeal that years later appeared in print, but it shows no particular talent for writing, and he had only the scantiest of journalistic experience when Cronican's death left him at the helm of the *Texian*.[10]

The future of the paper hung in the balance for a time, but at last new proprietors kept it alive. "The *Western Texian* after undergoing a series of transitions from one proprietor to another is at last safely moored in the possession of Messrs. Lewis & Groesbeeck," the *Texas State Gazette* reported on November 3, 1849. "Its editors evince more

[9] *Telegraph and Texas Register*, November 16, 1848; Larry Jay Gage, "The Editors and Editorial Policies of the *Texas State Gazette*, 1849–1879" (M.A. thesis, University of Texas, 1959), pp. 5–6.

[10] James M. Day, ed., "Diary of James A. Glasscock," *Texana* 1 (Spring, 1963): 86–88.

care and ability than formerly." Glasscock left San Antonio in 1850 to travel with Major Robert S. Neighbors to El Paso. From thence he worked his way to California, residing for a time in Siskiyou County. Reportedly, he died in 1876.

The new proprietors of the *Western Texian*, Nathaniel C. Lewis and John D. Groesbeeck, dropped the *i* in *Texian* and continued the paper, at least in part to advertise their mercantile wares. The leading merchants in the town, they prospered by supplying the army headquartered there. Long wagon trains from Indianola brought merchandise to stock their shelves and supply citizens and soldiers with necessities and luxuries.

Nat Lewis, born in Massachusetts on June 11, 1806, came to Texas in 1830 and engaged in the San Antonio–Gulf Coast trade at an early date. Reputedly, he slipped into the Alamo with supplies during the siege of the old mission and was the last Anglo-American to leave before its fall. A scout for the Texas Army in 1839–40, he represented Bexar County in the Fourth Congress. His partner and brother-in-law, John D. Groesbeeck, was born on April 13, 1816, in Albany, New York, and arrived at Galveston in 1837, first working as a surveyor and then establishing a wholesale drug company. Groesbeeck moved his business to Houston in 1841 and to San Antonio in 1846, where he joined Lewis in mercantile and banking enterprises.

The partners employed Henry M. Lewis, Nat's brother, a college-educated lawyer and recent arrival from Massachusetts, as editor of the *Western Texan*. He proved a capable editor, but the proprietors grew disillusioned with newspapering in less than three years, reportedly because they lost the city printing contract to their rival, the *Ledger*. By September, 1852, Dr. J. H. Lyons and J. S. McDonald and Company published the *Texan*; by the following year, Lyons had withdrawn, and by 1855 it had passed to E. G. Huston and J. M. Smith.[11]

The first competitor of the *Texan* appeared in 1850, the same year that Glasscock left San Antonio. Joseph Walker, sometime Texas Ranger and a practical printer from Austin, established a second printing office and issued the *Ledger*. Like the *Texan*, the *Ledger* existed precariously throughout the 1850s and passed through a series of owners.

[11] Jacobina Burch Harding, "A History of the Early Newspapers of San Antonio, 1823–1874" (M.A. thesis, University of Texas, 1951), pp. 46–48.

Walker returned to Austin a year after its founding, leaving lawyers David Campbell Van Derlip and Ira A. Hewitt as proprietors. They in turn sold to an English printer, Michael Bourke. Both the *Texan* and the *Ledger* began issuing dailies in 1858, and before the Civil War they merged under the ownership of Aeneas Macleod and N. A. Taylor to become the *Ledger and Texan*.

By then two additional presses had been established in San Antonio, and a number of newspapers had appeared to challenge the pioneers and to reflect the peculiarly cosmopolitan nature of the town. Indeed, during the 1850s San Antonio compensated for any previous tardiness in journalistic endeavors. In 1853, a group of German immigrants underwrote the establishment of a press and a newspaper, the *San Antonio Zeitung*, edited by Carl Daniel Adolph Douai. From the same press in 1855 came a Spanish-language paper, *El Bejareño*, edited by a French-born linquist, Xavier Blanchard DeBray, and Alfred A. Lewis. The following year a second Spanish-language paper, *El Ranchero*, appeared, edited by a Cuban-born refugee, José Agustín Quintero, and in 1858, yet another, *El Correo*, appeared.[12]

In 1855 John S. McDonald, once of the *Texan*, introduced a fourth press, from which came the *Sentinel*, a Know-Nothing paper edited by X. B. Sanders, an early schoolteacher in San Antonio. The *Sentinel* lasted only a short while, but the press in the hands of James Pearson Newcomb and later John D. Logan produced the *Herald*, the paper that gave the *Texan* and *Ledger* the greatest competition in the late 1850s.[13]

Newcomb learned his trade in the pioneer printing offices of San Antonio. Indeed, he grew up in the offices of the *Texan* and *Ledger* and dominated journalism in the town for a generation. Born in Amherst, Nova Scotia, on August 31, 1837, Newcomb arrived in Texas with his parents and younger brother in 1839. His mother died two years later at Victoria and his father, Captain Thomas Newcomb, a former sea captain, lawyer, and poet, remarried in 1847. The family removed to San Antonio, where Captain Newcomb died in April, 1849, of the same cholera epidemic that took Michael Cronican. His widow found the responsibility of two stepsons too much for her, and, arrang-

[12] Ibid., pp. 46–49; Carland Elaine Crook, "San Antonio, Texas, 1840–1861" (M.A. thesis, Rice University, 1964), pp. 133–35.
[13] Harding, "Early Newspapers of San Antonio," p. 50–52.

ing for them to board in a local home, she removed herself from their lives.

Of necessity, young James entered the working world at a tender age in order to earn his and his brother's keep. He apprenticed at age twelve to Henry Lewis of the *Western Texan*, thus setting the course of his career. Newcomb later fondly recalled his apprenticeship—how he swept the floor for Mrs. Lewis and operated the old Washington hand-press, using buckskin balls instead of rollers to ink the forms.

After Lewis and Groesbeeck sold the *Texan*, Newcomb moved to the *Ledger* office as a printer's devil. At age sixteen, he joined with another teen-age devil, Frank M. Whitemond, to found his first paper, the biweekly *Alamo Star*, which first appeared on March 25, 1854. The two used the press of the *Ledger* and did everything from composing the editorials to delivering the paper. They confessed to inexperience in their first issue, writing that "in commencing the Star, we labor under many disadvantages; neither of us ever before attempted to pen an arti-cle for a paper, . . . and our readers must not expect too much of us." Even so, the *Star* enjoyed instant success, and within a short while became a weekly. Initially "devoted to the advancement of the Youth in Literature and Morality," it promoted the Youths' Debating Club, to which both Newcomb and Whitemond belonged, and opened up sub-jects of debate such as women's suffrage and Know-Nothingism.[14]

But the *Star* soon advanced beyond youthful issues. Newcomb launched crusades against intemperance, gambling, and the Roman Catholic church, bringing a turnover in his associates. Whitemond left the *Star* after July 8, 1854, and later in the year founded the *San An-tonio Reporter*, described as "a kind of printers' enterprise," which ap-peared intermittently for about two years. Robert J. Lambert replaced Whitemond at the *Star* but remained only a few months, leaving New-comb as sole owner on October 1, 1854.

Newcomb left youthful things behind forever by discontinuing the *Alamo Star* on January 24, 1855, and replacing it on April 3 with the *San Antonio Herald*, a larger, more sophisticated, and even more con-troversial sheet. In partnership with J. M. West, a refugee from a murder charge in Ohio, Newcomb took up the cause of the American

[14] See John Fowler, *James P. Newcomb: Texas Journalist and Political Leader*, pp. 2–4.

or Know-Nothing party. Within a short while, the two made the *Herald* the leading paper in San Antonio but embroiled themselves in so explosive a political situation that Newcomb found it expedient to sell his interest in the paper to J. D. Logan.

West left in haste shortly thereafter just ahead of a law officer from Ohio with orders for his arrest. West joined William Walker's filibuster to Nicaragua and suffered a wound at the siege of Grenada. Upon his return, he settled in New Orleans, where he advocated the Confederacy and died in the mob riots of September, 1871.[15]

Newcomb's retirement from the San Antonio newspaper scene proved only temporary. After a brief respite, he returned to the *Herald* as editor and continued the course that made him one of the more important and controversial editors in Texas before—and after—the Civil War.

[15] Harding, "Early Newspapers of San Antonio," p. 53.

CHAPTER 13

More People, More Papers

SHEER population increases—from an estimated 142,009 people in 1847 to 604,215 by the census of 1860—brought corresponding increases in the number of papers. The press followed the frontier to the north as well as to the south; printers filled in the gaps in the settled portions of the state. A few literary and special-interest papers appeared, and religious journals flowered to surpass the secular in circulation.

In the same year the permanent press reached the old town of San Antonio, James Wellington Latimer and William Willis established the *Herald* at the new town of Dallas. They considered themselves on the outskirts of the frontier in 1849. The county contained only about two thousand people, and the outside settlement lay thirty miles to the west at Fort Worth. In nine years' time the population of the area multiplied 450 percent, and the frontier pushed fifty miles beyond Fort Worth, taking the press with it. Chilton and Collins established the *Western Express* at Birdville in 1856; C. E. Van Horn and Company, the *Frontier News* at Weatherford in 1858. By 1860 the *Chief* had appeared at Fort Worth and the *White Man* at Jacksboro. "Our own prosperity has not been in ratio with the advancement and prosperity of the country," complained Latimer. "We have labored under disadvantages that none but those who have attempted to publish a newspaper in a frontier country under similar circumstances can appreciate."[1]

Latimer spoke too modestly, for his press office had increased proportionally, at least in size. He and Wallis began publication of the *Herald* on a Ramage handpress that had previously printed several pa-

---

[1] *Dallas Herald*, July 3, 1858.

pers at Bonham and Paris. When the press office burned in the fateful
Dallas fire of 1860, a year after Latimer's death, the proprietors lost
four presses.

Wallis remained with the *Herald* only a short time, but Latimer,
scion of a prominent and prolific north Texas family, joined with J. W.
Swindells, a New York printer, to make the *Herald* one of the important papers in the state by the late 1850s. They made it a strong voice
for the Southern Democrats in northern Texas and once challenged the
Texas State Gazette for the state printing contract. After Latimer died
in a freak accident at age thirty-three, Swindells continued the paper
in the same style, with Charles Pryor, a Virginia doctor, as editor.[2]

While some newsmen pushed to the frontier, others brought additional presses to older areas. William D. Wood, founder of the *Leon
Pioneer*, represented many of them. He and his brother, a printer,
walked from Alabama to Texas, arriving at Centerville, Leon County,
on November 14, 1851. "As we had no means, and meat and bread,
clothes and shelter, were practical, pressing necessities that could not
well be ignored or put off, we concluded to start a newspaper at Centerville," he remembered. "We thought that the novelty of the thing,
in what was then almost a wilderness, would attract attention and patronage and thus give us an occupation that would enable us to earn our
daily bread."[3]

They persuaded a friend to lend them money and ordered a hand-
press and supplies from New York. After many delays and mishaps, the
press arrived in the spring of 1852, and they issued the first number of
the *Leon Pioneer*. "It was, indeed, a pioneer, for it was located in a
section of the country that had never before been invaded by a newspaper," Wood said. "The people came from far and near to see it, and
considering the paucity of the population, it was liberally patronised."[4]

The *Pioneer* carried legal advertising for several counties and
prospered, so that the brothers supported themselves and paid their
debt. But not without the usual difficulties that surrounded such offices. When the Trinity River failed, as it often did, newsprint came

[2] Ibid., April 13, 1859. For a more complete history, see Samuel Paul Maranto, "A
History of Dallas Newspapers" (M.S. thesis, North Texas State University, 1952).

[3] W. D. Wood, "Reminiscences of Texas and Texans Fifty Years Ago," *Quarterly of
the Texas State Historical Association* 5 (October, 1901): 113.

[4] Ibid., p. 114.

to them from Huntsville on horseback, and in times of extreme scarcity they printed only the legal advertisements in order to save that business.

Communication with the outside world also came to them primarily through Huntsville by way of a weekly mail—"that is, the mail came over the line on the back of a mule, once a week in dry weather," commented Wood. "When the floods came and Bidias Creeks became raging torrents, we were often without a mail. . . . All that was necessary to render the Bidias impassable was one or two lonesome thunders on the head of these creeks. In between mails, the editor of the Pioneer had to manufacture news out of his own consciousness as best he could."[5]

The Wood brothers published the *Pioneer* for three and a half years and then sold the office to John Gregg and Morris Reagan, a brother of John H. Reagan, who moved the press to Fairfield. W. L. Moody, patriarch of the prominent Galveston family, was publishing the paper by late 1855 and was succeeded by N. R. Barnes a year later.

Increased population brought a few specialty papers aimed at certain groups. For example, W. T. Yeomans and Andrew Jackson issued the *Texas Free Mason* from Rusk in 1858 by authority of "the Most Worshipful Grand Lodge of the State of Texas." Publishers in the larger towns often printed sheets designed for businessmen, papers such as the *Commercial Weekly and Prices Current* at Galveston and the *Price Current and Business Register* in Houston. At Austin, Irving Root and J. E. Park edited the *Texas Journal of Agriculture*, a monthly for farmers, from the office of the *Texas State Gazette*. At Galveston, B. F. Davis issued the *Texas Register* for stockraisers, promising to list strays and help owners recover lost or stolen animals. For the cause of education, the *Public School Advocate* came from the office of the *Democratic Telegraph and Texas Register* at Houston in 1847, and the *Texas Journal of Education* appeared in the same town in 1854. The cause of temperance inspired several sheets. The Huntsville *Texas Banner* noted the *Temperance Banner and Sunday School Advocate* at Rusk in 1849, and John Hannay and Francis D. Allen issued the *Good Samaritan and Temperance Messenger* at Galveston in 1855.[6] With few

---

[5] Ibid.

[6] Clarksville *Northern Standard*, April 22, 1847; *Galveston Directory*, pp. 90–92; Huntsville *Texas Banner*, February 3, 1849; Austin *Texas State Times*, February 3, 1855;

exceptions the special papers lasted only a short while. The census of 1860 listed only two miscellaneous publications, one weekly and one monthly.

On paper, literary publications fared somewhat better. The census counted twelve in 1860, nine weekly and three monthly. But the record shows little in the way of individual successes. The first literary paper, the *Telescope and Texas Literary Messenger* appeared at Richmond in 1839. It lingered for about a year under several editors, among them Nicholas Maillard, an Englishman who later wrote a book highly critical of Texas. Literary publications that followed included the *Horned Frog*, a humor sheet that appeared in Galveston in 1858; the *Rambler*, published by William Carleton, first at Austin and then at Lockhart; and the *Texas Portfolio*, founded at Galveston by Oscar H. Harpel and Francis D. Allen. Mrs. Eleanor Spann, also of Galveston, launched the most ambitious of this genre, the *Texian Monthly Magazine*. Editors throughout the state gave the magazine glowing reports when it appeared in 1858. But yellow fever appeared in Galveston about the same time as the *Texian Monthly Magazine*. Mrs. Spann published a few numbers and then suspended.[7]

Another publication, the *Southern Age*, stands in a category by itself. In late 1857, "two distinguished adventurers," calling themselves Mr. and Mrs. Weekes, arrived at Galveston and issued a single number of that journal. They canvassed the town selling subscriptions for cash in advance and doing far better in that regard than most other editors. Then they toured the state selling subscriptions on the same terms, even selling to many members of the legislature at Austin. There the *Texas State Gazette* gave a pleasant welcome to Mrs. Cora Ann Weekes, editress of the "New Texian Literary Paper." The pair returned to Galveston, issued another number of their paper, and departed for New Orleans, where they sold more subscriptions. As Galvestonians heard the end of the story, the couple then departed for San Francisco, where they collected subscriptions in advance for a proposed paper there before leaving for Hawaii just ahead of the law.[8]

The *Texas Almanac* also stands in a category by itself. Hailed as

---

Lynnell Jackson, *True Witnesses: A Check List of Newspapers, 1854–1861*, pp. 22, 29, 54.

[7] *Galveston Directory*, p. 91; *Dallas Herald*, July 3, 1858.

[8] *Galveston Directory*, p. 91; Austin *Texas State Gazette*, January 2, 1858.

"one of the most valuable publications ever issued from the Texas press," it was believed by its publishers to be the most widely circulated periodical in the South in 1859. David Richardson, a native of the Isle of Man, conceived the idea and persuaded Willard Richardson, not a kinsman, to publish the almanac under the auspices of the *Galveston News*. An annual, the first volume appeared in 1857 and contained historical sketches, information for prospective immigrants, and descriptions of Texas. The publication proved an instant success. The proprietors issued 10,000 copies of the first issue, 25,000 each of the next two, and proposed to issue 30,000 in 1860.[9]

In circulation, if not in financial returns, religious papers represented another journalistic success story of the early statehood period. The first religious papers in Texas, however, left few traces. A prospectus for the *Nazarene Advocate* appeared in the *Matagorda Bulletin* of October 25, 1837, but the paper probably was never published. The first of the genre to appear was probably the *Literary Intelligencer* at San Augustine, which diarist Adolphus Sterne of Nacogdoches noted on December 22, 1843: "Mr Reed from San Augustine came from that place brought me several prospectuses for a Paper to be called the San Augustine Literary Intelligencer, Edited or Fathered by L. A. L. Laird and T. M. Flatau, the Paper to be a Methodist Paper—(oh! dear)—& to be under the management of a Son of Abraham verily I am tempted to believe in Parson Miller's Doctrine—." The following February 2, Sterne received the first numbers of the paper and commented favorably that "it does honor to its Editor & proprietor and vice versa." The *Literary Intelligencer* then vanished without leaving further evidences of its existence.[10]

The real era of the religious publication began about the time of annexation. In late 1846, Andrew Jackson McGown, a veteran of the Battle of San Jacinto and a Cumberland Presbyterian minister, started the *Texas Presbyterian* at Victoria, using the press of the *Advocate*. The following year, Robert B. Wells, a Methodist minister, launched the *Texas Christian Advocate and Brenham Advertiser*. That same

[9] *Galveston Directory*, p. 92; A. C. Gray, "A History of the Texas Press," in *A Comprehensive History of Texas, 1685–1897*, ed. Dudley G. Wooten, II, 390; Ernest W. Winkler, *Check List of Texas Imprints, 1846–1860*, p. xx.

[10] Archie P. McDonald, ed., *Hurrah for Texas: The Diary of Adolphus Sterne, 1838–1851*, pp. 186, 195; Thomas W. Streeter, *Bibliography of Texas 1795–1845*, pt. 1, vol. II, 542.

year, Moseley Baker, whose troops had burned the *Telegraph* office at San Felipe in 1836 and who also had fought at San Jacinto, founded the *Texas True Evangelist* at Houston.

Moseley Baker had feuded not only with Francis Moore but also with Sam Houston during the years after the Texan Revolution. Houston blamed Baker for the firing of San Felipe, and Baker soundly denounced Houston's conduct of the San Jacinto campaign. Baker repented of his transgressions in the late 1830s and, joining the Methodist church, became a prominent Methodist minister at Houston. But in 1847 he created an uproar in church circles by falling under the influence of a prophet named Alley and taking up mesmerism and spiritualism. Withdrawing from the Methodist church, he started the *Texas True Evangelist* to propound his new doctrines.[11]

Reportedly, after founding the *Evangelist*, Baker wrote Houston a letter "saying he knew him to be an unmitigated scoundrel, a poltroon, utterly unprincipled, and full of guile." Even so, "he (Baker), having repented of his sins and become reconciled to his Maker, desired to be at peace with all mankind, and therefore tendered the olive-branch to Houston and hoped he would accept it in the same spirit, lay down the tomahawk, and smoke the calumet, and 'let the dead past bury its dead.'" By this time Houston had married the devout daughter of a Baptist minister, but he was several years away from entering the fold of that church. He replied shortly that he cared not what Baker thought of him and cared even less for Baker's friendship or enmity. Baker published the exchange in the *Evangelist* along with a prayer that God would soften Houston's hard heart, convert him from his wicked ways, and pardon his manifold transgressions. Baker continued the *Evangelist* somewhat erratically until his death of yellow fever in 1848. At that time Francis Moore, who had forgiven Baker even if Houston had not, published a warm obituary in the *Telegraph*.[12]

The *Texas Presbyterian* and the *Texas Christian Advocate and Brenham Advertiser* followed more closely than the *True Evangelist* the pattern of the religious journal of the era. Earlier in the nineteenth century, as publishing technology improved and the public grew more

[11]Macum Phelan, *A History of Early Methodism in Texas, 1817–1866*, pp. 310–11.

[12]Gray, "History of Texas Press," pp. 387–88 (Gray incorrectly gives the title of the paper as *True Witness*); Houston *Democratic Telegraph and Texas Register*, November 9 and 16, 1848.

literate, churchmen in the United States recognized the potential of
the press in spreading their message. Thus, they developed a journal
that combined the format of the general newspaper with their interpretation of events. They perfected the genre by 1830, and it reached
Texas about the time of annexation.

A. J. McGown, after an unsuccessful attempt to obtain backing in
the east, began the *Texas Presbyterian* as an independent effort but in
hopeful expectation that the Cumberland Presbyterian church would
assume responsibility. After only a few months at Victoria, he moved
to Houston, and after about three years he followed the synod head-
quarters to Huntsville. There he and an associate, Robert Waters,
bought the press of the *Texas Banner* from Francis L. Hatch. Despite
their efforts, the church declined to accept the paper. Financial difficulties forced Waters to abandon the enterprise early, but McGown
continued it under his own auspices until 1856, when the church refused once again to accept the *Texas Presbyterian*. The outspoken
McGown, bitter at the action of the church, announced his retirement
from the field and resumed his activities as a minister of the gospel.[13]

The *Texas Christian Advocate and Brenham Advertiser* also began as an independent project, but, unlike the *Texas Presbyterian*, it
eventually came under the auspices of a church, the Methodist. As the
title suggests, the paper initially was half-religious and half-secular.
The citizens of Brenham encouraged its founding, but, as Mary E.
Wells, wife of the founder, recalled: "When we came to the work, and
tried to get printers to set type and hands to work off the papers we
were at a loss to know what to do—a long ways from market, and news
of interest was scarce. . . . Houston was our nearest market, and in
rainy weather the road was almost impassable. We would have trouble
with our press, and it was hard to get paper." Although her husband
worked day and night and she along with him, the difficulties proved
too great for them. In 1848 her father, Orceneth Fisher, an influential
Methodist minister, assumed responsibility for the paper and moved it
from Brenham to Houston. At the same time, he shortened the title to

[13] William J. Stone, Jr., "Texas' First Church Newspaper: The Texas Presbyterian,
1846–1856," *Texana* 12 (Summer, 1973): 239–47. See also Wesley Norton, "Religious
Newspapers in Antebellum Texas," *Southwestern Historical Quarterly* 79 (October,
1975); and William J. Stone, Jr., "A Historical Survey of Leading Texas Denominational
Newspapers, 1846–1861" (Ph.D. diss., University of Texas, Austin, 1974).

the *Texas Christian Advocate*. The following year, Chauncey Richardson became editor, and the title became the *Texas Wesleyan Banner*. The Methodist General Conference accepted the paper as its official organ in 1850, and by the following year it boasted a circulation of 1,500, the largest of any paper in the state.[14]

Despite this circulation, financial problems plagued the paper, in part because of the low subscription rate of two dollars per year. A group of lay leaders assumed responsibility for finances in 1851, and Richardson resigned in a huff when they reduced his salary. Charles Shearn, one of the laymen, subsidized the paper for a time. Then another group headed by David Ayres moved it to Galveston in 1854, where it again became the *Texas Christian Advocate*.[15]

The mid-fifties brought another crop of religious papers, among them three at Galveston in the German language. In 1855, Peter A. Moelling, pastor of a German Methodist congregation, began *Der Deutsche Christliche Apologete* on the press of the *Texas Christian Advocate*. He replaced it the following year with the *Evangelische Apologete*, a paper that lasted until the Civil War. Also in 1855, Heinrich Wendt, a Lutheran minister, began *Der Pilger Im Sueden Der Union*. A monthly designed to promote the founding of a Lutheran seminary, *Der Pilger* continued for about a year.[16]

Other denominations entered the field in the same period. In 1855 at Houston, J. J. Nicholson started the *Texas Episcopalian*, and Jerome Twitchell and Joseph P. Wilson began the *Panoplist and Presbyterian* on behalf of the Old School Presbyterian church. At Anderson, George Washington Baines launched the *Texas Baptist*. The following year, the *Dallas Herald* noted the prospectus of the *Bible Union*, to be published at Paris "by Dr. Pandun of the Christian (Campbellite) Church."[17]

Of these, the *Texas Baptist* proved the most notable, in part because of the growth of the denomination during the decade. The paper appeared under the direction of the Texas Baptist Publication Society

[14] Phelan, *History of Early Methodism*, pp. 308–309.

[15] *Galveston Journal*, July 8, 1851.

[16] *Galveston Directory*, p. 91; Rudolph Leopold Biesele, *The History of the German Settlements in Texas, 1831–1861*, p. 225; T. Herbert Etzler, "German-American Newspapers in Texas," *Southwestern Historical Quarterly* 57 (April, 1954): 423–24.

[17] *Dallas Herald*, June 14, 1856; Houston *Tri-Weekly Telegraph*, May 30 and August 8, 1855.

but as a privately financed venture. Editor Baines "rendered valuable service," commented one pastor, and proved notable in his own right.[18] He left the *Texas Baptist* to become president of Baylor University, and his great-grandson, Lyndon Baines Johnson, became president of the United States in the following century.

As a rule, the religious journals in Texas printed general news stories but, with the exception of slavery, avoided political issues. Typically, they carried denominational news, inspirational stories, and theological discussions, and all of them accepted the responsibility of upgrading morals. They advocated temperance reform and the observance of the Sabbath and deplored vulgar language and crude manners. Appropriately, they gave unstinting encouragement to education, even at times giving special advertising rates to educational institutions.

By 1860 religious papers accounted for roughly one in every ten papers distributed in the state. *The Texas Christian Advocate* continued to lead all other papers, general or religious, in circulation. It boasted 4,500 subscribers; the *Texas Baptist*, 2,400; and the *Evangelische Apologete*, 2,000. Secular editors pointed to these figures with pride as evidence of the development of society. But these figures do not tell all of the story. Because of their high purpose, editors of religious papers even more than other editors fell behind in collections. The *Texas Christian Advocate* complained of 2,000 subscribers who failed to pay in 1859; and Justin Kimball, who succeeded Baines as editor and proprietor of the *Texas Baptist*, noted in 1861 that some 1,500 had received his paper for a year without paying.[19]

The Civil War brought an end not only to these specific religious papers but also to the genre. When church leaders resumed publication after the war, they discarded the secular aspects and instead made their papers more strictly denominational organs.

[18]Zachariah N. Morrell, *Flowers and Fruits in the Wilderness*, pp. 301–302; Tom Berger, *Baptist Journalism in Nineteenth-Century Texas*, pp. 1–23.

[19]Norton, "Religious Newspapers," p. 147; Berger, *Baptist Journalism*, p. 23.

CHAPTER 14

Zeitungen und Union

A growing and literate German population inspired the establishment of three presses and a corresponding number of newspapers before the Civil War. The brothers Christian H. and George Buechner of Galveston pioneered in the field, importing type from Germany shortly after annexation and launching a German-language newspaper. "A new journal styled the Galveston Zeitung is now published in Galveston," Francis Moore observed in the *Democratic Telegraph and Texas Register* of August 9, 1847, while Charles DeMorse greeted the paper in the *Standard* of September 4 by commenting that "the materials for it were imported from Germany, and are of superior quality."

Because of the language barrier, the English-speaking editors seldom excerpted items from the *Galveston Zeitung*, and because it aimed at a specific audience and gave them little competition for readers they paid it scant attention until the Know-Nothing and abolitionist issues developed in the 1850s.

George Buechner died of yellow fever November 23, 1847, but his brother continued the paper until 1855. Reputedly pressures from Know-Nothings caused him to discontinue the *Zeitung* and F. Muhr to begin in its stead in July, 1855, a Democratic paper, known variously as *Wochentliche* ("Weekly") *Union, Dreiwochentliche* ("Triweekly") *Union,* or *Wochentblatt* ("Weekly Paper") *der Union.* Ferdinand Flake purchased the paper in 1857 and made *Die Union* the most widely circulated paper in Galveston by the time of the Civil War.[1] Flake also

[1] Ben C. Stuart, "History of Newspapers in Texas" (manuscript, Houston Public Library), pp. [74, 98–99]; Rudolph Leopold Biesele, *The History of the German Settlements in Texas, 1831–1861*, p. 225; Earl W. Fornell, "Ferdinand Flake: German Pioneer Journalist of the Southwest," *American-German Review* 21 (February–March, 1955): 25; Lynnell Jackson, *True Witnesses: A Check List of Newspapers, 1845–1861*, pp. 15–16,

began publication of an English-language journal, *Flake's Bulletin*, which gained considerable importance and wide readership during and after the war.

By popular subscription, settlers in New Braunfels established the second German press in the state in 1852 and underwrote the founding of the historic *Neu-Braunfelser Zeitung*. The paper not only proved the most long-lived of the early German papers but also one of the most long-lived papers in the state generally. As New Braunfels *Herald and Zeitung*, it has continued into the last quarter of the twentieth century.

The *Zeitung* launched the journalism careers of two of the era's most interesting editors, Ferdinand Jacob Lindheimer and Adolph Douai. Both men were German intellectuals who found it politically expedient to leave home, and both achieved recognition in other fields—Lindheimer in botany and Douai in the labor movement and education. Both displayed a decided anticlericalism, and both exerted considerable influence over state affairs, but otherwise they had little in common. Lindheimer exerted a moderating influence in German-Anglo relations over a period of almost twenty years. Douai, by contrast, burst on the scene like a bombshell and in four years of residence promoted a scheme to divide the state and fueled the Know-Nothing movement, which in turn inspired the formal organization of the Democratic party. Along the way he also created the enduring but incorrect image that all Germans in the state advocated the abolition of slavery.

Lindheimer qualified as an old Texian. Born at Frankfort-on-the-Main on May 21, 1801, he attended the University of Bonn and emigrated to the new world after becoming involved in the student revolutions of 1833. He sojourned in Mexico for a time, beginning there the work that later brought him honor as a botanist. Upon the outbreak of the Texan Revolution he determined to join forces with the rebels. Taking the long route, he went to Mobile, where he joined a company of volunteers under Captain Jerome B. Robertson. He and his fellows landed at Galveston shortly before the Battle of San Jacinto and reached Sam Houston's army the day after the big battle.[2]

Throughout the 1840s Lindheimer collected botanical specimens

20, 67; Houston *Tri-Weekly Telegraph*, December 22, 1858; Houston *Texas Christian Advocate*, June 13, 1857; T. Herbert Etzler, "German-American Newspapers in Texas," *Southwestern Historical Quarterly* 57 (April, 1954): 423–24.

[2] Samuel Wood Geiser, *Naturalists of the Frontier*, pp. 132–47.

along the Texas frontier, giving his name to a score of plants, among them the *Opuntia lindheimeri*, familiarly the Texas prickly pear. "He bought a two-wheeled covered cart with a horse, loaded it with a pack of pressing-paper and a supply of the most indispensable provisions . . . and set forth into the wilderness," wrote one of his contemporaries. "Armed with his rifle and with no other companion than his two hunting dogs, he occupied himself with collecting and pressing plants. He depended for his subsistence mainly upon his hunting, often passing whole months at a time without seeing a human being."[3]

Lindheimer interrupted his collecting in 1844 to meet the first immigrants of the Adelsverein colony and guide them to the site chosen for the town of New Braunfels. Securing land as an immigrant, he built a house in the new town and in 1846 married Eleanore Reinarz.

The following year he joined forces with another group of recent arrivals from Europe, the Darmstadters or "The Forty," German intellectuals who intended to plant a communistic colony on the Texas frontier. Sparked by the leadership of Ferdinand Herff and Gustav Schleicher, this group of men attempted the settlement of Bettina, named for Bettina von Arnim, between the Llano and San Saba rivers. The colony "went to pieces like a bubble," recalled one of the settlers, because everybody worked only if he pleased, with the result that "less and less work was done as time progressed. Most of the professional men wanted to do the directing and ordering, while the mechanics and laborers were to carry out their plans. Of course, the latter failed to see the justice of this ruling."[4] The colonists scattered to the four winds in the summer of 1848, Herff going on to become a prominent physician in San Antonio, Schleicher to become a United States congressman and newspaperman, and Lindheimer to begin his career as editor of the *Neu-Braunfelser Zeitung*.

The movement to bring a press to New Braunfels began in 1851, when the citizens raised money by popular subscription to establish a newspaper that would advertise the town, attract immigrants, and enhance land values. Securing a third of the amount needed, they ordered the press from New York, but when it arrived at Indianola the shippers held it there awaiting settlement of the balance due.

[3] Ferdinand Roemer, *Texas: With Particular Reference to German Immigration*, p. 108.

[4] Louis Reinhardt, "The Communist Colony of Bettina (1846–8)," *Quarterly of the Texas State Historical Association* 3 (July, 1899): 33–40.

Carl Daniel Adolph Douai, fresh from troubles in Europe, arrived in the same season as the press. Four feet eight inches tall, he displayed throughout life a penchant for controversy inversely proportionate to his height. Before his death he could boast of being forced from his native land because of his revolutionary activities, from Texas because of his abolitionist stand, and from Boston because of his religion, or rather his lack of it. When he died in January, 1888, the *Workmen's Advocate*, the official journal of the Socialist Labor Party, lauded him as an "agitator," labor leader, socialist, and educator and noted that he had begun the kindergarten movement in the United States.[5]

Born in Saxon Altenburg on February 22, 1819, Douai married the Baroness Agnes von Beust and eventually fathered ten children. He participated in the abortive 1848 revolution, serving time in prison for his activities, and upon his release sailed for Texas. Arriving with his growing family in May, 1852, he proceeded to New Braunfels and began casting about for means to earn a livelihood. A gifted musician, he first organized a concert to help pay for the press. This effort raised half of the balance still due, and Lindheimer, who had accepted the position of managing editor, assumed the remainder of the debt. The press thus came to New Braunfels, and the *Neu-Braunfelser Zeitung* made its debut November 12, 1852. Something over a year later, a visitor from the northeastern United States declared it "of much higher character than most of the German American papers."[6] Lindheimer continued as editor until August 18, 1872, sprinkling its pages with Latin terms and classical references and treating his readers to learned discourses as well as pertinent news and editorials.

Strangely, in view of Lindheimer's long tenure, Douai later recalled him as being "poorly adapted to serve as editor" and for that reason having invited Douai to help put out the paper. "But my very first editorial misfired so greatly that I never again tried another," wrote Douai. With his usual knack for controversy, he mocked the townspeople for petitioning the legislature for a university and electing its president before one cent of money had been appropriated. In the en-

---

[5] Douai's height is gleaned from his passport, and other biographical information from his obituary in the *Workmen's Advocate*, January 28, 1888, and from his autobiography, translated by his grandson Richard H. Douai Boerker, hereafter cited as Douai, "Autobiography." All are in the Douai Papers at the University of Texas.

[6] Frederick Law Olmsted, *A Journey Through Texas*, p. 178.

suing hassle, Douai cut short his association with the paper and tried his hand, also unsuccessfully, at teaching school and manufacturing cigars.[7]

Moving to San Antonio, Douai earned a living for a time as a musician and made the acquaintance of a group of "forty-eighters" and other intellectuals who resided in the vicinity, among them Ottomar von Behr, Gustav Theissen, Ferdinand Herff, Gustav Schleicher, Hermann Spiess, and Charles N. Riotte.

As in New Braunfels, his arrival coincided with a popular movement to establish a German press. At the insistence of his friends Riotte and Theissen, he agreed to edit the new paper, and at a meeting of stockholders in the enterprise he explained that he would follow social-democratic ideals in matters of policy. Asked his choice for president had he been a citizen in 1852, he replied Franklin Pierce, for he considered Pierce a friend of the workingman. "That seemed to win unanimous approval," Douai wrote in his memoirs. He did not explain that he chose Pierce only as the lesser of two evils, for both candidates in the election endorsed slavery, which he opposed.[8]

The press arrived in good time, and the *San Antonio Zeitung* appeared in July, 1853, without mention of slavery in its early issues. "Julius Froebel, who at that time had just returned from a trip to Mexico, and who was stopping off at San Antonio, furnished the first number an account of his travels," Douai recalled. "I printed the paper myself and with the help of the typesetter printed it from the first to the very last issue."[9]

Ironically, Douai, the labor agitator and workingman's friend, immediately ran into labor troubles in his role as editor. "We had a German typesetter by the name of John whom we entertained for $40 per month until the paper paid its way," wrote Douai. "But after setting only a few numbers he wanted to get paid for setting by the 1000 numbers of issues which would have increased his wages to $70 per month."

When Douai refused, the typesetter not only quit the job but plastered the walls of the town with posters that accused Douai of unfair labor practices—posters printed, as a crowning indignity, by one of

---

[7] Douai, "Autobiography," pp. 105–106; *Neu-Braunfelser Zeitung*, December 17, 1852.

[8] Douai, "Autobiography," p. 109.

[9] Ibid., p. 113.

the competing English offices. Douai found another typesetter, named Kiedner, and began himself to learn typesetting.[10]

A more crucial problem developed with the arrival of Frederick Law Olmsted and his brother Dr. John Hull Olmsted in the winter of 1853–54. An ardent abolitionist, Frederick Law Olmsted had previously written a book of his tour of the southern states, and he came to Texas to gather material for a companion volume and to further his pet cause. His brother, suffering from tuberculosis, came in search of health. They formed a warm friendship with Douai, who introduced them to his friends in San Antonio and guided them to Sisterdale, where a number of German intellectuals had settled. "There are certain persons with whom acquaintance ripens rapidly," Olmsted wrote of the editor. "Our companion, we found, was one of these. We listened to some details of a varied and stormy life, in learning what brought him here, and were not long in falling into discussions that ran through deep water, and demanded all our skill in navigation."[11]

The "deep water" concerned a plan hatched by the Olmsteds, Douai, and his friends to create the free state of West Texas. At the time proslavery and antislavery forces contended for Kansas, and the Olmsteds had contacts with abolitionist groups in the North, who sent immigrants and supplies into Kansas. Why not, Frederick Law Olmsted suggested to his German friends, do something similar in Texas? The western area included a large number of Germans and Mexicans and very few slaveholders. If all the state could not be freed of slavery, then at least it could be divided as provided in the terms of annexation, and a new state of West Texas created as a free state.

The suggestion fired Douai's imagination, and even three decades later he remembered it with enthusiasm. "We Germans in West Texas enjoyed an impregnable strategic position," he wrote in his memoirs. To the south lay the Gulf of Mexico, to the north the desert, to the rear the antislavery Republic of Mexico. From north to south across Texas stretched a chain of German settlements, which could furnish from ten to fifteen thousand former soldiers ready to take the field on short notice. "We were not only impregnable behind the Colorado River, but we also could train and arm the fleeing negroes and advance from one river defense line to another; from the Colorado to the Brazos to the

---

[10] Ibid.
[11] Ibid., Olmsted, *Journey*, pp. 187–88.

Trinity to the Sabine. We would with the support of the North roll back slavery to Louisiana and even further to the East."[12]

The schemers pledged themselves to secrecy until the time ripened for action and laid their plans with care. The Olmsteds departed, promising to organize support for the movement in the North, and Douai promised to use his press for the cause when the moment came. Frederick Law Olmsted accordingly planted stories in New York papers designed to attract settlers of free-soil sentiment without alarming those of opposite sentiment. He hoped thereby to avoid creating another Kansas, where immigrants of both factions engaged in open warfare. In the same period, his brother, in fast-declining health, edited the classic book on their journey from the journal Frederick had kept, praising the natural resources of Texas, lauding the German element as uniformly opposed to slavery, and downgrading the slaveholding elements as coarse, wasteful, and inefficient. Both Olmsteds contacted abolitionist friends, asking for money to finance the project.[13]

Rumors of the plot surfaced in the spring of 1854 in connection with plans for a statewide meeting of German singing societies (Staats-Saengerfest) at San Antonio on May 14 and 15. Douai's friends at Sisterdale had organized a political club, Der frei Verein ("the Free Society") that opposed slavery. This club issued a call for all Germans in the state to meet in convention on the occasion of the songfest to secure their place in political affairs.

Various organizations sent delegates to the convention, and under the guidance of Der frei Verein at Sisterdale they issued a platform that called for political reforms such as the popular election of the president of the United States and pronounced that "slavery is an evil the removal of which is absolutely necessary according to the principles of democracy."[14]

Upon its publication, the platform stirred up a storm of protest and showed that Douai and the Olmsteds had misjudged German sentiment. They had, in fact, accepted the sentiment of a few intellectuals as representative of the entire German population. The first protests

[12] Douai, "Autobiography," pp. 111–12, 114.

[13] Charles Capen McLaughlin, ed., *The Papers of Frederick Law Olmsted: The Formative Years*, pp. 3–46; Laura W. Roper, "Frederick Law Olmsted and the Western Texas Free Soil Movement," *American Historical Review* 56 (October, 1950): 58–64.

[14] Biesele, *German Settlements*, pp. 196–204; "The Texas State Convention of Germans in 1854," *Southwestern Historical Quarterly* 33 (April, 1930): 247–61.

against the platform came from within the German community with Lindheimer in the lead. He printed letters from Alexander Rossy of New Braunfels and Friedrich Ernst of Mill Creek, which maintained that the San Antonio convention did not represent Germans in general and criticized the platform, especially the antislavery plank, as impolitic and detrimental to the interests of both the Germans and the state as a whole.[15]

Douai, ignoring the German opposition and obviously thinking that the moment had come for his and the Olmsteds' grand plan, endorsed the platform. As a result, the stockholders in the paper split among themselves over its policy and determined to sell it. By appealing to the Olmsteds for a loan of $350, borrowing money locally, and selling his home in New Braunfels, Douai managed to purchase the paper.[16]

But worse times lay ahead of him. Because of the language barrier, Anglo editors and readers became aware of the platform only slowly and only as Germans began assuring them that it did not represent the mass of the German population. The matter created a storm of controversy, as editors debated whether the Germans were or were not abolitionist. It also acted as catalyst in Anglo-American politics, for Douai endorsed the platform just as the American, or Know-Nothing, movement reached Texas, and he accounted in large measure for its rapid growth there. The Anglo editors almost to a man opposed anything that smacked of abolitionism, but they reacted differently to the circumstances. The rival Austin editors, John S. Ford and John Marshall, represented the division. Ford converted to the new party to demand that foreigners not tell Americans how to manage their affairs. Calling attention to the nearness of Douai's press to the San Antonio River, he urged the local citizens to "Pitch in!" By contrast, Marshall found the new party more alarming than the reported abolitionism of the Germans. He defended the mass of Germans from the charges and, spearheading the formal organization of the Democratic party, welcomed them into it.[17]

For a time, Know-Nothing threats of violence united the German

[15] *Neu-Braunfelser Zeitung,* May 26 and June 9, 1854.
[16] Douai, "Autobiography," pp. 117–18.
[17] Austin *Texas State Times,* May 19, 1855.

population of San Antonio behind Douai, and he kept his paper afloat. Indeed, things went well for a while. By submitting a low bid, he obtained a contract from the state to print the laws in German. He and his printer-partner Kiedner purchased lithographic equipment that promised to improve their business, and he contracted to print a Spanish-language newspaper, *El Bejareño*, published by Xavier Blanchard DeBray.

But just as Douai and the Olmsteds had misjudged the sentiment of the mass of Texas Germans, so Douai misjudged the support for the West Texas movement. Thus in the February 9, 1855, issue of the *San Antonio Zeitung*, he came out boldly in favor of the free state of West Texas. "If West Texas through the agitation of my newspaper became a slave-free state, then my business speculation would have have succeeded," he wrote later. "If the agitation failed, then it was immaterial how much I lost."[18]

His stand brought ruin to the paper. Subscribers cancelled their subscriptions, and businessmen their advertising. Rowdies threatened to lynch him and throw his press into the river; creditors called in their loans. His partner Kiedner joined forces with the enemy, and even his friends fell away. "My comrades in the movement, Riotte, Theissen, Behr, Degener and others should have supported me with cash donations but they said that at the moment they had no means," he recalled. To make matters worse, the lithographic business proved a failure.

"There began for me a time of the greatest peril," he later wrote. He reduced the size of the paper, set the type himself, continued printing *El Bejareño*, and took on job printing that kept him working fourteen hours a day and sometimes all night.[19]

At the same time he suffered harassment from his opponents. In his memoirs he remembered—perhaps constructively—an encounter with John S. Ford of the Austin *Texas State Times*, an encounter that Ford—perhaps conveniently—forgot in his memoirs. Ford accused Douai of being in the pay of abolitionists. Douai responded in an English editorial, accusing Ford of lying, whereupon Ford came to Douai's

[18] Douai, "Autobiography," p. 117.
[19] Ibid., p. 119.

office to demand a retraction. Douai declined and recalled that in the ensuing fight "I quietly beat him up until he bled, even though he was very much stronger and bigger than I was."[20]

He also recalled harassment from a border ruffian who stormed into his printing office yelling: "Are you the God-damned Abolitionist?" Douai laid down a large piece of type, stood erect and responded, "I am; what do you want?" The ruffian, taken aback by his openness, moved backward toward the door "mumbling unintelligible words" as Douai advanced from behind his composition table.[21]

But Douai's bravado availed nothing. By March, 1856, "my situation and that of my newspaper had become unbearable to the point of starvation," he recalled. He also learned through a friend that a group that included Germans in the legislature, Gustav Schleicher and Jacob Waelder, had organized to drive him and all other abolitionists from Texas. At this point, he decided to give up and accepted an offer from H. F. Oswald, of the opposition faction, for the printing press and paper. Together with his wife, six children, and father, he departed from Texas on May 10, 1856, exactly four years after his arrival, carrying with him bitter memories. The Anglo Texans he considered "very cowardly"; the mass of Germans he decided too late were "with very few exceptions a reactionary and ignorant lot"; and his friends had not properly supported him. "If the other German abolitionists had made as big financial sacrifices as I did, then I would have continued the fight," he wrote.[22]

Nor, unlike his friend Olmsted, did he find praise for the land itself. "Romance is cheap in a land where there are large rivers but little water and even scarcer bridges," he declared, "where there are half-broken roads and deep gulleys but no railroads; where there are plenty of wild animals and poisonous snakes; and where even domesticated animals and many humans are half or entirely wild."[23]

He later learned with ill-concealed satisfaction the fate of some of his enemies: H. F. Oswald, who had purchased the newspaper and engaged in a tirade with him, had died a lingering and painful death shortly afterward, and his brother Theodore Oswald, who edited the

[20] Ibid., p. 120.
[21] Ibid., p. 121.
[22] Ibid., pp. 110, 121, 124–28.
[23] Ibid., p. 130.

paper, had become an officer in the Civil War and disappeared from the earth without leaving a trace. Gus Schleicher, another owner, had lost his fortune despite his political triumphs.

Eleven years after Douai's departure—a period that saw secession, the Civil War, and emancipation—he received a copy of a newspaper that somewhat redeemed his Texas experience: "This newspaper, the first to be founded in Texas by Negroes, was printed on the same press which Dr. Adolf Douai founded in San Antonio in 1853 in order to combat slavery," said the first article. "It will be a great satisfaction to him that the freed slaves of Texas gratefully remember his dangerous and courageous agitation in their behalf."[24]

[24] Ibid.

CHAPTER 15

Of Press and Party: Whigs

TEXAS entered the Union with predilections for the Democratic party that lasted for more than a century. The established press reflected general sentiment. "The great question of annexation has necessarily thrown us with the Democratic party of the Union, for it has been mainly through the unwearied efforts of that party that this measure has been effected," Francis Moore wrote. He and Jacob Cruger then took their stand by changing the name of their paper to the *Democratic Telegraph and Texas Register*.[1]

Other editors followed their lead. At Austin John S. Ford and Michael Cronican discontinued the *National Register*, which reputedly had opposed annexation, launched the *Texas Democrat*, and issued a call for the organization of the Democratic party. At San Augustine A. W. Canfield averred in the *Red-Lander* that "no true friend of Texas" could adhere to the Whig party and that even people who had been the most ardent Whig partisans in the United States had changed their political creed after making Texas their home.[2]

The Mexican War and subsequent boundary dispute confirmed Texans in their political loyalties, for the Whigs generally opposed both the war and Texas' claims along the Rio Grande. Even so, the Whigs established several newspapers and campaigned actively during the presidential elections of 1848 and 1852. Whig papers sprouted in the areas where that party found most of its adherents—the Gulf Coast or northeast—and generally its adherents represented commercial in-

---

[1] Houston *Telegraph and Texas Register*, October 22, 1845.
[2] San Augustine *Red-Lander*, November 13, 1845. See also E. W. Winkler, ed., *Platforms of Political Parties in Texas*, pp. 11–17.

terests or those who wanted river and harbor improvements at the expense of the federal government.[3]

The most successful of the Whig editors played down party affiliation to urge Texans to vote for the man or issue rather than the party label. Thus, the old Whig newsmen John D. Logan and Thomas Sterne declared their Victoria *Texan Advocate* neutral in politics at the same time as they touted the military prowess of Zachary Taylor. Willard Richardson, reportedly a closet Whig in 1848, advised his readers to vote independently, for "both northern parties are united against us." The *Galveston Journal*, a Whig party organ, urged readers in 1850 to lay aside party organization until the agitation over slavery ended. "In other States the terms, Whig and Democrat, have almost been forgotten in the absorbing questions of union or disunion," wrote the editor. "The Whigs of Texas are for the Union, and, therefore, from the highest motives that can prompt men in their political views, desire no strict organization until that Union is safe from the agitation which at present threatens it."[4]

On the eve of the presidential election of 1848, Francis Moore found eastern Texas as much involved in party politics as any part of the United States but other parts of the state comparatively little interested in the contest. And in Houston on election day he reported little of the ill feeling that had characterized some previous elections. "The Whigs expected to be defeated, of course, and only wished a respectable minority," he observed in the *Telegraph*. "The Democrats, on the other hand, although confident of success, were desirous of obtaining a respectable majority. The result appears to have pleased both parties."[5]

Zachary Taylor received roughly one-third of the vote statewide, a respectable showing indeed in view of the image of his party. Moore attributed the showing to Democrats who, "dazzled by the military fame of General Taylor," wandered from their party by mistake and who would return to the fold in good season.[6] Only after Taylor took office did his derogatory remark about Texas—"Thank God, the last

[3] Randolph Campbell, "The Whig Party of Texas in the Elections of 1848 and 1852," *Southwestern Historical Quarterly* 73 (July, 1969): 17–34.

[4] *Galveston News*, April 27, 1848; *Galveston Journal*, December 24, 1850.

[5] Houston *Democratic Telegraph and Texas Register*, October 5 and November 9, 1848.

[6] Ibid., November 9, 1848.

Texan has been discharged"—receive wide circulation and his stand on the boundary issue arouse hostility to him.

Shortly before the election, Francis Moore counted twenty-one newspapers in Texas and, excluding three religious journals, listed them by party. He placed eight in the Democratic column: his own *Telegraph*, the *Texas Democrat* at Austin, the *Union* at San Augustine, the *Standard* at Clarksville, the *Banner* at Huntsville, the *Civilian* and *Zeitung* at Galveston, and the *Times* at Nacogdoches. Four openly supported the Whigs: the *Spirit of the Age* at Jefferson, the *Western Star* at Clarksville, the *Pioneer* at Rusk, and the *Western Argus* at Bonham. Four declared themselves neutral: the *Texian Advocate* at Victoria, the *Herald* at Port Lavaca, the *Corpus Christi Star*, and the *News* at Galveston. Two—the *Star State Patriot* at Marshall and the Matagorda *Tribune*—defied classification because of their equivocal stands.[7] Moore admitted that many observers disagreed with the neutral classification of the *Galveston News*, and indeed its exhortations that Texans remain independent of both parties smacked of expedient Whiggism and reflected the Calhoun brand of Southern Whiggery. In view of the record, observers might also have questioned the neutrality of the *Texian Advocate*, which boasted of having first mentioned Zachary Taylor for president.

Of the declared Whig papers, the *Spirit of the Age* proved the most ephemeral. A campaign sheet, it appeared only weeks before the election. Francis Moore received the first two numbers the second week in October and under the heading "Interesting Whig Paper" commented that "one side of each of the numbers is blank. These blank sides are very interesting and instructive. . . . They are the best example of the present 'Whig Platform' that we have seen in a coon's age." The paper disappeared as suddenly as it appeared. The following February the *Northern Standard* reported that the printing office had been sold and would be moved to Mount Pleasant, but instead it remained in Jefferson, where the *Independent Monitor*, a politically neutral paper edited by Dr. J. M. Baker, began in June, 1849.[8]

The *Western Star* stirred up more party controversy than any other Whig paper in 1848, in part because it challenged Charles De-

[7] Ibid., October 5, 1848.
[8] Ibid., October 12, 1848; Clarksville *Northern Standard*, February 24, 1849; Marshall *Texas Republican*, June 15, 1849.

Morse in Clarksville. The *Star* appeared on August 11, 1847, for the stated purpose of advocating "generally the doctrines of the Whig party in the United States." The proprietor, W. J. F. Morgan, formerly foreman of DeMorse's printing office, announced that the paper would appear weekly on an imperial sheet under the motto "The Constitution and Liberty." Edited by Judge William Trimble of Hempstead County, Arkansas, the paper promptly launched an attack on President Polk's conduct of the war and began boosting Zachary Taylor for president.[9]

Charles DeMorse, in deference to prominent Whigs among his readers, had announced the political neutrality of the *Standard*, but the appearance of the *Western Star* pushed him into heated editorial support of the "Great Party" that had brought Texas into the Union. Charging that his rival organ took part against its own country in regard to the war and that Whigs represented privileged groups, he declared that "the time has arrived for every man in this state to know his fellow, politically speaking." So that all would know him he added to the masthead of the *Standard* the words "A Democratic Republican Journal Advocating Equal Rights, Principles Before Men, and Opposed to All Chartered Monopolies." He then began a running attack on a shadowy "secret" editor of the *Star* as opposed to the announced editor. "Donning our armor and unfurling our banner, we stand in the arena armed for the strife," he wrote. The *Star* remained at Clarksville until 1850, giving competition and exchanging barbs with the *Standard*. Then it moved to Paris, where it continued under the same name, with the Reverend Thomas Lewelling serving as editor in 1851.[10]

The other two Whig papers on Francis Moore's list in 1848 owed much to Joseph Addison Clark, the Johnny Appleseed of such journals in that season. A preacher, lawyer, surveyor, miller, educator, and journalist, Clark made his most lasting contribution by establishing with his sons, Addison and Randolph, the institution Add-Ran College, which grew into Texas Christian University. Born in Illinois on November 6, 1815, he changed his name from Zachariah to Joseph Addison after reading the *Spectator Papers*. His father disappeared to Texas in 1826, and by the following year young Clark and other family members

[9] *Northern Standard*, August 14, 1847; Lynnell Jackson, *True Witnesses: A Check List of Newspapers, 1845–1861*, p. 66.

[10] *Northern Standard*, August 14, September 4 and 11, and November 4, 1847; *Galveston News*, March 11, 1850; Jackson, *True Witnesses*, p. 66.

resided in Selma, Alabama, where he worked with George W. Bonnell on the *Southern Argus*, a pro-Masonic newspaper. By 1841, Clark had joined Bonnell in Austin to work on the *Sentinel* and to publish, together with John Henry Brown and Martin Carroll Wing, Bonnell's *Topographical Description of Texas*.

Clark then shifted his activities to northern and eastern Texas, never remaining long in one place or in one calling. He contributed articles to the *Red-Lander*, speculated in land, and in 1847 resumed his journalistic career for the benefit of the Whig party. He joined with John Shaffer to establish the *Western Argus* at Bonham. "The paper at Bonham has again changed hands, and is now under the editorial charge of Jos. A. Clark . . . a gentleman of good capacity, and a practical printer," the *Northern Standard* noted on May 19, 1847. Later that year, after the editor of the *Shield* murdered the editor of the *Red-Lander* at San Augustine, Clark purchased the *Red-Lander* press. But he did not establish a Whig newspaper on that traditionally pro-Houston press. Instead in December, 1847, he sold the press to the Reverend William N. Harman, who also purchased the *Shield* press and combined both of the earlier papers into the *Texas Union*.

The following year Clark left the *Argus* and moved to Rusk, where he established the *Rusk Pioneer*, another Whig newspaper and one that soundly denounced both Andrew Jackson and his protégé Sam Houston. Clark's tenure at the *Pioneer* ended early and in violence. He practiced law in Rusk in partnership with Rufus Chandler, and, either because of a lawsuit or editorial policy, the partners aroused animosity. The malcontents ambushed and killed Chandler and threatened Clark's life, prompting him to carry a gun and make plans to relocate. On March 23, 1848, for the sum of $150, he sold the "Rusk Pioneer press, type and appurtenances" to John Shaffer, his former associate on the Bonham *Western Argus*. But Clark, together with W. R. Culp, continued to publish the paper until after the election. The *Telegraph* reported shortly thereafter that "The Rusk Pioneer, a Whig paper, has been sold to Messrs. Glidewell & Parsons, who intend to publish a Democratic paper at Rusk."[11]

By September, 1849, Joseph Addison Clark resided in Palestine, where he established another paper, first called the *Pioneer* and later

[11] *Democratic Telegraph and Texas Register*, November 30, 1848.

the *Trinity Advocate*. Party politics being in a lull, the paper began agitating for the improvement of the Trinity River by diverting to it water from the Red River. That project proving visionary, his son wrote years later, Clark "left the paper in charge of James Ewing who had been associated with him at Bonham and Rusk, and went to Galveston with the purpose of establishing a paper." James W. Ewing, in association variously with Matthew Dale and A. E. McClure, continued the *Advocate* until about the Civil War and together with McClure re-established it in 1867. Under a new owner it became a daily in 1893.[12]

Clark did not establish a paper at Galveston, for, his son related, he found Willard Richardson "of the same political faith occupying the territory." Clark worked for Richardson for a time and then moved on to other pursuits. Thereafter, from time to time he returned to journalism but confined his efforts to religious publications.[13]

The national success of the Whigs in 1848 encouraged the founding of several new Whig presses in Texas. The news of Taylor's election had scarcely reached the state when Launcelot Abbotts established the *Mercantile Advertiser* at Houston, for the stated purpose of advancing Whig principles. Francis Moore greeted the *Advertiser* with the tolerance he reserved for those newspapers that posed no particular threat to the *Telegraph*. "It is as large as the *Christian Advocate*," he commented, "and its typographic execution is not surpassed by any paper in the State. As it has no ostensible editor, we shall say nothing of its editorial department." Eighteen months later he bid the publisher a pleasant farewell. "A new paper to be called the Texas Monument will soon be published at Lagrange by Mr. L. Abbots of this city late publisher of the Mercantile Advertiser. Mr. Abbots is one of the old settlers of Texas and passed through many trying scenes in the days of our country's greatest peril. . . . Mr. Abbots is one of the best printers in the state."[14]

In the same season that the *Mercantile Advertiser* struggled to survive in Houston, R. C. Wheeler established a press at Henderson that produced a series of short-lived Whig or Whiggish papers. The

[12] Joseph Lynn Clark, *Thank God We Made It!*, pp. 207–17; Jackson, *True Witnesses*, p. 2.

[13] See Clark, *Thank God We Made It!*, pp. 207–17.

[14] *Democratic Telegraph and Texas Register*, December 28, 1848, and June 13, 1850.

Texas Statesman began publication in March, 1849, and gave way in July to the *Aegis of Truth*, whose editors, commented Robert W. Loughery of Marshall, had the reputation of being Whigs. The paper ended in March, 1850, when Editor F. A. Wingfield purchased the *Shreveport Journal*. Next came the *Texas Whig*, "printed with the same material of the Aegis of the Truth of which paper it is a fair representative," and edited by a young lawyer, Isaac Dansby. The *Texas Whig* existed only a few months, giving way to a Democratic paper, the *Flag of the Union*, which appeared October 12, 1850, published and edited by William M. Messenger. Messenger continued the paper in association first with William H. Estill and then with James R. Armstrong until his death. The paper swung back and forth in politics. In 1854 it declared itself politically neutral, whereupon local Democrats threatened to establish a rival press. In an attempt to please everyone, Messenger and Armstrong dissolved their partnership, and Messenger edited the *Flag*, again a Democratic paper, while Armstrong founded the *Texas State Intelligencer*, a Whig paper—"one of the old fashioned ultra sort"—which utilized the same press.[15]

By then the Whig party had hastened its ruin in Texas by nominating Winfield Scott, a free-soiler, for president. Several state leaders left the party; the *Victoria Advocate* announced that although it was Whig owned, it would not support Scott; other papers followed its lead; and only the *Star State Patriot* at Marshall and the *Galveston Journal* supported the Whig ticket in 1852.

Francis Moore had found the *Patriot* impossible to classify in 1848 because of the recent death of its editor, H. B. Kelsey. Begun in early 1848 on the press formerly used by the *Soda Lake Herald* and owned by T. A. and J. C. Harris, the paper lost its editor, a highly respected minister, temperance leader, and Mason, before the election. Kelsey had leaned toward the Democrats, but the next editor, Howard Burnside, made the paper neutral in politics, and a change in ownership in 1850 made it Whig. The Harrises sold the press office to A. N. Witherspoon, who employed W. A. Tarleton, professor at the local college, as editor, and launched an editorial war against Robert W. Loughery of the neighboring *Texas Republican*. Describing himself as a "compromise Whig," Witherspoon urged acceptance of the Compromise of

1850 and labeled the Whig party as the party of union. He placed at the masthead of the paper the words: "The loss of liberty, of all good government, of peace, plenty, and happiness must inevitably follow the dissolution of the Union."

By September, 1851, the economics of newspapering had forced A. N. Witherspoon to sell the paper to John F. Witherspoon and Josiah Marshall, who strained their resources to keep it going until after the election of 1852. Marshall became sole editor and proprietor in May, 1852, and not only endorsed "Windfield" Scott, a spelling error that excited considerable mirth among Democratic editors, but issued a *Campaign Patriot* to further the cause. At the close of the campaign, Marshall denied rumors that the paper would be suspended, but on April, 1853, he turned it over to S. H. Parsons and E. Junius Foster, also Whigs, and the following February he offered the office for sale.[16]

The story of the *Galveston Journal*, the leading Whig paper in the state in 1852, followed the same pattern, although it won unstinted praise for its makeup from Democratic editors. That veteran Galveston newsman and founder of the *News*, Wilbur Cherry, joined with John M. Gibson to publish the *Journal*, and the first issue appeared in February, 1850, edited by Robert H. Howard. By then the issues of abolition, disunion, and slavery in the territories were redrawing party lines, and Francis Moore welcomed the *Journal* with a warmth that reflected some of his own changing attitudes. Indeed, only a few months later Moore removed the word "Democratic" from the title of his paper. Moore noted with approval the "truly Democratic motto" adopted by the *Journal*—"Error ceases to be dangerous when truth is left free to combat it"—and declared that if all Whig papers in the Union were conducted with the same moderation as the *Journal* party animosity would vanish. "If this first number is a fair specimen, the party have just reason to feel proud of it," he wrote. "The editorial department evinces so much candor, liberalism and true patriotism that we might readily have supposed it to be a Democratic journal if the editor had not stated positively that it is devoted to the cause of the Whigs." Even more staunchly Democratic editors than Moore ad-

---

[16] *Democratic Telegraph and Texas Register*, November 30, 1848; Marshall *Star State Patriot*, June 7, 1851, January 17, March 13 and 20, April 10, May 22, and July 3, 1852, and January 29, 1853; *Texas Republican*, January 10, April 4, and July 6, 1850, April 3 and 27, May 9, 13, and 22, and July 3, 1851, April 2, 1853, and February 11 and September 30, 1854; Austin *Texas State Gazette*, July 20, 1850.

mired the *Journal*. It contained more good reading material than any paper in the state, said Robert W. Loughery, and "aside from its Whiggery and false notions . . . evinces talent and industry."[17]

But despite its excellent reports, the *Journal* suffered the usual hardships of new papers and especially new Whig papers. B. E. Tarver replaced Howard as editor only months after the founding of the paper, and Cherry bought out Gibson in July, 1851. When, the next January, the trustees threatened to foreclose the mortgage, Cherry kept the paper alive by appealing to his patrons to pay their bills and bringing in S. Carter as a new publisher. By June, 1853, Cherry had removed himself, leaving S. Carter and Company as publisher, and in early 1854 the paper went into the hands of T. J. Allen. In the meantime, H. H. Smith, who had become editor in June, 1852, had died of yellow fever in October, 1853.[18]

The Whigs received roughly 25 percent of the vote in Texas in the election of 1852, and shortly thereafter the party disintegrated nationwide. It never posed a real threat to the Democrats in Texas, and they had thus never found it necessary to organize or expend great effort to defeat it. "The state of parties in Texas does not demand at the hands of a Democratic paper any extravagant outlay of time or labor," commented the *Texas State Gazette* in the summer of 1852. "The Whigs are a helpless minority, and it is but time thrown away by a press to devote any unusual space to the men or the measures of either party."[19]

Whig newspapers in Texas reflected the weakness of their party—and its persistence. They vanished along with it, but they tended to reemerge under new names as organs of opposition to the Democrats.

[17] *Democratic Telegraph and Texas Register*, February 14, 1850; *Texas Republican*, January 25, 1851, and March 5, 1852.

[18] *Texas State Gazette*, January 24 and July 3, 1852; Washington *Texas Ranger*, January 12, 1854; *Galveston Journal*, March 15, 1850, January 28 and June 17, 1853; *Texas Republican*, October 24, 1854.

[19] *Texas State Gazette*, August 7, 1852.

CHAPTER 16

The Invincible Sam

A mysterious presence called "Sam" moved from the eastern United States into Texas early in the 1850s. He was, said one who knew him, "the embodiment of liberty," and, said another, he rode his war horse over the plains of the New World to wound both of the old parties and establish another—"an American Party that will live forever."[1] Sam's party, commonly called the Know-Nothing, did what the Whig party did not. It scared the Democrats of Texas into organizing. It also inspired a host of newspapers, some of them favoring the party and others opposing it.

The new party began as a secret movement, similar to the fraternal organizations that attracted Americans of the era. Complete with ritual, it opposed the foreign-born and the Roman Catholic church in the United States, and it took the high ground in regard to patriotism and preservation of the Union. Indeed, because of the secrecy and ritual, some early recruits did not recognize it immediately as a political party and withdrew when they discovered its true nature.

After its emergence as a political party, under the name American party, it attracted a variety of adherents other than nativists. Old Whigs, stranded by the disintegration of their party, saw it as a haven, as did Democrats disgruntled with theirs. In addition, it turned attention away from the slavery issue, thus appealing to those disturbed by the virulent sectionalism and the drift toward disunion.

Texas, with its large number of German immigrants and Spanish-speaking citizens, offered a promising field to the Know-Nothing party, and it arrived in the state at the most opportune of all moments—just

[1] See W. Darrell Overdyke, *The Know-Nothing Party in the South*, pp. 180–83.

as Adolph Douai launched his editorial move in the *San Antonio Zeitung* to create the free state of West Texas. Douai had intended to strike a blow for abolition, but instead he almost single-handedly launched the Know-Nothings in Texas. Douai labeled the German population—permanently—as anti-slavery and touched the nerve that determined the course of events. Some ardent Southerners saw the Germans as a threat to the peculiar institution and reasoned that a party opposed to foreign immigration must favor slavery. Thus in Texas the Know-Nothing party appealed to two diverse groups—those who saw it as a distraction from the divisive issue and those who saw it as favoring the Southern view.[2]

Leaders of the party gathered at Washington on the Brazos in June, 1855, ostensibly to attend a river improvement meeting. Secretly, they nominated a slate of candidates for office, drawing the lines between political party and patriotic organization. One early recruit, W. S. Oldham, co-editor of the *Texas State Gazette*, withdrew in anger upon learning the true purpose of the Know-Nothings, and his partner, John Marshall, promptly sounded the alarm among the Democratic faithful. Marshall perfected the formal organization of the Democrats and placed himself at their head. A spirited campaign along party lines followed, making the state for the first time, in the words of one editor, "only an abridged map of the state of politics throughout the Union."[3]

Still the lines of the American party remained somewhat blurred. It nominated for governor in 1855 the then lieutenant governor, David C. Dickson, who had already been endorsed for reelection by some of the leading Democratic newspapers. Some of those papers continued to support Dickson, at the same time denying support of the Know-Nothing party. Because of the anomalies, Democratic converts could recant after the disintegration of the Know-Nothings and return to the fold with the explanation that they had been deceived.

The most notable convert in Texas was Sam Houston, whose votes as senator had ruined him with the southern wing of the Democratic party. The word *Sam* thus took a double and sometimes confusing

[2] On the Know-Nothing party in Texas, see Litha Crews, "The Know Nothing Party in Texas" (M.A. thesis, University of Texas, Austin, 1925); and Ralph A. Wooster, "An Analysis of the Texas Know-Nothings," *Southwestern Historical Quarterly* 70 (January, 1967): 414–23.

[3] Austin *Texas State Times*, October 27, 1855.

meaning during the Know-Nothing years in Texas, referring inter-changeably to the party symbol and to the most important local recruit.[4]

Generally, the presses and editors who had been Whiggish switched allegiance to the American party. For example, the *Galveston Journal* combined with another struggling paper, the *Times*, in 1855 to become the *Confederate*, a Know-Nothing paper that vanished quietly when the party followed the Whigs into history. J. D. Logan, the Whig founder of the *Victoria Advocate*, purchased the *San Antonio Herald*, a Know-Nothing paper, in 1856; the *Star State Patriot* at Marshall be-came the Know-Nothing *Harrison Flag*, edited by J. W. Barrett; and the *Flag of the Union* at Henderson became the *Star Spangled Ban-ner*, with an old Whig, J. W. Flanagan, as proprietor and his son Web-ster Flanagan as editor.

But former Whigs composed only a portion of the Know-Nothing press support. Some Democratic editors converted to the new party, and it established a number of papers of its own. Because of the initial secrecy, the blurred lines, and the wavering loyalties, the exact num-ber of journalist supporters remains doubtful, as does the exact posi-tion of a few. The ultra-Democratic press considered some "mongrels." For example, the *Telegraph* and the *Nacogdoches Chronicle* supported the Know-Nothing candidate for governor in 1855, at the same time denying that they belonged to the party. The *Lamplighter*, founded at Daingerfield by Ward Taylor, Jr., and edited by D. J. Bean, professed to be neutral, although one observer at least thought it "touched lightly on the American Party." Another observer, strangely, thought *El Bejareño*, the Spanish-language paper printed on Douai's press, "sort of half sided with the Know-Nothing Party."[5]

Only weeks after the organization of the party at Washington on the Brazos, blatantly Know-Nothing papers began cropping up. In early July the *Confederate*, published by "Messrs. Waddell, Gossler and Holt" and edited by J. F. Waddell and John T. Holt, appeared in Galveston on the ruins of the *Journal* and the *Times*. By the end of the month the editor of the *Telegraph* had received the first number of a campaign paper, the *Invincible Sam*, published in Huntsville by W. S. Reynolds. The Americans took heart from their showing in the August election and immediately made plans for the national campaign of the

[4] See Llerena Friend, *Sam Houston, The Great Designer*, pp. 292–93.
[5] *Texas State Times*, July 28, 1855; Austin *Texas State Gazette*, July 18, 1857.

following year. By September, rumors abounded of Know-Nothing papers to appear at Palestine, Huntsville, Washington on the Brazos, Waco, Livingston, and Alto in Cherokee County. By mid-October, the editor of the *Telegraph* counted seventeen Know-Nothing papers in the state, among them the Waco *American Beacon*, published by George Miller and edited by J. L. L. McCall, and an American paper at Anderson. In addition, party members had acquired the plant of the *Bayou City News* at Houston and moved it to Washington on the Brazos to establish a paper.[6]

Among the established papers that became Know-Nothing, at least for a time, were the *Texas State Times*, edited by John S. Ford at Austin, the *True Issue* at La Grange, the *Central Texian* at Anderson, and the *Bastrop Advertiser*. Other papers that either supported the party or were founded to support it included the *American* at Palestine, edited by A. J. Fowler and G. W. Tuggle, the *Frontier Patriot* at Paris, the *Seguin Journal*, the *Huntsville Recorder*, published by Benjamin W. Cammer and W. A. McLaughlin, the *Texas Enquirer*, published by W. T. Yeomans at Rusk, the *True American* at Goliad, the *Herald* at Jefferson, the *Clarksville Messenger*, and the *Herald* and *Sentinel* at San Antonio.

The prominence of newsmen in the party leadership suggested the Know-Nothings' appreciation of the power of the press. At their first open convention, held at Austin in January, 1856, they elected William E. Jones, then Ford's partner in the *Times*, as president pro tempore. Jones, Ford, and J. W. Flanagan of the Henderson *Star Spangled Banner* served on the Committee on Resolutions, and Flanagan also served as a presidential elector. Delegates to the national convention included J. F. Waddell of the Galveston *Confederate*, A. J. Fowler of the *Palestine American*, and J. L. L. McCall of the Waco *American Beacon*.[7]

The energy of the Know-Nothings alarmed the Democrats, and they took steps to counteract their opposition. The established editors pushed for more subscribers. John Marshall, for example, offered the *Texas State Gazette* to clubs at special rates.[8] A few other Democrats established new papers, among them the *Chronicle of the Times* at

[6] Houston *Tri-Weekly Telegraph*, July 11 and 30 and October 15, 1855.
[7] Ernest W. Winkler, ed., *Platforms of Political Parties in Texas*, pp. 68–69.
[8] *Texas State Gazette*, May 17, 1856.

Matagorda, the *Henderson Democrat*, established by M. D. Ector, the *Lamar Inquirer* at Paris, and the *Democrat* at Washington on the Brazos.

Party rivalry, fanned by newspapers in three languages, erupted in violence in San Antonio during the summer of 1856. Douai left the city in late April, but it remained divided—though not along strictly party or ethnic lines. Indeed, the major ethnic groups divided among themselves. The Germans disagreed on the abolitionist issue raised by Douai, and the new German paper took a strong stand for the Democratic party. The older Anglo papers—the *Texan*, then owned and edited by E. G. Huston, and the *Ledger*, published by Michael Bourke —remained Democratic, while two new papers—the *Herald* and the short-lived *Sentinel*, edited by X. B. Sanders on a press owned by John S. McDonald—appeared to promote the cause of the Know-Nothings.

The Spanish-speaking population divided after the Democratic convention of Bexar County in June, 1856. A group of delegates walked out in protest of the proceedings and utilized *El Bejareño* to get their message to Hispanics. The rival group responded by founding *El Ranchero*, edited by José Quintero, to present their views. *El Ranchero* took an almost hysterical view of the Know-Nothings, warning that they planned violence against the Spanish-speaking and planned to tear down the Roman Catholic churches.

James P. Newcomb, the eighteen-year-old prodigy of the *Herald*, made matters worse by translating and printing a particularly incendiary editorial from *El Ranchero*. This aroused the Know-Nothings, who charged Quintero with printing false and libelous material and threatened his life if he did not retract. As the situation became explosive, Mayor James M. Devine stepped in, calling on responsible citizens, regardless of party, to arm themselves to maintain peace and protect the editor. John S. McDonald marched into Devine's drugstore to challenge him on the action, whereupon Devine killed him.

A mob headed by J. M. West of the *Herald* threatened to drag Devine from the jail where he had placed himself and lynch him, but cooler heads prevailed. The court promptly ruled that Devine had acted in self-defense, and, over all, the letting of blood eased tensions. The city mourned McDonald, at the same time conceding that he had been the aggressor. Young Newcomb came in for a round of criticism for translating the offending editorial and shortly thereafter sold the *Herald* to Logan. Newcomb worked for the paper until after the national elections and then, citing his desire for education, went east while the excitement blew over.[9]

More representative of Know-Nothing papers than the *Herald* was the *American*, edited at Washington on the Brazos by George W. Crawford. A restless man interested in railroads, filibustering, newspapering, politics, and the navigation of the Brazos River, Crawford came to Texas from Mississippi before 1846 and made his base in Washington County. He and B. E. Tarver issued a prospectus for the *Texas State Journal*, to be published at Washington, in 1848, but they gave up the project when Joseph Lancaster founded the *Texas Ranger* there. The following year Crawford reconsidered and decided to give competition to Lancaster. He purchased the *Lone Star*, which John B. Wilkins and D. H. Rankin had established at Brenham, and moved it to Washington, at the same time announcing that he had ordered a new Hoe press. The *Semi-Weekly Star* appeared in early 1850, published by Crawford and edited by W. H. Ewing. The paper opposed the division of the state and free-soilism and professed to be Democratic, although it advocated banks. Crawford left the *Star* in September, 1852, and shortly thereafter purchased an interest in the *Texas State Gazette* at Austin, an interest he retained only a year. In 1854 he joined the Know-Nothings and the following November issued the first number of the *American*.

Under the motto "Heaven and earth will witness, if America must fall, that we are innocent" the paper printed the platform of the American party and reported on party activities. An early issue carried an attack on foreigners, which brought protests from the foreign-born in Washington County and which Crawford later amended to exclude the local people. Foreigners were usually abolitionist, he explained, and "it would be just as reasonable to expect Heaven to produce devils, as for England, France, or Ireland and other nations to produce lovers of slavery." He professed to believe that there was not an abolitionist in Washington County. Generally, the Know-Nothings in Texas classified no one who resided in the state at the time of annexation as a foreigner regardless of the place of birth.

The *Washington American* carried full coverage of William Walk-

[9] *San Antonio Ledger*, August 2, 1856; *San Antonio Texan*, August 7 and 14, 1856.

er's filibustering in Nicaragua, and that adventure drew Crawford away from the paper at the end of a year. Leaving it in the hands of W. J. Pendleton in late 1856, Crawford recruited troops and joined Walker. He returned to Texas to recover from a wound early in 1857 and later in the year gave support to Sam Houston for governor and ran for state representative from Washington County. Crawford, like Houston, went down in defeat. He later raised troops for the Confederates during the Civil War and died in 1869. The *Washington American* continued for about a year after Crawford's departure and then disappeared, the victim of the disintegration of the party and the failure of Washington to develop as a river port.[10]

The most celebrated editor to convert to Know-Nothingism was John Salmon Ford, physician, ranger, and lawyer, who made his *Texas State Times* the foremost spokesman of the party during its heyday. Born in South Carolina on May 26, 1815, Ford arrived in Texas in 1836 and served in the army for two years before joining with Michael Cronican to purchase the press of the *Texas Register* in 1845 and move it to Austin to found the *Texas Democrat*. After interrupting his journalism career to fight in the Mexican War, he sojourned four years on the Rio Grande as soldier and Texas Ranger. Then he returned to Austin to serve in the legislature and in 1852 to resume his newspaper career.

By then, both he and the paper he had founded earlier had new names. As physician in Jack Hays's regiment during the Mexican War, Ford made out the death certificates for men killed in battle. Feeling that the task required an element of compassion, he wrote "Rest in Peace" on each certificate, and as the number of casualties increased, he shortened the notation to R.I.P. The men began calling him "Rip," and the name stuck to him for the rest of his life.[11]

His former paper in the meantime became the *Texas State Gazette*, owned and edited variously by William H. Cushney, Robert C. Matthewson, Joseph Wade Hampton, and Henry Percy Brewster.[12]

---

[10] *Washington American*, November 8, 1855, November 19, 1856, and July 14, 1857.

[11] Clarence J. LaRoche, "Rip Ford: Frontier Journalist" (M.A. thesis, University of Texas, 1942), p. 2. For a biography, see William J. Hughes, *Rebellious Ranger: Rip Ford and the Old Southwest*, and for Ford's memoirs, see *Rip Ford's Texas*, edited by Stephen B. Oates.

[12] For a detailed study of the *Texas State Gazette*, see Larry Jay Gage, "The Editors and Editorial Policies of the *Texas State Gazette*, 1849–1879" (M.A. thesis, University of Texas, 1959).

Thoughout the changes, the paper held the public printing contract Ford and Cronican had obtained for its predecessor—but not without challenge. From 1849, the office of the *South-Western American*, edited by Phineas DeCordova and located across the street, offered persistent competition. Phineas DeCordova's brother Jacob, one of the most enterprising land speculators of the era, had introduced the press to Houston in early 1849 and established there *DeCordova's Herald*, a monthly paper designed to promote land sales.[13] But after only a few issues, opportunity drew his eyes westward. From New Year's Day, 1847, when Dr. John G. Chalmers of the Austin *New Era* died in a street brawl, the *Texas Democrat* had faced only minimal competition for the public printing, and by late 1848 both Ford and Cronican had abandoned the *Democrat*, apparently leaving an open field for the public printing. Jacob DeCordova relocated his press, and his brother founded the *South-Western American* at Austin, but they found that Cushney had already preempted the field. Cushney staved off the competition and held the public printing contract despite DeCordova's efforts.

In late 1852 more changes pended at the *Gazette*. Cushney, in the last stages of tuberculosis, sold his interest to George W. Crawford on October 1 and died on November 24, much mourned in Austin. His illness and the sale of the *Gazette* opened the possibility of Ford's returning to his former office. But DeCordova also offered his office for sale—at a bargain, for he had again failed to get the public printing—and Ford chose it. He and Joseph Walker, an old Ranger buddy, printer, and founder of the *San Antonio Ledger*, purchased the *South-Western American* on November 1, 1852. They planned to rename it the *Texas Ranger* and to join forces with Joseph Lancaster, whose paper by that name at Washington on the Brazos had been suspended when his press burned. In December, 1852, Ford and Lancaster issued a prospectus for the new *Texas Ranger* to be published in Austin, but Lancaster changed his mind. Obtaining the press of the *Lone Star* he reestablished his paper at Washington. Ford and Walker continued with the *South-Western American* until late in 1853, when they renamed it the *Texas State Times*.[14]

[13] Houston *Democratic Telegraph and Texas Register*, May 10 and November 29, 1849.

[14] *Texas State Gazette*, May 29 and December 4, 1852; Ford, *Rip Ford's Texas*, p. 207.

Ford recalled with questionable accuracy that he and Walker made the *Times* "the largest weekly in the State, except the Galveston *News*," and that it "contained quite as much reading matter as the *News*." But they had no better luck than DeCordova in wresting the public printing away from the *Gazette*.

Ford remembered his competition tolerantly in his memoirs. "Of course the usual rivalry sprang up between the *Gazette* and the *Times*," he wrote. "Two newspaper firms seldom preserve harmonious relations when divided by a street only, and it is hard for either of the editors to do anything the other does not find out about." And when Hampton died, like Cushney, of tuberculosis after selling his interest in the *Gazette*, Ford eulogized him as "dignified and courteous, yet bold and manly."[15]

But at the time, the competition between the editors grew bitter. Although both were Democrats, they disagreed on the candidate for governor in 1853, and, although both favored the building of railroads in the state, they differed on the methods of financing. At the bottom of their differences lay the matter of the public printing. Ford expected to win the contract because of his service to the republic, state, and party, and when he failed in 1853 he charged Hampton and Crawford with using undue political influence.

Hampton proved a worthy opponent, having learned the tactics of editorial warfare in his native North Carolina. Born July 7, 1813, he imbibed the states' rights theories of John C. Calhoun and as a Calhoun Whig and then as a Southern Democrat supported those theories first in the Salisbury *Western Carolinian* and then in the *Mecklenburg Jeffersonian* at Charlotte. Hampton became an influential editor, but he met with little financial success, and in late 1848 he went to Texas in search of opportunity and relief from the lung disease that plagued him. He stopped for a year in Huntsville, where he served as trustee of Austin College and took an active part in the affairs of the Presbyterian church, the temperance society, and the Masonic Lodge. Then, seeing better opportunity at Austin, he moved there to join the *Gazette* and involve himself in political and civic activities.[16]

Hampton showed his editorial form during the summer of 1853,

[15] Ford, *Rip Ford's Texas*, p. 208; *Texas State Times*, June 16, 1855.
[16] For a biography of Hampton, see Ronnie C. Tyler, *Joseph Wade Hampton: Editor and Individualist*.

when he supported E. M. Pease and Ford supported M. T. Johnson as
the Democratic nominee for governor. In an exchange over Ford's
electioneering efforts in the Rio Grande, Hampton commented that a
"greaser" had popped Ford "on the head with grape shot" during his
adventures to the south, thereby causing a "hole . . . in his head that
caused considerable leakage of his not too plentiful brains." Ford took
exception to the comment, causing Hampton to retract some of his remarks and to affirm that he considered his rival to be neither a liar nor
a coward.[17]

Early in the following year the editorial feud flared over a scarcity
of paper. Both journals ran short because of a delayed shipment to
their supplier, Francis T. Duffau. Hampton learned that a small shipment had reached Lavaca and, without consulting anyone, took his
wagon to the coast and appropriated the paper for the *Gazette*. Ford
protested that Duffau had promised him the paper because Hampton
had failed to comply with an agreement to pay one-half of the purchase
price in advance. Duffau confirmed Ford's position and took the shipment away from Hampton. Hampton denied the charge and maintained further that Ford owed him two bundles of paper borrowed
earlier.[18]

But Hampton's newspaper career was drawing to a close because
of his declining health. In May, 1854, he sold his interest in the *Gazette* to John Marshall of Jackson, Mississippi. A few months later,
W. R. Scurry, who had purchased Crawford's interest in late 1853, sold
out to W. S. Oldham, giving the *Gazette* a new set of owners and
editors.

Still, to Rip Ford's frustration, the *Gazette* retained the printing
contract. He found it particularly galling that a rank newcomer to the
state like Marshall would receive the favor, and the matter figured into
his joining the American party. "A tide of new men, and with them
new measures have been constantly rolling into Texas, and much of the
primitive patriotism of the country is supplanted by a set of politicians
who know but little and care but little, about the hardship of the men
of former days," he wrote in the *Times* during the heat of the election
of 1855. "A large majority of those who attempt to mould and lead pub-

[17] *Texas State Gazette*, July 11, 16, and 25, and August 6, 1853.
[18] Ibid., February 7 and 14, 1854.

lic opinion in Texas at the present time are those who have sat down to the banquet after all the dangers and toil of preparing it was over."[19]

Ford's devotion to "Southern institutions" as well as his rivalry with the *Gazette* led him into the American party. Douai's *Zeitung* incensed him, and he, like Douai, believed that all Germans were abolitionists. While his rival at the *Gazette* welcomed the Germans into the Democratic party, Ford viewed them with alarm. He advocated a revision of naturalization laws that would require a residence of twenty-one years in the United States before the foreign-born could vote. Foreigners, he submitted, should not be allowed to tell Americans what to do in regard to their institutions. He reserved his sharpest attacks for Douai, urging the citizens of San Antonio to throw his press into the river.[20]

Ford also saw Mexico as a threat to slavery. He pointed out the number of slaves who escaped across the border and the fact that Mexico gave them haven. He continued his involvement in border intrigues such as the Sierra Madre filibuster and, also in support of Southern causes, sympathized with the filibustering enterprise in Cuba. Strongly anti-Catholic editorials appeared in the *Times*, but Ford later attributed them to his assistant editor James A. Beveridge.[21]

The *Times* duly supported the American party candidates, Millard Fillmore and Andrew Jackson Donelson, in the 1856 presidential elections, but Fillmore's reputed free-soilism and the moderate stand of the Texas party on slavery dampened Ford's enthusiasm. Shortly after the defeat of the party, Ford reconsidered his political affiliation, and the following spring he did an about-face. By then, in his opinion, abolitionists to the north posed a greater threat to "Southern institutions" than Mexicans to the south or Germans in Texas. When the Democratic party convened at Waco in May, 1857, Ford attended and received the welcome of a prodigal son. "We are happy to record that Captain John S. Ford made an open confession of his sins," reported one editor, "and that he was received into full fellowship amidst the most enthusiastic applause."[22]

In his memoirs, Ford called his joining the Know-Nothings "one

[19] *Texas State Times*, June 30, 1855.
[20] Ibid., May 19, 1855.
[21] Ford, *Rip Ford's Texas*, p. 211.
[22] Austin *Southerner Intelligencer*, May 13, 1857.

of those inconsiderate things men do sometime," but he reported his change of heart to his readers of the *Times* without apology and without criticizing the American party. He returned to the Democratic fold, he explained, because of his duty to the South.[23]

About the same time that he recanted, Ford sold the *Times*. During his five years as owner-editor a series of men had joined him at the press office. Jo Walker came in and went out several times; William E. Jones joined him for seven months in 1856. Others included W. T. Davidson, Ed Finnin, F. M. Gibson, and X. B. DeBray.

Ford and his last partners disagreed politically after the Know-Nothing party fell apart. While Ford joined the Calhoun wing of the Democratic party, his partners followed the more general course of old Know-Nothings into the independent wing. That is, in 1857 they supported Sam Houston, also a Know-Nothing defector, for governor. Previously a loyal follower of the old hero, Ford found Houston's lack of support of "Southern institutions" intolerable. Thus, he sold his interest in the *Times*. The new owners promptly changed the name of the paper to the *Sentinel* and made it a campaign organ for Sam Houston. Eventually it blended with another Austin paper, the *Southern Intelligencer*.[24]

Ford's sometime partner, Jo Walker, also repented of his dallying with the Know-Nothings and in the summer of 1857 reversed field by purchasing W. S. Oldham's interest in the *Texas State Gazette*. Ford made his own turnabout complete by joining his old partner as pro tem editor of the *Gazette* in 1858 during a lengthy absence of John Marshall.

As the saga of Ford and the *Texas State Times* suggests, the American party disappeared rapidly after 1856, and with it many of its papers. The *Huntsville Recorder* died of starvation; the Henderson *Star Spangled Banner* became the *Carthage Recorder*; the *Clarksville Messenger* moved to McKinney. Still, an opposition press survived. Old Democratic editors who had strayed away from their party tended to return, but, like Ford's partners, most of them joined the independent wing to challenge John Marshall's control. Generally, old-line Whigs remained Know-Nothing longer. The *Harrison Flag* still carried the

---

[23] Ford, *Rip Ford's Texas*, p. 211.
[24] Ibid., p. 218.

slogan "Americans Must Rule America" in 1858 and advocated Millard Fillmore for the next president. Two years later the *Flag*, following the classic course of old Whigs turned Know-Nothing, supported the Constitutional Union party, which, averred one rival editor, advocated "no North, no East, no South, no West, no everything, Know-Nothing, and more especially nothing in particular."[25] This persistent opposition to the Democrats paved the way for some editors to join the Republican party during the Reconstruction era. James Winwright Flanagan, for example, served as lieutenant governor under E. J. Davis, and James Pearson Newcomb, as secretary of state.

[25] *Dallas Herald*, July 6, 1860.

CHAPTER 17

Democrats of Varied Faiths

WITH few aberrations, the major editors of the early statehood era adhered to the Democratic party, but as crisis followed upon crisis to divide the Union during the 1850s the party divided into factions in Texas, as it did nationwide. One faction, the Southern or Calhoun Democrats, advocated states' rights and the protection of slavery; the other, the conservative or Jackson Democrats, placed the preservation of the Union above all other considerations.

The Calhoun Democrats held a decided advantage among the editors of Texas, and three major editors who rose to prominence in the 1850s—Robert W. Loughery, Edward Hopkins Cushing, and John Marshall—gave them substantial reinforcement. Together with Willard Richardson, these men gave powerful voice to the southern viewpoint and influenced the course of the state when crisis came in 1860–61.

Robert W. Loughery voiced ardent support for southern views in east Texas. Born in Tennessee on February 2, 1820, he learned the printing trade in Kentucky. As a sixteen-year-old boy, he started for Texas to join the revolution, but illness detained him in Louisiana, and he stopped there to publish the *Ouachita Courier* at Monroe before continuing his journey. In 1847 he arrived in Jefferson, Texas, to edit the *Jefferson Democrat*, a paper founded to promote "the principles of Thomas Jefferson, James Madison, and Andrew Jackson." Colonel Berry H. Durham, publisher of the paper, sold it to W. C. Baker and Company in early 1848, and the following year Loughery moved to Marshall to associate himself with the *Texas Republican*, a paper founded in the spring of 1849 by Trenton A. and Frank J. Patillo. Loughery became co-editor with Trenton and co-publisher with Frank

Patillo, and within a few years both of the founders had withdrawn, leaving him as sole editor and publisher.[1]

Some critics charged that Loughery had been a Whig before coming to Texas, but he had been a Calhoun Whig and remained true to man and principle while the party labels changed. Loughery stopped his press to mourn the death of Calhoun in the spring of 1850, and throughout the following decade he attacked the Whigs and Know-Nothings, making his paper, in the words of a fellow editor, "the Calhoun organ for Marshall." The *Republican*, observed another editor, was "none of your bogus, half-way sort of democratic" paper, but was "of the real Simeon-pure, ultra radical, Loco Foco stripe."[2]

Loughery defined the Democratic party according to his own beliefs, measuring editors and public men by their devotion to "southern causes" rather than by the party they professed. Some papers labeled as "Democratic," he charged, in fact opposed states' rights and advocated such Whiggish measures as banks and internal improvements by the federal government. In the interest of party purity, he kept a sharp eye on his fellow editors and often found them lacking. He questioned the party loyalty of Charles DeMorse, maintaining that, while the Clarksville *Standard* professed to be Democratic, DeMorse held an interest in the Whig paper at Bonham and that he was in fact "a died-in-the-wool-federalist." Marshall called the *Texas Union* at San Augustine a "free soil organ," a bad epithet indeed, and at one point he charged that all papers north of Marshall, with the notable exception of the *Dallas Herald*, were "purely antisouthern" in tone.[3]

On the issue of slavery, Loughery brooked no softness. No man imbued with anti-slavery sentiment, he maintained, should be allowed to remain in a slave state—"he should be driven out, and, where the case is one marked by aggravated circumstances, severely punished."[4]

Loughery prided himself on never dealing in personalities, but he considered political opinions legitimate subject for criticism, and, early and late, Sam Houston felt the sting of his pen. Soon after joining

[1] Walter Prescott Webb and H. Bailey Carroll, eds., *The Handbook of Texas*, II, 84–85.
[2] Marshall *Texas Republican*, October 18, 1849; *Galveston Journal*, June 17, 1853.
[3] *Texas Republican*, August 16 and October 18, 1849, April 4, 1850, and June 3, 1859.
[4] Ibid., November 19, 1859.

the *Texas Republican*, Loughery launched a running feud with F. L. Hatch of the Huntsville *Texas Banner*, "the General Houston organ," charging that Houston controlled Texas and wound it up like his watch. Throughout the decade Loughery tilted with other pro-Houston editors, at one time calling for Houston's resignation as senator because of his consistently following a course "in direct antagonism to the interests of the South." Houston responded on one occasion to Loughery's criticism by returning a copy of the *Republican* to him with the inscription across it: "I like a dog for he is faithful, but I detest the barking of puppies! You are paid in advance and I wish no more of your papers. You are welcome to the subscription!"[5]

For all his devotion to the South, Loughery lacked the extremism of some of his colleagues. The banner of his newspaper proclaimed his admiration for the Constitution of the United States, and he only slowly and with reluctance accepted the idea of disunion. He considered filibustering expeditions to Cuba and Nicaragua as flighty diversions, twitting his colleagues who joined them. When George W. Crawford departed for Nicaragua, for example, Loughery reminded him that J. M. West of the *San Antonio Herald*, refugee from a murder charge, had left just ahead of him—"having abandoned fair prospects of an *elevated* position in Ohio for fear that if ever *suspended*, his glory would be too *brief* for his ambition." And when General William Walker's book on his filibuster appeared, Loughery commented sourly that he doubted it would sell well enough to pay the printer, the "humbug of Nicaragua" having had its run.[6]

Loughery suffered serious misgivings when fellow editors began agitating for the reopening of the slave trade. Such agitation, he warned, had no chance of success in view of the militant abolitionism in the north, and it could only further divide the nation.[7]

Edward Hopkins Cushing lacked Loughery's emotional involvement in southern causes—and for good reason. Of Puritan stock, he came to Texas directly from New England, and, while he became an ardent Texan, he did not belong to the moonlight-and-magnolia tradition. He espoused southern causes, not because of romantic attach-

[5] Ibid., February 7, 1850, September 1, 1855, and May 10, 1856.
[6] Ibid., December 13, 1856, and February 4, 1860.
[7] Ibid., February 4, 1859.

ment, but because in his opinion they furthered the development of his adopted state.

Born in Vermont on June 11, 1829, Cushing arrived in Galveston a few months after his twenty-first birthday and after graduating from Dartmouth College. He taught school at Galveston, Brazoria, and Columbia for a time and then distinguished himself as editor and publisher of the *Columbia Democrat*, which, in partnership with W. F. Swain, he renamed the *Democrat and Planter*.

Cushing joined the *Telegraph* in 1856 and during the next few years made it again one of the important papers in the state. Under Harvey H. Allen, the *Telegraph* had become largely a promotion sheet for railroad enterprises. Cushing continued the emphasis on railroads, cheering on the builders as they made Houston the railroad center of Texas by the Civil War. But he did not limit himself to railroads. Making the *Telegraph* frankly a "commercial organ," he advocated the development of Buffalo Bayou to give competition to the railroads and the development of Houston as a port city to challenge the virtual monopoly of Galveston on sea-going trade. Competition between the two cities grew heated as Cushing attacked and the Galveston editors defended the entrepreneurs who controlled the island wharves.[8]

Cushing could well be accused of equating the growth of Houston with the growth of Texas. Yet he saw the larger picture. The vast, fertile, untilled lands fired his imagination. In his view, only the lack of labor and transportation prevented the state from realizing its agricultural potential. Because of the need for labor he accepted the existence of slavery without question and supported Latin American filibusters and the reopening of the slave trade. At the same time, he campaigned for a diversified economy, urging that the state and section become self-sufficient. "We send our cotton to Manchester and Lowell, our sugar to New York refineries, our hides to down-east tanneries and our children to Yankee colleges, and are ever ready to find fault with the North because it lives by our folly," he wrote. "We want home manufactures and these we must have, if we are ever to be independent."[9]

[8] See Earl W. Fornell, *The Galveston Era*, pp. 152–54; E. B. Cushing, "Edward Hopkins Cushing: An Appreciation by His Son," *Southwestern Historical Quarterly* 25 (April, 1922); and Emory M. Thomas, "Rebel Nationalism: E. H. Cushing and the Confederate Experience," *Southwestern Historical Quarterly* 73 (January, 1970).

[9] Houston *Weekly Telegraph*, November 12, 1856.

In less than a decade of residence, Cushing forgot his Yankee origins, as did his fellows. He advocated some causes that even native Southerners found extreme. Yet he tempered his positions with a certain objectivity, a rationality, and a touch of humor that kept him from being a fire-eater of the first order.

The same could not be said of John Marshall. Indeed, Marshall typified the fire-eating southern editor of the era, and more than any other Texas editor before the Civil War he influenced rather than reflected the course of events. From the time he purchased the *Texas State Gazette* in 1854, Marshall placed himself "almost at a single bound" at the head and front of the Democratic party and made the paper the unofficial organ of the party. "It was his prerogative almost from the beginning to ride upon the whirlwind and direct the storm of political commotion, to sit in the high place of power, or rather influence, and mould the destiny of Texas Democracy," observed his son-in-law, the son and namesake of his onetime partner Williamson Simpson Oldham.[10]

Yet details of Marshall's previous career are sketchy, and even his family professed to know little of his early life. "He was a silent man concerning matters which touched him personally," said Oldham. Born in Virginia about 1812, Marshall was a newsman in Louisiana by 1832 and by early 1844 had moved to Jackson, Mississippi. There he served as acting editor of the *Southern Reformer* and gave strong support to the annexation of Texas. Citing health reasons, he left the *Southern Reformer* in August, 1845, and for a time lived in Washington, D.C., where he worked in the Treasury Department under Robert J. Walker. When the Whigs came to power in 1849, Marshall returned to Jackson, where he purchased one-half interest in the *Mississippian*, the leading organ of the Democratic party in the state. He strongly opposed the Compromise of 1850, taking a stand at odds with most of the party leaders. In 1850 he married Anna P. Newman, daughter of a wealthy planter, and the following January he announced the sale of his interest in the *Mississippian*. According to Oldham, Marshall determined in 1852 to settle in Texas, but he retained business interests in Mississippi

---

[10] W. S. Oldham, "Colonel John Marshall," *Southwestern Historical Quarterly* 20 (October, 1916): 134.

and spent much time there, leaving the *Gazette* for months at a time in the hands of pro tem editors.[11]

Marshall studied law for his own edification after removing to Austin, and his writing indicates an excellent education. "His mind was a vast magazine admirably arranged," commented his son-in-law. "One could hardly ask for anything in history, biography or general literature that could not be found in that immense storehouse of knowledge. The article which you required was not only there; it was ready; it was in its own proper compartment; in a moment it was brought down, unpacked and displayed."

Described as a "rather undersized man, about five feet seven inches high, spare made," with a "fair complexion, aquiline features and an eye like an eagle's," Marshall never touched liquor of any kind and, winter or summer, arose at daybreak to take a dip in the river. He won fame afar for his temper and his duels, both editorial and otherwise. His son-in-law recalled a street fight in which Marshall and a Dr. Phillips, a prominent citizen of Austin, met with guns on Congress Avenue between Seventh and Eighth streets. Marshall withheld his fire, taking two shots from his opponent while he tipped his hat at a woman passing by and waited for her to move out of gun range. Then the two men "advanced from opposite sides of the Avenue, firing as they came. They emptied their revolvers; then shot their Derringers," wrote Oldham. "Then like Homer's Trojan heroes they picked up rocks and hurled them at each other until a huge, lone constable, a Mr. McAnally, reached them, seized each combatant by the collar and held him at arm's length until a crowd rushed up and separated them." No one was seriously injured in this fight, nor in other similar ones in which Marshall engaged. Obviously, more bluster than substance attended them.[12]

Marshall drew more blood with his pen. After organizing the Democrats to demolish the Know-Nothings in 1855 and 1856, he took aim at Sam Houston in 1857, orchestrating a campaign that gave the old general his only defeat at the hands of the Texas electorate.

Houston abandoned the American party earlier than Rip Ford,

[11]Olan Lonnie Sinclair, "Crossroads of Conviction: A Study of the Texas Political Mind, 1856–1861" (Ph.D. diss., Rice University, 1975), pp. 67–70.

[12]Oldham, "Colonel John Marshall," pp. 132–38.

but instead of going into the southern wing of the Democratic party he declared himself to be what he had always been—a Jackson Democrat. He decried the convention system of selecting candidates, and, after the party in convention at Waco nominated Hardin R. Runnels for governor, he announced his own candidacy as an independent.

John Marshall had pronounced the Know-Nothing party dead in 1856, as indeed it was, but former Know-Nothing papers and presses tended to support Houston in 1857, calling themselves Independent Democrats. The *Huntsville Recorder* at Houston's home town announced his candidacy, and he received press support from the *Washington American*, the Rusk *Texas Enquirer*, the Henderson *Star Spangled Banner*, the Marshall *Harrison Flag*, the *Jefferson Gazette*, the *Clarksville Messenger*, and the *San Antonio Herald*, all of the Know-Nothing persuasion. Rip Ford's old paper, renamed the *Texas Sentinel* and edited by F. M. Gibson, sounded the theme, vigorously supporting Houston and proclaiming itself "an independent, anti-Caucus, anti-Austin clique democratic journal."[13]

Houston received his strongest support in east Texas from the *Nacogdoches Chronicle*, then owned and edited by Eber Worthington Cave, a native of Philadelphia. Born on July 14, 1831, and trained as a printer in Burlington, New Jersey, Cave had arrived in Nacogdoches in January, 1853. He took the job of foreman at the *Chronicle*, a paper founded by J. C. Harrison and N. J. Moore the previous year, and purchased the paper several months later. "He soon raised the *Chronicle* above the ordinary plane of country weeklies by the vigor and pungency of his editorials and his ardent advocacy of the political cause of General Sam Houston," noted one commentator. Cave advocated Houston as president of the United States in 1855 and somewhat equivocally followed him into the Know-Nothing camp. After Houston announced for governor in 1857, Cave began issuing a *Campaign Chronicle* to support him.[14]

As in Sam Houston's previous campaigns, his opponents held the edge in the press. John Marshall, declaring "war to the hilt," charged Houston with betraying the South by his votes in the Senate. E. H.

[13] Austin *Texas Sentinel*, June 17, 1857.
[14] Eugene C. Barker and Amelia W. Williams, eds., *The Writings of Sam Houston*, VII, 387–88; A. C. Gray, "A History of the Texas Press," in *A Comprehensive History of Texas, 1685–1897*, ed. Dudley G. Wooten, II, 392.

Cushing reviewed Houston's record, bearing down on the negative aspects, while Willard Richardson, Charles DeMorse, and Robert Loughery renewed their criticism.

Houston showed his old form, giving the state the most exciting campaign it had seen. He attacked the Waco convention, maintaining that he could not take hold of it because it was "a muley and had no horns." Then compounding his metaphors, he imitated the squalling of a cat in pronouncing the word *Waco*, and called defenders of the convention dogs—"not *terriers* but *cur* dogs." He used some expressions his critics sanctimoniously declared unfit for the ears of ladies, reserving some of his choicest epithets for the partners of the *Texas State Gazette*. John Marshall, he submitted, was not only a disunionist who had attended the Nashville convention in 1850, but also "a vegitarian—he won't eat meat and a drop of his blood would freeze a frog." And Williamson S. Oldham "though he stole and sunk those bank books in the river and ran away to Texas, . . . is not yet in the penitentiary."[15]

Houston lost the election in part because of his Kansas vote and in part because of the taint of Know-Nothingism, but John Marshall took a full measure of credit. "Bring out the Waco Rooster, let him crow; the whole ticket triumphant!" he exulted after the election. The "Waco Rooster" had killed Sam Houston politically, the *Gazette* declared. "He will never again crow on this side of Mason and Dixon's line."[16]

With the party and state apparently under his control, John Marshall took a sharp turn toward extremism. Although he denied the persistent charge of disunion that the independents levelled at him, Marshall had in fact flirted long with the idea. As acting editor of the *Southern Reformer* in 1844, he saw opposition to the annexation of Texas as a northern conspiracy to reduce the South. A few years later as editor of the *Mississippian* and an opponent of the Compromise of 1850, he declared, "Our rights in the Union, or our independence out of it," and professed himself unafraid of meeting "the raw-head-and-bloody-bones DISUNION face to face."[17]

---

[15] Barker and Williams, *Writings of Houston*, VII, 29; Alexander W. Terrell, "Recollections of General Sam Houston," *Southwestern Historical Quarterly* 16 (October, 1912): 120.

[16] Austin *State Gazette for the Campaign*, August 22, 1857.

[17] *Mississippian* (Jackson, Miss.), June 22, 1849, as cited in Sinclair, "Crossroads of Conviction," p. 70.

The theme cropped up again and again during his association with the *State Gazette*. He had been owner for little more than a year when he called on southern men to stand to their arms and prepare to defend their institutions. He wrote that "in the Union or out of it, we say OUR INSTITUTIONS AND OUR RIGHTS UNDER THEM SHALL NEVER BE COMPROMISED!" Showing remarkable foresight, he anticipated the Confederate States of America as early as 1857. "We of Texas have lived outside of the Union when we were poor and needy. We are now comparatively rich, and we may be *powerful* in a Southern Confederacy," he wrote. "Yes, that word *Southern Confederacy*, shall be held in no soft murmuring whispers breathed to a lute upon a maiden's ear."[18]

After his victory over Sam Houston, Marshall took the offensive in his fight for southern rights. He began agitating for the reopening of the African slave trade, a cause guaranteed to push moderate northerners into the abolitionist camp and one that even dedicated Southerners saw as a threat to the existence of the Union. Marshall argued his point eloquently, gaining support from Willard Richardson, E. H. Cushing, and for a time Hamilton Stuart, but he failed to convince the majority of the citizenry. Over all, the issue further splintered the Democratic party, enlarging the faction that supported Sam Houston and eventually driving the German vote into the Houston camp.

Among those to part company with Marshall, was George Paschal, editor of the *Southern Intelligencer* at Austin, and until after the election of 1857 a loyal member of the organized party. Born in Georgia on November 23, 1812, Paschal studied law and then, taking a Cherokee wife, journeyed west with her family on the Trail of Tears. He resided for a decade in Arkansas, where he practiced his profession, served as legislator, and, before he reached thirty years of age, became chief justice of the Arkansas supreme court. He moved to Texas about 1847 and for a time practiced law at Galveston. Then, divorcing his Indian wife, he moved to Austin, where he played an active role in the Democratic party and in 1850 ran unsuccessfully for attorney general.[19]

Paschal entered journalism after Rip Ford turned Know-Nothing, thus forfeiting any chance of getting the printing contract and leaving the *Gazette* without a viable competitor. A group headed by S. M.

[18] Austin *Texas State Gazette*, June 9, 1855 and December 6, 1857.
[19] For a biography of Paschal, see Jane Lynn Scarborough, "George W. Paschal: Texas Unionist and Scalawag Jurisprudent" (Ph.D. diss., Rice University, 1972).

Swenson, a wealthy Austin merchant, proposed to fill the void by establishing a new printing office. Their paper, the *Southern Intelligencer*, first appeared on August 27, 1856, edited by Paschal and published by Irving Root and William Baker.

The *Intelligencer* proclaimed itself a Democratic paper, but Paschal, like other challengers before him, lost out in the contest for the public printing. In the party convention of 1857, Marshall also squeezed him out of the party leadership. Paschal supported the party ticket, joining in the tirades against Sam Houston, but during the campaign he and Marshall broke sharply for business, ideological, political, and personal reasons.

Throughout late 1857 and early 1858, the two Austin editors hurled insults at each other. Marshall warmed up by calling the *Southern Intelligencer* a "little bogus democratic banner," and inviting its editor—"a sneaking enemy in the disguise of a pretended friend"—to take "his small experiments in disorganization" to another party. He labeled Paschal as "Jerry Sneak" and S. M. Swenson as the "Yellow Dwarf," the head of the "Monied Dynasty of Austin."[20]

Paschal in return referred to the "noisy, fussing, self-constituted leaders" of the party who made up the "Austin clique" and who sought to assassinate every man's character who dared resist it. Marshall, said the *Intelligencer*, was known in Austin as "Hairy Nasty," "Vulture," and "Little Filthy"; he was "a brokendown politician from Mississippi," who had come to Texas to retrieve his fortunes, and he had drained money from the public treasury for printing.[21]

The feud heated up after the summer election of 1858, in which the editors backed different men. Marshall, thinking his man had won, printed a vicious attack on Paschal and then departed for a lengthy visit to Mississippi, leaving Rip Ford as acting editor of the *Gazette*.

Marshall had scarcely left the state when Paschal printed in the *Intelligencer* and separately as a pamphlet charges of gross misdeeds by the *Gazette* in regard to the public printing contract. John Marshall and Company, Paschal charged, had among other things failed to meet deadlines, overcharged the state, and shorted pages.[22] Paschal re-

[20] *Texas State Gazette*, November 28, 1857, and March 13, 1858.

[21] Austin *Southern Intelligencer*, August 25 and October 6, 1858.

[22] Ibid., September 8 and 15, 1858; George W. Paschal, *The Public Printing and the Public Printer*, pp. 1–5.

viewed the experience of previous editors who had competed for the
contract against the *Gazette*, calling on Rip Ford to bear him witness as
to irregularities. This, of course, placed Ford in an embarrassing position, and he declined to comment. In October, 1858, Ford departed for
the Indian frontier, leaving the *Gazette* under the acting editorship of
William Byrd.

Marshall resumed the editorial chair early in 1859 and in the issue
of January 8 replied to Paschal's charges. Denying all wrongdoing, he
accused Paschal of deliberate misrepresentation and heaped personal
insults on him. "With such an unscrupulous opponent, it has been impossible to be on terms of respect and I have necessarily named him
Jerry Sneak as the only suitable term by which his attributes can be
described," he wrote.

On the day the paper appeared, State Senator I. A. Paschal,
George's brother, and Major Robert S. Neighbors called on Marshall to
demand a retraction of all reflections on George Paschal's honor. Marshall refused to do so and referred them to his friend Dr. Josephus
Murray Steiner. The disputants avoided duel, unlawful in Texas, by
agreeing to submit to a board of honor composed of three friends of
each—Steiner, George F. Moore, and George Flournoy for Marshall
and F. M. Gibson, John C. Duval, and John Hemphill for Paschal.

On January 15, Marshall published the purported decision of the
board, clearing him of impropriety, but Paschal's friends denied having
reached such a decision. The matter thus flared again, with Paschal
submitting the charges regarding the public printing to another impartial board, which sustained him. At this point, two friends of the editors, Steiner and Robert S. Neighbors, came to near blows. Steiner
published a challenge to Neighbors in the *Gazette*, accusing him of
"low instinctive bullyism" for defending Paschal, "a wretched poltroon, whose cowardise has compelled him to dishonor himself."[23]

With that, the matter reached the gun-waving—though not the
shooting—stage. Steiner, a state Democratic committeeman, had killed
Major Ripley A. Arnold at Fort Graham on September 6, 1853, and
despite an acquittal by a jury controversy still swirled about the case.
He was not a man to be taken lightly, nor were the others involved. Yet
the *Gazette-Intelligencer* fracas took on the aspects of a comic opera.

---

[23] *Texas State Gazette*, March 12, 1859.

All parties engaged in more bombast than action, and at each crucial confrontation one party or the other delayed action long enough for the law to step in and prevent bloodshed.

Each editor kept the public informed of developments as he saw them. According to Paschal, he learned that Marshall, Steiner, and "one or two other valiant Knights," all "armed to the teeth," awaited him on Congress Avenue, chuckling at his failure to confront them. He, his eighteen-year-old son, and his law clerk took their double-barreled shotguns and went forth to settle the matter. As they approached, Marshall and his party retired to the safety of a nearby building and refused to show themselves when Paschal called for those who had "published him as a poltroon and a coward" to come out and face him. After the city marshal appeared to restrain Paschal, he left to write his account of the affair for the *Intelligencer* and to announce his intention of attending court in Georgetown, where his opponents could find him if they so desired. "If I fall by the assassin, let me," he said. "My cause is just."[24]

Marshall told a different story. According to him, he and his friends were unarmed when the Paschal party appeared, and they retired to the building while they waited for other friends to bring their guns. By the time they received arms, Paschal had gone, and the city marshal detained them and took them before Judge A. W. Terrell, who found no grounds for holding them.

Upon learning that Paschal had gone to Georgetown, Marshall and Steiner set out in pursuit, but word of the affray went before them. To forestall bloodletting, the sheriff at Georgetown took Paschal into protective custody. Marshall and Steiner, denied their prey, returned to Austin, where another sheriff arrested them, and Judge Terrell placed them under a peace bond to prevent their taking aggressive action against Paschal for a year. With that, the two editors put aside their guns to take up their pens and do political battle.[25]

By then many Texans had come to regret their repudiation of Sam Houston. Some found the drift toward disunion alarming and looked to Houston as a moderating force; others blamed Governor Runnels for unsettled conditions on the frontier and remembered the military glory of the old chief. Even as Marshall and Paschal engaged in their

[24] *Southern Intelligencer*, March 16, 1859.
[25] Clarksville *Standard*, April 9, 1859; *Texas State Gazette*, March 19, 1859.

personal vendetta, the gubernatorial campaign of 1859 took shape in the pages of their papers. Sam Houston, still senator from Texas, called Marshall the "Autocrat of the Texas Democracy" in midsummer of 1858, and Marshall responded with an attack on the "monied Dynasty" of Austin, meaning Paschal and Swenson, charging that they were attempting to organize an opposition to challenge the "Democracy proper." The Houston *Telegraph* and *Galveston News* echoed his charges, speaking of the Paschalian Democracy and the "new Paschalian Austin clique."[26]

The opposition drew strength from the continued agitation for the reopening of the slave trade. Marshall took up the cause with fresh energy after resuming his editorial chair early in 1859. Texas needed labor, he submitted, and had the natural sovereign right to obtain it from Africa or Virginia, wherever it was least expensive; federal laws opposed to that right should be repealed and slaves imported until every industrious white man could afford to own them.

He kept the issue hot in the pages of the *Gazette* in the weeks before the meeting of the state Democratic convention in May, reporting the newspapers that had joined him in supporting the trade— among them the *Eastern Texian* at San Augustine, *Centerville Herald*, and *Jefferson Herald*. But when the convention met in Houston, his adherents did not have the strength to make the issue a part of the party platform. When the matter came up on the floor, it inspired a heated debate, during which two Galveston editors, Hamilton Stuart and Ferdinand Flake, walked out, "declaring that the odor of the slave trade was too strong for their nostrils."[27]

Marshall secured the renomination of Governor Runnels, a sympathizer, but, sensing the danger to the party organization, he backed away from the divisive issue after the convention. In the *Gazette* he emphasized the harmony that had existed at Houston and played down the slave trade and the disunionism that it implied.

Even so, the reopening of the African slave trade became the most important issue of the campaign. Paschal hammered away at the thesis that it meant the destruction of the Union. Reopening the trade was an "impossible experiment," he declared, and, even if accomplished, it would work to the disadvantage of the white worker in the

[26] *Texas State Gazette*, June 4, 1859; *Galveston News*, June 28, 1859.
[27] See Fornell, *Galveston Era*, p. 225.

South by cheapening his labor. To counter the "Austin clique," he called for a meeting of the friends of National Democracy in Austin on May 20.[28] The meeting brought together the elements that would oppose secession the following year, elements the Clarksville *Standard* tagged as a "promiscuous, hetereogenious conglomeration . . . of Old Line Whigs, Know-Nothings, Independents, Renegades, Bolters, Faggots, Frazzels, Stubs and Tail-ends of all parties." Andrew Jackson Hamilton, candidate for representative of the Western District, made the key address, ending with a rousing call for Sam Houston to enter the race for governor and, observed one hostile reporter, pouring out "pathos that brought forth a quart of crocodile tears to every pint of whiskey drank on the occasion."[29]

In less than two weeks, Paschal announced in the *Intelligencer* that the "agony" was over—Sam Houston had taken the field once more. In contrast to the active campaign he had waged two years earlier, Houston made only one speech in 1859. The campaign took place largely in the newspapers, with several editors issuing special campaign sheets.

The Austin editors set the pace, both of them issuing special papers: Marshall, the *Gazette for the Campaign*, and Paschal, the *Campaign Intelligencer*. Marshall repeated his denunciations of Houston's votes on Kansas and bore down on his Know-Nothingism. Paschal, in return, equated Houston with the preservation of the Union and hurled back charges of Know-Nothingism by pointing to the defections of Marshall's erstwhile partner, W. S. Oldham, and his sometime pro tem editor, Rip Ford. The Democracy of Marshall and his friends, Paschal charged further, was in fact only a "narrower sort of Know Nothingism." They had substituted "Southrons and Fire-eaters shall rule the South" for "Americans shall rule America" and "intense Southernism for intense Americanism," making "Allegiance to the Union" as hateful as "spiritual allegiance to the Bishop of Rome."[30]

Throughout the state, newspapers divided along the lines drawn by the Austin editors. In the Galveston Bay area, the *Galveston News* and Houston *Telegraph* followed Marshall, while the *Civilian* and *Die Union* supported Paschal.

[28] *Southern Intelligencer*, May 20, 1859.
[29] *Standard*, June 4, 1859.
[30] *Southern Intelligencer*, June 1 and August 17, 1859.

At San Antonio Gustav Schleicher, then editor of the *Zeitung*, not only concurred with his fellow countryman of *Die Union*, but also joined with a group of like-minded men to issue the English-language *Union*, a paper designed to explain away Houston's Know-Nothingism. The German editors thus curiously placed themselves on the same side as most of the surviving Know-Nothing papers, among them the Rusk *Texas Enquirer*, the *Harrison Flag*, the *McKinney Messenger* (formerly the *Clarksville Messenger*), the Anderson *Central Texian*, the La Grange *True Issue*, and the *Jefferson Gazette*.[31]

The *San Antonio Herald* also supported Houston, but not because of the inclinations of its owner-editor. J. D. Logan, like Rip Ford, had converted to Calhoun Democracy, but he left the paper under the management of young James Pearson Newcomb at a crucial moment. Newcomb endorsed Houston, and when Logan returned he permitted the endorsement to stand.[32]

Houston again received his staunchest support in east Texas from E. W. Cave, who again put out the *Campaign Chronicle* at Nacogdoches. Other papers aligned with Houston included the Waco *Southern Democrat*, *Colorado Citizen* of Matagorda, *Richmond Reporter*, Brownsville *American Flag*, Birdville *Union*, *Washington Register*, *Seguin Journal*, and Henderson *New Era*.[33]

Houston's traditional critics, Robert Loughery and Charles DeMorse repeated their denunciations, but not without a slight wavering from the Marshall party line. Both opposed the reopening of the slave trade and dreaded secession. Loughery showed his independence by opposing John Reagan as representative from the east, and DeMorse, although he stressed the need of party unity, later confessed to a few misgivings about Runnels's stand on the Union.[34]

Houston's hometown paper, the *Huntsville Item*, again opposed him, as did the Washington *Texas Ranger*, Waco *Southerner*, Seguin *Texan Mercury*, *Jefferson Herald*, *Quitman Herald*, Gilmer *Upshur Democrat*, Henderson *Southern Beacon*, *Liberty Gazette*, Crockett *Argus*, Palestine *Trinity Advocate*, *Sherman Patriot* and *Dallas Herald*.[35]

[31] Austin *Campaign Intelligencer*, July 16, 1859.

[32] John Fowler, *James P. Newcomb: Texas Journalist and Political Leader*, p. 10.

[33] Houston *Tri-Weekly Telegraph*, August 10, 1859; *Campaign Intelligencer*, July 16, 1859.

[34] Marshall *Texas Republican*, June 24, 1859.

[35] *Campaign Intelligencer*, July 16, 1859.

The voters gave the Houston party a decisive victory in the August elections, and some of them took occasion to gloat over the papers that had opposed him. On the frontier, one group made a bonfire of such papers, among them the *Telegraph* and *Galveston News*. In the cities of Austin and Houston jubilant crowds serenaded the losing editors with groans after the trend became clear.[36]

The victorious editors promptly started a movement to nominate Sam Houston for president of the United States in 1860. George Paschal suggested that the Marshall faction disband to support Houston as the only man who could hold the Union together. E. W. Cave, who had promoted the idea, made plans to sell his newspaper and join the Houston administration in Austin as secretary of state. Houston, for his part, laid plans to separate John Marshall and the *Texas State Gazette* from the public printing.

The defeated editors reacted in different ways. Charles DeMorse, taking a jab at John Marshall, attributed the loss to the few leaders' pushing the issue of slave trade on the masses; while Robert Loughery good-naturedly headed a column "How the Democratic Editors take Defeat." E. H. Cushing took the gibes of the winners with as much grace as he could muster, informing them that he could do his own groaning. Under the heading "Three Groans for Old Harris," he printed a cannon upside down and wrote: "The city of Houston wrongside up!— The country ruined! What's news in Travis, Marshall? DeMorse, how about the Red River country? O, for a word from El Paso! Somebody please send us a Crumb of Comfort from Somewhere!"[37]

John Marshall accepted defeat with neither humor nor grace. Scoffing at the idea of Sam Houston as president, he attributed the election results to circumstances that could never recur. The loss spurred him to even more frenzied criticism of Houston and those who in his opinion threatened southern rights. His cause received an unexpected boost in October, when abolitionist John Brown led his raid on Harper's Ferry.

---

[36] *Tri-Weekly Telegraph*, August 17, 1859.
[37] Quoted in *Texas Republican*, August 13, 1859.

CHAPTER 18

The Mystic Red

JOHN BROWN, Indians, and the weather cooperated with fire-eating editors to create hysteria in Texas during the election year of 1860.

Brown's raid gave substance to fears that had cropped up time and again in newspapers throughout the 1850s, fears of slave insurrections incited by abolitionists. After the excitement created by Adolph Douai ran its course, the fears centered in northern Texas and reflected the disturbances in Kansas. In the summer of 1856, only months after Douai's hasty exit, a paper appeared at Quitman in Wood County that by its very name, the *Texas Free Press*, aroused apprehensions. Edited by Winston Banks and published by Banks and Turner, the paper professed to be Democratic, but its true purpose soon became apparent. It took a strong stand against William Walker's filibustering in Nicaragua and then published a letter by John E. Lemon that asked for a discussion of slavery.

The *Texas State Times*, which only months earlier had sounded the alarm in regard to German abolitionists, dismissed the *Free Press* as a "silly sheet," but the paper created a whirlwind of excitement in its more immediate environs. E. Junius Foster of the *Sherman Patriot* began seeing abolitionists all over north Texas, and Robert W. Loughery declared flatly that slavery was not a matter for discussion. "We are clearly of the opinion that the discussion of slavery ought not to be allowed in the South, and the abolitionist who attempts public utterance of his sentiments should be driven out of the country," he wrote. "The safety of families certainly demands it."[1]

---

[1] Austin *Texas State Times*, February 21 and April 25, 1857; Marshall *Texas Republican*, March 14 and April 25, 1857.

The editor of the *Free Press* announced that unless he obtained four hundred subscribers he would discontinue publication at the end of the first volume, and, either for that reason or because of local hostility, the paper disappeared in the summer of 1857. Only then did the Calhoun press in south-central Texas become alarmed. Before suspending, the editor informed his readers that certain persons in Austin had given him encouragement by letters and subscriptions. Belatedly the Calhoun editors identified John E. Lemon, an abolitionist, as the owner of the *Texas Free Press* and reported his expulsion from the state. E. H. Cushing learned further that after leaving Texas, Lemon removed to Danville, Illinois, where in the fall of 1857 he was conducting an abolitionist sheet. Reportedly, Lemon maintained in his new paper that "agitation is everywhere going on in Texas" and that he was distributing a large number of papers there.[2]

The report of Lemon's subscribers in Austin aroused John Marshall. "Cannot we get the names of those parties?" he asked in the *Gazette*. "The community is unsafe while they are living among us unknown for their active opposition to our slave institutions." Such people, he continued, "ought to be dealt with as pirates and outlaws." In addition, postmasters should be required to publish the names of the subscribers to such journals in the paper of the town nearest the post office.[3]

In the same season that the *Free Press* disappeared, reports circulated of abolitionist activity at several points in north Texas. The *Dallas Herald* carried the account of a slave uprising in Waxahachie, Ellis County. Allegedly, two preachers, the brothers Joseph and Thomas Donegan, incited the insurrection, which vigilantes put down. Joseph Donegan eluded them, but the vigilantes apprehended Thomas, whipped him five hundred lashes, and escorted him out of town. The *Texas Republican* repeated rumors of slave unrest near Marshall, and the *Sherman Patriot* reported insurrections brewing at several points. As the rumors multiplied and proved unsubstantiated, the *Texas State Gazette* twitted the *Patriot* for its excitability. Under the heading "Look Out for Abolitionists," one correspondent offered as proof "that he saw a man in white pants talking to his negro girl—ran him off—and

[2] Austin *Texas State Gazette*, October 3, 1857.
[3] Ibid., and January 30, 1858.

she would not tell what he had said to her." "Good Lord!" exclaimed the *Gazette*, "if that constitutes an abolitionist in Sherman, there are hundreds of gents in this vicinity who would do well to steer clear of that locality."[4]

Whether true or imaginary, the reports foretold the panic that gripped the state during the summer of 1860. As the Democratic party fell apart and the Republicans gained strength in the North, the hysteria spread to other southern states, creating one of the worst witch hunts in the nation's history and preparing the southern mind for secession. The panic resulted in the death of some fifty persons in Texas in 1860 and came to a climax in 1862 with the mass hanging of thirty-nine accused culprits at Gainesville.[5]

The burden for spreading the panic falls on the press of the ultra–states' rights school. Earlier the ultraists who supported the reopening of the slave trade of necessity discounted rumors of slave rebellions. But circumstances had changed by 1860. Editors such as John Marshall forgot the reopening of the trade as they watched the growth of the free-soil Republican party. They saw John Brown's raid both as confirmation of the worst fears of the South and as a political weapon. Equating Brown with the Republican party—which they always called the Black Republican to distinguish it from that of Thomas Jefferson, they invoked Brown's name first to force the nomination of a presidential candidate sympathetic to their views and then to work for secession in the event of a Black Republican victory.

During the course of the campaign, a spate of new states' rights papers reinforced the older ones. M. A. Royal and William Edwards began the *True Southron* in Houston; W. H. Smith and G. Miller Johnson, the *States Rights Sentinel* at Tyler; James W. White, the *Belton Democrat*; Victor M. Thompson, the *States Rights Democrat* at La Grange. John Marshall revived the *State Gazette for the Campaign* at Austin, and Willard Richardson issued a similar sheet, the *Crisis!* at Galveston.[6]

The most extreme of the new papers, the *White Man*, appeared at Jacksboro, on the northwestern frontier. Established by H. A. Ham-

---

[4] *Texas Republican*, October 24, 1857; *Texas State Gazette*, September 4, 1858.
[5] Donald E. Reynolds, *Editors Make War*, p. 107.
[6] *Dallas Herald*, December 11, 1859, and January 4, 1860; *Texas Republican*, May 24 and June 30, 1860; Clarksville *Standard*, March 5, 1860.

ner and Isaac C. Worrall, the *White Man* reflected the peculiar passions of its time and place. It opposed abolitionists to the east, but even more vigorously it opposed the Indian to the west and the Mexican to the south. Hamner, a seasoned Indian fighter, blasted both the federal and state governments for failing to defend settlers on the frontier and heaped recrimination on Sam Houston. Houston returned Hamner's dislike in full measure, once flying into a rage upon seeing Hamner's name on a list of minute men and striking it from the list.[7]

The pro-Houston, pro-Union papers—called the Opposition in 1860—steadily lost ground during the campaign. They, no less than the states' righters, opposed the Black Republicans, but they argued that a Republican victory did not mean the end of southern rights within the Union. The two factions waged bitter war against each other during the campaign, and, if they sometimes seemed to forget their common political enemy, it was for good reason. The Republican party existed only as a specter in Texas. When E. H. Cushing learned that several delegates represented the state at the Republican convention in Chicago, he expressed doubts that they were bona fide Texans and asked that their names be printed. "Let the people of Texas know the men who have so foully slandered our State as to represent that Anti-Slaveryism has a foothold here," he wrote.[8] Later, after the national conventions, the editor of the *Goliad Messenger*, an independent journal, stirred up a row by printing the names of *all* the presidential candidates—Abraham Lincoln for the Republicans, along with John Breckinridge for the Southern Democrats, Stephen Douglas for the National Democrats, and John Bell for the Constitutional Unionists. "We do not believe the editor of the Messenger means to countenance to any degree that contemptible ticket," commented John Marshall, "and yet he may subject himself to some very unpleasant imputations if he allows that piratical flag to fly among the lawful ensigns of the legitimate parties." Yielding to public pressure, the *Messenger* dropped Lincoln's name.[9]

[7] *Texas State Gazette*, February 25, 1860; *Dallas Herald*, February 22 and 29 and May 2, 1860; E. C. Barker and Amelia W. Williams, eds., *The Writings of Sam Houston*, VIII, 13; Lynnell Jackson, *True Witnesses: A Check List of Newspapers, 1845–1861*, p. 66.

[8] Quoted in *Dallas Herald*, June 6, 1860.

[9] *Texas State Gazette*, September 8, 1860; Corpus Christi *Ranchero*, September 15, 1860.

As in 1859, the *Southern Intelligencer* spearheaded the opposition to the states' righters, but under a different editor. George Paschal retired in early March, 1860, explaining in his valedictory that his law practice and private affairs had suffered because of his editorial duties.[10]

John Marshall bid a fond farewell to "Jerry Sneak," but he might well have restrained his elation. Paschal yielded his chair to Anthony Bannon Norton, of the same political persuasion and a full-blown eccentric to boot. Norton announced in an early issue his intention to maintain any position he might take, "the world, the flesh, and the devil to the contrary." At this, Robert W. Loughery, who had long kept a wary eye on him, warned, "Be careful not to offend his Satanic majesty."[11]

Norton never told his age, even to members of his family. "My body was born sometime before the war, but my heart is that of the generation that has grown to manhood since Appomattox," he told his children late in life. They believed him to be about eighty years old when he died on December 31, 1893.[12]

Born in Ohio, Norton received his education at Kenyon College and studied law in his native state. Becoming an ardent Whig, he vowed in 1844 that he would never cut his hair or shave until Henry Clay became president of the United States. Norton kept his vow, and, as Clay never reached the presidency, remained unshorn for almost fifty years. The long, flowing hair and beard became his hallmark and never failed to inspire comment by those who saw him.

Norton edited several Whig papers in his native state. Then converting to Know-Nothingism, he removed to Texas about 1855. He campaigned actively for Fillmore in 1856, creating a sensation when he appeared at a Know-Nothing rally in Marshall looking like one of the "ancient prophets." He made an indelible impression on Robert W. Loughery, who watched from the audience. "The man from Ohio" certainly said nothing "in defense of the South," Loughery reported, applying his customary standard of judgment, and "the savageness of his appearance was relieved" by only two things: "first, by his size, for he

[10] *Texas State Gazette*, March 10, 1860; *Dallas Herald*, March 11, 1860.
[11] *Texas Republican*, March 17, 1860.
[12] Barker and Williams, *Writings of Houston*, VIII, 6–7.

was rather under medium height; secondly by a pair of keen, penetrating, mischievous Yankee eyes, which spoke more of 'speculating' than of war, and of good nature than malice."[13]

Entering state politics, Norton transferred the loyalty he had previously given Henry Clay to Sam Houston. The voters of Henderson and Kaufman counties elected him to the state legislature in 1857 and again in 1859. Briefly, he edited the *Fort Worth Chief.* Then shortly before the adjournment of the legislature in the spring of 1860, he purchased the *Southern Intelligencer* to become, in Robert W. Loughery's words, "the organist" of the state government and "chief bugleman of Old Sam." A few weeks after Norton's acquisition of the *Intelligencer*, Houston appointed him state adjutant general. In another few weeks, Norton, his hair and beard "half a yard long," clad in homespun, and carrying a "great buckhorn handled cane," nominated Houston for president of the United States at the convention of the Constitutional Union party at Baltimore.[14]

But 1860 was not a good year for Sam Houston. His presidential boom died young, and peculiar problems beset his state. The newspapers carried account after account of Indian hostilities on the frontier; Juan Cortina kept the Mexican border in an uproar; Knights of the Golden Circle agitated a filibuster expedition; and summer, coming early, proved the hottest and driest in memory. Temperatures soared over the one-hundred-degree mark for days at a time and sometimes reached one hundred ten.

Worst of all, rumors of slave insurrections and abolitionist activity began cropping up after John Brown's raid and grew in crescendo as the elections approached. Late in 1859, vigilantes at Dallas whipped and expelled two Northern Methodist preachers, William Blunt and Solomon McKinney, for allegedly inciting slave rebellion. At the turn of the year a group of slaveholders in Marshall convicted one E. C. Palmer of being an abolitionist and asked that such views be made treason. About the same time the *Trinity Advocate* reported a terror that seized Palestine in regard to the distribution of abolitionist literature. In March a slave woman near Dallas allegedly attempted for the third

[13] *Texas Republican*, October 11, 1856.

[14] Ibid., June 2, 1860; Barker and Williams, *Writings of Houston*, VIII, 6; Llerena Friend, *Sam Houston, The Great Designer*, p. 315.

time to burn her master's barn; in early June, papers reported the dis-
covery of a grand conspiracy to kill eight families in Fannin County.[15]

Along with the stories of the Fannin conspiracy came one that particularly terrified the citizenry. Reportedly, a slave woman near Bonham killed her master's six-year-old son. Charles DeMorse, who was
near the scene when the tragedy occurred, reported that the woman
killed the boy because a few days previously he had brought punishment to her own son. But DeMorse customarily took a more rational
approach to events than his fellows. The other papers in the state generally interpreted the murder as part of a larger conspiracy. "This child
is the fourth or fifth person that has been murdered by negroes recently in that county," reported the *Dallas Herald*. "It is all attributed
to the pernicious effects of Abolitionist emissaries."[16]

The time was thus ripe for hysteria when, on Sunday afternoon,
July 8, three fires broke out almost simultaneously at Dallas, Denton,
and Pilot Point, all within a forty-mile radius. The worst fire, that at
Dallas, demolished the business district, destroying, among other
buildings, the office of the *Dallas Herald*. J. W. Swindells, publisher
and associate editor of the *Herald*, immediately wrote Charles De-
Morse of the disaster, reporting that the fire had begun in a trash heap
outside a store and that the citizens had already begun rebuilding.
Such fires were all too common in Texas. The inhabitants dwelt primarily in wooden buildings. They had only the most primitive of fire-
fighting equipment and depended on open flame for light and heat.
DeMorse reported several other fires that had occurred about the
same time and blamed them on the spontaneous combustion of phos-
phorous matches, which at the time were unstable and sometimes ig-
nited during hot weather.[17]

But within days, the local citizenry attributed the Dallas fire to
incendiaries and, linking it to those at Denton and Pilot Point, saw the

[15] *Texas Republican*, December 24, 1859, and July 14, 1860; *Dallas Herald*, May 16
and June 20, 1860; *Texas State Gazette*, June 16, 1860; Palestine *Trinity Advocate*, January 4, 1860; *Matagorda Gazette*, January 4 and July 4, 1860. See also William W. White,
"The Texas Slave Insurrection of 1860," *Southwestern Historical Quarterly* 52 (January,
1949); and Wendell G. Addington, "Slave Insurrections in Texas," *Journal of Negro History* 35 (October, 1950).

[16] Clarksville *Standard*, June 30, 1860; *Texas Republican*, June 23, 1860; *Dallas
Herald*, June 20, 1860.

[17] Clarksville *Standard*, July 14, 1860.

outlines of a gigantic abolitionist conspiracy to lay waste to northern Texas. Charles Pryor, editor of the *Herald*, sounded the alarm to the rest of the state by dispatching three letters to fellow editors in varied sections. One went to John Marshall at Austin, another to L. C. De-Lisle of the *Bonham Era*, and the third to E. H. Cushing.

"It was determined by certain Abolition preachers, who were expelled from the country last year, to devastate, with fire and assassination, the whole of Northern Texas, and when it is reduced to a helpless condition, a general revolt of the slaves aided by the white men of the North in our midst, was to come off on the day of election in August," he wrote Marshall. "Arms have been discovered in the possession of negroes, and the whole plot of insurrection revealed for a general civil war at the August election."[18]

A similar letter to DeLisle described a well-organized conspiracy, "systematically conceived and most ingeniously contrived." "You and all Bonham are in as much danger as we are," Pryor warned. "Be on your guard and make these facts known by issuing extras to be sent in every direction."[19]

The letter to Cushing added the details that the conspirators planned to use poison as well as fire and to slaughter the old females along with the men, while sparing the young and handsome women to be parcelled out among themselves. "They had even gone so far as to designate their choice," wrote Pryor, "and certain ladies had already been selected as the victims of these misguided monsters."[20]

Marshall, DeLisle, and Cushing lost no time in publishing the news. Other editors, both in Texas and out, picked it up, and the hysteria began. R. W. Loughery reprinted Pryor's letter to DeLisle under a heading that at the time passed for screaming headlines: "Fearful Abolition Raid—Negro Insurrection—Northern Texas to be Laid in Waste —Intense Excitement."[21]

Reports of fire filled the newspapers for the next few weeks. Estimates placed the loss of the Dallas fire at $400,000, of the Denton fire at $80,000, and of the Pilot Point fire at $10,000. On the same after-

---

[18] *Texas State Gazette*, July 28, 1860.

[19] *Texas Republican*, July 28, 1860.

[20] Houston *Tri-Weekly Telegraph*, July 21 and 26, 1860; Houston *Weekly Telegraph*, July 17, 1860.

[21] *Texas Republican*, July 28, 1860.

noon, too, according to reports, fires broke out but were extinguished at Honey Grove, Waxahachie, Lancaster, Jefferson, and Austin. Nor did the fires cease. The office of the *White Man* at Jacksboro burned on July 28; much of the town of Henderson went up in smoke on August 5; and citizens reported the loss of barns or other property throughout the summer.[22]

More numerous than actual fires were the rumors of fires. Indeed, the rumors became a matter of bitter jest among journalists as they read with surprise of the destruction of their own towns in their exchange papers. Editors at Marshall, Paris, Mount Pleasant, Austin, and Weatherford denied that their towns had fallen to incendiaries. "Rumor," commented Hamilton Stuart in the Galveston *Civilian*, "has burned almost every town in Texas this season."[23]

Along with reports of fire, the newspapers carried accounts of other activities of the conspirators. The *San Antonio Ledger* wrote of large quantities of arms and ammunition discovered in slave cabins near Bastrop. The *Tyler Reporter* told of "over one hundred bottles of strychnine found in the possession of the Negroes. The Rusk *Texas Enquirer* wrote that slaves of a nearby plantation were instructed "to poison all the wells and springs" before election day and "to fire the dwellings, secure the arms and kill the white men as they returned from the election." From Henderson came news of a plot "for an indiscriminate, wholesale destruction by poison and arms" on election day; from Fort Worth, reports that abolitionists had distributed fifty six-shooters to slaves there. And so the terror spread. "By our Texas exchanges we receive further particulars in regard to the excitement growing out of the suspected Abolition conspiracy," said the New Orleans *Daily Picayune*.[24]

Throughout the state, citizens organized to stand guard around the clock, and newsmen kept busy not only reporting the danger but standing watch against it. "We are all completely worn out," declared the *Tyler Reporter* after every man on the staff had stood duty for four nights in a row, "and if this excitement still continues to exist, we must

---

[22] *Texas State Gazette*, July 28, 1860; *Texas Republican*, August 18, 1860; White, "Slave Insurrection," pp. 260–61.

[23] Quoted in Reynolds, *Editors Make War*, p. 108.

[24] See *Texas Republican*, August 11, 1860; and White, "Slave Insurrection," p. 277.

stop our regular issues, and furnish the news in the form of extras, for it is impossible for us to watch all night and work all day."[25]

At the peak of the excitement, John E. Lemon, late of the *Texas Free Press*, surfaced again in Wood County. Vigilantes apprehended him and made ready to hang him, but they relented to the tears of his wife. Instead of hanging him, they forced him to sign documents saying that on penalty of death he would never return or circulate abolitionist documents in Texas. Then they escorted him out of the county.[26]

Lemon fared better than most suspects. Vigilantes used the rope freely, with only a passing nod at the formalities of law. They hanged three blacks for the Dallas fire, a white tavern keeper and his slave girl for the burning of Henderson, a Negro at Georgetown for burning a stable and kitchen. From Waxahachie came the report that "two white men were hanged on Sat. July 21, and some twenty-odd negroes were to be hung also next week," and from Tennessee Colony word came that two white men were hanged on August 5 for allegedly furnishing Negroes with firearms and strychnine.[27]

Reports confirm thirty deaths during the terror, and the total probably ran well over fifty. The vigilantes preferred to act secretly and thus avoid alerting other suspects before catching them.[28]

As the total increased, some editors showed concern about the lack of due process. Robert W. Loughery, for example, expressed reservations about the guilt of the tavern keeper and his slave girl who died for the Henderson fire.[29] But generally editors and public alike agreed that the circumstances justified the risks of a few miscarriages of justice. "It is better for us to hang ninety-nine innocent (suspicious) men than to let one guilty one pass," said a correspondent in the *Telegraph*, "for the guilty one endangers the peace of society."[30]

The state awaited the August election with apprehension, but only one incident occurred. At Marshall a man returned from voting to find his wife missing. Suspecting foul play on the part of his servants, he sounded the alarm, and friends and family launched a frantic

---

[25] Quoted in Reynolds, *Editors Make War*, p. 102–103.
[26] *Texas State Gazette*, August 18, 1860.
[27] Ibid; *Texas Republican*, September 1, 1860; White, "Slave Insurrection," p. 277.
[28] Reynolds, *Editors Make War*, pp. 105–106.
[29] *Texas Republican*, September 8, 1860.
[30] Quoted in Reynolds, *Editors Make War*, pp. 103–104.

search. After some hours, they found the woman a few miles away "in a wretched condition." Left alone with the servants, she had become fearful of them, and, terror-stricken, had set out afoot for a neighbor's house only to become lost.[31]

When the state election passed without the heralded insurrection, a few observers moved the date up to the national election in November. But a number of editors decided that the matter had been blown out of proportion. The supposed poison found on blacks turned out to be whiskey, snake root, or paregoric, and some alleged abolitionists turned out to be merely citizens away from home. "There have been exaggerations," admitted Loughery, who had done his part to spread the alarm but who had displayed some doubts even during the height of the panic. The editor of the *True Issue* at La Grange called most of the accounts he received from the northern part of the state "falsehoods and sensation tales," while Thomas J. Crooks of the *Paris Press* announced that he was tempted to disbelieve all reports of "attempted insurrections, well poisoning, diabolic plans of abolitionists, &c," because the majority "when fully investigated turn out to be totally false."[32]

Others gave a harsher interpretation to the "exaggerations." At a Union rally in Austin, Governor Sam Houston accused those "whipsters and demagogues" who spread the stories of deliberately publishing falsehoods to further their political ends. "We all know how every occurrence has been magnified by the disunion press and leaders and scattered abroad," he declared, "and for no other purpose than to arouse the passions of the people and drive them into the Southern Disunion movement."[33]

A. B. Norton endorsed Houston's stand and elaborated on the theme in the *Southern Intelligencer*. Why, he asked, had rumors of the burning of Austin appeared just before the election? He particularly indicted the *Gazette*, the *Galveston News*, the Houston *Telegraph*, and the *Belton Democrat* for using rumor for political effect and promised that if his readers would investigate the facts they would see through "the transparent veil" of the "political editors."[34]

[31] *Texas Republican*, August 11, 1860.
[32] Reynolds, *Editors Make War*, pp. 110–11; *Texas Republican*, September 8, 1860; La Grange *True Issue*, October 18, 1860.
[33] Barker and Williams, *Writings of Houston*, VIII, 155–56.
[34] *Texas State Gazette*, August 25 and September 1, 1860.

Norton's stand brought a storm of criticism on his head. "We would ask, 'Are these men right on the issue of slavery?'" asked the *Telegraph*, a question that other states' rights papers picked up. At Fort Worth a meeting of citizens followed up on the question. "We look upon the course of the Austin Intelligencer and other papers and persons who attribute the late fires to accident and who assert that the hue and cry about abolition incendiarism has been raised for political effect, as insulting to the intelligence of Texas," they declared, "and as justly subjecting the editor of the Austin Intelligencer or any other papers or persons guilty of the like offense, to be placed at once on the list of persons whose future course is to be carefully watched by the proper committee."[35]

In the brouhaha, John Marshall and A. B. Norton exchanged personal insults, and Marshall again issued a challenge to physical combat to an editor of the *Southern Intelligencer*. Norton accepted the challenge but added his own touch. As dueling was still illegal in Texas, he proposed to meet Marshall at Tah-la-quah, five hundred miles distant and two hundred miles into Indian Territory. If Norton expected the distance to cool Marshall's belligerence, he miscalculated. Marshall agreed to the place and in company with Junius W. Smith and a few other friends set out for the battlefield.

Arriving at Sherman, near the state line, on September 4, he conferred with his old antagonist, George W. Paschal, who had ridden north as Norton's second. They confirmed arrangements for the meeting, agreeing, as Marshall understood, to change the place to a point just across the border in Indian Territory. Marshall and his friends headed for the border, but before they reached it a deputy sheriff from Sherman arrested them and detained them until Marshall made bond. He then proceeded to Indian Territory by way of the Preston Crossing of the Red River.

But as in his affair of honor with Paschal, Marshall and his opponent somehow arranged to miss each other. Authorities detained Norton in Sherman as they had Marshall, and when they released him Norton took a different crossing of the river. The two awaited each other at different points, and when they returned to Austin without fighting each charged that the other had failed to keep the rendezvous.[36]

[35] Ibid., September 22, 1860.
[36] Ibid., September 9, 1860.

While the two editors vented their personal hostilities, a letter, allegedly found near Fort Worth, whipped the conspiracy hysteria to new heights. Addressed to William Buley and purportedly written by one William A. Bailey, the letter described the activities of an abolitionist organization called the Mystic Red. "I found many friends who had been initiated, and understood the Mystic-Red," said the letter. "If we can break Southern merchants and millers, and have their places filled by honest Republicans, Texas will be an easy prey. . . . Texas we must have, and our only chance is to break up the present inhabitants, in whatever way we can."[37]

At first some editors, among them R. W. Loughery, questioned the authenticity of the letter, but it received wide circulation and the public accepted it as genuine. Citizens near Fort Worth identified the addressee as Anthony Bewley, a Northern Methodist preacher and abolitionist who fled Texas after the Dallas fire. Vigilantes apprehended him in Arkansas and returned him to Fort Worth, where he was hanged.[38]

John Marshall returned from his jaunt to north Texas to dispel any doubts his readers entertained about whether a conspiracy existed. "A plot has been formed in the Northern States embracing a large number of conspirators, which has as its object the expulsion or destruction of the entire pro-slavery population of Texas," he wrote. The plot involved not a single man like John Brown, he explained further, but many men, who planned to act in unison in various parts of the state to create chaos.[39]

Whether the conspiracy existed or not, it served the purpose of the ultra–states' righters. Even the opposition press tended to defect to their camp. J. D. Logan, for example, the old Whig turned Know-Nothing who owned the *San Antonio Herald*, switched sides after the August election and gave his support to Breckinridge. The move so outraged James Pearson Newcomb, then editor of the *Herald*, that he resigned and started another paper, the San Antonio *Alamo Express*, to support John Bell.

In addition, the two ultraist presses that burned in the summer resumed operation before the national elections. H. A. Hamner pur-

---

[37] Ibid., September 22, 1860.
[38] Walter Prescott Webb and H. Bailey Carroll, eds., *The Handbook of Texas*, I, 153–54.
[39] *Texas State Gazette*, September 22, 1860.

chased the press of the *Fort Worth Chief* at a sheriff's sale in late August and moved it to Weatherford, where, together with George W. Baylor, he reestablished the *White Man*. In October Swindells and Pryor resumed publication of the *Dallas Herald*.[40]

In November Breckinridge won a resounding victory in Texas; Lincoln received not a single vote there, or in nine other southern states, for the simple reason that his name was not on the ballot. As word reached Texas of his election, the press divided on the issue of secession—with the secessionists having by far the majority.

[40] Ibid., September 1 and 22, 1860; *Dallas Herald*, October 10, 1860.

CHAPTER 19

Closing the Era

NEWS of Lincoln's victory created a sensation as it spread across Texas. The news reached Galveston only two days after the election, prompting Willard Richardson to declare that "the time of waiting is past" and to call a meeting to consider dissolution of the Union.[1]

A telegraph line completed only months earlier flashed the news to Houston, where E. H. Cushing issued an extra of the *Telegraph* that carried word to the interior. The lone star flag flew in Galveston, said the extra, and a declaration of independence circulated at Houston. Throughout the state the ultraist editors accepted the news as the signal for secession. The editors of the *States Rights Sentinel* at Tyler placed at their masthead a five-pointed star with the words, "The Lone Star—she will never submit to Black Republican rule." The *Gulf Key* at Lavaca also hoisted the lone star, declaring for the dissolution of all connections with the North rather than submission. Robert W. Loughery, still exulting over Breckinridge's victory in Texas, could hardly believe the news when he received the *Telegraph* extra. A Unionist second only to a Southron, he recovered from his shock to declare that "the people of Texas will never consent to Black Republican domination" and to urge "Resistance to the Black Republicans."[2]

In no place did the news create more excitement than at the office of the *State Gazette* in Austin. John Marshall had departed early in November for Mississippi, where his wife lay ill in the last stages of con-

---

[1] Earl W. Fornell, *The Galveston Era*, p. 278; *Galveston News*, November 13, 1860.
    [2] Houston *Tri-Weekly Telegraph*, December 20, 1860; *Dallas Herald*, November 14, 1860; Marshall *Texas Republican*, November 24 and December 1 and 15, 1860.

sumption, but he directed affairs from afar. The *Gazette* continued in his style under the editorship of William Byrd, a scion of the renowned Virginia family and the grandfather of three famous Americans of the next century—Harry, governor of Virginia; Richard, aviator, explorer, and the first to fly over the North Pole; and Tom, a hero of World War I.[3]

The *Gazette* demanded that Governor Houston call the legislature into session, and when he dallied a group of men who clustered around the press office took matters into their own hands. The *Gazette* of December 8 carried and endorsed a call for an election on January 8 to choose delegates to a convention to meet in Austin on January 28.[4]

Throughout the state other papers joined the call for secession: the *Herald* and the *Ledger and Texan* at San Antonio, the *Ranchero* at Corpus Christi, the *Herald* at Dallas, the *Democrat* at Kaufman, the *Reporter* at Tyler, the *States Rights Democrat* at La Grange, the *Countryman* at Bellville. The *Colorado Citizen* at Columbus, a Bell paper before the election, converted to the cause, and during the crisis several new papers appeared to urge first secession and then Texas' joining the southern Confederacy. Thomas Crooks, who had doubted the wild stories of the Mystic Red while editor of the *Paris Press*, left that paper when it turned Unionist and founded the *Paris Advocate*, which carried the motto "The Confederate States of America—Our Home." W. E. Goodrich launched the *Southern Confederacy* at Seguin, as successor to Myddleton S. Dunn's *Mercury*; James A. Warner and Tom P. Ochiltree founded the *Star State Jeffersonian* at Jefferson; A. H. Appleton, the *Texas Patriot* at Gilmer; Richardson and Ramsey, the *Lone Star Banner* at Carthage.[5]

As no newspaper of record in Texas—indeed no voter—had supported Lincoln, no victors celebrated his election or formed a nucleus to oppose the secessionists. All alike went down in defeat in the presidential election of 1860, and, while the fire-eaters took up the shout for disunion, the more moderate elements nursed their wounds for a fatal

[3] Austin *State Gazette*, November 17 and 24 and December 1, 1861; Larry Jay Gage, "The Editors and Editorial Policies of the *Texas State Gazette*, 1849–1879" (M.A. thesis, University of Texas, 1959), pp. 52–58.

[4] Ernest W. Winkler, *Journal of the Secession Convention of Texas, 1861*, pp. 9–14.

[5] Columbus *Colorado Citizen*, February 16, 1861; *Dallas Herald*, March 20, 1861; *State Gazette*, March 23, 1861; Seguin *Southern Confederacy*, February 8, 1861.

moment. Only slowly did they rally to oppose secession and then only in broken ranks and sometimes halfheartedly.

The obvious rallying point for the Unionists, Sam Houston, at first adopted a wait-and-see attitude, advising those who asked him that he stood by the Constitution and that the Constitution had not yet been violated. At last on December 17, under pressure from the ultraists, he called a special session of the legislature to meet on January 21. But by then he had lost the initiative, and he never regained it. During late 1860 and early 1861, he progressively lost control of events to the fire-eaters.[6]

Hamilton Stuart and Charles DeMorse represented the dilemma of the moderate editors. Although they differed in their regard for Sam Houston, both considered themselves Democrats, and neither followed the party line unquestioningly. Both supported Breckinridge in the 1860 election, but Stuart publicly voiced his belief that Douglas was the better choice, and DeMorse deplored the stalemate of the Democrats at Charleston that led to the breakup of the party.

When Stuart learned the results of the election, he wrote a reasoned editorial arguing that Lincoln had won a "barren victory" because of the strength of the Democrats in other branches of the government. He defended Sam Houston's stand as the crisis developed, reminding his readers that "wise men and patriots often differ."[7]

DeMorse took a gloomy view of events, conceding the necessity of secession but at first making no effort to remove the United States flag from his mast or to change his motto, "The Constitution and the Union —the Union Under the Constitution." Even after the convention passed the secession ordinance on February 1, DeMorse expressed hope that the Union would reconstruct. When the issue was put to the voters on February 23, he announced his choice with scant conviction: "Everybody who reads the Standard knows that we are no extremist or disunionist. We have not yet abandoned the hope that the glories and benefits of the Union are to be perpetuated. Yet, so hoping, we give this day our vote 'For Secession.'" A few weeks later, after the voters had chosen disunion by a large majority, he replaced the stars and stripes with the lone star at the mast of the *Standard*, but still sadly. "There can be no propriety in the continuing of the Standard of the

---

[6] See Llerena Friend, *Sam Houston, The Great Designer*, pp. 330–31.
[7] Galveston *Civilian and Galveston Gazette*, November 13 and December 1, 1860.

late Union at our editorial head," he explained. "It is not with pleasure that we furl the old flag although we have done it before, and in 1836 sailed a few days under the white, red, and green of the Constitution party of Mexico and subsequently under the Lone Star." Sometime later, when critics asked whether he supported those who maintained that Texas had resumed her status as a republic, he explained that he did not raise the Confederate flag because he could not obtain a woodcut.[8]

Eventually a number of presses rallied to the Union cause, most of them located in areas with a large northern- or German-born population and many of them with records of opposing the Democrats or supporting the Houston faction of the party. In northern Texas, the *Quitman Clipper* and the *Weatherford News* opted for the Union, as did the *Sherman Patriot*, which alleged that the fire-eaters had nothing to lose by secession. The *Mount Pleasant Union*, after a brief suspension, resumed under a new editor, J. A. Carpenter, to urge citizens to fight for southern rights within the Union and to deride the "one-horse" convention called by the secessionists. The *McKinney Messenger* took Loughery of the *Texas Republican* to task for trying to destroy the Union, and the *Paris Press* suggested that Fannin County secede from Texas to form or join another state.[9]

At Marshall, J. W. Barrett of the *Harrison Flag* predictably took a stand opposite that of his local competitor, Robert W. Loughery. Under previous owners and in earlier papers, Barrett's press had advocated the Whig cause. He himself had abetted the Know-Nothing party and then the Constitutional Union. But Barrett did not live to fight the last political battle. He suspended the *Flag* in mid-January, 1861, because of poor health and died of a lingering illness shortly thereafter. Even Loughery, with whom he had carried on a long but gentlemanly feud, forgot political differences to remember the problems they shared as editors. "He has been sick nine months with little chance of improvement, . . ." wrote Loughery. "He has a large family depending on him, with children to educate. He needs every dollar coming to him. Those owing him should not be insensible to his condition."[10]

[8]Clarksville *Standard*, January 19, February 9 and 23, and March 11, 1861.

[9]*Texas Republican*, January 26, February 9, and May 25, 1861; *Dallas Herald*, December 5, 1860; Austin *Southern Intelligencer*, January 30, 1861.

[10]Marshall *Harrison Flag*, January 12, 1861; *Texas Republican*, January 17, 1861.

At Galveston Ferdinand Flake vigorously opposed secession in *Die Union*, thus voicing the general sentiment of the German citizenry. In central Texas, the La Grange *True Issue* and the *Bastrop Advertiser*, both once of Know-Nothing inclinations, took stands for the Union, as did the Seguin *Union Democrat* and the Waco *Southern Democrat*.[11]

At San Antonio, James Pearson Newcomb revived the *Alamo Express* to oppose the fire-eaters. "War of the direst description now threatens the land—Civil War," he warned. "And when the flame is fanned by every partizan sheet in the land by misrepresentation and inflammatory appeals, it behooves every man who can reach the public ear to soften if possible the sectional feeling."[12]

At Austin, A. B. Norton again made the *Southern Intelligencer* the most prominent opponent to the Marshall Democrats. "Who was the first fire eater?" he asked in the *Intelligencer*. Then he gave the answer: "The Devil, who is the first fire eater as well as the first secessionist on record, though he did secede, gained nothing but lost all by his attempt at revolution. . . . We don't belong to his party."[13]

When legislators and convention delegates gathered at Austin in late January, newsmen of both persuasions joined them in what grew into an informal editors' convention. A. B. Norton, as a host editor, extended professional greetings to all alike: to George H. Sweet, the fire-eater of the *San Antonio Herald*; Henry A. Maltby, the states' righter but reluctant secessionist of the Corpus Christi *Ranchero*; A. P. Shuford, a legislator as well as editor of the Unionist *Quitman Clipper*; William J. Cain of the Unionist *Bastrop Advertiser*; and Myddleton S. Dunn of the *Seguin Mercury* and E. W. Kinnan of the *Belton Independent*, both indecisive.[14]

The editors fraternized with one another at Austin, but intolerance lay not far beneath the surface, and already the press had experienced violence. The fire-eaters initially labeled the Unionists "submissionists," but as the crisis worsened so did the denunciations. "The submissionist sheets are apologists for Abraham Lincoln . . . forerunners of Black Republicans," charged the *Dallas Herald*. A. B. Norton

---

[11] *Southern Intelligencer*, January 30, 1861.
[12] San Antonio *Alamo Express*, February 6, 1861.
[13] *Southern Intelligencer*, January 30, 1861.
[14] Ibid.; *Southern Confederacy*, February 22, 1861.

was at heart a "Black Republican," said R. W. Loughery, and the *Intel-ligencer* "a quasi Black Republican sheet." "Are they traitors?" he asked. "Ought such treasonable, mendacious sheets as the Austin Intelligencer be allowed to exist in our State?"[15]

When news arrived at the turn of the year that South Carolina had seceded, the opposition to the Unionist papers took a violent turn. The fire-eaters exulted over the news. "South Carolina like a star of radiant glory has shot not madly but wisely from her sphere," effused the *Dallas Herald*. "She now shines as a Star whose glory fills the land."[16]

But at Galveston Ferdinand Flake took a different view, writing a sorrowful editorial that began "Poor South Carolina." The editorial infuriated the fire-eaters, and that night a crowd gathered in the streets, shouting derisively, "Poor South Carolina! Poor South Carolina!" The mob converged on the office of *Die Union* and using the ruse of a fake fire alarm broke into the office, wrecking the press and scattering the type. The act did not catch Flake by surprise. He had sensed the growing resentment of his Unionism and had set up duplicate printing equipment in his home. He continued to issue the paper from his residence until he repaired his office, sending out a greatly reduced sheet to explain what had befallen his press.[17]

The attack on *Die Union* embarrassed even some of the more ardent secessionists in the city. A few of them collected funds to repair the damage, and the fire-eater among the local editors attempted to shift the blame from his adherents. It was generally understood in Galveston, Willard Richardson said in the *News*, that the destruction was "the work of some of Mr. Flake's own countrymen. How true this general belief is we cannot say of our knowledge but such was and is the impression." The *Gazette* in Austin also felt enough embarrassment over the incident to credit it to Germans expressing their opposition to "that abolition concern," *Die Union*. George H. Sweet of the *San Antonio Herald* followed the same line.

The La Grange *True Issue* did not accept Richardson's conjecture, nor did James P. Newcomb of the *Alamo Express*. "Die Union was no

[15] *Dallas Herald*, December 5, 1860; *Texas Republican*, January 26, March 2, and May 11, 1861.

[16] *Dallas Herald*, January 2, 1861.

[17] Earl W. Fornell, "Ferdinand Flake: German Pioneer Journalist of the Southwest," *American-German Review* 21 (February–March, 1955): 25; *Galveston Era*, pp. 288–89.

abolition concern, but a Union paper," he wrote, "and the editor, Mr. Flake is an old Texan, a slave holder, and a better Southern man than any of the editors of the Herald. Mr. Flake's crime was a devotion to the Union."[18]

The next act of violence hit another German editor, and Germans did commit that. Ferdinand Lindheimer of the *Neu-Braunfelser Zeitung* in deference to the Anglo majority adopted the states' rights position. His readers took issue with his stand and attacked his press office, dumping his type into the Comal River. Lindheimer, like Flake, took the deed in stride. He fished his type out of the river and continued publication throughout the war.[19]

After Texas officially joined the Confederacy and the secessionists forced Houston to resign as governor, most of the Unionist editors accepted the fact and, like Houston, went with the state. But a few still raised their voices. At Waco a sheet called the *Sword of Gideon* appeared to lambast the secession convention and the Confederate States of America. It carried a crude woodcut of a man hanging by the neck and suggested such was the proper fate of traitors.[20] Opposition also came from the *Crockett Printer* under an editor, James Beveridge, who had come to his position by a tragic turn of events. Oscar Dalton, founder of the *Printer*, had been shot in his office in October, 1860, and died of his wound the following March. Beveridge filled in for Dalton and took a strong stand for Sam Houston, aiming sharp barbs at R. W. Loughery and other anti-Houston editors.[21]

Both James Pearson Newcomb and A. B. Norton continued their opposition to secession and left the state not far ahead of those who wanted to hang them. Newcomb insisted on his right to free speech and his credentials as an old Texan. "We have been raised in Texas from early infancy and her sod covers much whose memory is dear to us," he wrote. "She has become our father and mother and we believe

[18] *Alamo Express*, February 4, 1861.

[19] Selma Metzenthin-Raunick, "One Hundred Years: *Neu-Braunfelser Zeitung*," *American-German Review* 19 (August–September, 1953): 15.

[20] *Standard*, April 6, 1861.

[21] *Texas Republican*, June 6, 1861; *Southern Confederacy*, April 12 and October 12, 1861; *Southern Intelligencer*, May 15, 1861. The very prototype of the peripatetic printer, Beveridge had worked variously on the *Galveston News*, the Corpus Christi *Nueces Valley*, the *Bastrop Advertiser*, and the Austin *Texas State Times*. Known among his peers for his poetry and his caustic pen, he had written bitter anti-Catholic editorials for the *Times* during the Know-Nothing period. Beveridge's career at the *Printer* lasted only a short time. He died at Galveston "of dissipation" in October, 1861.

we know our duty to her and we will perform it to the best of our ability."[22]

After the federal troops in the state surrendered to state officials, Newcomb continued his tirades. He printed the census figures for 1860, showing the entire population of the seven seceding states at one million less than the population of New York alone and pointing out further that the large slave population would be worse than a dead-weight in case of war. When the flag of the Confederacy went up over the Alamo, he commented, "We advise these brave flag raisers to look sharp or the ghost of Crockett and Travis will haunt them."[23]

Newcomb went too far when on May 13 he issued an extra giving a sarcastic account of a "great victory" in which 1,500 Confederates captured 300 "U.S. troops who had already agreed to leave the state." That night a mob, identified by Newcomb as "Knights of the Golden Circle and rangers," broke into the *Express* office, destroyed his press and materials, and set fire to the building. By morning nothing remained but ruins. Rumors circulated that 150 Union men would be hanged or banished, Newcomb among them, and the *Ledger* applauded the destruction of the *Express*. "It should have been destroyed long since by an outraged community," said the *Ledger*. "It is high time that the world should know that this community will not brook the presence of traitors nor tolerate the existence of nuisances."[24]

On the advice of his friends, Newcomb left the city for the Rio Grande. He left openly, announcing that he would return in two weeks, but on his return trip he met friends who warned him that the secessionists regretted having let him go and would hang him on his return. He also met Confederate troops en route to New Mexico, among them his only brother, who further warned him. Newcomb turned back toward the Rio Grande and made his way through Mexico to California. He remained in exile for the duration of the war—but still unsilenced. From the far west he issued another of his warnings: "The present Southern Confederacy must perish—it is founded on no principle of liberty or right—it is the work of satanic ambition, and terrible will be its end."[25] Nor was the *Alamo Express* completely extinguished. Newcomb returned after the war to found another paper, the *San Antonio*

[22] *Alamo Express*, February 19, 1861.
[23] Ibid., March 15 and 20, 1861.
[24] Ibid., May 13, 1861; *Ledger* quoted in *Texas Republican*, June 8, 1861.
[25] James Pearson Newcomb, *Sketch of Secession Times in Texas*, p. 12.

Express, which continued the name and which continued still in 1981.

Norton remained in Texas only slightly longer than Newcomb. About the time that Newcomb printed his sarcastic account of the "great victory" of the Confederate troops, the *Intelligencer* carried a "Letter to the People," which the *Gazette* branded as "treasonable." The *Gazette* called for a public meeting to consider the matter but called off the meeting when the *Intelligencer* recanted and said the letter was published by mistake. Growing fearful for his safety, Norton announced the continuation of the *Intelligencer*, thus hoping to throw off his enemies. Then he slipped away from Austin "to seek a more healthful latitude." He made his way through the lines to Ohio, where he waited out the war.[26]

Newcomb's predictions of doom proved all too correct. Indeed, in retrospect the gathering of editors at Austin in January, 1861, appeared as an editorial wake not only for the state and nation as they had been, but also for newspapering as it had been in Texas. The Union blockade thrown about the southern coast made the old problem of obtaining newsprint almost insurmountable. Editors and printers went off to war, some of them never to return. Most of the printing presses in the state fell silent for the duration. Only a few papers persisted to carry the news, and those appeared on reduced sheets or irregularly and sometimes on makeshift newsprint—wallpaper, wrapping paper, or letterhead.

Appropriately, John Marshall, who had done so much to bring about secession and war, left for the battlefront early in the hostilities. As if symbolizing his lost cause, he died in Virginia leading a charge during the Seven Days Battles.[27]

In the last year of the war, the deaths of two other newsmen put a symbolic period at the end of the pioneer era of Texas newspapers. The Houston *Telegraph*, which Francis Moore and Jacob W. Cruger had nursed to maturity, printed their obituaries in successive issues on December 7 and 9 of 1864.

Moore, a Unionist in 1860 as in 1845, went north after secession. He died in Michigan on September 1, 1864, while in the employ of a

---

[26] A. B. Norton, "A History of Early Newspapers in Texas," in *A History of the Texas Press Association*, ed. Ferdinand B. Baillio, p. 362; *State Gazette*, May 18, 1861.

[27] W. S. Oldham, "Colonel John Marshall," *Southwestern Historical Quarterly* 20 (October, 1916): 137–38; *State Gazette*, July 5, 1862.

copper mining company. Old Texians cherished the notion that the war caught Moore in the north and that he tried valiantly to return through the lines to lend support to the state. But the facts do not bear out that belief. Moore, the state geologist in early 1861, was on the frontier on official business when the crisis developed. Fearing the consequences of a bitter war, he took his family north.[28]

His former partner, Jacob W. Cruger, chose the different course. Cruger joined the Confederate army and distinguished himself in action with Richard Montgomery Gano's company of Texas cavalry in the trans-Mississippi west. Camp life broke his health, and he retired to his brother's home at Belton, where he died of tuberculosis on November 30, 1864.[29]

E. H. Cushing interrupted his reports on the war to pay tribute to his predecessors, who had recorded "the birth, the infancy, the youth and the full manhood" of Texas. The files of the *Telegraph*, he mused, recorded the "struggles and failures . . . the successes and triumphs," indeed, the history, of an era. The same could be said of the files of the other Texas newspapers before the Civil War.

[28] Samuel Wood Geiser, "Note on Dr. Francis Moore (1808–1864)," *Southwestern Historical Quarterly* 47 (April, 1944): 425; *Tri-Weekly Telegraph*, December 7, 1864.

[29] Madeleine B. Stern, "Jacob Cruger: Public Printer of Houston," in *Imprints on History: Book Publishers and American Frontiers*, pp. 134–35; *Tri-Weekly Telegraph*, December 9, 1864.

Appendix: A Checklist of Texas Newspapers From Annexation to the Civil War

THOMAS W. STREETER, *Bibliography of Texas, 1795–1845*, lists definitively the newspapers of Texas before annexation, but the papers of later periods have not been so treated. The following checklist is designed to fill in part the gap for the period from annexation to the beginning of the Civil War.

The list is based primarily upon an examination of the newspapers available and upon references in contemporary papers. Supplementing those sources are early histories by journalists close to the era: A. B. Norton, "A History of the Early Newspapers of Texas"; Ben Stuart, "History of Newspapers in Texas" (manuscript); and A. C. Gray, "A History of Texas Press." Because of incompleteness and a tendency to error, however, these histories must be used with caution. Norton, a Texas newsman before and after the Civil War, compiled his work primarily from personal recollections, and, predictably, his work is rich in human interest but garbled in fact. Stuart, a Galveston newsman and son of a pioneer newsman, is most authoritative when writing of the newspapers of his city. Gray, the last editor-owner of the historic Houston *Telegraph*, is best when dealing with Houston papers and journalists.

More recent works are also of use, but again some of them must be used cautiously. The most recent checklist, Lynnell Jackson, *True Witnesses: A Check List of Newpapers, 1845–1861*, incorporates most of the errors of the early histories and adds a few new ones by confusing Texas cities—for example, Albany, Buffalo, Fredericksburg, and Montgomery—with cities in other states. Ernest W. Winkler, *Check List of Texas Imprints, 1846–1860*, provides a usually accurate check on names and titles, even though he does not list newspapers as such.

Ike H. Moore, comp., *Texas Newspapers: A Union List of Newspaper Files, 1913–1939*, although dated, is still useful in locating copies of newspapers.

Streeter included 101 items in his checklist. Of those, only one, the *Galveston News*, has continued to the present. The following list includes 347 items, of which six in addition to the *News* have published continuously since their founding: *Victoria Advocate*, *Huntsville Item*, *Bastrop Advertiser*, Columbus *Colorado Citizen*, *Gonzales Inquirer*, and *Neu-Braunfelser Zeitung* (now *Herald and Zeitung*). Other late-twentieth-century papers can trace their origins to antebellum newspapers and pioneer presses.

The list is alphabetized first by town and then by title. Variant titles are shown with the more common or better known title of a paper. The extant copies are not systematically and exhaustively located, but the reader is directed to sample copies and collections when that information is available.

The University of Texas at Austin has the largest collection of newspapers for the period, and the Texas State Library, the second largest. Other depositories with notable holdings include the San Jacinto Museum of History, Rosenberg Library at Galveston, Library of Congress, Houston Public Library, and San Antonio Public Library. The more important papers are on microfilm and thus generally available.

[Anderson] *Central Texian*

The brothers T. D. and R. A. Van Horn began this weekly in May, 1854. It carried the motto "Independent on All Subjects—Neutral on None," but Democratic editors considered it to be Know-Nothing in 1855. R. A. Van Horn purchased his brother's interest in June, 1856. W. B. Rennolds [*sic*] served as editor until September, 1856, when Alfred A. Pittuck, a printer, succeeded him. John C. Hepperla replaced Pittuck in January, 1857, and Van Horn suspended the paper with the issue of March 7, 1857, "after three years of battling adverse storms of poverty and non appreciation." Van Horn sold the press later in the year. In October, 1859, he established the *Navarro Express* at Corsicana. Pittuck and Reynolds revived the *Texian* in May, 1858, with David C.

Dickson, once Know-Nothing candidate for governor, as editor. The San Jacinto Museum of History has an excellent run from 1855 to 1857.

[Anderson] *Texas Baptist*

Volume I, number 1, of this weekly appeared March 7, 1855, with George Washington Baines as editor, J. B. Stiteler, associate editor, and R. W. Taliaferro and John H. Rowland, corresponding editors. The paper carried the motto "Devoted Expressly to the Religious and Educational Interests of the Baptist Denomination in Texas." Printed at first in the office of T. D. and R. A. Van Horn, the paper appeared from an office owned by the Texas Publication Society in 1858. Justin A. Kimball became editor in early 1861 when Baines, the great-grandfather of Lyndon Baines Johnson, became president of Baylor University. The Southwestern Baptist Theological Seminary at Fort Worth has a full run of the paper.

[Austin] *Campaign Intelligencer*

George Paschal, editor of the *Southern Intelligencer*, issued this sheet during the campaign of 1859 to advocate Sam Houston for governor. He discontinued it at the end of the campaign. Four issues for June and July, 1859, are in the Newspaper Collection, University of Texas at Austin.

[Austin] *Democratic Platform*

This semiweekly campaign sheet appeared June 2, 1859, from the office of the Austin *Texas State Gazette*. Edited by John Marshall, it advocated H. R. Runnels for governor. The issues of June 2 and July 14 and 26, 1859, are in the Newspaper Collection, University of Texas at Austin. The issue of June 28, 1859, is in the Texas State Library.

[Austin] *New Era*

Joel Miner and Jacob Cruger established this weekly on July 23, 1845, to print the proceedings of the Convention of 1845. They suspended it after the convention adjourned, but Dr. John G. Chalmers bought the press in October and revived the *New Era*. He continued publication erratically until his death on New Year's Day, 1847, in a street incident.

[Austin] *Rambler*

The first issue of this weekly appeared on September 28, 1858, with William Carleton as editor and publisher. Carleton, born in England on May 7, 1812, came to Texas in January, 1835, with his wife, child, and three servants. After distinguishing himself in the Texan Revolution, he resided in New Orleans for twenty years. The Texas Legislature passed a special act giving him land for his revolutionary service. He moved back to Texas, sold his land, and bought a printing press to issue this paper. He moved the paper to Lockhart in mid-1859. Copies for November 9, 1858, and January 25, 1859, are in the Newspaper Collection, University of Texas at Austin.

[Austin] *Scorpion*

This sheet, "devoted to everything in general and nothing in particular," appeared in the late spring of 1860, with John Squibob, obviously a pseudonym, as editor and publisher. The issue of May 7, 1860, is in the Newspaper Collection, University of Texas at Austin.

[Austin] *Southern Intelligencer*

This weekly began August 27, 1856, with William Baker and Irving Root as publishers and George W. Paschal as editor. The paper supported the Independent Democrats in 1859 in opposition to the Austin *Texas State Gazette*. By February 1, 1860, R. J. Lambert, John S. Perry, and Joel Miner owned the paper. Shortly thereafter, A. B. Norton acquired an interest and replaced Paschal as editor. Both Paschal and Norton engaged in bitter feuds with John Marshall of the *Texas State Gazette*. The paper opposed secession in 1861 and suspended when Norton fled to the north. The Newspaper Collection, University of Texas at Austin, has scattered issues from 1856 to 1861.

[Austin] *South-Western American*

The brothers Jacob and Phineas DeCordova established this weekly in November, 1849. Initially, Phineas DeCordova and Lewis M. H. Washington edited it. Jacob DeCordova wrote extensively about Texas, gaining the title of "Land Merchant of Empire." John S. Ford and Joseph Walker purchased the office in November, 1852, and a year later changed the name to the *Texas State Times*. Copies from December 21, 1849, to November 5, 1853, are in the Newspaper Collection, University of Texas at Austin.

[Austin] *State Gazette and General Advertiser*

This daily edition of the *Texas State Gazette* appeared on October 12, 1859. That issue and the one for November 8, 1859, are in the Newspaper Collection, University of Texas at Austin.

[Austin] *State Gazette for the Campaign*

John Marshall of the *Texas State Gazette* issued this sheet to promote the Democrats over the Know-Nothings in the summers of 1855, 1857, and 1860. The issues from July 24 to August 4, 1855, and June 24, July 29, 1857, are in the Newspaper Collection, University of Texas at Austin.

[Austin] *Texas Democrat*

John S. Ford and Michael Cronican purchased the Washington *Texas National Register* in 1845 and moved it to Austin, where they changed the name and began issuing the *Texas Democrat* in January, 1846. Ford and Cronican dissolved their partnership after Ford left to fight in the Mexican War. Joel Miner and Samuel Cummings acquired the paper and sold it to William Cushney, who changed the name to *Texas State Gazette*. Scattered issues from January, 1846, to July, 1848, are in the Newspaper Collection, University of Texas at Austin.

[Austin] *Texas Journal of Agriculture*

The Austin *Texas State Times* of February 3, 1855, noted receipt of the first number of this paper. It was published in the office of the Austin *Texas State Gazette* and edited by Irving Root and J. E. Park.

[Austin] *Texas National Register*

John S. Ford and Michael Cronican purchased this paper at Washington from William Cushney and George Washington Miller in the fall of 1845. They moved it to Austin and early the following year changed the name to the *Texas Democrat*. The issues from November 15 to December 27, 1845, are in the Newspaper Collection, University of Texas at Austin.

[Austin] *Texas Ranger*
In late December, 1852, Joseph Lancaster and John S. Ford issued a
    prospectus for this paper to be published in Austin, but it never
    appeared. Lancaster, publisher of a paper by the same name at
    Washington, revived his paper there. Ford purchased the Austin
    South-Western American.

[Austin] *Texas Sentinel*
This weekly, the successor to the *Texas State Times*, began publication
    on June 20, 1857, and continued until July, 1858. William G.
    O'Brien and Company purchased the *Times* from John S. Ford.
    Other proprietors in the firm included P. W. Humphreys, A. G.
    Compton, and X. B. DeBray. Fenton M. Gibson, formerly of the
    Richmond Recorder, edited the paper. The *Sentinel* gave vigor-
    ous support to Sam Houston during the election of 1857. Copies
    from June 27, 1857, to July 24, 1858, are in the Newspaper Collec-
    tion, University of Texas at Austin.

[Austin] *Texas State Gazette, Tri-Weekly State Gazette*
William H. Cushney purchased the *Texas Democrat* and began this
    paper, first a weekly and later a triweekly, in 1849. Robert C.
    Matthewson was the first editor. Other men associated with the
    Gazette before the Civil War included H. P. Brewster, J. W.
    Hampton, George W. Crawford, W. R. Scurry, and John Mar-
    shall. Marshall made the paper the organ of the Southern Demo-
    crats in the late 1850s, and largely because of his opposition Sam
    Houston lost the election of 1857. One of the most important pa-
    pers of the period, it has been more fully treated in Larry Jay
    Gage, "The Editors and Editorial Policies of the *Texas State Ga-
    zette*, 1849–1879" (Master's thesis, University of Texas at Austin),
    and "The Texas Road to Secession and War: John Marshall and the
    Texas State Gazette, 1860–1861"; Lonnie Sinclair, "Crossroads of
    Conviction"; and Ronnie C. Tyler, *Joseph Wade Hampton: Editor
    and Individualist*. The Newspaper Collection, University of Texas
    at Austin, has a full run from August 25, 1849.

[Austin] *Texas State Times, Tri-Weekly State Times*
John S. Ford and Jo Walker purchased the *South-Western American*
    from Jacob and Phineas DeCordova in 1852 and changed the

name to *Texas State Times* on November 14, 1853. Others associated with the paper during the next few years were W. T. Davidson, James A. Beveridge, W. E. Jones, Ed Finnin, X. B. DeBray, and Fenton M. Gibson. The paper vigorously supported the American party from 1855 to 1857, when Ford returned to the Democratic party. He sold the paper to a group headed by William O'Brien, who changed the name to the *Texas Sentinel*. Issues from 1854 to 1857 are in the Newspaper Collection, University of Texas at Austin.

Bastrop Advertiser

The first issue of this weekly appeared on March 4, 1853, with the motto "Devoted to Agriculture, Education, Temperance, Internal Improvements and General Information." The successor to the *Colorado Reveille*, the *Advertiser* was published by William J. Cain and initially edited by H. Armington. Armington withdrew in 1854, and Cain became editor. The paper supported the Know-Nothing party during the mid-1850s and then supported the Independent Democrats. The editor served in the Confederate army. The copy of May 23, 1854, and scattered copies from 1857 to 1858 are in the Newspaper Collection, University of Texas at Austin. The paper still continues.

[Bastrop] *Colorado Reveille*

The Clarksville *Standard* of July 3, 1852, noted receipt of the first two issues of this paper, edited by B. Desha, Jr., a newcomer to the state. The prospectus and first issue were printed at Washington, the second at Bastrop. William J. Cain purchased the press in late December, 1852, and began the *Advertiser* the following year. Volume I, number 6, for June 24, 1852, is in the Texas State Library.

Beaumont Banner

This weekly began in April, 1860, with A. N. Vaughn as editor. An independent paper, it cost three dollars per year. Volume II, number 1, for May 30, 1861, is in the San Jacinto Museum of History. The issues of December 11, 1860, and January 8 and May 21, 1861, are in the Newspaper Collection, University of Texas at Austin.

Bellville Countryman

This weekly appeared on July 20, 1860, with John P. Osterhout, editor
    and proprietor, and W. W. Thayer, publisher. It regularly carried
    a column in German. Its motto was "Independent in All Things—
    Neutral in None," but it leaned toward the southern wing of the
    Democratic party. Osterhout, born in Pennsylvania about 1825,
    continued the paper throughout the war, publishing on half-
    sheets. The Texas State Library has an excellent run from July 28,
    1860, to August 21, 1865. The Newspaper Collection, University
    of Texas at Austin, has a run from April 21, 1861, through August
    21, 1865.

Belton Argus

J. A. Kirgan and W. B. Beckwith issued a prospectus, dated Decem-
    ber 7, 1857, and printed at Fairfield, for this paper. It probably
    never appeared. A copy of the prospectus is in the San Jacinto
    Museum of History.

Belton Democrat

The Marshall *Texas Republican* of February 4, 1860, noted receipt of
    the first number of this weekly. James W. White was proprietor
    and John Henry Brown, editor. A handsome masthead carried
    Patrick Henry's words, "Give Me Liberty or Give Me Death."
    The paper advocated the cause of the South. The issue of March
    8, 1861, is in the Newspaper Collection, University of Texas at
    Austin; that of September 27, 1861, in the Texas State Library.

Belton Independent

Andrew Marschalk moved this paper from Georgetown to Belton in
    1857. He edited it, and his son Francis published it. The Houston
    Tri-Weekly Telegraph of December 22, 1858, reported that "the
    Independent being printed in a very open building has to suspend
    in long continued cold weather." Edward W. Kinnan acquired the
    paper in the spring of 1859, and the Marschalks moved to Hemp-
    stead to found the *Courier*. The paper supported Sam Houston
    and opposed secession. The Newspaper Collection, University of
    Texas at Austin, has the issues of May 2, 1857, March 13, 1858,
    and June 4, 1859.

[Birdville] *Union*

This paper appeared in 1857, with Albert Gallatin Walker as editor and W. L. Edwards as publisher. It was Democratic and opposed the removal of the county seat from Birdville to Fort Worth. In a dispute over the removal, Walker killed John J. Courtney, editor of the rival *Western Express*. Walker, a native of Virginia, served several terms in the Texas legislature.

[Birdville] *Western Express*

The Marshall *Texas Republican* of November 22, 1856, welcomed this paper, published by Chilton and Collins. John J. Courtney, the editor, was killed by Albert Gallatin Walker, editor of the *Union*, in 1859.

Bonham Advertiser

Charles DeMorse of the Clarksville *Standard* and Richard S. Hunt started this paper in 1849. Hunt purchased DeMorse's interest late in the year. Hunt, Canadian-born, aroused the ire of the Marshall *Texas Republican* by supporting Sam Houston. Hunt sold the paper to N. P. Clark and Moody, who proposed to change the name to *Western Star* in 1853 but reconsidered and continued the paper with Hunt as editor. After Moody's death, Clark sold the office to E. J. Foster, who took it first to Paris and then to Sherman. Copies for July 8, 1851, and July 9, 1853, are in the Library of Congress.

Bonham Era

After the death of John M. Crane, editor of the *Independent*, L. C. DeLisle and Phelps purchased the office and began the *Era* in 1859. DeLisle, born in Virginia about 1835, sold to Richard S. Hunt and Matteson in July, 1860.

Bonham Independent

John M. Crane established the *Independent* in April, 1858. The Marshall *Texas Republican* of April 8, 1859, reported that Crane had been shot on the streets of Bonham by one Saddler, whom Crane had previously caned. After Crane's death, L. C. DeLisle and Phelps bought the office of the *Independent* and established the *Era*.

[Bonham] *Northern Standard*

Charles DeMorse acquired the office of the *Sentinel* and issued the
   Standard simultaneously at Clarksville and Bonham from August
   23, 1846, until the following April. He then discontinued the
   Bonham office with the explanation that the experiment was not
   financially feasible. By the summer of 1847, J. A. Clark and John
   Shaffer had bought the press and established the *Western Argus*.

Bonham Sentinel

Thomas J. Langdon established the *Sentinel* in July, 1846. He issued
   only a few numbers and then sold the office to Charles DeMorse,
   who published the *Standard* at both Clarksville and Bonham for
   eight months.

[Bonham] *Western Argus*

Joseph Addison Clark and John Shaffer acquired the office that had
   previously issued the *Bonham Sentinel* and the *Northern Standard* in 1847. They published the *Western Argus*, a Whig paper.
   They sold to James Sharp before the year was out, and the following year Sharp sold to Robert C. Matthewson and James W. Latimer. The new owners moved the press to Paris, where they issued
   the *Texas Times* for a short while. Latimer moved the press to
   Dallas in 1849 and started the *Herald*, while Matthewson became
   editor of the Austin *Texas State Gazette*.

[Bonham] *Western Star*

The Marshall *Texas Republican* of November 5, 1853, reported that
   "Moody and [N. P.] Clark of the Bonham Advertiser have purchased the office and changed the name of the paper to Western
   Star." Before the end of the year, that name was dropped in favor
   of the original, and the former editor, Richard S. Hunt, had become publisher.

Boston Bee

The Houston *Democratic Telegraph and Texas Register* of March 28,
   1850, welcomed the first number of the *Bee*, established by
   Joseph Lynch and G. W. Wright.

[Boston] *Bowie Inditer*

The Marshall *Texas Republican* of March 19, 1853, greeted this paper published by Charles R. Joslin. The *Republican* of March 3, 1854, noted receipt of the last number of the *Inditer*, which had appeared in half-sheet and mourning and was to be discontinued because of insufficient patronage.

[Brazoria] *Texas Planter*

This paper appeared in the summer of 1852, with Samuel L. Fowler as editor and proprietor and J. A. Hyslop as publisher. By late 1853, James H. Bell and A. S. Lathrop were editors and proprietors, and by the fall of 1854 they had been replaced by Henry and James R. Wilkes. In the summer of 1855, the paper blended with the *Columbia Democrat* to form the Columbia *Democrat and Planter*. The Newspaper Collection, University of Texas at Austin, has scattered issues from July 28, 1852, to July 18, 1855.

Brenham Enquirer

The Austin *Texas State Gazette* of July 9, 1853, welcomed the *Enquirer*, published by D. H. Rankin. M. F. C. Barber joined Rankin in 1856 and was replaced by J. T. Norris in 1857. Rankin continued the paper alone in 1858. The Newspaper Collection, University of Texas at Austin, has scattered issues from January 24, 1854, to July 16, 1858.

[Brenham] *Lone Star*

The Houston *Telegraph* of October 25, 1849, noted receipt of the first three numbers of the *Lone Star*, with W. H. Ewing as editor. John B. Wilkins owned an interest in the paper. He sold that interest to George W. Crawford in 1850, and Crawford and Ewing moved the office to Washington, where they began the *Semi-Weekly Star*. That paper became the *Lone Star and Southern Watchtower* in 1851.

[Brenham] *Texas Christian Advocate and Brenham Advertiser*

Robert B. Wells, a Methodist minister, founded this paper as an organ of his church in 1847. The paper moved to Houston in December, 1847, where it became the *Texas Christian Advocate*. It is fully treated in Wesley Norton, "Religious Newspapers in Antebellum Texas."

[Brenham] *Texas Ranger*

Joseph Lancaster founded this paper at Washington on the Brazos on
January 16, 1849, but moved its office back and forth between that
place and Brenham after 1856. By February, 1857, the *Ranger* was
published simultaneously at Brenham, Washington, Chappell
Hill, and Independence. A number of men joined Lancaster
through the years, among them John M. Gibson, G. B. Rives,
and Irwin Johnson. By late 1860, S. G. Ragsdale edited the paper,
and it appeared only at Brenham. The *Ranger* supported the
Southern Democrats. The Newspaper Collection, University of
Texas at Austin, has scattered issues from February, 1857, to December 17, 1860.

[Brownsville] *American Flag*

I. N. Fleeson and J. R. Palmer began the *Flag* in 1846 at Matamoros as
a Mexican War paper. After Fleeson's death in 1848, Palmer
moved the office across the Rio Grande to Brownsville. Edwin B.
Scarborough acquired the paper in 1849 and continued it for ten
years. Scarborough, born in Virginia about 1821, served several
terms in the Texas legislature. Four issues from May 19, 1855, to
March 16, 1859, are in the Newspaper Collection, University of
Texas at Austin.

[Brownsville] *Boletin Extraordinario*

This Spanish-language sheet appeared from the office of the *American
Flag* in 1855. The issue of August 29, 1855, is in the Newspaper
Collection, University of Texas at Austin.

[Brownsville] *Rio Bravo*

This paper appeared in 1851. The following year the Marshall *Texas
Republican* of May 1, 1852, reported on a bitter personal feud between the newspaper publishers at Brownsville. Reportedly, General Wheat of the *Rio Bravo* cowhided Dr. Adams of the *American Flag*.

[Brownsville] *Rio Grande Sentinel*

This paper, printed in both Spanish and English, appeared in the fall of
1849. It suspended publication about 1851 but was revived by Edwin B. Scarborough in late 1860 to advocate Breckinridge for
president. Scarborough had previously sold his *American Flag*.

Scarborough was editor, publisher, and proprietor of the revived paper, and José A. Puente was editor of the Spanish-language section. The paper suspended with the issue of June 26, 1861, which is in the Newspaper Collection, University of Texas at Austin.

Caldwell Times

The Austin *Texas State Gazette* of May 30, 1857, noted that this Democratic paper was to be established by Jo Littlefield. He had previously established short-lived papers at Washington and Independence.

Cameron Centinel

N. W. Warfield and John A. Moore established this paper in August, 1859. The Austin *Texas State Gazette* of September 8, 1860, classed it as an opposition paper, and the *Bellville Countryman* of September 15, 1860, called it "independent" in politics.

Canton Times

The Clarksville *Standard* of October 20, 1860, noted the first issue of the *Times*, published by Sid S. Johnson and Company.

[Carthage] *Lone Star Banner*

The *Galveston Weekly News* of January 15, 1861, noted the appearance of this paper, published by F. M. Bowers and owned and edited by A. M. Sanford and J. M. Ramsey. The paper opposed Sam Houston and supported secession.

[Carthage] *Panola Farmer*

The Marshall *Texas Republican* of June 26, 1858, noted this new Democratic paper published by J. W. Mason.

[Carthage] *Panola Harbinger*

M. L. McCormick changed the name of the *Carthage Recorder* to *Panola Harbinger* in 1859. Early the next year McCormick moved his office to Shelbyville, where he established the *Echo*. At that time he complained of "several failures" at Carthage and called the town "a graveyard, not a nursery of newspapers."

Carthage Recorder

M. L. McCormick acquired the office of the *Star Spangled Banner* at Henderson and moved it to Carthage, where he established the

Recorder in early 1858. The next year the paper was renamed the *Panola Harbinger*.

[Carthage] *Texas Bulletin*

This paper, edited by Tom Cooley and published by H. P. O. Dulaney, appeared in 1859. The San Augustine *Red Land Express* of July 28, 1860, noted that Cooley had suspended publication.

Centerville Herald

The Houston *Tri-Weekly Telegraph* of March 2, 1859, noted receipt of the first number of this "independent on all subjects paper." Despite that profession of independence, the Austin *Texas State Gazette* of March 19, 1859, reported that the *Herald* advocated the reopening of the slave trade.

[Centerville] *Leon Pioneer*

This weekly, published by Wood, Horn, and Company, appeared in 1852. William D. Wood gives an amusing account of his association with the paper in his "Reminiscences of Texas and Texans Fifty Years Ago." Wood, born in North Carolina on March 11, 1828, served several terms in the Texas legislature. He and his brother sold the *Pioneer* to Morris R. Reagan and John Gregg in 1855, and the new owners moved the office to Fairfield. The Newspaper Collection, University of Texas at Austin, has copies from 1852 to 1854.

[Centerville] *Texas Times*

The Austin *Texas State Gazette* of October 1, 1859, says that the name of the *Centerville Herald* had been changed to *Texas Times*. A. B. Norton associates Benjamin W. Cammer, formerly of the *Huntsville Recorder*, with the *Times*.

[Chappell Hill] *Minerva*

This paper, edited by James Wallis and published by Louis Jennings, appeared in July, 1859, and continued for at least a year.

[Chappell Hill] *Texas Ranger*

Joseph Lancaster published the *Texas Ranger* simultaneously at Chappell Hill, Brenham, Independence, and Washington from 1857 to 1859.

Clarksville Messenger

The San Augustine *Red-Lander* of August 19, 1854, noted the appearance of this paper, published by Colvin and Darnall. Initially a democratic paper, it became Know-Nothing in 1855. The Marshall *Texas Republican* of March 15, 1856, reported that C. L. Sutton and J. T. Darnall had purchased the paper and that J. W. Thomas edited it. The owners moved the paper to McKinney in 1858, where it became the *McKinney Messenger*.

[Clarksville] *Northern Standard*; after October, 1852, *Standard*

Charles DeMorse began this important paper in 1842 and continued it with interruptions until after the Civil War. The paper is more fully considered in the text. For a biography of the editor, see Ernest Wallace, *Charles DeMorse, Pioneer Editor and Statesman.* The Newspaper Collection, University of Texas at Austin, has a full run of the *Standard*, and it is available on microfilm.

[Clarksville] *School Monthly*

The *Bellville Countryman* of September 22, 1860, noted this educational paper.

[Clarksville] *Western Star*

This weekly appeared August 11, 1847, with W. J. F. Morgan as publisher and proprietor and William Trimble, formerly of Hempstead County, Arkansas, as editor. It supported the Whig Party and criticized President Polk's conduct of the Mexican War. The paper carried the motto "The Constitution and Liberty" and supported Zachary Taylor for president. The owner moved the *Star* to Paris in 1850 after engaging in a series of word battles with Charles DeMorse of the rival *Standard*. The issue of October 7, 1848 (Volume II, number 5), is in the Newspaper Collection, University of Texas at Austin.

Columbia Democrat

E. H. Cushing, later the noted editor of the Houston *Telegraph*, began publication of this weekly in 1853. Horace Cone served as co-editor until early 1854, when W. F. Swain replaced him. In 1855 the paper combined with the Brazoria *Texas Planter* to become the Columbia *Democrat and Planter*. Swain continued the paper

under that title after Cushing moved to Houston in 1856. The
Newspaper Collection, University of Texas at Austin has a good
run from 1853 to 1854.

[Columbia] *Democrat and Planter*
This paper, which appeared in 1855, resulted from the combining of
the *Democrat* at Columbia with the *Texas Planter* at Brazoria.
E. H. Cushing and W. F. Swain edited it until Cushing became
editor of the Houston *Telegraph* in 1856. A few issues from 1855 to
1861 are in the Newspaper Collection, University of Texas at
Austin.

[Columbia] *Texas Advertiser*
This sheet was "Published Quarterly at the Columbia Democrat Office
for Gratuitous Circulation Among the Texas Merchants." E. H.
Cushing and W. F. Swain were publishers. The issue of August 1,
1854 (Volume I, number 2), is in the Newspaper Collection, University of Texas at Austin.

[Columbus] *Colorado Citizen*
J. D. Baker and his brothers, Ben and A. Hicks, moved the office of
the Lockhart *Southern Watchman* to Columbus in 1857 and established this weekly. The paper supported Sam Houston. An extra
dated May 30, 1860, carried the motto "Our Country, Our State,
the South and the Union." The three Baker brothers fought in the
Confederate army, and the youngest, A. Hicks, died in service.
The two who survived reestablished the paper after the war, and it
continues at the present. The Newspaper Collection, University
of Texas at Austin, has scattered copies from 1859 to 1869.

Corpus Christi Gazette
This paper appeared on January 1, 1846, published by Samuel Bangs
and Dr. George W. Fletcher and edited by José de Alba. A war
paper, it served Zachary Taylor's army at Corpus Christi. It ceased
publication April 2, 1846, when Taylor's troops moved to the Rio
Grande. Lota M. Spell, *Pioneer Printer: Samuel Bangs in Mexico
and Texas*, considers the *Gazette* more fully. Copies from January
8 to March 8, 1846, are in the Newspaper Collection, Univeristy
of Texas at Austin.

[Corpus Christi] *Nueces Valley*

This paper began in February, 1849, and continued with interruptions for a decade. Among those associated with it were H. L. Kinney, Somers Kinney, Gideon K. Lewis, James R. Barnard, George W. Kinney, James A. Beveridge, B. F. Neal, Charles C. Bryant, and a Scott. Scattered copies from 1850 to 1858 are in the Newspaper Collection, University of Texas at Austin.

[Corpus Christi] *Ranchero*

The first number of this weekly appeared October 22, 1859, with Henry A. Maltby as editor. He was born in Ohio about 1830 and came to Texas in 1851. He served as mayor of Corpus Christi and resigned that office to join H. L. Kinney's filibuster to Nicaragua. Maltby represented Nueces County in the Secession Convention in 1861. His brother, William H. Maltby, joined the *Ranchero* on October 20, 1860. The paper supported Breckinridge for president in 1860 but only reluctantly went along with secession. Many ranchers listed their brands in the paper. During the Civil War the paper moved to Santa Margarita, Texas. After the war it continued in Brownsville. Scattered issues from 1859 to 1863 are in the Newspaper Collection, University of Texas at Austin.

Corpus Christi Star

This weekly appeared on September 11, 1848, with John H. Peoples as editor. He had previously edited several Mexican War papers. The *Star* carried a Spanish-language section called "La Estrella." Charles Callahan and then James R. Barnard succeeded Peoples as editor. The paper continued until the fall of 1849. Copies from September 11, 1848, to September 8, 1849, are in the Newspaper Collection, University of Texas at Austin.

[Corsicana] *Navarro Express*

Volume I, number 1, of this paper appeared October 29, 1859, with R. A. Van Horn, formerly of the Anderson *Central Texian*, as publisher and proprietor. He edited the paper together with N. P. Modrall, a Cumberland Presbyterian minister. In March, 1860, Modrall withdrew, and the paper became more Democratic politically, with William H. Neblett as editor and J. T. Spence and R. A. Van Horn as associate editors. Issues from 1859 to 1861 are in the Newspaper Collection, University of Texas at Austin.

[Corsicana] *Prairie Blade*

The Marshall *Texas Republican* of November 18, 1854, welcomed the
Prairie Blade, published by J. O. Shook. Shook, formerly a Whig,
supported the Know-Nothing party. The *Liberty Gazette* of
March 19, 1855, reported his withdrawal in favor of one Mills and
Dan Donaldson, Shook having made "his blade too sharp." By November, 1855, J. R. Loughridge was editor, and he and A. M.
Byers were publishers. The Austin *Southern Intelligencer* of January 7, 1857, reported that A. M. Byers had sold the *Prairie Blade*
to W. H. Fowler, who planned to change the name to *Prairie Intelligencer* and make it neutral in politics. Issues of November 17,
1855, and February 29, 1856, are in the Texas State Library.

[Corsicana] *Prairie Intelligencer*

The Austin *Southern Intelligencer* of January 7, 1857, reported that
A. M. Byers had sold the *Prairie Blade* to W. H. Fowler, who
planned to issue the *Prairie Intelligencer*, a neutral paper.

[Corsicana] *Southern Presbyterian*

The Clarksville *Standard* of July 7, 1860, carried a prospectus for this
paper, to be edited by N. P. Modrall and published by R. A. Van
Horn. The two had formerly co-edited the Corsicana *Navarro Express*. They proposed in the *Southern Presbyterian* to promote
the Cumberland Presbyterian Church and to "encourage and promote the morality, literature and general elevation of our common
country."

Corsicana Times

The Austin *Texas State Gazette* of February 21, 1857, mentioned this
paper, as did the Columbia *Democrat and Planter* of May 26, 1857.
It possibly succeeded the *Prairie Blade*, which W. H. Fowler purchased early in 1857 with the intent of issuing the *Prairie
Intelligencer*.

Crockett Argus

The Austin *Texas State Gazette* of April 24, 1858, welcomed this paper,
edited by Preston Hay and published by James M. Hall. Hall
killed Isaac Peacock in the spring of 1859 and abandoned the paper. John C. Hepperla, formerly editor of the Anderson *Central
Texian*, purchased the *Argus* and became editor and publisher.

Shortly after acquiring the paper, he engaged in a feud with Oscar Dalton, of the rival *Crockett Printer*, and shot Dalton. Dalton died of his wounds the following year. In February, 1860, the *Argus* merged with the Galveston *Texas Register*, published by B. F. Davis. Davis withdrew some months later, leaving Hepperla at the helm of the paper. A. B. Norton says that Hepperla died in the Civil War.

Crockett Printer

The Marshall *Texas Republican* of December 17, 1853, welcomed this weekly, edited and published by Oscar Dalton. In early 1859 the *Printer* appeared at both Crockett and Sumpter, with Dalton as the Crockett publisher and J. L. Cottrell, the Sumpter. Dalton and his rival editor, John C. Hepperla of the *Argus*, engaged in a bitter editorial war in the early summer of 1859, which resulted in Dalton's being shot in the mouth. He died the following March. A. B. Norton gives a sympathetic picture of Dalton and his family working at the *Printer*. James A. Beveridge served as pro tem editor of the *Printer* after Dalton's injury. Dalton was born in Louisiana about 1821 and came to Texas before 1850. The *Printer* opposed secession in 1861. The issue of November 14, 1860, is in the Newspaper Collection, University of Texas at Austin.

[Daingerfield] *Lamplighter*

The Austin *Texas State Times* of July 28, 1855, welcomed this paper published by Ward Taylor, Jr. It supported the Know-Nothing party. The issue of August 31, 1855 (Volume I, number 9), is in the Newspaper Collection, University of Texas at Austin. It lists D. J. Bean as editor and carries the slogan "Independent in all things— Devoted to Education, General Improvements and Progression."

Dallas Herald

James Wellington Latimer and William Willis established this weekly in 1849. Latimer had previously purchased the press of the Bonham *Western Argus* and moved it to Paris, where he and Robert C. Matthewson issued the *Texas Times* for a short while. John W. Swindells replaced Willis at the *Herald*, and he and Latimer made the paper the voice of Southern Democracy in their area. Latimer died in 1859 and was replaced by Charles Pryor. Copies from 1855 to 1861 are in the Newspaper Collection, University of Texas at Austin.

[Dallas] *Texas Echo*
The Clarksville *Standard* of July 7, 1849, noted that W. P. Watson, joint publisher of the Jefferson *Independent Monitor*, planned to establish this paper when he obtained subscribers. Subscriptions were two dollars in advance or four dollars at the end of the year. The paper never appeared.

[Fairfield] *Freestone Journal*
The Austin *Texas State Gazette* of August 11, 1855, noted the appearance of this paper, edited by Morris R. Reagan, brother of John H. Reagan. Subscriptions cost $2.50 in advance. Although it professed to be Democratic, the paper supported W. G. W. Jowers, the Know-Nothing candidate, for lieutenant governor.

[Fairfield] *Republican*
The Marshall *Texas Republican* of February 18, 1854, reported that the "Republican is the name of a new paper to be published at Fairfield by Friend & Moody. We protest the name."

[Fairfield] *Texas Farmer and Stockman Journal*
The Corsicana *Navarro Express* of November 17, 1859, carried the prospectus of this journal, to be published by J. L. Caldwell and Anderson, with W. B. Moore as editor. It was to be published "at Fairfield or Springfield or Cotton Gin, Freestone County." The publication appeared at Fairfield the following spring under the title *Texas Pioneer and Stock Journal*.

[Fairfield] *Texas Pioneer*
W. L. Moody and Morris R. Reagan established this paper in the fall of 1855. It succeeded the *Freestone Journal*. The Marshall *Texas State Gazette* of December 5, 1856, noted that Moody had been succeeded by N. R. Barnes and that the paper was Democratic in politics. In late 1858 the paper was published at both Fairfield and Springfield, with J. L. Caldwell as the Springfield publisher. The issues of June 1 and July 3, 1859, are in the Texas State Library.

[Fairfield] *Texas Pioneer and Stock Journal*
This monthly appeared in the spring of 1860. Edited by J. L. Caldwell, it was sent free of charge to county clerks for the purpose of
recovering lost or stolen livestock. The issue of October 11, 1862,
is in the Newspaper Collection, University of Texas at Austin.

Fort Worth Chief
A. B. Norton, author of an early history of Texas newspapers, published this paper during 1859 and 1860. After purchasing an interest in the Austin *Southern Intelligencer* in the spring of 1860, he
left George Smith as editor of the *Chief*. The paper took the unpopular side during the excitement of the summer of 1860 and,
wrote Norton, "the hostility of the people, growing out of secession views, compelled its discontinuance after the hanging of Rev.
Anthony Buley and Crawford." The press was sold at auction late
in the summer. H. A. Hamner, who had lost the press of the
White Man at Jacksboro to fire, purchased it and reestablished his
paper at Weatherford.

[Galveston] *Beacon*
Benjamin F. Neal, formerly of the *Galveston News* and several other
Galveston papers, established this daily in January, 1846. The
Clarksville *Standard* of February 18, 1846, noted receipt of issue
number 22, "edited with sprightliness and independence." Neal
later moved to Corpus Christi, where he served as the first mayor
and associated himself with the *Nueces Valley*.

[Galveston] *Civilian and Galveston Gazette*; title varies: *Civilian and
Galveston City Gazette, Civilian and Gazette, Daily Civilian, Tri-
Weekly Civilian*
Hamilton Stuart began this paper in the fall of 1838 and continued it
with various associates and with slight variations in title until after
the Civil War. It consistently supported Sam Houston. One of the
important papers of the period, it is more fully considered in the
text. Unfortunately, the files of the *Civilian* burned. There are in-
complete holdings in a number of depositories, among them the
Rosenberg Library, Galveston; the Newspaper Collection, University of Texas at Austin; the Texas State Library; and the San
Jacinto Museum of History.

[Galveston] *Commercial Weekly and Prices Current*

This weekly sheet for businessmen was issued from the office of the
    Civilian from early 1854 until at least 1859. Scattered issues from
    December 14, 1854, to June 4, 1859, are in the Newspaper Col-
    lection, University of Texas at Austin.

[Galveston] *Confederate*

This paper appeared in 1855 on the ruins of two other Galveston pa-
    pers, the *Times* and the *Journal*. Published by Waddell, Holt, and
    Gossler, it was edited by J. F. Waddell and J. T. Holt. It was a
    Know-Nothing paper and carried the motto "Put None but Ameri-
    cans on Guard." The issue of January 5, 1856, is in the Newspaper
    Collection, University of Texas at Austin.

[Galveston] *Crisis!*

Richardson and Company issued this campaign sheet to advocate the
    election of John C. Breckinridge to the presidency. The first issue
    appeared in July, 1860. Issues of August 13, September 10 and 17,
    and October 8, 1860, are in the Texas State Library.

[Galveston] *Der Deutsche Christliche Apologete*

A sample copy of this German Methodist paper appeared August 21,
    1855, and regular publication began October 4, 1855, with Peter
    A. Moelling as editor. The name of the paper was changed to
    Evangelische Apologete on January 3, 1856.

[Galveston] *Der Pilger im Sueden der Union*

This paper was established by a Lutheran minister, Heinrich Wendt,
    in 1855 to promote a Lutheran seminary. Wilhelm Strobel and
    Heinrich Bohnenberger assisted Wendt. The paper lasted for
    about a year.

[Galveston] *Educational and Literary Magazine*

The *Galveston Journal* of January 3, 1852, carried the prospectus of
    this journal over the name of J. Hesse. Hesse proposed to issue
    the publication monthly to aid the cause of education.

[Galveston] *Evangelische Apologete*

Peter A. Moelling, pastor of a German Methodist congregation in Gal-
    veston, edited this paper. The name was changed from *Der
    Deutsche Christliche Apologete* with the issue of January 3, 1856.

Printed at the office of the *Texas Christian Advocate*, the *Evangelische* continued until the Civil War, by which time it boasted of a circulation of about two thousand.

[Galveston] *Gazette*

The Columbia *Democrat and Planter* of October 23, 1855, reported, "The Galveston Gazette is the title of a new paper which has succeeded the Galveston Zeitung." This paper apparently lasted only a short time, for *Die Union* is generally considered the successor to the *Zeitung*.

[Galveston] *Good Samaritan and Temperance Messenger*

John Hannay and Francis D. Allen began this paper in 1855 for the purposes suggested by the title. It lasted for a year.

Galveston Herald

The Marshall *Texas Republican* of May 16, 1857, reported that "printers at Galveston recently struck for New Orleans prices, and, many being unemployed, five went in business for themselves to establish the Daily and Weekly *Herald*." The printers were headed by Wilbur Cherry, a pioneer Galveston newsman, and included J. J. Dunn, A. M. Dunn, J. C. Hepperla, and George Copeland. The *San Antonio Herald* of October 20, 1857, noted that the *Galveston Herald* had suspended, "not from choice, but from necessity," and that of the five printers who started the paper only two remained. The issue of May 2, 1857, is in the Newspaper Collection, University of Texas at Austin.

[Galveston] *Horned Frog*

This humor sheet appeared in the summer of 1858. Gustavus Gas was senior editor, and Godfrey Gitout, junior editor. The issues of July 4 and 14 and August 2, 1858, are in the Rosenberg Library, Galveston.

[Galveston] *Ignis Fatuus, or Jack O' the Lantern*

The first number of this humor sheet appeared April 12, 1856. A weekly, it was published by the "Order of Malta" through its "Supreme Council of Sons who Compose the Conclave of One Thousand and One." The first issue is at Rosenberg Library, Galveston.

[Galveston] *John Donkey*

Ben C. Stuart, "History of Newspapers in Texas," says that this "humorous or satirical" publication appeared in the 1850s and that it, like the *Horned Frog*, lampooned well-known local characters. Public opinion credited J. M. Conrad with writing most of the squibs that appeared in both papers, and both were short-lived.

Galveston Journal

Wilbur Cherry, pioneer Galveston printer and newsman, joined with John M. Gibson to found this Whig paper, a weekly and semiweekly, in February, 1850. Others associated with the paper were R. H. Howard, B. E. Tarver, H. H. Smith, T. J. Allen, and S. Carter. The *Journal* combined with the Galveston *Texas Daily Times* to become the *Confederate* in 1855. Scattered copies from December 24, 1850, to February 3, 1855, are in the Newspaper Collection, University of Texas at Austin.

Galveston News; title varies: *Evening News, Semi-Weekly News, Tri-Weekly News, Weekly News*

The oldest surviving paper in Texas, this paper is considered more fully in the text. The *News* was begun in June, 1843, by M. Cronican and Company. Willard Richardson joined the paper in 1845 and made it one of the most influential papers in the state. David Richardson, no relation to Willard and a native of the Isle of Man, joined the *News* in the 1850s. Like its rival, the *Civilian*, the *News* lost its files to fire. Issues are scattered in many depositories, among them the Newspaper Collection, University of Texas at Austin, the Rosenberg Library, Galveston, the San Jacinto Museum of History, and the Texas State Library.

[Galveston] *Newsletter and Price Current*

This sheet for businessmen appeared in late 1851 from the office of the *Galveston News*. The issue of April 9, 1852, is in the San Jacinto Museum of History.

[Galveston] *Southern Age*

The Austin *Tri-Weekly State Times* of January 2, 1858, noted receipt of the first number of this semimonthly and commented, "It is a neat quarto sheet devoted to Southern Literature and edited with marked ability by Mrs. Anna Cora Weeks of Galveston." The *Galveston Directory* says that "two distinguished adventurers," a Mr. and Mrs. Weekes, issued a few numbers of this journal, collected subscriptions in advance, and then departed.

[Galveston] *Temperance Banner*
The *Galveston Directory* of 1859 says that Charles Hanson started this sheet in 1857. The *Bastrop Advertiser* of May 29, 1858, reports its suspension for lack of means to continue.

[Galveston] *Texas Christian Advocate*
Methodist leaders moved the *Texas Wesleyan Banner*, the official organ of the general conference, from Houston to Galveston in 1854 and changed the name to *Texas Christian Advocate*. It was edited first by C. C. Gillespie and then by John Carnes. By 1860, it boasted the largest circulation of any paper in Texas. It is fully considered in John Daniel Barron, "A Critical History of the Texas Christian Advocate" (M.A. thesis, University of Missouri, 1952). Copies from August 13, 1856, to July 14, 1858, are in the Perkins School of Theology Library, Southern Methodist University.

[Galveston] *Texas Daily Times*
Holt, Ferguson, and Parker began this paper on January 31, 1854, with John T. Holt as editor and S. H. Ferguson as manager of the mechanical department. The paper suspended publication after a few months and eventually blended with the *Journal* to become the *Confederate*. The issues of March 25 and May 7, 1854, are in the Rosenberg Library, Galveston.

[Galveston] *Texas Land Register and Advertiser*
The first number of this journal appeared on February 8, 1855. Published by Jacob DeCordova and James C. Frazier, it listed land for sale in various parts of Texas. The first issue is in the Western Americana Collection, Yale University.

[Galveston] *Texas Portfolio*
The Anderson *Central Texian* of December 22, 1855, noted the first issue of this journal, published by Francis D. Allen and edited by Oscar H. Harpel. The paper, a semimonthly, was devoted to "general literature, education, entertainment, miscellany, intel-

lectual progress, and utility." Mrs. Virginia R. Allen edited the paper in 1856, and Jo Kirgan became editor and proprietor in 1857. It suspended that same year. A copy for April 16, 1857, is in the Newspaper Collection, University of Texas at Austin.

[Galveston] *Texas Register*

The Houston *Telegraph* of June 3, 1859, noted receipt of the first number of this semimonthly. B. F. Davis issued the paper for the special purpose of listing strays and returning them to their rightful owners. The paper blended with the *Crockett Argus* in early 1860.

[Galveston] *Texian Monthly Magazine*

The first number of this periodical appeared in July, 1858. Edited by Mrs. Eleanor Spann, it was first printed by Cherry, Dunn, and Company and then by the Civilian Steam Book Press. It was a literary journal that contained "romances, original tales, etc." and a number of translations from the French. Issues for July and September, 1858, are in the Texas Collection, University of Texas at Austin.

[Galveston] *Union, Die*; name varies: *Dreiwochentliche Union, Wochentblatt Union, Wochentliche Union*

F. Muhr began this German-language paper, the successor to the *Zeitung*, in 1855. Ferdinand Flake succeeded Muhr in 1857 and continued the paper until the Civil War. The paper had a large circulation in Galveston. A mob attacked the press office in 1861 in protest against Flake's opposition to secession. The issues of July 17, 1860, and July 18, 1861, are in the Texas State Library.

Galveston Zeitung

The brothers Christian H. and George Buechner established this German-language paper in the summer of 1847. George Buechner died only a few months after the paper began, but his brother continued it until 1855, when he ran into trouble with the Know-Nothing party. He sold the press to F. Muhr, who began the *Union*. Scattered copies from January, 1851, to February, 1855, are in the Texas State Library.

[Georgetown] *Weekly Independent*

Volume I, number 1, of this weekly appeared September 6, 1856, edited by Andrew Marschalk, Sr., and published by his son Andrew Marschalk, Jr. The Marschalks had formerly been associated with the *Indianola Bulletin*. Francis Marschalk, Jr., replaced the younger man, his brother, as publisher before the family moved the paper to Belton. Later they moved to Hempstead to establish the *Courier*. A few issues from September 6, 1856, to February 21, 1857, are in the Newspaper Collection, University of Texas at Austin.

[Gilmer] *Texas Patriot*

The Austin *Texas State Gazette* of March 23, 1861, noted the appearance of this paper. It was edited by A. H. Appleton and published by I. Richardson and J. E. Smith. An advocate of southern rights, it carried the motto, "Texas, Our Home." The issue of August 2, 1861 (Volume I, number 25), is in the Newspaper Collection, University of Texas at Austin.

[Gilmer] *Texas Star*

The Marshall *Star State Patriot* of March 19, 1853, noted the plans of J. A. Kirgan and Ben A. Vansickle to publish this paper. The *Columbia Democrat* of February 27, 1855, reported that the *Texas Star* had been moved to Tarrant, Hopkins County.

[Gilmer] *Texas Tribune*

The Marshall *Texas Republican* of February 18, 1860, noted the appearance of this weekly. B. W. Reilly was publisher, and J. H. Trowell, editor and proprietor. The *Bellville Countryman*, of September 22, 1860, classed it as uncommitted and Whig in the election of 1860.

[Gilmer] *Upshur Democrat*

The Marshall *Texas Republican* of March 28, 1857, noted receipt of the first number of this weekly, published by A. H. Abney and J. T. Harrison. By December 2 of that year, Abney was the sole proprietor. The Austin *Texas State Gazette* of December 18, 1858, reported that Abney had sold to A. K. Mitchell and noted on February 25, 1860, that Mitchell had withdrawn, leaving William K. Hart as editor.

Goliad Express

This weekly appeared in the spring of 1855, with A. M. Wigginton as editor and Ben F. King as publisher. It carried the motto "Pledged to the Truth, to Liberty and Law. No Favor Sways Us and No Fear Can Awe." By July, 1857, J. R. Parker had replaced King as publisher. The Newspaper Collection, University of Texas at Austin, has scattered copies from September 17, 1856, to September 5, 1857.

Goliad Guard

Although several sources indicate that this paper began in 1855, the earliest copy available is dated June 13, 1874, and is Volume 7, number 28. The volume number suggests that the paper began in late 1866.

Goliad Messenger

This weekly appeared in 1859, edited by A. F. Cox and published by Robert W. Pierce. The *Bellville Countryman* of September 22, 1860, lists it as a religious paper that took no stand on political issues. The *Messenger* created a flurry of excitement in 1860 by listing the names of all presidential candidates, including Lincoln. Under pressure from other editors, it withdrew his name. Copies for March 31, 1860, and October 26 and November 12, 1864, are in the Newspaper Collection, University of Texas at Austin.

[Goliad] *True American*

The Marshall *Texas Republican* of May 10, 1856, classed this paper as Know-Nothing. It was edited by a man named Crane. The Austin *Southern Intelligencer* of September 9, 1857, quoted from the *True American*.

Gonzales Inquirer

The Austin *Texas State Gazette* of February 19, 1853, noted a prospectus for this paper issued by Charles Sexton. The *Galveston Journal* of June 17, 1853, acknowledged receipt of the first issue. A weekly, it was published by Smith and Darst and edited by S. W. Smith. The paper is still in existence. Scattered copies from June 4, 1853, to December 9, 1864, are in the Newspaper Collection, University of Texas at Austin.

[Greenville[*Gladiator*

A. B. Norton says, "The Greenville Gladiator was published by B. W. Reilly in the year 1860; it was neatly executed, but inadequately supported and the publisher abandoned the field."

[Hallettsville] *Lone Star*

The Houston *Tri-Weekly Telegraph* of December 20, 1860, noted the appearance of this paper, with S. A. Benton as editor. The Columbia *Colorado Citizen* of August 3, 1861, reported that the editor of the *Lone Star* planned to complete a volume and "set for a time."

Hempstead Courier

This paper appeared on June 1, 1859, with Andrew Marschalk, Sr., as editor and proprietor. His son Francis Marschalk, Jr., later joined him as publisher. The elder Marschalk, born in Mississippi about 1817, had previously been associated with the *Indianola Bulletin*, a paper in San Antonio, the *Georgetown Weekly Independent*, and the *Belton Independent*. His sons, Francis and Andrew, Jr., assisted him in his printing ventures. The Marshall *Texas Republican* of December 2, 1859, reported that Marschalk had lost five members of his family to yellow fever. Shortly thereafter, he offered the *Courier* for sale. Copies for 1859 and 1860 are in the Newspaper Collection, University of Texas at Austin.

[Henderson] *Aegis of Truth*

This Whig paper, formerly the *Texas Statesman*, appeared in 1849, edited by F. A. Wingfield. It discontinued in the spring of 1850, when Wingfield moved to Shreveport. The *Texas Whig* succeeded the *Aegis of Truth*.

Henderson Democrat

This weekly appeared in early 1855, with Sparks and Martin as publishers, and Ector and Company, proprietors. Mathew Duncan Ector edited it until early 1858, when he retired in favor of John McClarty. McClarty changed the name to *Southern Beacon*. Ector served as brigadier general in the Confederate army. The issue of May 23, 1856, is in the San Jacinto Museum of History. Several issues from June 2, 1855, to June 27, 1857, are in the Newspaper Collection, University of Texas at Austin.

[Henderson] *East Texas Times*

The *Dallas Herald* of February 1, 1860, noted that this weekly had replaced the Henderson *Southern Beacon*. George H. Gould and
George W. Diamond edited it initially, and J. M. Dodson later
purchased an interest. Diamond later wrote an account of the
great hanging at Gainesville, which appeared in the *Southwestern
Historical Quarterly* of January, 1963. Issues of the paper for
March 1 and July 18, 1862, are in the Newspaper Collection, University of Texas at Austin.

[Henderson] *Flag of the Union*

This weekly, edited and published by William M. Messenger, replaced
the *Texas Whig* on October 12, 1850. It initially supported the
Democratic party, but after James R. Armstrong acquired an interest in February, 1854, the proprietors proposed to make it neutral. When local Democrats threatened to found their own paper,
Armstrong and Messenger dissolved their partnership, and Messenger continued the *Flag* as a Democratic paper, while Armstrong founded the *Texas State Intelligencer*, a Whig paper. Messenger died October 11, 1854. James W. Flanagan purchased the
office in April, 1855, and established the *Star Spangled Banner*, a
Know-Nothing paper. The issue of February 2, 1854, is in the
Newspaper Collection, University of Texas at Austin.

[Henderson] *Southern Beacon*

John McClarty purchased the press of the *Democrat* and began this
paper in January, 1858. The Marshall *Texas Republican* of August
20, 1859, reported that the *Beacon* had been discontinued for
want of patronage. The *East Texas Times* replaced it early the next
year. The issue of May 21, 1859 (Volume II, number 18), is in the
Newspaper Collection, University of Texas at Austin.

[Henderson] *Star Spangled Banner*

James W. Flanagan, later lieutenant governor of Texas under Edmund
J. Davis, purchased the press of the *Flag of the Union* and started
this Know-Nothing weekly in April, 1855. His son, Webster Flanagan, edited it. The Houston *Tri-Weekly Telegraph* of December
30, 1857, noted that the *Banner* had been discontinued and the
office moved to Carthage to print the *Recorder*.

[Henderson] *Texas New Era*

The Marshall *Harrison Flag* of November 19, 1858, noted the appearance of this new paper at Henderson. Edited and published by S. G. and Leon Swan, it was independent in politics. It supported Sam Houston, and A. B. Norton called it "a wide awake American journal." The Austin *Texas State Gazette* of October 15, 1859, noted the death of Leon Swan on September 25, 1859. The paper continued until at least the fall of 1860.

[Henderson] *Texas State Intelligencer*

James R. Armstrong, formerly a partner of William M. Messenger in the *Flag of the Union*, began this Whig paper in the spring of 1854. The two papers came from the same office, but the *Flag* supported the Democrats, while the *Intelligencer* supported the Whigs. Armstrong represented Rusk County in the secession convention of Texas in 1861.

[Henderson] *Texas Statesman*

R. C. Wheeler and J. C. Harris issued a prospectus for this paper that appeared in the San Antonio *Western Texan* of December 29, 1848. They proposed to begin publication on January 1, 1849. The Clarksville *Standard* of April 7, 1849, noted receipt of the first two numbers. A Whig paper, the *Statesman* became the *Aegis of Truth* in July, 1849.

[Henderson] *Texas Whig*

The Marshall *Texas Republican* of July 6, 1850, noted this new paper, started by R. C. Wheeler and Company on equipment of the *Aegis of Truth*. The *Republican* of July 20, 1850, noted that the paper was to be enlarged and edited by a young lawyer, Isaac Dansby. The *Texas Whig* was replaced by the *Flag of the Union* in the fall of 1850.

[Henderson] *Young America*

The Richmond *Texas Sun* of February 16, 1856, reported: "We have on our table a neat little paper, published in Henderson, Rusk County, called 'Young America.' The fighting editors rejoice in the euphoneous name of Fisticuffs and Hardskull. The publishers promptly answer to the appellation of Doesticks and Ivanhoe."

Hillsboro Express

A. B. Norton says, "At Hillsboro, in 1859– '60, a paper was published under the management of J. P. Weir. Its career terminated with the commencement of the War. The only vestige of the office left in 1870 was the legs of the press standing in the street at the corner of Ratcliff's lot on the public square as a warning or sign-board to travelers."

[Houston] *Age of Commerce*

This paper, first a weekly and then a daily, appeared in 1857, with C. H. Hanson as proprietor and Hanson and Andrew Daly as editors. The issue of April 22, 1857, is in the Texas State Library.

[Houston] *American Union*

The Houston *Tri-Weekly Telegraph* of November 3, 1856, reported, "The American Union, a Fillmore paper, for sometime published in this city, foreseeing the death and burial of Know Nothingism on the 4th, took the precaution to die itself in time, issuing its last number last Saturday." C. H. Hanson was the editor.

[Houston] *Bayou City Advertiser*

The Austin *Texas State Gazette* of May 17, 1856, noted the appearance of this paper. Published by Fairbairn and McClellan, it was edited by W. B. McClellan. A minister, McClellan was associated with several papers in La Grange.

[Houston] *Bayou City News*

The *Liberty Gazette* of September 10, 1855, noted receipt of the first number of this paper and reported that it was to appear regularly after yellow fever disappeared from Houston. The paper, established by G. W. Perkins and Company, lasted for three weeks. The press was moved to Washington on the Brazos to print the *American*. The Houston *Telegraph* of October 19, 1855, commented that the *News* had "changed owners, location, name, politics, and religion in three weeks." Perkins, born in Georgia about 1828, had worked as a printer in Galveston. He and Launcelot Abbotts issued the prospectus of the Liberty *Herald of Liberty* in 1852. Perkins joined the filibuster to Nicaragua in 1856.

[Houston] *Beacon*

This weekly appeared in 1850, with A. C. Gray as publisher and William J. Darden as editor. The Houston *Telegraph and Texas Register* of May 30, 1851, noted that Darden had retired and that "Charles A." Gray had succeeded him. George W. Miller purchased the office in late 1853 and began the *Spirit of the Age*. Copies for May 30 and August 15, 1851, and October 1, 1852, are in the Newspaper Collection, University of Texas at Austin.

[Houston] *Commercial Bulletin*

G. W. Perkins and Company issued this monthly for businessmen in 1854. The issue of April 1, 1855 (Volume I, number 8), is in the Newspaper Collection, University of Texas at Austin.

[Houston] *Commercial Express*

Ben C. Stuart, "History of Newspapers in Texas" (manuscript, Houston Public Library), says this paper began in 1858. The *Bellville Countryman* of September 22, 1860, lists the *Express* as politically uncommitted.

[Houston] *Commercial Telegraph and Business Register*

This paper for businessmen succeeded the *Houston Price Current and Business Register* in January, 1858. Like its predecessor, it was edited and published by E. H. Cushing of the Houston *Telegraph*. The Houston Public Library has issues from January 7, 1858, to December 22, 1859.

[Houston] *DeCordova's Herald and Immigrants' Guide*

This monthly appeared in the summer of 1849 from a press introduced to Houston by Jacob DeCordova. The paper encouraged immigrants to come to Texas and promoted the sale of DeCordova's land. He moved the press to Austin in the fall of 1849. There he and his brother Phineas began the *South-Western American*. The Newspaper Collection, University of Texas at Austin, has copies for July 21 and August 20, 1849.

[Houston] *Democratic Telegraph and Texas Register*

Francis Moore and Jacob Cruger added the word "Democratic" to the title of their paper with the issue of March 4, 1846. Moore dropped the word after he purchased Cruger's interest in the spring of 1851. See [Houston] *Telegraph and Texas Register*.

Houston Gazette

S. D. Hay and J. B. Lynch issued a prospectus for this paper, which appeared in the *Galveston News* of December 29, 1848. By the following summer, J. C. Harrison and G. W. Perkins published the *Gazette*, and S. D. Hay and Harrison edited it. The paper supported temperance and the Democratic party. The Austin *Texas State Gazette* of July 20, 1850, noted that the office was for sale. The San Jacinto Museum of History has the issues of August 25, November 10, and December 22, 1849.

[Houston] *Mercantile Advertiser*

The Houston *Telegraph* of December 28, 1848, noted this new paper, "devoted to the advancement of Whig principles," and published by Launcelot Abbotts. Abbotts was born in England about 1810 and had worked as a printer on the San Felipe *Telegraph and Texas Register* before the Texan Revolution. He moved the press of the *Advertiser* to La Grange to start the *Texas Monument* in 1850. Abbotts returned to England before 1860. The Library of Congress has scattered issues of the paper from April 14 to December 29, 1849.

[Houston] *Morning Star*

This paper, first a daily and later a tri-weekly, began publication on April 8, 1839. An important paper before annexation, it is considered more fully in the text. It came from the office of the *Telegraph*. The *Morning Star* diminished greatly in importance after annexation, becoming in its last years merely an advertising sheet. Francis Moore continued it until he sold the *Telegraph* office in 1854. The new owners discontinued it the following year. Copies from 1839 to 1846 are in the Texas State Library.

[Houston] *Panoplist and Presbyterian*

The Houston *Tri-Weekly Telegraph* of May 25, 1855, noted the appearance of this Old School Presbyterian paper. It was edited by Jerome Twitchell and published by J. P. Wilson. The editor drowned in August, 1856, and the paper ceased.

Houston Price Current and Business Register

This weekly for businessmen appeared on January 8, 1857. It was
edited and published by E. H. Cushing of the Houston *Telegraph*. Cushing continued the paper for a year, then replaced it
with the *Commercial Telegraph and Business Register*, which
continued the sequence. The Houston Public Library has issues
from January 8 to December 22, 1857.

[Houston] *Public School Advocate*

The Clarksville *Standard* of April 29, 1847, noted the appearance of
this monthly journal published by the Texas Literary Institute. It
came from the office of the *Democratic Telegraph and Texas Register* for the purpose of promoting public education.

Houston Quarterly Advertiser

Klein and Clark, owners of a dry goods store in Houston, began this
sheet in 1852 to advertise their wares and those of other local
merchants.

Houston Republic

This weekly, edited by Andrew Daly and published by Daly and J. T.
Capron, appeared on July 4, 1857. It supported Sam Houston for
president and later in 1860 supported the "Belleveritt" ticket.
The Newspaper Collection, University of Texas at Austin, has a
good run from 1857 to 1860.

[Houston] *Spirit of the Age*

The Washington *Lone Star and Texas Ranger* of December 3, 1853,
welcomed the first number of this paper. A weekly and tri-weekly,
it was published by George W. Miller from the office of the *Beacon*. The paper ceased in the spring of 1854, when Miller moved
to Waco to publish the *American Beacon*, a Know-Nothing paper.
The issue of January 18, 1854, is in the Newspaper Collection,
University of Texas at Austin.

[Houston] *Telegraph and Texas Register*; name varies: *Democratic
Telegraph and Texas Register, Telegraph, Tri-Weekly Telegraph,
Weekly Telegraph*

This historic paper began in 1835 and is considered in detail in the
text. Begun by the Borden brothers, it passed to Francis Moore

and Jacob Cruger in 1837. They published it under the title *Demo-cratic Telegraph and Texas Register* from 1846 to 1851. Moore purchased Cruger's interest in 1851 and resumed the former name. Moore, who had fallen on hard times because of a series of bad investments, was forced to sell to a group headed by H. H. Allen in 1854. W. J. Brocket purchased an interest in April, 1855, and E. H. Cushing joined it as owner and editor later in the year. The Newspaper Collection, University of Texas at Austin, has an excellent run from the beginning of the paper until 1860.

[Houston] *Texas Christian Advocate*
Orceneth Fisher, a prominent Methodist minister, acquired the Brenham *Texas Christian Advocate and Brenham General Advertiser* in late 1847 and the next year moved it to Houston, where it continued under this title for a time. The Texas and East Texas conferences agreed to publish the paper jointly, and in April, 1849, it became the *Texas Wesleyan Banner*. The paper was moved to Galveston in 1854, where it again became the *Texas Christian Advocate*. See John Daniel Barron, "A Critical History of the *Texas Christian Advocate*."

[Houston] *Texas Episcopalian*
The Houston *Tri-Weekly Telegraph* of May 30, 1855, noted the appearance of this religious sheet published by J. J. Nicholson. The paper lasted only a short time. *The Liberty Gazette* of August 13, 1855, noted that Nicholson had resigned as pastor of the Episcopal church at Houston because of ill health.

[Houston] *Texas Journal of Education*
The first issue of this journal appeared in July, 1854. A monthly, it was published by a committee appointed by the State Educational Convention. The first number is in the Texas Collection, University of Texas.

[Houston] *Texas Presbyterian*
Andrew Jackson McGown, a veteran of the Battle of San Jacinto and a Cumberland Presbyterian minister, moved this paper from Victoria to Houston in 1847. He moved it to Huntsville in 1850. The paper is more fully treated in William J. Stone, Jr., "A Historical Survey of Leading Texas Denominational Newspapers, 1846–

1861" (Ph.D. diss., University of Texas). Issues of June 12 and December 18 and 25, 1847, are in the Newspaper Collection, University of Texas at Austin.

[Houston] *Texas True Evangelist*

Moseley Baker, a hero of the Texan Revolution, began this paper in late 1847. He was assisted by his son-in-law, A. D. Darden. Baker, a prominent Methodist preacher in Houston in the early 1840s, broke with that church and issued this paper to propagate his theology. The paper ended shortly after Baker's death of yellow fever on November 4, 1848. A. C. Gray incorrectly gives the title as *True Witness*.

[Houston] *Texas Wesleyan Banner*

This paper began as the *Texas Christian Advocate and Brenham General Advertiser* in 1847. It became the Houston *Texas Christian Advocate* late in that year and the *Texas Wesleyan Banner* in April, 1849, after the Texas and East Texas conferences of the Methodist Church agreed to publish it. Chauncey Richardson served as editor until October, 1853. He was succeeded by George Rottenstein, who gave way to Simon B. Cameron in July, 1853. The paper was moved to Galveston in 1854, where it again became the *Texas Christian Advocate*. See John Daniel Barron, "A Critical History of the *Texas Christian Advocate*" (M.A. thesis, University of Missouri, 1952), and William J. Stone, Jr., "A Historical Survey of Leading Texas Denominational Papers, 1846–1861" (Ph.D. diss., University of Texas). Copies from April, 1850, to January, 1852, are in the Perkins School of Theology Library, Southern Methodist University.

[Houston] *True Southron*

The Austin *Texas State Gazette* of April 14, 1860, noted receipt of the first number of this states' rights paper. It was published by M. A. Royal and William Edwards. The issue of June 16, 1860, is in the Texas State Library.

[Huntsville] *Invincible Sam*

The Houston *Tri-Weekly Telegraph* of July 30, 1855, noted this Know-Nothing paper published by W. S. Reynolds. Two other Know-

Nothing papers, the *Union Advocate* and the *Recorder*, succeeded it.

Huntsville Item

George Robinson began this paper in 1850, and it still continues. Robinson, born in England October 12, 1820, immigrated to the United States, stopping first at New Orleans and then at Galveston, where he worked on the *News*. He opposed Sam Houston and was known for his irascible temperament. His fellows called him "Item George" and said there was always something interesting in the *Item*. He died January 31, 1888, and was succeeded at the *Item* by his son Fred. Copies from January 5 to June 7, 1856, are in the Library of Congress. The Newspaper Collection, University of Texas at Austin, has the issues of January 1, 1853, and November 18, 1864.

[Huntsville] Patriot

John M. Wade, a veteran of the Battle of San Jacinto and an early member of the Typographical Union in Texas, began this paper at Montgomery in April, 1845. He moved it to Huntsville in the summer of that year. Because of poor health, he sold the office to Francis L. Hatch, who began the *Texas Banner* in the fall of 1846. The issue of July 14, 1846, is in the Rosenberg Library at Galveston.

Huntsville Recorder

This paper, the successor to the *Union Advocate*, was begun by Benjamin W. Cammer and W. A. McLaughlin in early 1857. It supported Sam Houston and announced his candidacy for governor in May, 1857. The paper carried the motto "The Virtue and Intelligence of the People—the Only Safe-Guard of our Liberties." A Know-Nothing paper, it died "of actual starvation" in late 1857. The issue of October 15, 1857 (Volume I, number 47), is in the Newspaper Collection, University of Texas at Austin.

[Huntsville] Texas Banner

Francis L. Hatch began this paper in the fall of 1846 in association with S. D. Hay. The paper succeeded the Huntsville *Patriot*. Hatch, born in Alabama about 1822, gave strong support to Sam Houston. He sold the press to A. J. McGown and Robert Waters in the spring of 1850, and they used it to print the *Texas Presbyterian*.

Hatch moved to California shortly after selling the paper. The Newspaper Collection, University of Texas at Austin, has four issues from October 21, 1847, to November 24, 1849. The Library of Congress has copies from April 14 to December 1, 1849.

[Huntsville] *Texas Medium*

The first number of this paper appeared April, 1852. It was edited and published by Andrew Jackson McGown of the *Texas Presbyterian*. It continued erratically until mid-1856, when McGown suspended the *Texas Presbyterian*.

[Huntsville] *Texas Presbyterian*

Andrew Jackson McGown began this paper in Victoria in 1846 and moved it to Houston the following year. He moved it to Huntsville in 1850 after joining with Robert Waters to buy the office of the *Texas Banner*. McGown continued the paper until 1856, when the Cumberland Presbyterian Church declined to accept responsibility for it. See William J. Stone, Jr., "Texas' First Church Newspaper: The Texas Presbyterian, 1846–1856." Scattered copies from 1851 to 1853 are in the Newspaper Collection, University of Texas at Austin.

[Huntsville] *Texas Pulpit*

A. J. McCown and Robert Waters issued a prospectus of this monthly in July, 1851. They also issued a sample copy. It contained sixteen pages and cost one dollar a year. Regular publication began in 1852 under the title *Texas Medium.*

[Huntsville] *Union Advocate*

The Marshall *Texas Republican* of May 10, 1856, noted the appearance of this Know-Nothing paper. A. B. Norton says McCreary and Collins issued it. It advocated the cause of Sam Houston and was succeeded by the *Recorder*.

[Independence] *Baylor University Magazine*

A prospectus for this literary monthly appeared in the Austin *Texas State Gazette* of January 5, 1861.

[Independence] *Southern Star*

The Austin *Texas State Gazette* of April 25, 1857, noted the appearance of this paper, edited by Jo Littlefield, formerly of the *Washington*

Democrat. Littlefield, commented the *Gazette*, "phoenix-like has risen again." The *Washington American* of July 14, 1857, defended George W. Crawford from attacks by the *Southern Star*. In the summer of 1857, Littlefield proposed to establish a paper at Cameron.

[Independence] *Texas Literary Journal*

The *Washington American* of May 19, 1857, noted the publication of this journal by Rufus C. and Richard Burleson of Baylor University. The Austin *Texas State Gazette* of January 10, 1857, mentioned an educational journal to be published at Independence and edited by the faculty of Baylor University.

[Independence] *Texas Ranger*

This paper, published by Joseph Lancaster, appeared simultaneously at Brenham, Chappell Hill, Independence, and Washington in 1857 and 1859.

Indianola Bulletin

This weekly began in January, 1852, with John Henry Brown as editor and Robert C. Brady as foreman of the printing shop. Brown and Brady were publishers. By the end of its first year the *Bulletin* boasted a circulation of seven hundred, but it suspended temporarily in the summer of 1854. Brown left in September, 1854, to join the *Civilian* at Galveston. Andrew Marschalk, Sr., revived the paper in the spring of 1855. By August of that year W. H. Woodward had purchased an interest in it, and Andrew Marschalk, Jr., had replaced his father. C. A. Ogsbury succeeded Woodward and the younger Marschalk. The *Galveston Tri-Weekly News* of January 24, 1857, reported that the office had been sold at a sheriff's sale and printed Ogsbury's bitter farewell: "Alas, poor Bulletin, and must we mourn, / You died a martyr to Powderhorn." The *Indianolan* succeeded the *Bulletin*. Copies from April 26 to August 24, 1855, are in the Newspaper Collection, University of Texas at Austin.

Indianola Courier and Commercial Bulletin

This paper, edited by William T. Yancey, replaced the *Indianolan* in the spring of 1858. It continued until after the outbreak of the Civil War. Scattered issues from May 21, 1859, to May 24, 1861, are in the Newspaper Collection, University of Texas at Austin.

[Indianola] *Indianolan*

The *Galveston Tri-Weekly News* of June 30, 1857, noted receipt of the first number of this paper, the successor to the *Bulletin*. A Democratic sheet, it was owned and edited by Alfred P. Bennett, formerly of the *New Orleans Times*. The issue of July 18, 1857 (Volume I, number 3), is in the Newspaper Collection, University of Texas at Austin.

[Jacksboro] *White Man*

H. A. Hamner and Isaac Worrall established this paper in March, 1860. It agitated for the defense of the Indian frontier and criticized Governor Sam Houston for his defense policy. The printing office burned on July 29, 1860, in the midst of the hysteria over slave uprisings. Hamner purchased the office of the *Fort Worth Chief* at auction and reestablished the *White Man* at Weatherford in September, 1860.

[Jasper] *Eastern Texian*

The Houston *Telegraph and Texas Register* of September 19, 1851, lists this paper. The Austin *Texas State Gazette* of April 10, 1852, reported that Dr. John C. Lawhon of Newton County had purchased the office of the Jasper journal with the intent of continuing publication under a new name.

[Jasper] *East Texas Clarion*

The Clarksville *Standard* of November 12, 1859, noted that W. A. Leonard had established this paper with materials formerly used by the San Augustine *Eastern Texian*. The *Bellville Countryman* of September 22, 1860, classed the *Clarion* as Democratic in politics. The issue of July 21, 1860 (Volume I, number 36), is in the Newspaper Collection, University of Texas at Austin.

Jefferson Democrat

The Houston *Democratic Telegraph and Texas Register* of June 28, 1847, welcomed this new Democratic-Republican paper. The Clarksville *Standard* of September 4, 1847, noted the sale of the paper to Berry H. Durham. Robert W. Loughery, later of the Marshall *Texas Republican*, became editor at that time and continued as editor until early 1848, when W. C. Baker and Company bought the paper and J. M. and F. C. Baker became editors. The paper became the *Independent Monitor* in June, 1849.

[Jefferson] *Eastern Texas Gazette*

The Marshall *Texas Republican* of November 15, 1856, noted that this weekly would appear the following January. Published by Nimmo and Morgan, it was edited by D. S. McKay and J. W. Nimmo. Michael Farley bought the paper in the fall of 1857, and by November 7 he edited it, and it was published by Morgan and Farley. A Know-Nothing paper, it supported Sam Houston in 1857. Farley sold his interest to S. E. Eggers, a printer, in April, 1858, and the paper became simply the *Gazette* the following September. The issues of March 14 and November 7, 1857, are in the Newspaper Collection, University of Texas at Austin.

Jefferson Gazette

S. E. Eggers purchased the *Eastern Texas Gazette* from Michael Farley in the spring of 1858 and made it the *Gazette* in September. It continued to support Sam Houston. The Houston *Tri-Weekly Telegraph* of March 2, 1859, reported that "the Jefferson Gazette wants it distinctly understood that it still belongs to the American Party." The *Gazette* blended with the *Jefferson Herald* in 1860.

Jefferson Herald

This weekly appeared in the fall of 1850, with Charles W. Westmoreland as editor. It continued for a decade under a number of men, among them Samuel F. Moseley, W. A. Wortham, J. W. Ferris, Frank Clark, W. P. Watson, C. L. Norris, B. F. Baker, H. L. Grinsted, and Ward Taylor. The paper also varied in politics, alternately supporting the Democratic party and the American party. R. H. and J. S. Ward purchased the paper in 1858, and by September 22, 1860, the *Bellville Countryman* classed it as independent and uncommitted. The Wards sold to A. M. Walker and Allan Kirbie, who combined it with the *Jefferson Gazette* to become the *Herald and Gazette* in early 1861. The issue of May 29, 1855, is in the Newspaper Collection, University of Texas at Austin. At that time Frank Clark was editor, and the paper carried the motto, "The Union—The World's Best Hope and Our Own."

Jefferson Herald and Gazette

A. M. Walker and Allan Kirbie purchased the *Herald* in 1861 and combined it with the *Gazette* to issue this paper. The issues of August

16 and November 29, 1861, are in the Newspaper Collection, University of Texas at Austin.

[Jefferson] *Independent Monitor*

The Clarksville *Standard* of June 16, 1849, welcomed this paper, published by W. P. Watson and J. M. Baker and edited by Baker. The Marshall *Texas Republican* of October 18, 1849, reported that the *Independent Monitor* had died "of congestive chill." W. P. Watson announced plans to issue the *Echo* in Dallas in 1849, and by 1854 was part-owner of the *Jefferson Herald.*

[Jefferson] *Spirit of the Age*

The Houston *Democratic Telegraph and Texas Register* of October 12, 1848, noted receipt of the first numbers of this paper. It was a Whig paper, and, commented the *Telegraph,* "One side of each of the numbers is blank." A campaign sheet, the paper vanished after issuing only a few numbers. The press was used to print the *Independent Monitor* the following summer.

[Jefferson] *Star State Jeffersonian*

The *Dallas Herald* of March 20, 1860, noted receipt of the first number of this paper. Published by James A. Warner and Tom P. Ochiltree, it supported Southern causes.

Kaufman Democrat

The *Dallas Herald* of November 14, 1860, welcomed this paper. Published by J. B. and B. W. Reilly, it supported states' rights.

Kimball Herald

Volume I, number 1, of this paper appeared May 20, 1860. It was a quarterly "devoted to the interests of our state." The paper carried a large advertisement for lands Jacob DeCordova had for sale in the area. Kimball was located in Bosque County and is now a ghost town. The issue of May 20, 1860, which is in the Newspaper Collection, University of Texas at Austin, gives a glowing description of the town.

[La Grange] *Far West*

This paper succeeded the *Intelligencer* on February 13, 1847. J. Austin Martin was editor, and William G. Webb worked on the paper. By August, 1847, it had become the *Lavaca Journal* at Port Lavaca. A few copies for early 1847 are in the Texas State Library.

La Grange Intelligencer

William P. Bradburn and James P. Longley established this weekly
in January, 1844. Longley became the sole owner the following
month, and William B. McClellan became editor. Smallwood
S. B. Fields became editor and proprietor with the issue of May
30, 1844. He sold to William B. McClellan and W. D. Mims in
the summer of 1845. The paper continued until September 19,
1846. The *Far West* replaced it in February, 1847. See Julia Sinks,
"Editors and Newspapers of Fayette County." The Texas State Library has a run from February 15, 1844, to September 19, 1846.

La Grange Paper

William B. McClellan, formerly of the *Intelligencer*, purchased the office of the *Texas Monument* and began publication of this paper on
February 24, 1855. He suspended on the following September 29
because of ill health. Ben Shropshire and R. M. Tevis acquired
the press and changed the name to *True Issue*. The Texas State
Library has copies from February 24 to August 4, 1855.

[La Grange] *States Rights Democrat*

Victor M. Thompson began this weekly early in 1860 for the obvious
purpose of supporting the Southern Democrats. The paper carried an elaborate masthead showing the figure of Democracy
fighting an octopus of enemies. Because of the masthead, contemporaries, especially those who disagreed with Thompson's ultra-
Southern stand, called the paper "Snakes." A copy for February
21, 1861 (Volume II, number 2), is in the Newspaper Collection,
University of Texas at Austin. The Texas State Library also has
several copies.

[La Grange] *Texas Monument*

This weekly appeared July 29, 1850, under the auspices of the Texas
Monumental Committee, for the purpose of honoring Texan mar-
tyrs and publishing Texas history. Launcelot Abbotts, a veteran
Texas printer, moved the press of the Houston *Mercantile Adver-
tiser* to La Grange to print the *Monument* and remained with it
until early 1854. Five men in turn edited the paper—John W.
Dancy, J. K. Kuykendall, William P. Smith, Albert P. Posey, and
A. R. Gates. Posey purchased the paper in 1852 after the Monu-

mental Committee became disillusioned with it. He died on April 22, 1854, and A. R. Gates bought the press. He sold it to William B. McClellan, who began the *La Grange Paper* the following year. See Leonie Rummel Weyand and Houston Wade, *An Early History of Fayette County*, and James M. Day, *Black Beans and Goose Quills*. Both the Texas State Library and the Newspaper Collection, University of Texas at Austin, have good runs of the paper.

[La Grange] *True Issue*

Ben Shropshire and R. M. Tevis acquired the press of the *La Grange Paper* in the fall of 1855 and began this weekly. Initially, it supported the Know-Nothing party and carried the motto "Americans Must Rule America." J. J. Gossler replaced Tevis early in 1856, and Gossler and Shropshire sold to J. V. Drake and R. A. Davidge in 1861. The paper supported Sam Houston in the late 1850s. T. S. Cook edited it in September, 1860. See Leonie Rummel Weyand and Houston Wade, *An Early History of Fayette County*. The Texas State Library has copies from 1855, and the Newspaper Collection, University of Texas at Austin, has scattered issues from December 12, 1857, to November 12, 1864.

Lampasas Chronicle

Charles A. Wooldridge established this independent weekly in the summer of 1859. The issue of October 1, 1859 (Volume I, number 4), in the Newspaper Collection, University of Texas at Austin, carries the motto "Truth Without Fear."

[Lavaca] *Commercial*

The Houston *Democratic Telegraph and Texas Register* of June 20, 1850, welcomed this new weekly. W. Ogden edited it until 1851, when Nelson replaced him. The Austin *Texas State Gazette* of February 12, 1853, mentioned Prim as the editor, and the *Gazette* of September 10, 1853, announced that the *Commercial* had been discontinued for want of patronage. The issue of November 30, 1850 (Volume I, number 28), is in the Newspaper Collection, University of Texas at Austin.

Lavaca Courier

The Austin *Texas State Gazette* of August 14, 1852, noted that Nelson and West had issued a prospectus for this paper. It was to be politically neutral. The paper probably never appeared.

Lavaca Express

The *Galveston Journal* of April 11, 1853, noted the prospectus of this paper, and the *Journal* of August 15, 1853, reported that the *Express* had removed to Goliad after issuing only one number at Lavaca.

[Lavaca] *Gulf Key*

The Austin *Texas State Gazette* of April 14, 1860, noted that the *Gulf Key* was the new name of the *Herald* and that it was conducted by R. A. Davidge and Fetter. The paper took the Southern view in the crises of the period.

Lavaca Herald

This weekly appeared in the spring of 1855, with James C. Rowan as editor and proprietor. It was independent in religion and politics. Rowan withdrew in April, 1857, because of lack of patronage, but James Attwell, an early newsman at Matagorda, purchased the office and continued the paper until the end of 1859. It then became the *Gulf Key*. The issues of September 13, 1856, and April 3, June 27, and December 5, 1857, are in the Newspaper Collection, University of Texas at Austin.

Lavaca Journal

J. A. Martin acquired the materials of the La Grange *Far West* and established this paper at Lavaca. The Houston *Democratic Telegraph and Texas Register* of August 23, 1847, noted receipt of the first number. Several Lavaca citizens purchased the paper from Martin, and it continued with H. Beaumont as editor. The issue of January 14, 1848 (Volume I, number 22), is in the Newspaper Collection, University of Texas at Austin.

Lavaca Register

The Austin *Tri-Weekly State Times* of March 18, 1854, acknowledged receipt of the first number of this paper. Edited by Edward B. Mantor and published by James Attwell, the *Register* continued for about a year.

Leona Signal

The Clarksville *Standard* of October 30, 1847, carried a prospectus of this paper, to be published at Leona, the county seat of Leon County. Johnson and Keigwin were the publishers, and Dr. J. C. Boggs, the editor. The paper probably never appeared.

Liberty Gazette

W. J. Brocket and H. C. Shea began this weekly on February 27, 1855, with Brocket as editor. It carried the motto "Let all the ends thou aim'st at be thy country's, thy God's, and Truth's." Brocket withdrew in April to join H. H. Allen at the Houston *Telegraph*. Shea continued the paper until the summer of 1859, when Thomas Jefferson Chambers, Jr., a nephew of the old Texan by that name, replaced him. Chambers supported the Southern Democrats in 1860 and adopted the motto "Equality in the Union or Independence Out of It." Chambers continued the paper after the Civil War. The San Jacinto Museum of History has a good run from 1855 to 1869.

[Liberty] *Herald of Liberty*

George W. Perkins and Launcelot Abbotts issued a prospectus for this paper in early 1852. It was to be politically neutral and edited by Abbotts. Both men later established short-lived papers in Houston. Perkins also became publisher of the *Washington American*. Abbotts furnished the press for the La Grange *Texas Monument*.

[Lick Skillet] *Texas Times*

The Clarksville *Standard* of December 18, 1852, noted that "we have been favored with a copy of the Texas Times, a manuscript journal published at Lick Skillet, which is, we believe, in the Southwest corner of Grayson County." It favored the Democratic party.

Linden Reporter

H. F. O'Neal began this paper in early 1860. The *Dallas Herald* of November 28, 1860, reported that O'Neal had moved to the Jefferson *Herald and Gazette* and that M. M. Mitchell edited the *Reporter*.

Linden Times

The Clarksville *Standard* of February 26, 1859, noted the prospectus of this paper, issued by H. F. O'Neal and Company.

[Livingston] *Rising Sun*

The Austin *Texas State Gazette* of September 15, 1860, noted the establishment of this paper by B. H. Hervey and Company. *The Bellville Countryman* of September 22, 1860, classed it as independent.

[Lockhart] *Rambler*

William Carleton began this paper in Austin and moved it to Lockhart in mid-1859. The copy of July 1, 1859, which is in the Newspaper Collection, University of Texas at Austin, is shown as Volume I, number 7, in Lockhart, and number 35 in Austin.

[Lockhart] *Southern Express*

The Austin *Tri-Weekly State Times* of December 3, 1853, acknowledged receipt of the first number of this paper, published by J. Hubbard Stuart and edited by Mrs. Mary E. Stuart. The *Times* of March 18, 1854, reported that the name of the paper had been changed to *Western Clarion.*

[Lockhart] *Southern Rights*

The *Galveston Tri-Weekly News* of January 24, 1857, noted the prospectus of this paper, issued by J. D. Baker and his brothers. The Bakers were the sons of J. M. Baker, who had issued several papers in Jefferson. Instead of publishing this paper, they moved their press to Columbus to begin the *Colorado Citizen.*

[Lockhart] *Southern Watchman*

The Clarksville *Standard* of December 29, 1855, welcomed this weekly. Roger Lawson Fulton and Edgar Huntley Regan were editors and proprietors. It was, said the *Standard,* "what its name implied—a true Southern Anti-Know Nothing journal." J. D. Baker and his brothers, Ben H. and A. Hicks, bought the paper in early 1857 and issued a prospectus for the *Southern Rights.* With the June 6, 1857, issue they announced their removal to Columbus, because of lack of support in Lockhart. The issue of June 6, 1857 (Volume II, number 19), is in the Newspaper Collection, University of Texas at Austin.

[Lockhart] *South-Side Democrat*

The Austin *Tri-Weekly State Times* of February 2, 1854, reported, "The Bastrop Advertiser learns of the contemplated establishment of a new paper at Lockhart by Mr. Crane and others. It is to be called 'The South-Side Democrat.'"

[Lockhart] *Western Clarion*

The Marshall *Texas Republican* of January 27, 1855, noted this paper, edited by I. G. L. McGehee. The issue of June 2, 1855, is in the Newspaper Collection, University of Texas at Austin.

McKinney Messenger

The Clarksville *Standard* of January 22, 1859, noted the first issue of this weekly, formerly the *Clarksville Messenger*. The proprietors continued the sequence of the earlier paper. James W. Thomas and J. T. Darnall edited it. At Clarksville the paper had been Know-Nothing politically. The *Standard* of November 26, 1859, said that the *Messenger* "has sloughed off some of the madness of its former heresies, and is disposed to be moderate and let parties alone." Yet, the *Bellville Countryman* of September 22, 1860, called it Know-Nothing, and Democratic editors labeled it "submissionist" in 1861. The issue of October 18, 1861 (Volume VII, number 32), is in the Newspaper Collection, University of Texas at Austin. The paper continued after the Civil War.

[Marshall] *Campaign Patriot*

Josiah Marshall of the *Star State Patriot* issued this Whig sheet in 1852 to promote the election of Winfield Scott.

[Marshall] *Grapeshot*

The Marshall *Texas Republican* of July 4, 1857, took note of this pro–Sam Houston sheet that came from the office of T. A. Harris and was edited by Thomas Cooley.

[Marshall] *Harrison Flag*

This paper succeeded the *Star State Patriot* in June, 1856. John W. Barrett, former editor of the *Patriot*, was editor and publisher. The *Flag* supported the Know-Nothing party, Sam Houston, and in 1860 the Constitutional Union party. The Democratic press classed it as opposition and submissionist in 1861. Barrett continued the paper until early 1861, when poor health forced him to suspend. He died shortly thereafter. His son William revived the paper after the Ciivl War. The elder Barrett was born in South Carolina about 1816. The Texas State Library has scattered issues from July 10, 1858, to October 28, 1868.

[Marshall] *Meridian and Pacific Railway Advocate*

The Austin *Texas State Gazette* of August 13, 1853, noted that this paper was to be published by W. R. D. Ward. The paper appeared the following November, edited by Ed Clark, and published by Ward and Company. Clark edited only three issues before political affairs called him to Austin. Herbert Helby replaced Clark. The paper was owned by more than twenty individuals, and its purpose, as the title suggests, was to promote railroads in northeast Texas. Its motto was "Devoted to the Railroad, Agricultural, Commercial, Social, and Moral Improvement of Our Country." By June, 1855, the paper was Know-Nothing. The Marshall *Texas Republican* of August 11, 1855, announced that the *Meridian* was to cease. The owner of the *Republican* later purchased the press of the *Meridian*. The issue of January 28, 1854 (Volume I, number 11), is in the Newspaper Collection, University of Texas at Austin.

[Marshall] *Raging Tad*

The Marshall *Texas Republican* of February 7, 1857, noted that this "scurrillous, vulgar newspaper . . . its editor and publisher anonymous, made its appearance during the dark hours of Saturday night last, and was distributed at the doors of some of our dwellings." The *Republican* commented that many of the articles in the new paper were "not devoid of humor, but the offensive personal character and vulgarity of others rendered it exceedingly reprehensible."

[Marshall] *School Girls' Greeting*

A prospectus for this "original Literary Journal" appeared in the Marshall *Harrison Flag* of February 10, 1860. The "editoresses"—all young ladies from the Marshall Masonic Female Institute—included Fannie Barrett, daughter of the proprietor of the *Flag*, Mary Bradfield, Fanny Van Zandt, and Eliza Rain. They proposed to issue the journal monthly.

[Marshall] *Soda Lake Herald*
This paper appeared in the fall of 1845, with E. C. Beazley as editor,
and T. A. Harris and Zach. Wills as publishers. The *Star State Patriot* came from the same office in the spring of 1848.

[Marshall] *Star State Patriot*
This weekly succeeded the *Soda Lake Herald* in April, 1848, and came
from the press office of T. A. and J. C. Harris. H. B. Kelsey, the
first editor, made the paper Democratic in politics. He died late in
1848 and was succeeded by Howard Burnside, who made it politically neutral. The Harrises sold to A. N. Witherspoon in 1850,
and he made it Whig. W. A. Tarleton served briefly as editor.
John F. Witherspoon and Josiah Marshall became owners in September, 1851, and Marshall became sole owner and editor the following May. He gave ardent support to Winfield Scott and issued
the *Campaign Patriot* to advocate the Whig candidate. S. H. Parsons and E. Junius Foster joined the *Patriot* briefly in 1853,
and Marshall offered the office for sale early the following year.
John W. Barrett, the last editor of the *Patriot*, purchased the office and renamed the paper the *Harrison Flag* in June, 1856. The issues of June 7, 1851, and March 19, 1853, are in the Newspaper
Collection, University of Texas at Austin.

[Marshall] *Texas Republican*
The brothers T. A. and F. J. Patillo began this weekly on March 30,
1849. Robert W. Loughery joined the paper the following July as
associate editor. He became editor in the fall of 1849 and purchased the paper in 1851. A staunch Calhoun Democrat, Loughery made the paper one of the important journals of the 1850s. It
is more fully treated in the text. The Texas State Library has an
excellent run.

[Matagorda] *Chronicle of the Times*
Dugald MacFarlane, who was born in Scotland in 1797, began publication of this paper in 1855 in partnership with his son-in-law Joseph
Theall. It carried an interesting masthead, which included a star
and snake. The issue of March 6, 1858 (Volume III, number 21), is
in the Newspaper Collection, University of Texas at Austin.

[Matagorda] *Colorado Herald*

James W. Dallam began this weekly in the summer of 1846, as the successor to his *Despatch*. The Houston *Democratic Telegraph and Texas Register* of August 30, 1847, noted that Dallam planned to discontinue the *Herald* and move the office to the new town of Indian Point. There he planned to establish a paper called the *Emigrant*, printed in both German and English. Dallam died before he could move, and Edward F. Gilbert purchased the press and renamed the paper the *Colorado Tribune*. The issue of August 19, 1846, is in the Texas State Library. Several mutilated copies, probably for early 1847, are in the Newspaper Collection, University of Texas at Austin.

[Matagorda] *Colorado Tribune*

The Houston *Democratic Telegraph and Texas Register* of November 4, 1847, reported that Edward F. Gilbert had purchased the materials of the *Colorado Herald* and planned to issue the *Tribune*. The paper supported Zachary Taylor for president in 1848. Gilbert offered the office for sale in late 1853. The issues of April 17, 1848, and May 10 and June 2, 1851, are in the Newspaper Collection, University of Texas at Austin. The Texas State Library has a good run from June, 1849, to July, 1854.

Matagorda Gazette

This paper appeared on July 31, 1858, with Galen Hodges as proprietor and E. J. Lipsey as editor. In 1859 Lipsey purchased Hodges's interest. The Austin *Texas State Gazette* of March 9, 1861, noted that Swope and Lewis were editors and that the *Gazette* was a states' rights paper. The Newspaper Collection, University of Texas at Austin, has a good run from July, 1858, to January, 1860.

[Meridian] *Bosque Times*

The *Galveston Weekly News* of October 16, 1860, welcomed this paper, established by W. R. D. Ward and C. E. Cantley. The paper supported Breckinridge and Lane.

[Mount Pleasant] *Texas Register*

The Clarksville *Standard* of April 21, 1849, carried the prospectus of this paper, to be published the following month by J. C. Chisholm and A. S. Gray.

Mount Pleasant Union

This weekly appeared during the summer of 1860, with B. Ober, formerly of the Paris *Family Visitor*, as editor and Enoch Marple as
proprietor. The Clarksville *Standard* of June 30, 1860, called it a
"Sam Houston sort" of Democratic paper. Marple retired, and the
paper suspended briefly after the election of November, 1860.
J. A. Carpenter revived the paper in January, 1861, to oppose the
secession convention and agitate for "rights within the Union."
The *Bellville Countryman* of September 22, 1860, called it "uncommitted and Whiggish."

[Nacogdoches] *Campaign Chronicle*

E. W. Cave issued this campaign sheet in 1857 and again in 1859 to
promote Sam Houston for governor. Copies of July 19 and 26 and
August 5, 1859, are in the Newspaper Collection, University of
Texas at Austin.

Nacogdoches Chronicle

The Austin *Texas State Gazette* of March 13, 1852, noted the first number of this paper, published by J. C. Harrison and N. J. Moore
and edited by Harrison. It carried as its motto Andrew Jackson's
toast, "The Union—It Must Be Preserved." Eber Worthington
Cave replaced Harrison as editor in 1853 and purchased the paper
in early 1854. The paper supported Sam Houston for president
and leaned toward the American party in the mid-1850s. The
Marshall *Texas Republican* of June 24, 1859, said, "The Nacogdoches Chronicle which we had supposed dead and buried in its
own putridity, is alive once more and wallowing in its own slime."
After Houston was elected governor in 1859, Cave became his
secretary of state and sold the paper to H. C. Hancock. The Austin *Southern Intelligencer* of May 5, 1861, reported that S. H. B.
Cundiff had replaced Hancock. Scattered issues from January 4,
1852, to October 17, 1854, are in the Library of Congress. Both
the Texas State Library and the Newspaper Collection, University
of Texas at Austin, have a few issues.

[Nacogdoches] *Nacogdoches*

The San Augustine *Red-Lander* of April 2, 1846, carried a prospectus
of this paper to be published in June, 1846, by John H. Moffette.

Nacogdoches Times

The Clarksville *Standard* of July 31, 1847, reported, "We perceive by
a notice in the Shield that Mr. Kendall of that paper is about to
start a new paper in old Nacogdoches." Henry A. Kendall of the
San Augustine Shield killed his rival of the *Red-Lander* shortly
thereafter and fled to New Orleans, where he died of yellow fever
in October, 1847. Floyd H. Kendall in fact issued the prospectus
of the *Nacogdoches Times*. He began the paper about July 31,
1847. A Mr. Hammond and John H. Cohoon later joined him. Cohoon bought the paper in April, 1849, and discontinued it with
the issue of August 4. See Lois Fitzhugh F. Blount, "Nacogdoches
Notes." The Texas State Library has a good run from April, 1848,
to August, 1849.

[New Braunfels] *Neu-Braunfelser Zeitung*

Ferdinand Jacob Lindheimer began this paper on November 12, 1852,
and it continues with a slightly different title to the present. The
paper is considered more fully in the text. Both the Newspaper
Collection, University of Texas at Austin, and the Texas State Library have excellent files.

Palestine American

The Clarksville *Standard* of December 22, 1855, noted receipt of this
Know-Nothing paper edited by Andrew Jackson Fowler and
George Washington Tuggle. The Marshall *Texas Republican* of
June 21, 1856, listed A. D. McCutchan as the publisher. J. L.
Caldwell, co-owner of the Fairfield *Texas Pioneer*, purchased the
office in September, 1858, with plans to issue the *Pioneer* simul-
taneously at Fairfield and Springfield.

[Palestine] *Christian Philanthropist*

The Austin *Texas State Times* of September 29, 1855, noted the appearance of this monthly, edited by C. Kendricks. It took a strong
anti-Catholic stand.

Palestine Pioneer

The Houston *Democratic Telegraph and Texas Register* of October 25,
1849, noted that the *Pioneer* was now in Palestine. A Whig paper,
it was established by Joseph Addison Clark, who had previously

edited a paper by the same name at Rusk. The *Pioneer* lasted only a short while. It was succeeded by the *Trinity Advocate*. Copies for October 31 and November 7, 1849, are in the Library of Congress.

[Palestine] *Students' Friend*
A prospectus for this publication appeared in the *Harrison Flag* of September 23, 1859.

[Palestine] *Trinity Advocate*
The Marshall *Texas Republican* of January 25, 1851, noted receipt of this paper "on the ruins of the Wonder upon which it is a decided improvement." The press had earlier printed the *Pioneer*. By June, 1852, the *Advocate* was published by Rogers, Ewing, and Martin and edited by J. A. Hyslop. James W. Ewing had formerly been associated with Joseph Addison Clark on the *Pioneer*. Matthew Dale joined the paper in 1852, and A. E. McClure joined it in 1856. Ewing sold his interest in 1857. Dale joined the Confederate army and died in the Battle of Shiloh. The issue of June 19, 1852, is in the Texas State Library; those of December 10, 1853, and May 20, 1857, are in the Newspaper Collection, University of Texas at Austin; and the Library of Congress has scattered issues from April 22, 1857, to December, 1860.

Paris Advocate
The *Dallas Herald* of March 20, 1861, noted receipt of this paper, edited by Thomas J. Crooks. It carried the motto "The Confederate States—Our Home." Crooks had once been a correspondent of the Clarksville *Standard* and had edited the *Paris Press*, which F. W. Miner published. Crooks and Miner disagreed politically in late 1860, prompting Crooks to establish this new paper.

[Paris] *Bible Union*
The *Dallas Herald* of June 14, 1856, noted that "Dr. Padun of the Christian (Campbellite) Church" was planning to establish this paper.

[Paris] *Family Visitor*
The Clarksville *Standard* of January 15, 1859, welcomed this paper, which had replaced the *Lamar Enquirer*. The *Visitor* was pub-

lished by B. Ober and L. S. Gooding and edited by B. Ober. The *Standard* of February 26, 1859, suggested that the *Family Visitor* was Know-Nothing in disguise.

[Paris] *Frontier Patriot*

E. Junius Foster purchased the press of the *Bonham Advertiser* and moved it to Paris to establish this paper in early 1856. Foster, an old Whig turned Know-Nothing, had formerly been associated with the Marshall *Star State Patriot*. In early 1858 he moved the press to Sherman, where he founded the *Patriot*.

[Paris] *Lamar Enquirer*

The Marshall *Texas Republican* of June 28, 1856, noted this new paper edited by John T. Mills and published by R. Q. Terrill and Richard Peterson. The paper supported the Democrats in 1856. B. Ober and L. S. Gooding bought the press and changed the name to *Family Visitor* in January, 1859. The issue of October 16, 1856, is in the Newspaper Collection, University of Texas at Austin.

Paris Press

This paper appeared in 1859, with Fred W. Miner as publisher and Thomas J. Crooks as editor. The two disagreed politically after Lincoln's victory in the presidential election of 1860. Crooks founded the *Advocate* to support secession, while Miner continued the *Press* as a Union paper.

[Paris] *Texas Times*

Robert Campbell Matthewson and James Wellington Latimer purchased the Bonham *Western Argus* in late 1848 and moved the office to Paris, where they briefly published the *Times*. The Marshall *Texas Republican* of November 22, 1849, reported that the paper had been discontinued. Latimer moved the equipment to Dallas, where he started the *Herald*. Matthewson moved to Austin to edit the *Texas State Gazette* for a time. Matthewson had come to Texas with the Peters Colony and had edited several Mexican War papers. A man given to controversy, he disagreed with the publisher of the *Gazette* and left for California in 1850.

[Paris] *Western Star*

W. J. W. Morgan established this paper in Clarksville in 1847 and moved it to Paris in 1850. A Whig paper, it was edited for a time by the Reverend Thomas Lewelling. After a suspension, Morgan revived it in September, 1852. The Library of Congress has a few copies from June 29 to December 19, 1851.

Quitman Clipper

A. P. Shuford established this weekly about 1859. It supported the Bell-Everitt ticket in 1860 and was called a "submissionist" paper in 1861. Shuford represented Wood County in the secession convention. He was born in North Carolina about 1836 and came to Texas in 1855.

Quitman Herald

This weekly appeared in June, 1857, with W. J. Sparks, J. J. Jarvis, and J. M. Clark as proprietors. Sparks and Jarvis edited it. The Marshall *Texas Republican* of October 29, 1858, noted that Jarvis and Clark had sold their interest to Sparks and A. and W. W. Gunter. The paper opposed Sam Houston. The issue of July 1, 1857, is in the Newspaper Collection, University of Texas at Austin.

[Quitman] *Texas Free Press*

This paper appeared in the summer of 1856, edited by Winston Banks and published by Banks and Turner. John E. Lemon contributed to it, calling for a discussion of slavery. The Free-Soil sentiments of the paper stirred up excitement, and it discontinued in 1857. It is considered more fully in the text.

[Richmond] *Brazos Delta*

This weekly appeared in 1851, edited by J. G. Wright. He killed Richard Hanson in July, 1852, and a few months thereafter sold the paper to Fenton M. Gibson and Dunn, who renamed it the *Recorder*.

Richmond Recorder

The Austin *South-Western American* of December 1, 1852, noted the first two issues of this weekly, edited by Fenton M. Gibson. It succeeded the *Brazos Delta*. Gibson participated in the Mier Expedition and wrote an account of his misadventures. He became editor of the Austin *Texas State Times* in March, 1857, and continued as editor of the Austin *Texas Sentinel*, which replaced the *Times* in the summer of 1857. The issue of December 8, 1852, is in the Texas State Library.

Richmond Reporter

The Austin *Texas State Gazette* of June 7, 1856, noted the appearance of this paper, published by William F. Ferguson. He was assisted by his brother, Samuel H. Ferguson. Samuel A. Benton became editor and proprietor in the summer of 1858, and William F. Ferguson remained with the paper as printer. The *Texas State Gazette* of June 16, 1860, reports that Gustav Cook had joined the *Reporter*. Later that year Benton established the *Lone Star* at Hallettsville. The issues of August 2, 1856, July 12, 1857, and January 29, 1859, are in the Newspaper Collection, University of Texas at Austin.

[Richmond] *Texas Sun*

This paper began in January, 1855, with R. H. Rawlings and Co. as publishers and proprietors. The *Galveston Weekly News* of October 31, 1854, identified the proprietors as R. Herndon Rawlings, J. S. Sullivan, T. H. and G. W. McMahan, W. G. Foot, J. H. Herndon, J. S. Duval, William E. Kendall, and H. B. Wallar. The *Sun* supported E. M. Pease for governor and carried the motto "The Tool of No Man; the Slave of No Party." It was discontinued in 1856. The issues of February 17 and 24 and March 10, 1855, and April 26, 1856, are in the Newspaper Collection, University of Texas at Austin.

[Rusk] *Cherokee Sentinel*

The Houston *Democratic Telegraph and Texas Register* of March 28, 1850, noted the appearance of this weekly. Initially published by Andrew Jackson and John B. Long, it was published by Jackson and William R. Wiggins and edited by Thomas J. Johnson in 1855. Johnson retired in late 1856, and shortly thereafter Jackson, Wiggins and Company sold to Reagan and Noland, and M. R. Reagan became editor. The issues of May 10, 1856, and August 1, 1857, are in the Newspaper Collection, University of Texas at Austin.

Rusk Pioneer

The Houston *Democratic Telegraph and Texas Register* of March 2, 1848, noted that Joseph Addison Clark of the Bonham *Western Argus* planned to establish this paper. Clark ran into trouble in Rusk, as described in Joseph Lynn Clark, *Thank God We Made It!* The *Telegraph* of November 30, 1848, reported that Glidewell and Parsons had purchased the paper and that it would be Democratic. Even so, by August, 1849, the paper still carried the names of Clark and W. R. Culp. The issue of August 3, 1849, is in the Texas State Library. The Library of Congress has several copies from April to August, 1849.

[Rusk] *Temperance Banner and Sunday School Advocate*

The Huntsville *Texas Banner* of February 3, 1849, carried a prospectus for this monthly, to be published by J. B. Mitchell.

[Rusk] *Texas Enquirer*

The Marshall *Texas Republican* of March 8, 1856, noted receipt of the first issue of this weekly, edited and published by W. T. Yeomans. It supported the Know-Nothing party. After a suspension it resumed in 1857 to support Sam Houston. It also supported Houston in 1859.

[Rusk] *Texas Free Mason*

W. T. Yeomans of the Rusk *Texas Enquirer* and Andrew Jackson of the *Cherokee Sentinel* issued a prospectus dated January 4, 1858, for this Masonic paper. The Grand Lodge of Texas accepted it as the official paper of the lodge, and it continued until 1861.

Sabine Pass Times

The Clarksville *Standard* of November 12, 1859, noted receipt of the second number of this paper. Edited by J. Thomas Fuller, it advocated the advantages of Sabine Pass over Galveston. It supported John Breckinridge for president in 1860. The San Augustine *Red Land Express* of February 2, 1861, reported Fuller's death of consumption at Ocean Springs, Mississippi, on December 31, 1860.

[San Antonio] *Alamo Express*

James Pearson Newcomb established this paper, first a weekly and then a tri-weekly, on August 18, 1860, to advocate the Constitutional Union ticket in the presidential election. He had previously

been associated with the *Herald* and left that paper because of political differences with the publisher. The *Express* suspended after
the election in November but resumed publication early the next
year, with J. B. Baccus as publisher. It advocated the cause of the
Union so vigorously that a hostile mob burned the press office and
Newcomb fled to California. Copies from August 18, 1860, to May
3, 1861, are in the San Antonio Public Library.

[San Antonio] *Alamo Star*
Two teen-age boys, James Pearson Newcomb and Frank M. Whitemond, began this weekly on March 25, 1854. It boasted a circulation of 240 by May 20. Whitemond left the paper in the summer
of 1854 but remained in San Antonio and the area as a printer and
journalist for many years. Robert J. Lambert replaced Whitemond at the *Star* but also left before Newcomb discontinued the
paper in early 1855. Newcomb replaced the *Star* with the *Herald*.
Copies from March 24, 1854, to January 29, 1855, are in the San
Antonio Public Library.

[San Antonio] *El Bejareño*
The first number of this Spanish-language paper, first a semi-monthly
and then a weekly, appeared on February 7, 1855. It was edited
and published by X. B. DeBray and A. A. Lewis, and carried the
motto "For the Constitution of the United States and Freedom of
Religion." It reflected the political division of the city at that time,
and, said the Austin *Texas State Times*, it leaned toward the
Know-Nothing party. DeBray later associated himself with the
Austin *Texas State Times* and its successor, the *Texas Sentinel*,
both of Know-Nothing sentiments. He headed a regiment in the
Civil War. Copies from February 17, 1855, to June 28, 1856, are in
the Newspaper Collection, University of Texas at Austin.

[San Antonio] *El Correo*
This Democratic paper in the Spanish language appeared in April,
1858. A weekly, it was edited by José Ramos de Zuñiga and Alfred A. Lewis. Lewis had previously co-edited *El Bejareño*. Copies for April 28, May 19, and July 8, 1858, are in the Newspaper
Collection, University of Texas at Austin.

[San Antonio] *El Ranchero*
J. A. Quintero began this Spanish-language paper in July, 1856, to take issue with *El Bejareño*. A campaign sheet, it created a sensation by charging that the Know-Nothings planned to burn Roman Catholic churches in San Antonio. Quintero stepped down in favor of G. Leal, and the paper ceased shortly thereafter. Quintero, a Cuban refugee, was engaged in the cotton trade during the Civil War. The issues of July 4, 11, 19, and 28, 1856, are in the Newspaper Collection, University of Texas at Austin.

San Antonio Herald
James Pearson Newcomb founded this paper on April 3, 1855, as the successor to the *Alamo Star*. J. M. West assisted him. After running into political trouble in the summer of 1856, Newcomb sold to J. D. Logan. The following year S. C. Thompson joined Logan. Newcomb returned to edit the paper in 1857, but left it after disagreeing with Logan on politics in 1860. S. C. Thompson sold his interest to G. W. Palmer in January, 1859. George H. Sweet replaced Newcomb as editor in 1860. Both the San Antonio Public Library and the Newspaper Collection, University of Texas at Austin, have good holdings.

San Antonio Ledger
Jo Walker, a printer and sometime Texas Ranger, founded this paper, a weekly and later a daily, in the summer of 1850. During the next decade many men were associated with it, among them I. A. Hewitt, David Campbell Van Derlip, Michael Bourke, Michael R. Finck, B. F. Neal, Robert J. Teel, a Schobell, and a Howard. The paper suspended for six months in 1859 and revived with N. A. Taylor as editor and A. E. Macleod, Robert J. Teel, and Taylor as publishers. Both the San Antonio Public Library and the Newspaper Collection, University of Texas at Austin, have scattered copies from 1851 to 1860. The paper merged with the *San Antonio Texan* to become the *Ledger and Texan*.

San Antonio Ledger and Texan
N. A. Taylor and A. E. Macleod of the *Ledger* bought the *San Antonio Texan* in the fall of 1859 and issued this paper from January 7 to December 1, 1860. Robert J. Teel owned part interest. By Febru-

ary, 1861, Macleod and J. Y. Dashiell were publishers. Scattered
copies are at the San Antonio Public Library and Newspaper Collection, University of Texas at Austin.

[San Antonio] *Mallet and Shooting Stick*

A group of printers founded this paper in 1857, after a strike by their
union for New Orleans wages left them unemployed. The printers
included F. M. Whitemond, Robert Lambert, John M. Smith,
Robert J. Teel, and one McKinney. The paper lasted only a short
while.

San Antonio News

Jacobina Burch Harding, "A History of the Early Newspapers of
San Antonio, 1823–1874" (M.A. thesis, University of Texas), says
this was edited by Jeremiah Yellott Dashiell and published by
R. Finck in 1860 and that it merged with the *Ledger and Texan*.
Dashiell was connected with the *Ledger and Texan* by February,
1861, and later edited the *San Antonio Herald*. E. G. Huston
published the *Semi-Weekly News* by March, 1862.

San Antonio Reporter

After Frank M. Whitemond dissolved his partnership with James Pearson Newcomb in the *Alamo Star*, he founded this paper, in association with B. M. Banker. It carried the motto "Nothing Suffers
from Free Discussion but Ignorance and Error." Issues from
March 18 to September 9, 1856, are in the San Antonio Public Library.

[San Antonio] *Sentinel*

The Austin *Texas State Times* of May 26, 1855, noted receipt of the first
number of this weekly. Published by X. B. Sanders and Company,
it was edited by Sanders and J. Varian Smith. The issue of July 14,
1855, is in the San Antonio Public Library.

[San Antonio] *Texas Staats-Zeitung*

This paper succeeded the *San Antonio Zeitung* and initially was edited
by H. F. Oswald. After his death, his brother Theodore Oswald
became editor. Gustav Schleicher edited it in 1859 and was replaced the next year by Herzberg and R. Finck. The issue of April
9, 1859, is in the Texas State Library.

[San Antonio] *Union*

This paper appeared on June 29, 1859. It was a "campaign chronicle for the coming canvas, edited by an association of Union men for Houston." Backed by Gustav Schleicher and Jacob Waelder, it took as its purpose explaining away Sam Houston's flirtation with the Know-Nothing party and enlisting the German vote for him. The issue of July 29, 1859, is in the Newspaper Collection, University of Texas at Austin.

[San Antonio] *Western Texian*; title varies: *Daily Texan, San Antonio Texan, Western Texan*

Michael Cronican and J. A. Glasscock began this paper in October, 1848. Cronican died shortly after founding it, and it passed through a number of hands during the next few years. The men associated with it included Nathaniel Lewis, John D. Groesbeeck, J. H. Lyons, J. S. McDonald, E. G. Huston, and John M. Smith. The paper merged with the *San Antonio Ledger* to become the *Ledger and Texan* in late 1859. See Jacobina Burch Harding, "A History of the Early Newspapers of San Antonio, 1823–1874" (M.A. thesis, University of Texas). Scattered copies from 1848 to 1859 are in the Newspaper Collection, University of Texas at Austin, and the San Antonio Public Library.

San Antonio Zeitung

A group of Germans purchased the press for this paper, and it appeared in July, 1853, edited by Adolph Douai. He later purchased the press. The paper precipitated a crisis by advocating the creation of the state of West Texas as a free state. The paper is treated more fully in the text. The Texas State Library has scattered issues.

[San Augustine] *Campaign*

The Marshall *Star State Patriot* of April 10, 1852, noted that Alexander H. Evans of the San Augustine *Red Land Herald* had issued a prospectus of this paper. He proposed to issue the paper from June "till (somewhere this side of) January." The paper was devoted to Democracy in general and "old Sam in particular."

[San Augustine] *Eastern Texian*

The Austin *Texas State Gazette* of April 25, 1857, noted the appearance of this paper, edited by George W. King. It advocated the cause of Sam Houston. It ceased in 1859, when W. A. Leonard purchased the office and moved it to Jasper to establish the *East Texas Clarion*. The Texas State Library has a good run from April 11, 1857, to July 10, 1858.

San Augustine Herald

C. L. Collins purchased the *Red Land Herald* and made it simply the *Herald* in 1852. The Marshall *Texas Republican* of July 15, 1854, noted that it had changed hands and that the new proprietors, M. C. McDaniel and James F. Martin, had begun the *Red-Lander*. The issues of January 21 and May 6, 1854, are in the Newspaper Collection, University of Texas at Austin.

[San Augustine] *Red-Lander*

The first paper by this name appeared in San Augustine in September, 1838, and was discontinued in December, 1839. A. W. Canfield revived the name in May, 1841, and made the *Red-Lander* one of the important papers in Texas at the time of annexation. Canfield sold the paper to James Russell and H. M. Kinsey after annexation. Russell was killed by a rival editor, Henry Kendall of the *Shield*, on August 10, 1847. William N. Harman purchased both press offices and combined the *Red-Lander* and the *Shield* to issue the *Texas Union*. The *Union* became first the *Red Land Herald* and then the *Herald* and then under two new owners, M. C. McDaniel and James F. Martin, again the *Red-Lander* in the summer of 1854. F. H. Dixon replaced McDaniel in late 1858. Scattered copies from 1841 to 1854 are in both the Texas State Library and Newspaper Collection, University of Texas at Austin.

[San Augustine] *Red Land Express*

The Marshall *Harrison Flag* of May 18, 1860, welcomed the first number of this paper, edited by A. D. McCutchan. Initially it advocated Sam Houston for president. After his chances vanished, it supported John C. Breckinridge. Scattered issues from May 19, 1860, to February 2, 1861, are in the Texas State Library.

[San Augustine] *Red Land Herald*

The Austin *Texas State Gazette* of November 17, 1849, noted that Benjamin F. Benton and B. F. Price had purchased the San Augustine *Union* and changed the name to *Red Land Herald*. In the spring of 1851, Benton and Price sold the paper to Alexander H. Evans who made it, in the words of the Houston *Telegraph and Texas Register* of July 4, 1851, the "organ of Mr. Greer." C. L. Collins purchased the paper in 1852 and made it simply the *Herald*. Benton, a nephew of Thomas Hart Benton, was killed at Gaines Mill during the Civil War.

San Augustine Shield

This weekly appeared in the summer of 1846, with Henry A. Kendall as publisher and F. H. Blades and J. G. Brooke as editors. The Clarksville *Standard* of August 7, 1847, announced the retirement of the Reverend Blades as editor. On August 10, 1847, Kendall killed James Russell, editor of the San Augustine *Red-Lander*. Kendall left for New Orleans, where he died of yellow fever in the fall of 1847.

[San Augustine] *Texas Union*

The Reverend William N. Harman, formerly of the *Red-Lander* office, purchased the presses of the *Shield* and *Red-Lander* in October, 1847, and united the papers under this name. The editor of the *Shield*, Henry A. Kendall, had killed the editor of the *Red-Lander*, James Russell. Henry W. Sublett edited the *Texas Union* in the spring of 1848. Harman sold the paper to Benjamin F. Benton and B. F. Price in the fall of 1849. The Austin *Texas State Gazette* of November 18, 1849, noted that the new owners had changed the name of the paper to the *Red Land Herald*. The *Gazette* of August 30, 1851, gives a brief history of the paper. A few copies from April 1 to July 15, 1848, are in the Newspaper Collection, University of Texas at Austin.

Seguin Journal

The Houston *Telegraph* of December 27, 1857, noted receipt of Volume II, number 2, of this paper, published by S. Wright and Frank Whitemond. By May, 1858, S. Wright was editor and proprietor, and the paper, then entitled the *Journal and Recorder*, carried the motto "Union and Liberty, One and Inseparable, Now and Forever." The Texas State Library has several issues from July 11, 1857, to March 27, 1858. The issue of May 15, 1858, is in the Newspaper Collection, University of Texas at Austin.

[Seguin] *Mirror*

The Austin *Texas State Gazette* of October 8, 1859, noted this "neat literary work devoted to the interest of Seguin Male and Female College."

[Seguin] *Southern Confederacy*

This paper first appeared on February 8, 1861, replacing the *Seguin Mercury*. W. E. Goodrich was editor and D. R. Freeman, publisher. As the title suggests, it advocated secession and the joining of Texas to the Southern Confederacy. The first issue is in the Newspaper Collection, University of Texas at Austin.

[Seguin] *Texan Mercury*; later, *Seguin Mercury*

This weekly, published by J. D. Buchanan and edited by H. T. Burke, appeared in the fall of 1853. By June of 1855, R. W. Rainey had replaced Buchanan as publisher, and by the end of the year Burke had withdrawn. Rainey changed the name of the paper to *Seguin Mercury*. The Austin *Texas Sentinel* of August 8, 1857, reported Rainey's death at age thirty. The paper was suspended for several months and then revived by William and Myddleton S. Dunn. W. E. Goodrich edited the paper for a time. The "sterling democratic Seguin Mercury" was replaced by the *Southern Confederacy* in early 1861. The issues of October 15, 1853, and March 10, 1855, are in the Newspaper Collection, University of Texas at Austin. Scattered copies from 1855 to 1860 are in the Texas State Library.

[Seguin] *Union Democrat*

The Houston *Weekly Telegraph* of October 5, 1859, noted this paper, edited by S. Wright, formerly of the *Seguin Journal*. The paper opposed lending money to railroads and was classed as Know-Nothing by the *Bellville Countryman* of September 22, 1860. It opposed secession but felt that the South had been wronged in early 1861. An extra dated February 23, 1861, carries the motto "Our Country, Right or Wrong." That extra is in the Newspaper Collection, University of Texas at Austin.

Shelbyville Echo

The Marshall *Texas Republican* of January 28, 1860, noted that M. L. McCormick of the Carthage *Panola Harbinger* had established this paper. In the spring of 1860, the *Echo* advocated W. R. Poag of east Texas for president and John C. Breckinridge for vice president. The paper supported the Breckinridge ticket later in the year. The paper was printed on a small sheet from an office "upstairs over J. M. Lucky's Family Grocery Store on Main Street." The issue of July 7, 1860 (Volume I, number 21), is in the Newspaper Collection, University of Texas at Austin.

[Shelbyville] *Shelby Reville*

The Austin *Texas State Gazette* of May 13, 1854, reported: "The Shelby Reville [*sic*] is the title of a new paper just started at Shelbyville, Texas, edited and published by J. F. Martin. The Reville is neutral in Politics." James F. Martin purchased an interest in the *San Augustine Herald* in July, 1854. In the July 29, 1854, issue of that paper, Martin explains why he left Shelbyville and also gives the above spelling to the title.

[Shelbyville] *Tenehaw Beacon*

The Austin *Texas State Gazette* of August 20, 1853, noted receipt of the first number of this paper, dated August 8, 1853, and edited and owned by Harry White. Two weeks later, the *Gazette* reported, "It seems that Mr. White's labors were cut short by the Sheriff of San Augustine County arresting him on capias, sent from Brazoria County for stealing a rifle gun!"

[Sherman] *Advance Guard*

The Houston *Tri-Weekly Telegraph* of March 25, 1859, noted receipt of the first number of this paper. Published by Wallace A. Price and Clay C. Wells, it lasted only a short time. By May 28, 1859, the Clarksville *Standard* had received the successor to the *Advance Guard*, the *North Texian*.

[Sherman] *Harbinger*

The Houston *Tri-Weekly Telegraph* of January 14, 1859, reported that the Reverend DeSpain planned to issue the "Harbinger (Campbellite)" from Sherman.

Sherman Journal

The *Journal*, edited by J. P. Whitaker, succeeded the *Monitor* in the
    spring of 1861. The issue of August 21, 1862 (Volume II, number
    12), is in the Newspaper Collection, University of Texas at Austin.

Sherman Monitor

The Austin *Texas State Gazette* of December 15, 1860, noted receipt of
    the first number of this paper. It was published by J. P. Whitaker
    of Vermont and J. H. Crabtree of North Carolina. The *Monitor*
    had become the *Journal* by 1861. See Graham Landrum and Alan
    Smith, *Grayson County*.

[Sherman] *North Texian*

The Clarksville *Standard* of May 28, 1859, noted receipt of this paper,
    the successor to the *Advance Guard*. A Union journal, it sup-
    ported Sam Houston and was edited by Tom Grant and one Mar-
    shall. The *Bellville Countryman* of September 22, 1860, classed it
    as independent.

Sherman Patriot

The Austin *Texas State Gazette* of July 3, 1858, welcomed this paper,
    published by E. Junius Foster. Foster had previously been con-
    nected with the Marshall *Star State Patriot*. He purchased the
    Bonham Advertiser and moved the office first to Paris, where he
    issued the *Frontier Patriot* for two years, and then to Sherman
    to found this paper. Foster, born in North Carolina about 1814,
    was an old Whig who leaned toward the Know-Nothings in the
    mid-1850s and supported the cause of the Union in 1860. His pa-
    per was "submissionist" in early 1861 and suggested the forming
    of a new state in north Texas that would remain in the Union.
    Upon hearing erroneously that Foster had died, the Houston *Tri-
    Weekly Telegraph* of March 16, 1859, commented, "He was doubt-
    less troubled enough by the devil when alive, and we trust he has
    escaped him now." Foster in fact was killed in 1862 as a result of
    his editorial comments on the violence that wracked north Texas
    at that time. See Graham Landrum and Alan Smith, *Gray-
    son County*.

[Sherman] *Texas Farmer*

The Houston *Tri-Weekly Telegraph* of January 14, 1859, reported that James T. Maddux and Company planned to issue this paper at Sherman.

[Springfield] *Texas Pioneer*

This paper appeared simultaneously at Fairfield and Springfield in late 1858, with J. L. Caldwell as the Springfield publisher. The *Bellville Countryman* of September 22, 1860, called it independent in politics.

[Sulphur Springs] *Bright Star*

The Austin *Texas State Gazette* of September 26, 1857, noted receipt of the second number of this paper.

[Sulphur Springs] *Independent Monitor*

The Marshall *Texas Republican* of July 30, 1859, noted that "our young friend John Garrison is connected with W. M. Payne in publishing the Independent Monitor." The *Bellville Countryman* of September 22, 1860, classed it as independent. By late 1860, Ashcroft, Davis, and Company owned the paper, and W. H. Ashcroft and William L. Davis were editors. The issue of December 1, 1860 (Volume II, number 17), is in the Newspaper Collection, University of Texas at Austin.

[Sulphur Springs] *Texas Telegraph*

The Marshall *Texas Republican* of April 3, 1858, noted the appearance of this paper, edited by S. B. Callahan and D. N. Smith, and commented that the publishers had made a "bad selection of title." It was a Democratic paper. The Austin *Texas State Gazette* of July 3, 1858, noted that W. M. Payne had joined the *Telegraph*.

[Sumpter] *Printer*

The Clarksville *Standard* of January 15, 1859, noted that the *Printer* appeared simultaneously at Crockett and Sumpter, with Oscar Dalton as editor in Crockett and J. L. Cottrell in Sumpter. Sumpter, in central Trinity County, was the county seat in 1850 but is now a ghost town.

[Sumpter] *Trinity Valley*

A. B. Norton says, "There was a Sumpter, in the fall of 1860, a small paper styled the Trinity Valley, published by Jo A. Kirgan, which eked out for a short time a miserable existence, and its industrious publisher, for the support of his family, turned his attention to making hide-bottom chairs."

[Tarrant] *Democrat Herald*

A. B. Norton says that William Amos Wortham published this paper from 1858 to 1860. Wortham had formerly published the *Jefferson Herald* and after the Civil War published several papers at Sulphur Springs.

[Tarrant] *Hopkins Democrat*

A. B. Norton wrote that E. D. McKenney published this paper from 1857 to 1860. McKenney sometimes wrote articles for the Clarksville *Standard*.

[Tarrant] *Texas Star*

The *Columbia Democrat* of Feburary 27, 1855, reported: "The Texas Star, whillom [*sic*] of Gilmer, Upshur County, comes to us now from Tarrant, Hopkins County. The paper is somewhat improved in appearance." Ben A. Vansickle was the editor.

[Tyler] *Hornet*

Sid S. Johnson, *Some Biographies of Old Settlers*, describes this sheet, saying it appeared in 1859, published by two young printers, Irwin Cowsar and Matt Hays. The editor in chief was Benjamin Rismuswigglewroggle, and the paper carried the motto "Touch Me and I'll Sting." The paper created a stir locally, and there was much speculation as to the real editor.

Tyler Reporter

C. L. Collins, formerly of the San Augustine *Red Land Herald*, purchased the *Tyler Telegraph* in 1854 and renamed it the *Reporter*. Collins withdrew in 1855, and during the next few years a number of men were associated with the paper, among them J. C. Shook, Jack Davis, B. T. Selman, W. A. Hendricks, and Stanley M. Warner. By May 16, 1860, Warner was editor and James P. Douglas, assistant editor. Douglas distinguished himself in the Confederate army and continued with the *Reporter* after the Civil War. See Lucia Rutherford Douglas, ed., *Douglas's Texas Battery, C.S.A.* Scattered issues from 1855 to 1860 are in the Newspaper Collection, University of Texas at Austin.

[Tyler] *States Rights Sentinel*

The Clarksville *Standard* of March 5, 1860, noted the appearance of this sheet, edited by William H. Smith and George Miller Johnson. It followed the political line suggested by the title. Smith, a native of Georgia, graduated from Georgia Military Institute. He died in the Civil War. Johnson also served in the Confederate army.

Tyler Telegraph

This Democratic weekly appeared on May 31, 1851, with Lucius C. Clopton as editor and Thomas Davis, publisher. In 1852 Davis, Clopton and Company sold to a group that included William Henry Parsons, James C. Hill, David Hill, Everett H. Lott, and B. T. Selman. Parsons edited the paper and became involved in an argument with H. L. Grinsted of the *Jefferson Herald*. When Parsons attended his father-in-law's funeral in Jefferson in early 1854, he was shot in the legs. Contemporary newspapers identify his assailant as John Morgan, a Jefferson printer, but Sid S. Johnson, *Some Biographies of Old Settlers*, says Parsons did not know who shot him. The incident ended Parson's Tyler career. He moved to Waco, where he edited the *South-West* in 1860. C. L. Collins of the San Augustine *Red Land Herald*, purchased the *Telegraph* and made it the *Reporter*. The first issue is in the Texas State Library.

[Tyler] *Temple of Honor*

The Huntsville *Texas Presbyterian* of September 23, 1854, noted the prospectus of this monthly magazine. Devoted to the cause of temperance, the magazine was edited by Dr. William Chilton. The Marshall *Texas Republican* of May 12, 1855, noted that the magazine had been discontinued.

[Tyler] *Texas Legal Directory*

The Austin *Texas State Gazette* of April 30, 1859, noted this new monthly, to be published at the office of the *Tyler Reporter* by

Stanley Warner. The paper cost one dollar per year, which included a copy of the *Reporter* and the insertion of a card. "Mr. Warner is making a valuable contribution to the legal profession," commented the *Gazette*.

[Victoria] *Der Texas Demokrat*

This German-language paper began in 1859, with Frederick Dietzel as editor. A Unionist paper, it moved to Houston before May, 1863. Several issues from December 9, 1862, to May 25, 1863, are in the Texas State Library.

[Victoria] *Texan Advocate*; title varies: *Texian Advocate, Victoria Advocate*

John D. Logan and Thomas Sterne, formerly of Arkansas, established this paper on May 8, 1846. They claimed to be the first to advocate Zachary Taylor for president. George W. Palmer and John J. Jamieson became owners in 1853, and Samuel Addison White in 1859. White continued the paper throughout the Civil War, and it continues today as the second-oldest continuous paper in Texas. Scattered issues from 1848 to 1858 are in the Newspaper Collection, University of Texas at Austin. The paper is more fully considered in Geraldine Talley, "The *Victoria Advocate*: A History of Texas' Second Oldest Continuous Newspaper, 1846–1888" (M.S. thesis, Trinity University).

[Victoria] *Texas Presbyterian*

Andrew Jackson McGown, a Cumberland Presbyterian minister, issued a sample number of this paper on November 3, 1846, and began regular publication on the following January 2. He issued ten numbers at Victoria and then moved the paper first to Houston and then to Huntsville. The issues of November 3, 1846, and January 2 and March 24, 1847, are in the Newspaper Collection, University of Texas at Austin.

[Victoria] *Texas Volksfreund*

This German-language paper appeared from the office of the *Victoria Advocate* in 1860. The *Bellville Countryman* of August 18, 1860, mentioned it.

[Waco] *American Beacon*

The Houston *Tri-Weekly Telegraph* of October 15, 1855, noted receipt of the first number of this paper. A Know-Nothing sheet, it was published by George Miller, formerly of the Houston *Spirit of the Age*, and edited by J. L. L. McCall.

[Waco] *Brazos Statesman*

The Marshall *Texas Republican* of May 3, 1856, welcomed this paper, founded by Franklin Lodowik Denison. The paper, a weekly, supported the Democratic ticket. By early 1857 H. B. Granbury was editor, and J. O. Shook as agent offered one-half of the office for sale. The Austin *Texas State Times* of May 2, 1857, noted that the *Brazos Statesman* had become the *Southerner*. The issues of September 5, 1856, and January 3, 1857, are in the Newspaper Collection, University of Texas at Austin.

Waco Era

The *Handbook of Waco and McLennan County*, edited by Dayton Kelley, says this first newspaper in Waco was established by George Lambdin in 1854. The *Columbia Democrat* of February 27, 1855, mentioned it, as did the Houston *Telegraph* of June 20, 1855. The Columbia *Democrat and Planter* of October 23, 1855, noted that the *Era* was "now strictly neutral" and that it was published on a letter sheet.

[Waco] *Southern Democrat*

The Austin *Texas State Gazette* of January 30, 1858, noted the first number of this paper. It was edited and published by J. O. Shook, formerly of the Waco *Southerner* and *Brazos Statesman* and still earlier of the Corsicana *Prairie Blade*. The *Gazette* called it the "Sam Houston kind of Democrat." In January, 1860, Shook was making plans to buy a power press, but on November 9 of that year he was killed in his office by a printer, Tom McCordell. The issues of April 15 and 22 and November 18, 1858, are in the Newspaper Collection, University of Texas at Austin.

[Waco] *Southerner*

The Austin *Texas State Times* of May 2, 1857, noted that the *Brazos Statesman* had become the *Southerner*. J. O. Shook and Com-

pany published the paper, and H. B. Granbury edited it in 1857.
Shook left the *Southerner* early in 1858 to establish the *Southern
Democrat*. By the summer of 1858, W. D. Chambers edited the
Southerner, and by December, 1858, it was published by Wil-
liams and Kimbrough. The Houston *Telegraph* of April 10, 1860,
associated N. P. Clark with the *Southerner*. The paper was
replaced by the *South-West* in the fall of 1860. The issues of
May 9 and June 6, 1857, August 7 and September 4, 1858, and
June 8, 1859, are in the Newspaper Collection, University of
Texas at Austin.

[Waco] *South-West*

William Henry Parsons, formerly of the *Tyler Telegraph*, began this
pro-Southern sheet on October 17, 1860. When it entered its second volume, the Houston *Tri-Weekly Telegraph* called it one of
the best papers in the state. By January 16, 1861, it was published
by Brandon and Parsons, and by the next August by Pryor and
Parsons. Parsons distinguished himself in the Confederate army.

[Waco] *Sword of Gideon*

The Clarksville *Standard* of April 6, 1861, noted receipt of this sheet,
which criticized the recent state convention and the new Confederacy. It carried a woodcut of a man hanging and stated that
that secession was treason.

[Waco] *Temperance Banner*

The Columbia *Democrat and Planter* of August 16, 1859, noted receipt
of the second number of this sheet, published by Williams and
Kimbrough. A monthly, it cost fifty cents per year.

Washington American

George W. Crawford and George W. Perkins began this Know-Nothing
sheet on November 1, 1855. Crawford had formerly been associated with the Washington *Semi-Weekly Star* and the Austin *Texas
State Gazette*. Both Crawford and Perkins joined the Walker filibuster to Nicaragua in 1856. W. J. Pendleton continued the paper until the summer of 1857. The Newspaper Collection, University of Texas at Austin, has a near-complete run from November 1,
1855, to August 18, 1857.

Washington Democrat

The Marshall *Texas Republican* of February 7, 1857, noted the appearance of this paper, edited by Jo Littlefield. The Austin *Texas State Gazette* of March 28, 1857, reported the demise of the paper after "some two months of sickly existence."

[Washington] *Lone Star*

This paper was founded by W. H. Ewing and John B. Wilkins at Brenham in 1849 and moved to Washington in 1850, where it first became the *Semi-Weekly Star* and then the *Lone Star and Southern Watchtower*. By the fall of 1852, it was again the *Lone Star*, a weekly, published by J. D. Buchanan and edited by J. W. Wynne. It continued the sequence of the Brenham paper. In 1853, Joseph Lancaster of the Washington *Texas Ranger* purchased the press and combined the papers to issue the *Texas Ranger and Lone Star*. Issues of June 26, July 11, and September 9, 1852, are in the Newspaper Collection, University of Texas at Austin.

[Washington] *Lone Star and Southern Watchtower*

In 1851, the *Semi-Weekly Star*, formerly the Brenham *Lone Star*, became the *Lone Star and Southern Watchtower*, edited by George W. Crawford. The following year it again became the *Lone Star*. The Newspaper Collection, University of Texas at Austin, has copies from April 5, 1851, to September 18, 1852.

Washington Register

This paper, edited by John A. Moore, appeared in 1858 and lasted about a year. The Houston *Tri-Weekly Telegraph* of August 10, 1859, reported that the *Register* supported Sam Houston.

[Washington] *Semi-Weekly Star*

This paper, formerly the Brenham *Lone Star*, moved to Washington in 1850 and continued under this title, with W. H. Ewing as editor and George W. Crawford as publisher. In 1851, the paper became the *Lone Star and Southern Watchtower*. Issues of June 26, July 11, and September 9, 1850, are in the Newspaper Collection, University of Texas at Austin.

[Washington] *Texas Ranger*; title varies: *Texas Ranger and Brazos Guard*, or *Texas Ranger and Lone Star*

Joseph Lancaster, English-born, started the *Texas Ranger and Brazos Guard* on January 16, 1849. He had first come to Texas in 1836 and had served in the Texas Rangers. After sojourning in Mississippi for six years, he returned to Texas to start this paper. His particular purpose was to promote navigation on the Brazos River. His new press office burned in late 1852, possibly the work of arsonists. Lancaster considered moving his paper to Austin to join forces with John S. Ford, but instead he acquired the press of the *Semi-Weekly Star* and resumed publication in 1853 under the title *Texas Ranger and Lone Star*. Lancaster moved the paper back and forth between Brenham and Washington in the late 1850s and from 1857 to 1859 published it simultaneously at Washington, Brenham, Independence, and Chappell Hill. A number of different men joined him in editing and publishing the paper. Scattered issues from 1849 to 1856 are in the Newspaper Collection, University of Texas at Austin.

[Washington] *Texas State Journal*

B. E. Tarver and George W. Crawford issued a prospectus for this sheet in the fall of 1848. They decided against publishing it.

[Weatherford] *Frontier News*

The *Dallas Herald* of July 3, 1858, welcomed the first number of this paper, published by C. E. Van Horn and Company. The Marshall *Texas Republican* of August 5, 1858, noted that D. O. Norton and C. L. Jackson had purchased it. The *Dallas Herald* of April 4, 1860, noted that the paper had been revived by Judge D. O. Norton, editor, and J. D. Keely. The issue of August 19, 1858, is in the Newspaper Collection, University of Texas at Austin.

[Weatherford] *White Man*

H. A. Hamner and Isaac C. Worrall first established this paper in Jacksboro. After their press burned on July 29, 1860, Hamner purchased the office of the *Fort Worth Chief*, and he and George W. Baylor reestablished the paper at Weatherford on September 13, 1860. H. Smythe, *Historical Sketch of Parker County and Weatherford*, says B. L. Richey, John Devons, and T. Obenchain bought the office in October, 1860, and that it was destroyed in December, 1861. The paper advocated a harsh Indian policy, criticized Sam Houston, and supported states' rights. The single copy in the Newspaper Collection, University of Texas at Austin, September 13, 1860 (Volume I, number 18), carries the motto "The Frontier and Its Defense."

Woodville Messenger

The Marshall *Texas Republican* of June 21, 1856, welcomed this new paper, published by Dr. S. B. Johnson and Company and edited by N. A. Penland. It continued until at least the fall of 1857.

Bibliography

Archival Collections

Austin, Texas. County Clerk's Office. Deed Records of Travis County.

Austin, Texas. General Land Office. Muster Roll.

Austin, Texas. Texas State Library. Archives. Audited Military Claims. Civil Claims. Civil Service Claims. Republic of Texas, Domestic Correspondence, 1836. Republic of Texas, Executive Record Book. Republic of Texas, Records Relating to Public Printing.

Austin, Texas. University of Texas. Archives. Bexar Archives. Adolph Douai Papers. James F. Perry Papers. Ernest W. Winkler Papers.

Austin, Texas. University of Texas. Nettie Lee Benson Latin American Collection. Alexandro Prieto Collection.

Galveston, Texas. County Clerk's Office. Deed Records of Galveston County.

Houston, Texas. County Clerk's Office. Deed Records of Harris County.

Huntsville, Texas. County Clerk's Office. Deed Records of Walker County.

Washington, D.C. National Archives. State Department Manuscripts, Special Agents, William Shaler, 1810.

Worcester, Massachusetts. American Antiquarian Society. Biographical File.

Unpublished Manuscripts

Barron, John Daniel. "A Critical History of the Texas Christian Advocate. M.A. thesis, University of Missouri, 1952.

Crews, Litha. "The Know Nothing Party in Texas." M.A. thesis, University of Texas, 1925.

Crook, Carland Elaine. "San Antonio, Texas, 1846–1861." M.A. thesis, Rice University, 1964.

Frantz, Joe B. "The Newspapers of the Republic of Texas." M.A. thesis, University of Texas, 1940.

Frazier, Mary Glasscock. "Texas Newspapers During the Republic." M.A. thesis, University of Texas, 1931.

Gage, Larry Jay. "The Editors and Editorial Policies of the *Texas State Gazette*, 1849–1879." M.A. thesis, University of Texas, 1959.

Hann, Charles E. "A History of the *Tribune* in Matagorda County." M.S. thesis, East Texas State University, 1978.

Harding, Jacobina Burch. "A History of the Early Newspapers of San Antonio, 1823–1874." M.A. thesis, University of Texas, 1951.

Jones, Sister Martin Joseph. "An Analytical Index to the Standard (Clarksville, Texas) for the Years 1842 through 1850." M.S.L.S. thesis, Catholic University, 1965.

Lale, Max S. "The Influence of the Media on the Discerning Public." Manuscript in possession of author, Marshall, Texas.

LaRoche, Clarence J. "Rip Ford: Frontier Journalist." M.A. thesis, University of Texas, 1942.

McCalib, Paul T. "Moore and Stuart: Rival Editors in Early Texas (1837–1862)." M.A. thesis, University of Texas, 1948.

Maranto, Samuel Paul. "A History of Dallas Newspapers." M.A. thesis, North Texas State University, 1952.

Scarborough, Jane Lynn. "George W. Paschal: Texas Unionist and Scalawag Jurisprudent." Ph.D. dissertation, Rice University, 1972.

Sharp, Lawrence R. "A History of Panola County." M.A. thesis, University of Texas, 1940.

Sinclair, Olan Lonnie. "Crossroads of Conviction: A Study of the Texas Political Mind, 1856–1861. Ph.D. dissertation, Rice University, 1975.

Stone, William J. "A Historical Survey of Leading Texas Denominational Newspapers, 1846–1861." Ph.D. dissertation, University of Texas, Austin, 1974.

Strickland, Rex Wallace. "Anglo-American Activities in Northeastern Texas, 1803–1845." Ph.D. dissertation, University of Texas, 1936.

Stuart, Ben C. "History of Newspapers in Texas." Manuscript, Houston Public Library.

Talley, Geraldine. "The *Victoria Advocate*: A History of Texas' Second Oldest Continuous Newspaper, 1846–1888." M.S. thesis, Trinity University, 1967.

United States. "Census of Jefferson County, Texas. Population Schedule." Microfilm copy in Clayton Library, Houston Public Library.

Wallace, John M. "George W. Bonnell, Frontier Journalist in the Republic of Texas." M.A. thesis, University of Texas, Austin, 1966.

Whitehead, Marie Hall. "A History of *The Rusk Cherokeean*, 1847–1973." M.A. thesis, Stephen F. Austin State University, 1974.

Newspapers

Austin *Campaign Intelligencer*
Austin City Gazette
Austin *New Era*

Austin *Southern Intelligencer*
Austin *Texas Democrat*
Austin *Texas Sentinel*
Austin *Texas State Gazette*
Austin *Texas State Times*
Brazoria *Constitutional Advocate and Texas Public Advertiser*
Brazoria *Texas Republican*
Brownsville *American Flag*
Clarksville *Northern Standard*
Columbus *Colorado Citizen*
Corpus Christi *Nueces Valley*
Corpus Christi *Ranchero*
Corpus Christi Star
Corsicana *Navarro Express*
Crockett Printer
Daingerfield *Lamplighter*
Dallas Herald
Galveston *Civilian and Galveston Gazette*
Galveston *Crisis!*
Galveston Journal
Galveston News
Galveston *Texas Daily Times*
Henderson *Flag of the Union*
Houston *Morning Star*
Houston *Telegraph and Texas Register*
Huntsville Item
Huntsville Recorder
Huntsville *Texas Banner*
Jasper *East Texas Clarion*
Jefferson Herald and Gazette
La Grange Intelligencer
La Grange *States Rights Democrat*
McKinney Messenger
Marshall *Harrison Flag*
Marshall *Star State Patriot*
Marshall *Texas Republican*
Matagorda Bulletin
Matagorda Gazette
Matagorda *Weekly Despatch*
Nacogdoches *Campaign Chronicle*
Nacogdoches Chronicle
Natchitoches, La., *El Mexicano*
Natchitoches, La., *Gaceta de Texas*
New Braunfels *Neu-Braunfelser Zeitung*
New Orleans, La., *Picayune*

Palestine *Trinity Advocate*
Paris *Lamar Enquirer*
Quitman Herald
Richmond Telescope and Register
San Antonio *Alamo Express*
San Antonio *El Bejareño*
San Antonio Herald
San Antonio Ledger
San Antonio *Union*
San Antonio *Western Texan*
San Augustine Herald
San Augustine *Red-Lander*
San Felipe *Telegraph and Texas Register*
San Felipe *Texas Gazette*
San Luis Advocate
Seguin *Southern Confederacy*
Victoria Texan Advocate
Waco *South-West*
Washington American
Washington *Semi-Weekly Star*
Washington *Texas National Register*
Washington *Texas Ranger and Brazos Guard*
Washington *Texas Ranger and Lone Star*
Washington *Texian and Brazos Farmer*
Weatherford *Frontier News*
Weatherford *White Man*

Books and Articles

Acheson, Sam. *35,000 Days in Texas: A History of the Dallas News and Its Forebears.* New York: Macmillan Co., 1938.

————, and Julie Ann Hudson O'Connell, eds. "George Washington Diamond's Account of the Great Hanging at Gainesville, 1862." *Southwestern Historical Quarterly* 66 (January, 1963): 331–414.

Addington, Wendell G. "Slave Insurrections in Texas." *Journal of Negro History* 35 (October, 1950): 408–34.

Allen, William Youel. "Allen's Reminiscences of Texas, 1838–1842." *Southwestern Historical Quarterly* 17 (April, 1914): 302–10.

American Dictionary of Printing. Detroit, Ill.: Gale Research Co., 1967.

Bacarisse, Charles. "The *Texas Gazette*, 1829–1831." *Southwestern Historical Quarterly* 56 (October, 1952): 239–53.

Baillio, Ferdinand B., ed. *A History of the Texas Press Association.* Austin: Texas Press Association, 1913.

Bancroft, H. H. *A History of the Northern Mexican States and Texas.* 2 vols. San Francisco: History Co., Publishers, 1890.

Barker, Eugene C., ed. *The Austin Papers.* Vols. I and II. Washington, D.C.: American Historical Association, 1919–22. Vol. III. Austin: University of Texas, 1926.

――――. *The Life of Stephen F. Austin, Founder of Texas, 1793–1836.* Nashville, Tenn.: Cokesbury Press, 1925.

――――. "Notes on Early Texas Newspapers, 1819–1836." *Southwestern Historical Quarterly* 21 (October, 1917): 127–30.

――――, and Amelia W. Williams, eds. *The Writings of Sam Houston.* 8 vols. Austin: University of Texas Press, 1938–48.

Bass, Feris A., Jr., and B. R. Brunson, eds. *Fragile Empires: The Texas Correspondence of Samuel Swartwout and James Morgan: 1836–1856.* Austin: Shoal Creek Publishers, 1978.

Beretta, J. W. *The Story of Banco Nacional de Texas and 136 Years of Banking in San Antonio de Bexar, 1822–1958.* San Antonio: Claude Aniol, 1959.

Berger, Tom. *Baptist Journalism in Nineteenth-Century Texas.* Austin: Department of Journalism, University of Texas, 1970.

Biesele, Rudolph Leopold. *The History of the German Settlements in Texas, 1831–1861.* Austin: Von Boeckmann–Jones Co., 1930.

――――. "The Texas State Convention of Germans in 1854." *Southwestern Historical Quarterly* 33 (April, 1930): 247–61.

Binkley, William C., ed. *Official Correspondence of the Texas Revolution.* 2 vols. New York: D. Appleton–Century Co., 1936.

Blount, Lois F. F. "Nacogdoches Notes." *East Texas Historical Journal* 4 (March, 1966): 46.

Bonnell, George William. *Topographical Description of Texas.* Waco: Reprint. Texian Press, 1964.

Bonquois, Dora F. "The Career of Henry Adams Bullard, Lawyer, Jurist, Legislator, and Educator." *Louisiana Historical Quarterly* 23 (October, 1940): 999–1101.

Branda, Eldon Stephen. *The Handbook of Texas: A Supplement.* Vol. III. Austin: Texas State Historical Association, 1976.

[Brigham, Clarence S.] "From the Texas Republican." *Southwestern Historical Quarterly* 51 (April, 1948): 366–69.

――――. *A History and Bibliography of American Newspapers, 1690–1820.* 2 vols. Worcester, Mass.: American Antiquarian Society, 1947.

Brindley, Anne A. "Jane Long." *Southwestern Historical Quarterly* 56 (October, 1952): 211–38.

Campbell, Randolph. "Texas and the Nashville Convention of 1850." *Southwestern Historical Quarterly* 76 (July, 1972): 1–14.

――――. "The Whig Party of Texas in the Elections of 1848 and 1852." *Southwestern Historical Quarterly* 73 (July, 1969): 17–34.

Carroll, H. Bailey. *The Texan Santa Fe Trail.* Canyon, Tex.: Panhandle-Plains Historical Society, 1951.

Castañeda, Carlos Eduardo, ed. *The Mexican Side of the Texan Revolution,*

1836, by the Chief Mexican Participants. Dallas: P. L. Turner Company, 1928.

Christian, Asa Kyrus. "The Tariff History of the Republic of Texas." *Southwestern Historical Quarterly* 20 (April, 1917): 317–40, and 21 (July, 1917): 1–35.

Clark, Joseph Lynn. *Thank God We Made It!* Austin: University of Texas, 1969.

Cope, Millard. *The Texas Press, 1813–1836.* Dallas: Texas Harte-Hanks Newspapers, 1954.

Copeland, Fayette. *Kendall of the Picayune.* Norman: University of Oklahoma Press, 1943.

Creighton, James A. *A Narrative History of Brazoria County.* Waco: Texian Press, 1975.

Crenshaw, Ollinger. *The Slave States in the Presidential Election of 1860.* Baltimore: Johns Hopkins Press, 1945.

Crocket, George Louis. *Two Centuries in East Texas.* Dallas: Southwest Press, 1932.

Cushing, E. B. "Edward Hopkins Cushing: An Appreciation by His Son." *Southwestern Historical Quarterly* 25 (April, 1922): 261–65.

Dabney, L. E. "Louis Aury: The First Governor of Texas Under the Mexican Republic." *Southwestern Historical Quarterly* 42 (October, 1938): 108–16.

Day, James M. *Black Beans and Goose Quills.* Waco: Texian Press, 1970.

———, ed. "Diary of James A. Glasscock." *Texana* 1 (Spring, 1963): 86–96.

DeBray, Xavier Blanchard. *A Sketch of the History of DeBray's Regiment of Texas Cavalry.* Austin: E. Von Boeckman, 1884.

Dillon, Charles H. "The Arrival of the Telegraph in Texas." *Southwestern Historical Quarterly* 64 (October, 1960): 200–11.

Dorsey, Florence. *Master of the Mississippi.* Boston: Houghton-Mifflin, 1941.

Douglas, Lucia Rutherford, ed. *Douglas's Texas Battery, C.S.A.* Waco: Texian Press, 1966.

Duval, John C. *The Adventures of Big-Foot Wallace.* Macon, Ga.: J. W. Burke & Co., 1870.

Erath, George Bernard. "Memoirs of Major George Bernard Erath." *Southwestern Historical Quarterly* 27 (July, 1923): 40–49.

Etzler, T. Herbert. "German-American Newspapers in Texas." *Southwestern Historical Quarterly* 57 (April, 1954): 423–31.

Falconer, Thomas. *Letters and Notes on the Texan Santa Fe Expedition.* Edited by Frederick Webb Hodge. New York: Dauber & Pine, 1930.

Foote, Henry Stuart. *Texas and the Texans.* 2 vols. Philadelphia: Thomas Cowperthwait & Co., 1841.

Ford, John Salmon. *Rip Ford's Texas.* Edited by Stephen B. Oates. Austin: University of Texas Press, 1963.

Fornell, Earl W. "Ferdinand Flake: German Pioneer Journalist of the Southwest." *American-German Review* 21 (February–March, 1955): 25–28.

―――. *The Galveston Era.* Austin: University of Texas Press, 1961.

Fowler, John. *James P. Newcomb: Texas Journalist and Political Leader.* Austin: Department of Journalism, University of Texas, 1976.

Franklin, Ethel Mary. "Joseph Baker." *Southwestern Historical Quarterly* 36 (October, 1932): 130–43.

Frantz, Joe B. *Gail Borden, Dairyman to a Nation.* Norman: University of Oklahoma Press, 1951.

Friend, Llerena. *Sam Houston, The Great Designer.* Austin: University of Texas Press, 1954.

Gage, Larry Jay. "The City of Austin on the Eve of the Civil War." *Southwestern Historical Quarterly* 63 (January, 1960): 428–38.

―――. "The Texas Road to Secession and War: John Marshall and the Texas State Gazette, 1860–1861." *Southwestern Historical Quarterly* 62 (October, 1958): 191–226.

Galveston Directory. Galveston: News Book and Job Office, 1859.

Gambrell, Herbert. *Anson Jones, the Last President of Texas.* Austin: University of Texas Press, 1964.

―――. *Mirabeau Buonaparte Lamar, Troubadour and Crusader.* Dallas: Southwest Press, 1934.

Garrett, Julia Kathryn. "The First Newspaper of Texas: Gaceta de Texas." *Southwestern Historical Quarterly* 40 (October, 1937): 200–15.

―――. *Green Flag Over Texas.* New York: Cordova Press, 1939.

―――, trans. "Gaceta de Texas: Translation of the First Number." *Southwestern Historical Quarterly* 42 (July, 1938): 21–27.

Garrison, George P. *Diplomatic Correspondence of the Republic of Texas.* 3 vols. Washington: Annual Report of the American Historical Association, 1908, 1911.

Geiser, Samuel Wood. *Naturalists of the Frontier.* Dallas: Southern Methodist University, 1948.

―――. "Note on Dr. Francis Moore (1808–1864)." *Southwestern Historical Quarterly* 47 (April, 1944): 420–21.

Gray, A. C. "A History of the Texas Press." In *A Comprehensive History of Texas, 1685–1897.* Vol. II. Edited by Dudley G. Wooten. Dallas: William G. Scarff, 1898.

Gray, William Fairfax. *From Virginia to Texas.* Houston: Fletcher Young Publishing Co., 1965.

Green, Thomas J. *Journal of the Texian Expedition against Mier.* New York: Harper & Bros., 1845.

Gregory, Winifred. *American Newspapers, 1821–1936: A Union List of Files Available in the United States and Canada.* New York: H. W. Wilson Co., 1937.

Grimes, Roy, ed. *300 Years in Victoria County.* Victoria, Tex.: Victoria Advocate Publishing Co., 1968.

Gulick, Charles A., et al., eds. *The Papers of Mirabeau Buonaparte Lamar.* 6 vols. Austin: Texas State Library, 1921–27.

Hayes, Charles W. *Galveston: History of the Island and the City*. Austin: Jenkins Garrett Press, 1974.

Hatcher, Mattie Austin, ed. "Joaquín de Arredondo's Report of the Battle of Medina, August 18, 1813." *Quarterly of the Texas State Historical Association* 11 (January, 1908): 220–36.

Henderson, Harry McCorry. "The Magee-Gutiérrez Expedition." *Southwestern Historical Quarterly* 55 (July, 1951): 43–61.

Hogan, William Ransom. *The Texas Republic: A Social and Economic History*. Norman: University of Oklahoma Press, 1956.

Hollon, W. Eugene, and Ruth Lapham Butler, eds. *William Bollaert's Texas*. Norman: University of Oklahoma Press, 1956.

Honig, Lawrence E. *John Henry Brown, Texian Journalist, 1820–1895*. El Paso: Texas Western Press, 1973.

Houstoun, Mrs. [M. F. C.]. *Texas and the Gulf of Mexico, or Yachting in the New World*. 2 vols. London: John Murray, 1844.

Hughes, William J. *Rebellious Ranger: Rip Ford and the Old Southwest*. Norman: University of Oklahoma Press, 1964.

Jackson, Lynnell. *True Witnesses: A Check List of Newspapers, 1845–1861*. Austin: Department of Journalism, University of Texas, 1971.

Jefferson, Thomas. *The Writings of Thomas Jefferson*. Edited by Albert Ellery Bergh. 20 vols. Washington, D.C.: Jefferson Memorial Association, 1903–1907.

Jenkins, John H., ed. *Houston Displayed*. Austin: Brick Row Book Shop, 1964.

Johnson, Sid S. *Some Biographies of Old Settlers*. Tyler, Tex.: Sid S. Johnson, 1900.

Jones, Anson. *Memoranda and Official Correspondence Relating to the Republic of Texas*. New York: D. Appleton and Co., 1859.

Kelley, Dayton, ed. *The Handbook of Waco and McLennan County, Texas*. Waco: Texian Press, 1972.

Kemp, L. W. *The Signers of the Texas Declaration of Independence*. Salado, Tex.: Anson Jones Press, 1959.

Kendall, George Wilkins. *Narrative of an Expedition Across the Great South-Western Prairies, from Texas to Santa Fe*. 2 vols. London: David Bogue, 1845.

Kennedy, Joseph C. G. *Preliminary Report on the Eighth Census*. Washington, D.C.: Government Printing Office, 1862.

Landrum, Graham, and Alan Smith. *Grayson County: An Illustrated History of Grayson County*. Fort Worth: Historical Publishing Company, 1967.

Lane, Walter P. *The Adventures and Recollections of a San Jacinto Veteran. . . .* Marshall, Tex.: Tri-Weekly Herald Job Print, 1887.

[Langworthy, Asahel]. *A Visit to Texas. . . .* New York: Goodrich & Wiley, 1834.

Lea, Tom. *The King Ranch*. 2 vols. Boston: Little, Brown and Co., 1957.

Loomis, Noel M. *The Texan–Santa Fe Pioneers*. Norman: University of Oklahoma Press, 1958.

Lubbock, Francis Richard. *Six Decades in Texas; or, Memoirs of Francis Richard Lubbock*. Edited by C. W. Raines. Austin: Ben C. Jones & Co., Printers, 1900.

Lundy, Benjamin. *The Life, Travels and Opinions of Benjamin Lundy*. Philadelphia: Thomas Earle, 1847.

McCaleb, Walter F. "The First Period of the Gutierrez-Magee Expedition." *Quarterly of the Texas State Historical Association* 4 (January, 1901): 218–29.

McDonald, Archie P., ed. *Hurrah for Texas: The Diary of Adolphus Sterne, 1838–1851*. Waco: Texian Press, 1969.

McLaughlin, Charles Capen, ed. *The Papers of Frederick Law Olmsted: The Formative Years*. Baltimore: Johns Hopkins University Press, 1977.

McLean, John H. *Reminiscences*. Dallas: Smith & Lamar, 1918.

McMurtrie, Douglas C. "The First Texas Newspaper." *Southwestern Historical Quarterly* 36 (July, 1932): 41–46.

———. "Pioneer Printing in Texas." *Southwestern Historical Quarterly* 39 (October, 1935): 83–99.

Members of the Legislature of the State of Texas from 1849–1939. Austin, 1939.

Metzenthin-Raunick, Selma. "One Hundred Years: *Neu Braunfelser Zeitung*." *American-German Review* 19 (August–September, 1953): 15–16.

Moore, Francis, Jr. *Map and Description of Texas*. Reprint. Waco: Texian Press, 1965.

Moore, Ike H. "The Earliest Printing and First Newspaper in Texas." *Southwestern Historical Quarterly* 39 (October, 1935): 83–99.

———, comp. *Texas Newspapers: A Union List of Newspaper Files, 1913–1939*. Houston: San Jacinto Museum of History Association, 1941.

Morrell, Zachariah N. *Flowers and Fruits in the Wilderness*. Irving, Tex.: Griffin Graphic Arts, 1966.

Mott, Frank Luther. *American Journalism: A History, 1690–1960*. New York: Macmillan Co., 1962.

Muir, Andrew Forest. "Algernon P. Thompson." *Southwestern Historical Quarterly* 51 (October, 1947): 143–53.

Neighbours, Kenneth F. "The Expedition of Major Robert S. Neighbors to El Paso in 1849." *Southwestern Historical Quarterly* 58 (July, 1954): 36–59.

Neville, A. W. *A History of Lamar County*. Paris, Tex.: North Texas Publishing Co., 1937.

———. *The Red River Valley, Then and Now*. Paris, Tex.: North Texas Publishing Co., 1948.

Newcomb, James P. *Sketch of Secession Times in Texas*. San Francisco, 1863.

Norton, A. B. "A History of the Early Newspapers of Texas." In *A History of the Texas Press Association*. Edited by Ferdinand B. Baillio. Austin: Texas Press Association, 1913.

Norton, Wesley. "Religious Newspapers in Antebellum Texas." *Southwestern Historical Quarterly* 79 (October, 1975): 145–65.

Oldham, W. S. "Colonel John Marshall," *Southwestern Historical Quarterly* 20 (October, 1916): 132–38.

Olmsted, Frederick Law. *A Journey Through Texas*. New York: Dix, Edwards & Co., 1857.

Overdyke, W. Darrell. *The Know-Nothing Party in the South*. Baton Rouge: Louisiana State University Press, 1950.

Parsons' Texas Cavalry Brigade Association. *A Brief and Condensed History of Parsons' Texas Cavalry Brigade. . . .* Waxahachie, Tex.: J. M. Flemister, Printer, 1892.

Paschal, George W. *The Public Printing and the Public Printer*. Austin: Southern Intelligencer Press, 1858.

————. *Some Facts and Figures Relative to the Public Printing. . . .* Austin: Southern Intelligencer Office, 1859.

Paxton, John Adams. *Supplement to the New Orleans Directory and Register*. New Orleans: Benjamin Levy & Co., Printers, 1824.

Peña, José Enrique de la. *With Santa Anna in Texas*. Translated and edited by Carmen Perry. College Station: Texas A & M University Press, 1975.

Phelan, Macum. *A History of Early Methodism in Texas, 1817–1866*. Nashville: Cokesbury Press, 1924.

Pike, Zebulon. *Sources of the Mississippi and the Western Louisiana Territory*. Readex Microprint Corp., 1966.

Reinhardt, Louis. "The Communist Colony of Bettina (1846–48)." *Quarterly of the Texas State Historical Association* 3 (July, 1899): 33–44.

Reynolds, Donald E. *Editors Make War*. Nashville: Vanderbilt University Press, 1966.

Roach, Hattie Joplin. *A History of Cherokee County, Texas*. Dallas: Southwest Press, 1934.

Robinson, Duncan W. *Judge Robert McAlpin Williamson: Texas' Three-Legged Willie*. Austin: Texas State Historical Association, 1948.

Robinson, William Davis. *Memoirs of the Mexican Revolution Including a Narrative of the Expedition of General Xavier Mina*. Philadelphia: Lydia R. Bailey, Printer, 1820.

Roemer, Ferdinand. *Texas: With Particular Reference to German Immigration*. San Antonio: Standard Printing Co., 1935.

Roper, Laura W. "Frederick Law Olmsted and Western Texas Free Soil Movement," *American Historical Review* 56 (October, 1950): 58–64.

Rowland, Dunbar, ed. *Official Letter Books of W. W. C. Claiborne, 1801–1816*. 6 vols. Jackson, Miss.: State Department of Archives and History, 1917.

Russell, Traylor. *History of Titus County, Texas*. Waco: W. M. Morrison, 1965.

Ruthven, A. S. *Proceedings of the Grand Lodge of Texas. . . .* 2 vols. Galveston: Richardson & Co., News Office, 1860.

Sibley, Marilyn McAdams, ed. *Samuel H. Walker's Account of the Mier Expedition.* Austin: Texas State Historical Association, 1978.

Siegal, Stanley. *A Political History of the Texas Republic, 1836–1845.* Austin: University of Texas Press, 1956.

Sinks, Julia. "Editors and Newspapers of Fayette County," *Quarterly of the Texas State Historical Association* 1 (July, 1897): 34–47.

———. "Journalists of Austin in 1840," *Dallas Morning News*, May 7, 1876.

Slauson, Allan B. *A Checklist of American Newspapers in the Library of Congress.* Washington: Government Printing Office, 1901.

Smith, Justin H. *The Annexation of Texas.* New York: Baker and Taylor Co., 1911.

Smither, Harriett, ed. "The Diary of Adolphus Sterne." *Southwestern Historical Quarterly* 30 (October, 1926): 219–32.

Smithwick, Noah. *The Evolution of a State.* Austin: Gammel Book Co., 1900.

Smythe, H. *Historical Sketch of Parker County and Weatherford, Texas.* St. Louis: Louis C. Lavat, 1877.

Somers, Dale A. "James P. Newcomb: The Making of a Radical." *Southwestern Historical Quarterly* 72 (April, 1969): 449–69.

Sonnichsen, C. L. *Ten Texas Feuds.* Albuquerque: University of New Mexico Press, 1957.

Sowell, A. J. *The Life of Big-Foot Wallace.* Bandera, Tex.: Frontier Times, 1927.

Speers, William S., ed. *Encyclopaedia of the New West.* Marshall, Tex.: United States Biographical Publishing Co., 1881.

Spell, Lota M. "The Anglo-Saxon Press in Mexico—1846 1865." *American Historical Review* 38 (October, 1932): 20–31.

———. *Pioneer Printer: Samuel Bangs in Mexico and Texas.* Austin: University of Texas Press, 1963.

———. "Samuel Bangs: The First Printer in Texas." *Southwestern Historical Quarterly* 35 (April, 1932): 267–78.

Stambaugh, J. Lee, and Lillian J. Stambaugh. *A History of Collin County.* Austin: Texas State Historical Association, 1958.

Stern, Madeleine B. "Jacob Cruger: Public Printer of Houston." In *Imprints on History: Book Publishers and American Frontiers.* Edited by Madeleine B. Stern. Bloomington: Indiana University Press, 1956.

Stiff, Edward. *The Texian Emigrant.* Cincinnati: George Conclin, 1840.

Stone, William J., Jr. "Texas' First Church Newspaper: The Texas Presbyterian, 1846–1856." *Texana* 12 (Summer, 1973): 239–47.

Streeter, Thomas W. *Bibliography of Texas, 1795–1845.* 3 vols. in 5. Cambridge, Mass.: Harvard University Press, 1955–60.

Stuart, Ben C. "Hamilton Stuart: Pioneer Editor." *Southwestern Historical Quarterly* 21 (April, 1918): 381–88.

Talley, Geraldine. "The Story of the *Advocate.*" In *300 Years in Victoria County.* Edited by Roy Grimes. Victoria, Tex.: Victoria Advocate Publishing Co., 1968.

Terrell, Alexander W. "Recollections of General Sam Houston." *Southwestern Historical Quarterly* 16 (October, 1912): 113–36.

Texas, Republic of. *Journals of the Fourth Congress of the Republic of Texas, 1839–1840.* Edited by Harriett Smither. 3 vols. Austin: Von Boeckmann–Jones Co., [1929].

Texas, Republic of. *Journal of the House of Representatives. Second Congress—Adjourned Session.* Houston: 1838.

Thomas, Emory M. "Rebel Nationalism: E. H. Cushing and the Confederate Experience." *Southwestern Historical Quarterly* 73 (January, 1970): 343–48.

Tyler, Ronnie C. *Joseph Wade Hampton: Editor and Individualist.* El Paso: Texas Western Press, 1969.

Walker, Henry P., ed. "William McLane's Narrative of the Magee-Gutierrez Expedition, 1812–1813." *Southwestern Historical Quarterly* 66 (October, 1962, and January, April, 1963): 234–51, 457–79, 569–88.

Wallace, Ernest. *Charles DeMorse, Pioneer Editor and Statesman.* Lubbock: Texas Tech Press, 1943.

Wallace, John Melton. *Gaceta to Gazette: A Check List of Texas Newspapers, 1813–1846.* Austin: Department of Journalism, University of Texas, 1966.

Wallis, Jonnie L., and Laurence L. Hill, eds. *Sixty Years on the Brazos: The Life and Letters of Dr. John Washington Lockhart, 1824–1900.* Los Angeles: Dunn Bros., 1930.

Warren, Harris Gaylord. "José Alvarez de Toledo's Initiation as a Filibuster, 1811–1813." *Hispanic American Historical Review* 20 (February, 1940): 56–82.

———. "José Alvarez de Toledo's Reconciliation with Spain." *Louisiana Historical Quarterly* 23 (July, 1940): 827–63.

———. "The Origin of General Mina's Invasion of Mexico." *Southwestern Historical Quarterly* 42 (July, 1938): 1–20.

———. *The Sword Was Their Passport.* Baton Rouge: Louisiana State University Press, 1943.

Webb, Walter Prescott, and H. Bailey Carroll, eds., *The Handbook of Texas.* Vols. I and II. Austin: Texas State Historical Association, 1952.

West, Elizabeth, trans. and ed. "Diary of José Bernardo Gutiérrez de Lara, 1811–1812." *American Historical Review* 34 (October, 1828): 55–77, 281–94.

Weyand, Leonie Rummel, and Houston Wade. *An Early History of Fayette County.* La Grange, Tex.: La Grange Journal, 1936.

White, Gifford, ed. *The 1840 Census of the Republic of Texas.* Austin: Pemberton Press, 1966.

White, William W. "The Texas Slave Insurrection of 1860." *Southwestern Historical Quarterly* 52 (January, 1949): 259–85.

Whiting, William. *Memoir of the Reverend Samuel Whiting.* Boston: Privately printed, 1873.

Winkler, Ernest W. *Check List of Texas Imprints, 1846–1860.* Austin: Texas State Historical Association, 1949.

──────. "The First Newspaper in Texas." *Quarterly of the Texas State Historical Association* 6 (October, 1902): 162–65.

──────. *Journal of the Secession Convention of Texas, 1861.* Austin: Austin Printing Company, 1912.

──────. "The Mexican Advocate." *Quarterly of the Texas State Historical Association* 7 (January, 1904): 243; 8 (January, 1905): 272–73.

──────. "Note on the Texas Republican." *Quarterly of the Texas State Historical Association* 7 (January, 1904): 242–43.

──────. "The Texas Republican." *Southwestern Historical Quarterly* 16 (January, 1913): 329–31.

──────, ed. *Platforms of Political Parties in Texas.* Bulletin of the University of Texas, No. 53. Austin, 1916.

Wood, W. D. "Reminiscences of Texas and Texans Fifty Years Ago." *Quarterly of the Texas State Historical Association* 5 (October, 1901): 113–17.

Wooster, Ralph A. "An Analysis of the Texas Know-Nothings." *Southwestern Historical Quarterly* 70 (January, 1967): 414–23.

Wooten, Dudley G., ed. *A Comprehensive History of Texas, 1685–1897.* 2 vols. Dallas: William G. Scarff, 1898.

Zuber, William P. *My Eighty Years in Texas.* Austin: University of Texas Press, 1971.

Index